Global and Transnational Business: Strategy and Management

Second Edition

Global and Transnational Business: Strategy and Management

Second Edition

George Stonehouse
Northumbria University

David Campbell
University of Newcastle-upon-Tyne

Jim Hamill
University of Strathclyde

Tony Purdie
Northumbria University

John Wiley & Sons, Ltd

Other Wiley Editorial Offices

John Wiley & Sons Inc., 111 River Street, Hoboken, NJ 07030, USA

Jossey-Bass, 989 Market Street, San Francisco, CA 94103-1741, USA

Wiley-VCH Verlag GmbH, Boschstr. 12, D-69469 Weinheim, Germany

John Wiley & Sons Australia Ltd, 33 Park Road, Milton, Queensland 4064, Australia

John Wiley & Sons (Asia) Pte Ltd, 2 Clementi Loop #02-01, Jin Xing Distripark, Singapore 129809

John Wiley & Sons Canada Ltd, 22 Worcester Road, Etobicoke, Ontario, Canada M9W1L1

Wiley also publishes its books in a variety of electronic formats. Some content that appears in
print may not be available in electronic books.

Library of Congress Cataloging-in-Publication Data

Global and transnational business : strategy and management / George
Stonehouse ... [et al.]. – 2nd ed.
      p. cm.
Includes bibliographical references and index.
ISBN 0-470-85126-0 (Paper : alk. paper)
1. International business enterprises – Management.   2. Strategic planning.
3. Marketing – Management.   4. Competition, International.
I. Stonehouse, George.
HD62.4 .G528 2004
658.4′012 – dc22   2003025487

British Library Cataloguing in Publication Data

A catalogue record for this book is available from the British Library

ISBN 0-470-85126-0

Project management by Originator, Gt Yarmouth, Norfolk (typeset in 11/14pt Garamond)
Printed and bound in Great Britain by TJ International, Padstow, Cornwall
This book is printed on acid-free paper responsibly manufactured from sustainable forestry
in which at least two trees are planted for each one used for paper production.

CONTENTS

PREFACE TO THE SECOND EDITION

International business is one of the most fertile areas of academic research in British and American university business schools, and the number of research articles and textbooks produced in the area in recent years is testimony to this intellectual fecundity. The eclecticism of the field, drawing as it does on studies in general strategy, politics, economics and philosophy presents another set of challenges to authors such as ourselves – what to include for completeness and what to leave out or excise in the interests of accessibility and brevity. We acknowledge this tension and hope we have pitched this second edition about right.

Two issues distinguish this edition from the first: an increased emphasis on knowledge as a source of transnational competitive advantage and a modification to the way in which case materials are used.

We felt it important in this edition to reflect the debate in the strategy literature on the sources of competitive advantage to international businesses. In explaining competitive advantage from the perspective of knowledge management and organization learning, we have dismissed neither the competitive positioning school nor the core competence/resource-based perspective. We view the understanding of competitive advantage from a knowledge-based perspective as an enrichment of both of the previous explanations and seek to explain this synergy at several points in the text as the context requires. This has meant substantial revisions to Chapters 1, 2, 6 and 9.

The second change made for the second edition is in the way in which case materials are presented. The first edition contained a suite of six 'long' cases at the end of the text. After feedback from our adopters and some discussion, including with the publisher, we decided to change the focus of the cases. We have reduced the number of cases at the conclusion of the book to two (retaining the Nike case and adding a new one on McDonald's) and added several shorter ones as 'in-chapter' examples. We hope this new format provides for an effective learning experience.

ACKNOWLEDGEMENTS

The authors are grateful to colleagues who contributed case materials for this edition. Nigel Evans and Sonal Minocha (both of Newcastle Business School, Northumbria University) provided a number of well-researched cases of varying lengths for illustrative purposes and their contributions appear throughout the text.

Nigel Evans (principal lecturer in travel and tourism) contributed material on Nokia (Chapter 2), Holiday Inn (Chapter 7), airlines (Chapters 4 and 14), British Airways (Chapter 12) and DaimlerChrysler (Chapter 14). Sonal Minocha (lecturer in strategic management) contributed notes on pharmaceuticals (Chapter 4), Body Shop (Chapter 9) and Aventis (Chapter 14). All other cases and illustrations were written by the authors.

PART

STRATEGIC AND MANAGEMENT ISSUES IN GLOBAL AND TRANSNATIONAL BUSINESS

1

Learning objectives

After studying this chapter students should be able to:

- define the key terms used in the study of international business;
- describe the changes in international business behaviour in the second half of the 20th and early 21st century;
- explain the causes, nature and problems of globalization;
- describe some of the key issues in global and transnational business management;
- define and distinguish between the 'big controversies' in strategic management in relation to global business;
- explain the management processes involved in successful global and transnational business management.

Global and transnational business – an introduction

Some important definitions

Globalization is pehaps the single most important force at work in contemporary society, business, management and economics. For this reason, it is strategic management in a global context that forms the central theme of this book. Globalization is a complex phenomenon, and this chapter explores its causes, nature, effects and implications for managers in modern business organizations. Alongside the exploration of globalization, this chapter examines recent developments in strategic management and identifies their impact on transnational management, setting out the analytical frameworks which will form the core of the subsequent chapters.

It is useful to begin by clarifying some of the terminology used in the literature of international business. The terms *international, multinational, transnational* and *global* business are often used interchangeably. This can be a cause of serious confusion, so it is important to define and distinguish between the terms. A spectrum of international business activity can be identified depending on the nature and extent of a business's involvement in international markets and the degree of co-ordination and integration of geographically dispersed operations. The importance of making this distinction lies in the fact that the strategic and management issues facing an organization will vary considerably depending on the breadth of its international presence.

International, multinational, global and transnational business

The term *international business* simply implies that an organization is operating in more than one country or, to put this another way, organizations from different countries are trading across their national boundaries. In this sense it is a generic term. A business that is *multinational* is one conducting international business and operating in several countries; but, in addition, Bartlett and Ghoshal (1989) suggested the term implies some decentralization of strategy and management decision making to overseas subsidiaries, with little co-ordination of activities and subsidiaries across national boundaries. In other words subsidiaries operating in different countries are allowed considerable autonomy in terms of their strategies, which are largely determined by local conditions. In contrast, a *global business* is one conducting its activities in a large range of countries across the world with a single strategy that is highly co-ordinated and integrated throughout the world. Company strategy is determined centrally and subsidiaries have little autonomy in their operations. Finally, the term *transnational business* describes the situation when an organization conducts its activities across national boundaries, with varying degrees of co-ordination, integration and local differentiation of strategy and operations, depending on market and business conditions.

Globalization

One of the most used yet complex terms in international business is *globalization*. The word is used to describe a range of related but distinct, sociological, economic, political and business phenomena. In general terms, globalization refers to the development of global or worldwide business activities, competition and markets and the increasing global interdependence of national economies.

In economic terms, globalization refers to the increasing interdependence between national economies and markets. From a sociological perspective, it describes an increasing degree of cultural interaction and convergence between the countries of the world. From the standpoint of business, globalization describes the increasingly global nature of markets, the tendency for transnational businesses to configure their business activities on a worldwide basis, and to co-ordinate and integrate their strategies and operations across national boundaries.

Definitions of globalization

Globalization of economies – increasing interdependence between national economies throughout the world.

Globalization of markets – increasing homogenization of consumer tastes and product preferences in certain markets, as evidenced by the popularity of global brands in certain markets, like Armani, Hugo Boss and Calvin Klein in fashion clothing, McDonald's, Burger King and Pizza Hut for fast food, and Coca-Cola and Pepsi-Cola for soft drinks.

Globalization of industries – the increasing globalization of the productive process, with firms choosing to concentrate or disperse value-adding activities around the world according to the locational advantages to be obtained.

Globalization of strategy – the extent to which an international business configures and co-ordinates its strategy globally. A global strategy will normally include a global brand name and products, presence in major markets throughout the world, productive activities located so as to gain maximum advantage, and co-ordination of strategy and activities throughout the world.

Although the origins of globalization can be traced back to the early history of international business, its rapid acceleration in the 19th and 20th centuries can be attributed to relatively recent developments in:

- *manufacturing technology*, which began during the industrial revolution, making mass production possible;

- *transportation technology*, like railways, motor transport, steam shipping and aeroplanes, allowing the movement of people, materials and finished products from country to country and continent to continent more quickly and cheaply;
- *information and communications technology*, like the telephone, computers, the Internet, satellite television, which have together contributed to both the globalization of markets and the global co-ordination of worldwide business activities;
- *trade liberalization*, through GATT (the General Agreement on Tariffs and Trade) and its successor, the WTO (the World Trade Organization), which have reduced tariff and other barriers to trade between countries;
- *rising real term incomes*, which have contributed to an increase in demand for products and services worldwide.

GATT and the WTO

The most prominent international trade agreements are the *General Agreement on Tariffs and Trade* (GATT) and its successor, the *World Trade Organization* (WTO). The GATT agreement began life as the Havana Charter 1948 when 23 countries acted as signatories to what they hoped would become an international trading organization (ITO). As negotiations progressed, it became clear that such a worldwide trading block was too ambitious and so a 'general agreement' was arrived at. The main points of the agreement were as follows:

❑ tariffs should not be increased above current levels;
❑ quotas should be reduced and eventually abolished;
❑ each signatory was a 'most favoured nation' (this meant that trading privileges extended by one member nation to another must be widened to include all of the others);
❑ the general agreement recognized that other trading blocks may exist, such as the EU and NAFTA (North American Free Trade Area), but these were encouraged to be outward-looking rather than insular as far as trading restrictions were concerned.

The WTO has evolved over the years through the staging of several 'rounds' of lengthy and complicated negotiation. The number of countries subscribing to the WTO has grown as the various rounds have progressed. With over 100 members, the WTO now accounts for about 80% of international trade. Overall, the WTO has succeeded in generally reducing import tariffs and significantly cutting down on quotas. Recent rounds have focused on attempting to reduce the stark variations in prosperity between wealthy and poorer countries – the 'north–south dialogue'.

Globalization and business

From the perspective of business, interest in globalization centres on two major facets: the globalization of markets and the globalization of production and the supply chain. Levitt's seminal work of 1983, 'The globalization of markets' (Levitt, 1983), suggested that technological change, social, political and economic developments have, in recent decades, driven the world toward a 'global village' or 'converging commonality' – a homogenized, unified global market in terms of consumer tastes and product preferences. For Levitt, the main beneficiaries of this convergence would be global organizations producing globally standardized products in order to achieve world economies of scale. Such global businesses are able (because of scale economies) to undercut the prices of more nationally orientated competitors. Levitt concluded that a global strategy must be based on standardization of product, branding and advertising.

While there is strong evidence that many markets are becoming increasingly global in certain respects, an approach to strategy that concentrates almost exclusively on standardization and costs represents an oversimplification of the situation. The global environment is becoming increasingly complex and requires more sophisticated approaches to strategy. There are important variations in consumer needs regionally and locally, as well as globally. At the same time as markets become more global, consumers are becoming more sophisticated, demanding products (goods and services) that are differentiated rather than standardized. Thus, although the market may be essentially global, the sophistication of consumers' needs and wants will dictate that strategy must be flexible and responsive, rather than rigidly standardized.

A further complexity is that globalization is not confined simply to consumer markets but also relates to the global scope of all of an organization's business operations and its ability to compete on a global scale (Yip, 1992). Yip used the term 'total global strategy' to describe an approach to strategy that embraces the worldwide scope of an organization's activities, a view that the whole world is a potential market. Yip, however, recognized the need to adapt aspects of strategy where local conditions dictate.

Porter (1990) focused on the globalization of an organization's value-adding activities. Globalization has given business the opportunity to configure its activities so as to take account of locational and other advantages arising from differences in resources, skills and economic conditions in different parts of the world. By configuring its activities to take advantage of these differences and by co-ordinating its global activities effectively, an organization can gain global competitive advantage. Bartlett and Ghoshal (1989) used the word *transnational* to describe the configuration, co-ordination and control of global business activities across national boundaries in the pursuit of global competitiveness, at the same time as encompassing local adaptation and differentiation of organizational strategy and structures. Such an approach to business allows an organization to take advantage of both global and local advantages and opportunities.

Both markets and the ways in which international businesses configure and co-ordinate their activities are becoming increasingly *global in scope* and *transnational in nature*. It is the process of developing global and transnational strategies, and the management and co-ordination of worldwide operations that provide the main focus to this text.

It should be obvious that definitions of the term globalization that are either overly prescriptive or vague are not particularly useful. Few markets and industries are fully global although many display global characteristics (Yip, 1992). A global strategy of complete world standardization is therefore unlikely to be successful and, as a result, very few (if any) organizations adopt such strategies. Otherwise 'global' corporations like McDonald's and Coca-Cola make minor adjustments to their strategies as national circumstances demand. Using the term 'globalization' to describe the strategy of any company expanding abroad is too wide in scope since it would encompass all businesses with any interests overseas, and clearly not all such organizations are global.

Globalization – is it a blessing or a curse?

Globalization has become one of the most contentious political and economic issues of modern times. It is the subject of debate, demonstrations and even violence. So what is it that gives rise to such passions and are there any answers to the problems?

There is no single form of globalization; rather there are many. Globalization of markets is the development of products satisfying customer needs that are common throughout the world ('market' in this context refers to the demand side of an economic system of exchange). This may be the need for fast food, soft drinks, films, popular music, sport, fashion clothing, fragrances, computers, consumer electronics and so on. In these circumstances consumer needs throughout the world appear to have grown more similar, perhaps based on cultural convergence (i.e., national cultures growing more similar to each other). The advantage to consumers is that their choice of products has widened and that prices have fallen. The advantage to producers is that they are able to earn much higher revenues, which in turn finance research and development of new products, and that they are able to achieve economies of scale, which then reduce unit costs of production. Sony, the Japanese electronic giant, is able to introduce a constant stream of new and improved products, financing the development out of global sales revenues and keeping prices low on the basis of the huge economies of scale obtained.

The second form of globalization relates to the way in which firms organize their value-adding activities on a worldwide basis, according to availability of resources, cost levels, skills, quality and so on. The firms benefit from much lower unit cost levels and often higher quality manufacturing. Consumers benefit from lower prices and increased choice, together with better quality. Designer clothing, including labels like Ralph Lauren, Calvin Klein, Armani and Yves St Laurent, is produced in the Far East and thus made affordable to consumers because of low production costs (because labour costs are often cheaper in the Far East than in the West).

Both the globalization of markets and production have led to the development of huge transnational organizations or global companies whose revenues exceed the national incomes of many medium-sized countries. Such organizations produce and sell throughout the world. Organizations like General Electric, Microsoft, Procter and Gamble, Unilever, Sony, Ford, General Motors, Toyota and their activities span the globe.

At the same time technological developments like the Internet and air travel have considerably increased the interdependence between the countries of the world. Increased travel and improved communications have increased awareness of ethnic products and of political, social and economic events and changes. Satellite television, films and package holidays have all increased consumers' awareness of and demands for foreign products.

The blessings

Many people argue that these types of globalization have brought many benefits. Consumers have access to a much wider range of products, which are constantly being updated, and at relatively low prices. Increased global trade has made people wealthier and allowed them to lead more diverse lifestyles. Companies benefit from access to global markets and low cost production in developing countries. Developing countries like Thailand, Vietnam and Cambodia, it is argued, benefit from increased levels of employment and increasing wage levels. Transnationals like Nike pay wages well above the local average but well below those in the USA.

Globalization is not entirely a new phenomenon, however. Trade between nations goes back centuries and even millennia, but the extent of globalization and its rate of increase have been most marked in the years following World War II (1939–45). There are many reasons that may account for this change. Rising real term (i.e., after inflation) incomes and living standards have led to a dramatic increase in demand for consumer products while international travel and communications have introduced consumers to products from other countries. Western democracies have played an important role by placing increasing emphasis on the market economy as a vehicle for economic growth and by building and strengthening international ties as a way of fostering trade and good international relations.

The developing of international ties, increasing travel and the development of the Internet have diminished the importance of national borders and brought about greater interdependence and fusing of individual national markets. At the same time the reduction in protectionist barriers, resulting from the work of organizations like GATT and its successor, the WTO, has stimulated free movement of products and capital and paved the way for the development of transnational organizations with centres throughout the world.

So, globalization has been welcomed by consumers and by capitalists who believe in international free trade between nations as a matter of principle. For consumers, international trade has increased competition, driven down prices, given greater choice in High Street stores, and these factors have, in turn, resulted in greater spending, rising living standards and increased international travel. In addition, sympathizers with globalization say it has increased information flows between countries, assisted cross-cultural understanding, promoted democracy and furthered world peace. The fall of communism in Eastern Europe and the absence of a major war in Western Europe since 1945 are all attributed, at least in part, to increased international trade and understanding between the nations of the world.

The curses

In the face of all these economic, social and political benefits, it may be difficult to understand why several anti-globalization demonstrations have taken place. What is it that arouses such anti-globalization passions? The groups of demonstrators who protested against globalization in Seattle in November 2000 at the World Trade Organization conference in London, at the G8 meeting in Genoa, and in Prague at the annual meetings of the International Monetary Fund and the World Bank clearly believe that globalization is essentially a harmful phenomenon.

The demonstrators argue that the gains in living standards in the developed countries has been at the expense of the developing countries. While living standards have risen for many as a result of globalization, more than a billion people live in extreme poverty throughout the world. Globalization has brought no benefits for these people. In fact, the share of the global income of the poorest people in the world fell throughout the 1990s. The already impoverished countries are becoming even poorer. The gap between rich and poor is becoming ever wider. They argue that although transnational organizations may have brought employment to some developing countries, some are accused of employing child labour, condoning inhumane working conditions and paying slave wages among producers in developing countries. In addition to this, what of the underdeveloped countries in Africa that have enjoyed little or no investment by transnationals and whose economies show little or no sign of development?

Even in the developed economies, globalization has been the cause of problems. In developed countries there have been huge job losses among unskilled workers as transnationals shift production to low-wage economies in the developing world. Some small businesses in developed countries are afraid of transnationals, fearing that they may be forced out of business if they are unable to emulate the economies of scale and low costs of these global juggernauts.

Globalization brings threats to the national cultures and identities of developing and developed countries alike through the spread of satellite TV, the development of international media networks and increased personal travel. Some traditional customs, industries and languages are disappearing.

Huge transnational companies are seen as a threat to democracy as they have greater economic power than the governments of the developing countries in which they are operating. They may fatally damage the economy of a country by attaching greater importance to shareholder value than to social, cultural and national economic concerns. It is suggested that they threaten human rights through their selfish pursuit of profit.

The transnationals are also accused of damaging the ecological environment in the pursuit of profits. Developing countries contribute little to the world's pollution problems while the developed countries contribute much. Transnationals may bring the problem to the developing countries as they seek ever increasing levels of low-cost production. Increasing levels of global consumption also threaten the world's non-renewable resources. Our living standards today may be at the expense of future generations. Our growth in living standards may not be sustainable.

The opposition groups

The protesters who have gathered in Seattle, London, Genoa and Prague to highlight these fundamental issues represent a disparate group of causes, unified only by their opposition to globalization. They are an unlikely coalition of environmentalists, anti-poverty campaigners, trade unionists, anti-capitalist groups and anarchists who tend to view globalization and transnational companies as a major threat to people, the developing countries and the environment. One umbrella group that sought to unite these anti-globalization groups in Prague was the Initiative Against Economic Globalization (INPEG). It provided the campaigning groups with training in demonstration management, making human chains, first aid, tree climbing, street theatre and communicating with the media. INPEG described itself as 'a loose coalition of various Czech environmental, human rights and autonomist/

anarchist groups, organizations and individuals who are ready to stand up critically against the summit of the world financial oligarchy.'

The record of these demonstrations is not itself good. They have been marred by violence, death and destruction of property. These acts may only be perpetrated by a small minority of demonstrators, but they feature heavily in the portrayal of the demonstration by the world's media. The heavy media coverage of these acts of violence tends to cloud the basic issues of social justice, sustainability and ecology that underpin the globalization debate. It is ironic, however, that it is the world's media, the epitome of globalization itself, that allows the debate to take place across national and continental boundaries. Perhaps this is indicative of the fact that the global village, predicted by Marshall McLuhan, has already arrived.

Can globalization be managed?

If globalization is a trend that can be traced back far into our history and that is inextricably intertwined with so many people's lives, can its march be halted? Indeed, is it desirable to halt its march? It is likely that it is impossible to halt the driving forces behind globalization. The vast majority of people throughout the world, especially in developed countries, are addicted to consumerism and actively seek new products at low prices. They may well be concerned about the conditions under which the products are produced, but are unwilling to completely boycott their purchase. Nevertheless, companies like Nike have been forced to monitor and improve the conditions under which the workers producing their products are employed. They have sought to eliminate child labour, raise wage levels and provide social and medical benefits to workers in the factories producing the products as a result of the pressure of public opinion.

People in developing countries lived in poverty before globalization, and it is unlikely that poverty can be meaningfully tackled without the assistance of foreign governments and without investment from transnationals. The wages paid by transnationals in developing countries may be well below those paid to workers in developed countries but they are, nevertheless, often well above average wage levels throughout the developing world.

The answer to the problems posed by globalization may therefore not be to try to prevent change, but to seek to ameliorate and eliminate its harmful consequences. In other words governments, international bodies like the WTO, IMF and World Bank, and transnational businesses must work together to create conditions under which the potential benefits of globalization are realized while its potentially damaging outcomes are eradicated.

Free trade between countries is often presented as necessary for global business. Yet free trade need not mean a complete absence of regulation. The dangers of the monopoly power of developed countries and huge transnationals must be controlled. Developing countries must be assisted in achieving economic prosperity. Free trade need not be unregulated trade. Bodies like the WTO seek to develop rules through which developing countries and their populations are protected. The problem is that developing countries are a majority of the WTO's members and can dominate its proceedings. This is not surprising when half the least developed countries have no representation at the WTO headquarters in Geneva. The WTO must find mechanisms for representing the opinions of developing countries and for implementing rules that prevent developed countries and transnational businesses from striking deals that harm the developing world. Furthermore, the WTO must set and achieve development targets that reduce poverty, create sustainable development and protect the environment.

The world's governments have agreed to targets like halving the number of people living in poverty by 2015, universal primary education in all countries by 2015, gender equality, a reduction of two-thirds in infant mortality rates by 2015, improved primary health care and the implementation of national strategies for sustainable development in all countries by 2005.

The reduction of poverty is not simply a social and moral issue it is also economic and political. Globalization means increasing interdependence between nations. If the poorer countries become richer then they become markets for the products and services of transnationals. If developing countries have social and political problems then they also affect developed countries. As a consequence it is in the interests of developed countries to assist their development. The uneven spread of the benefits of globalization, as illustrated by the development of East Asian countries compared with the failure to improve the lives of millions of people in rural Africa, remains an issue.

It remains a challenge for the governments of poorer countries to create domestic conditions that attract foreign investment. This means the elimination of corruption, the development of education, the regulation of working conditions and the provision of primary health care. These governments cannot achieve these goals on their own and must be assisted by developed countries and by international bodies. There are many causes of poverty, but it is widely accepted that education is an important factor in its reduction. Recent research suggests that investing in primary education, particularly for girls, is the most effective path to economic development and the elimination of poverty. Education creates a skilled and adaptable workforce that attracts inward investment and rising levels of income. At the present time (2003) it is estimated that worldwide 113 million children of primary school age have never gone to school and a further 150 million drop out before achieving basic literacy and numeracy skills.

Transnational businesses can themselves play a much greater role in reducing poverty and creating sustainable development. They can insist on best practice in relation to child labour, corruption, corporate governance, human rights, health and safety, and the environment, so creating employment, eliminating poverty and improving conditions in poor countries. Many companies have already realized the benefits to their reputations and productivity levels that can be achieved by investing and setting standards in poor countries.

Developed countries might also set a better example in terms of protecting the environment, reducing pollution and preserving natural resources. Developing countries might then, in turn, ensure that their newly emerging industries conform to global environmental agreements (such as the Rio and Kyoto Protocols).

A key way in which developed countries can assist the poorer nations is through aid. Developing countries have already been given huge amounts of aid, but it has often been given unwisely and used equally as badly. Lending governments have often tied aid to contracts for their countries' products. The governments of developing countries have often not made the best use of the money that they have received. It is generally accepted that aid should be used to create conditions in developing countries which not only help the poor but also attract inward investment that assists in promoting economic growth.

Globalization cannot be prevented but can be managed by governments, international bodies and global businesses to raise living standards for all.

Global and transnational strategy

Yip (1992) used the term *total global strategy* more broadly than many other writers, arguing that '*a* [global] *strategy can be more or less global in its different elements.*' To avoid confusion with more limited definitions of global strategy this book uses the term *transnational strategy*. A transnational strategy is one that combines a global configuration and co-ordination of business activities with local responsiveness, based on continuous organizational learning, and consists of:

- global knowledge-based core competences giving access to global markets;
- extensive participation in major world markets;
- global configuration of value-adding activities which exploits both national similarities and differences;
- global co-ordination and integration of activities;
- local responsiveness where required;
- differentiated structure and organization.

The definition of globalization and transnational strategy above provide the focus of this book.

Table 1.1 shows how international business has developed over recent decades. Note how the configuration of international activities has increased over time.

Structure of the book

The emphasis of this book – on global and transnational strategy, rather than international or multinational strategy and management – reflects the major changes that have taken place in the environment of international business since the early 1980s. These changes accelerated in the 1990s and have continued into the 21st century (see Chapter 2). The overarching theme is the link between the trend toward globalization of competition, markets and products, and the consequent imperative to adopt global and transnational strategies and approaches to management.

Competition in many industries and markets has become increasingly global rather than international in scope (Porter, 1990; Yip, 1992). As a consequence, many established international businesses have replaced their traditional country-centred multidomestic strategies with ones that involve closer co-ordination and integration of geographically dispersed

Table 1.1   The evolution of international and global strategy (1950–21st century)

Period	International strategy of the period
1950s/1960s	Multinational expansion through the establishment of miniature replica subsidiaries abroad. Predominance of multidomestic strategies, with largely autonomous foreign subsidiaries supplying local/regional markets. Limited global co-ordination or integration of geographically dispersed operations.
1970s	Multinationals in retreat: divestments, rationalizations and host country plant closures.
1980s	Shift toward co-ordinated and integrated global strategies by established MNEs (multinational enterprises); focus on global competitiveness and use of global scope as a competitive weapon in global industries involving plant specialization and national interdependency.
1990s	Transition to global and transnational strategies. Businesses focus on developing core competences with outsourcing of other non-core activities. This results in the development of global networks and strategic alliances that are both horizontal and vertical. Increasing emphasis on knowledge as an asset and early forms of learning organization begin to develop.
2000s	The era of the 'virtual corporation' and the 'intelligent organization'.

operations. In other words organizations and strategies are no longer best described as multinational but as global and transnational.

The extent of globalization, however, varies both within and between industries and markets and its effects vary from country to country. Indeed, there are still many industries and markets where local conditions dictate local adjustments to strategy and management. These factors raise major implications for management within businesses. It is therefore necessary to adopt a co-ordinated approach to global production, technology, marketing, financial, human resource management and so on, combined with differentiated structures and strategies where and when local conditions require. A global or transnational strategy, therefore, implies taking advantage of both global and local conditions through a differentiated, rather than standardized, approach to business.

Part II of the book (Chapters 2–5) is concerned mainly with developing an understanding of global business and the globalization of the business environment. The implications of globalization for business strategies are examined in Part III (Chapters 6–8). Part IV (Chapters 9–14) examines global and transnational business management. The remainder of this chapter develops the concept of globalization further and explains the approach adopted to the processes of strategic management.

Increasing global co-ordination in Philips Electronics

In 1991, Philips of the Netherlands – one of the world's largest electronics multinationals – celebrated its one-hundredth anniversary. The celebrations coincided with the announcement of a major change in Philips' corporate mission and strategy for the 1990s aimed at improving global competitiveness.

Although operating on a global scale with a very large number of geographically dispersed activities, Philips was not a global company. Historically, the company had adopted a multidomestic or country-centred strategy with national subsidiaries being responsible mainly for the domestic markets in which they operated and with a lack of global co-ordination and integration of activity in different countries. By the late 1980s, it had become obvious to senior executives that this multidomestic strategy was becoming increasingly inappropriate given the rapid changes taking place in the world's electronics industry. The most important of these were:

❑ the globalization of the market and the emergence of strong global competitors, especially from the Far East;
❑ rapid technology change leading to a stream of new product developments and closer convergence between consumer and professional electronics;
❑ changes in production processes (e.g., CADCAM) that were becoming much less labour-intensive;
❑ new patterns of industry competition and co-operation through strategic alliances; and
❑ fluctuating exchange rates.

In response to these changes, electronics companies required global sales to achieve economies of scale and learning curve effects. They also needed to spread R&D costs and to justify new product developments.

The major change in Philips' corporate strategy and mission was the adoption of a global orientation or strategic vision with the objective of becoming a leading global electronics company with strengths in the major 'triad' markets of the USA, Europe and the Far East. The adoption of a global philosophy and a reorientation of strategy toward global markets was to be achieved through the implementation of several changes in the worldwide strategy and management of the company. The major measures included:

- the adoption of globalization and an orientation to global markets;
- restructuring of product development and production for global market distribution through the establishment of international production centres (IPCs) as manufacturing centres for products aimed at world markets;
- centralization of product policy and planning aimed at achieving a coherent, integrated global marketing strategy covering product planning, design, development, etc (national marketing, sales and service programmes should complement the overall global product strategy);
- organizational restructuring to conform to global orientation;
- production restructuring, especially a shift from local production for local markets to highly efficient factories for large-volume production for world markets through IPCs;
- improving the management of resources through decentralizing the organization through the establishment of business units and project teams;
- an effective human resource management development programme;
- greater attention paid to the management of external relationships; and
- improving the management of operating systems.

These changes were aimed at achieving a balance between global integration and national responsiveness (i.e., a balance between centralization to achieve global integration and decentralization to achieve national responsiveness).

Global and transnational strategies and management – the issues

The Philips' case illustrates many of the complex strategic and management issues involved in global business including:

- the importance of organizational learning in a turbulent international business environment (industry globalization had made Philips' traditional country-centred strategy inappropriate);

- global strategies involving co-ordination and integration of geo-graphically dispersed operations were becoming essential to maintain competitiveness in global electronics;
- the adoption of global strategies requires an underlying global philosophy or strategic vision;
- the shift from country-centred to global strategies required major changes in the internal management of Philips – especially in production, logistics, R&D, human resource management and development, etc.;
- the shift to global strategies implied significant changes in organization and control.

In this complex area we need to draw a distinction between the conception of strategy and that of management. Strategy concerns organizational learning about the business and its environment and the development of knowledge that produces core competences which position the organization favourably with regard to the variables in the environment (which in the case of international business are usually very complex and turbulent environments). Management is concerned with how the company configures and oversees its internal value-adding and support activities to implement its strategy and achieve competitive advantage. The key issues surrounding global and transnational strategy and management are summarized in Table 1.2.

A framework for global and transnational strategic management

The controversies in strategic management

Strategic management is a comparatively young discipline and, in consequence, there is considerable debate over which approach managers should adopt in devising their strategies. The alternative approaches are considered here before the frameworks used in this book are developed. McKiernan (1997) identified four well-established approaches to strategic management. The approaches can be broadly identified as:

1. *the prescriptive approach* (also called the deliberate or planned approach);
2. *the emergent (or learning) approach*;
3. *the competitive positioning approach*;
4. *the resource, competence and capability approach.*

Table 1.2 Global and transnational business strategy and management: the issues

	Issues involved
(a) *Global and transnational strategy*	
Global transnational strategy (how the organization positions itself with regard to the global business environment and how it formulates its strategies).	Knowledge, global core competence and capability. Global generic/hybrid strategy. Competence and strategy relationships. Global, transnational, regional and multidomestic strategies. Collaborative network strategies – the virtual corporation. Learning organizations – knowledge-based competition.
Global/transnational marketing servicing (how the global organization sets about responding to and servicing its markets – its groups of customers in various parts of the world).	Market-servicing strategies – the alternatives: exporting; contractual agreements; joint ventures strategies, foreign direct investment (FDI); cross-border mergers, acquisitions and strategic alliances.
Subsidiary strategies (how the organization deals with its subsidiaries in other parts of the world).	Types of subsidiaries – subsidiary and global strategies. Evolution of subsidiary strategies. Subsidiary strategies and management.
(b) *Global and transnational management*	
Human resource management (how the global organization manages its people).	Transformational leadership. Staffing and expatriate policies. Cross-cultural management and global management development.
Production and logistics management (how the organization manages its main value-adding activities, such as manufacturing and distribution).	Global production. Global logistics. Plant location. Global procurement (purchasing).
Technology management (how the organization invests in and employs all technologies)	Technology accumulation, development, diffusion and deployment. Technology and competitiveness.
Marketing management (how the organization understands and communicates with its customers).	Role of marketing in global strategy. Global marketing. Global marketing strategies. Segmentation and positioning for global markets. Global marketing mix.
Financial management (how the organization raises funds for global activity and how it manages its financial resources in a complex environment).	Financing international development. Strategies for managing exchange rate risk. Transfer pricing. Financial strategies for global competitiveness.
Organizational structure and global control (how the organization is structured and controlled to achieve its global objectives).	Organizational structures – types and evolution of. Organizational culture. Decision making and control. Global strategy, structure and competitiveness.

More recently the focus in the literature has shifted to a *knowledge-based approach* to competitive advantage (Nonaka et al., 2000; Stonehouse and Pemberton, 1999). This approach combines elements of the various methodologies of strategic management, particularly learning and resource-based strategy and is the basis of this book.

Each of these approaches to strategic management has its distinct characteristics and emphases. Equally, however, the approaches are interlinked and share certain concepts. No single approach presents a prescription for a complete methodology of strategic management. As a consequence, we draw on certain of the frameworks developed by each school of thought, in order to develop a methodology for devising transnational strategies. Global strategic management is by its nature an eclectic academic discipline.

The prescriptive or deliberate approach to strategy

This approach focuses on long-term planning aimed at achieving a 'fit' between an organization's strategy and its environment (Ansoff, 1965; Learned et al., 1965; Argenti, 1974; Andrews, 1987). Internal competences are matched to opportunities and threats in the environment. Strategic management is presented as a highly systematized and deterministic process, from the setting of objectives through external and internal analysis, to the formulation and implementation of a grand organizational strategy aimed at achieving a 'fit' between the organization and its environment. Each stage of the process is highly structured and prescribed.

The major advantage of such systematized planning is that it structures complex information, defines and focuses business objectives, establishes controls, and sets targets against which performance can be measured.

There are, however, dangers inherent in an approach that is overly prescriptive. The business environment (particularly complex international environments) can be very chaotic and complex. The information on which planning is based can accordingly be uncertain and often inaccurate. To adopt rigidly defined plans based on incomplete information may result in flawed decision making. Accordingly, strategies must be adapted to take advantage of unanticipated opportunities and to deal with unanticipated threats.

The emergent or learning approach to strategy

The complexity and dynamism of modern business organizations and their environments has led many writers to suggest that strategy will emerge and evolve incrementally over time (Lindblom, 1959; Mintzberg and Waters, 1985; Mintzberg et al., 1995). It has been suggested that organizations simply 'muddle through' in the face of complexity. The research of Quinn (1978), however, suggests that, rather than 'muddling through', many organizations continually adapt their strategies to changing circumstances. He termed this approach *logical incrementalism*. In other words strategy evolves rationally in response to changes in the environment.

Mintzberg argued that strategy is a combination of deliberate plans and emergent adjustments over time. There is likely to be a substantial difference between planned (or intended) strategy and the strategy that is actually realized by an organization. Some aspects of intended strategy will not be realized, while other elements of emergent strategy, will evolve as the strategy is carried out. Logical incrementalism is therefore a fusion of planning and the incremental adaptation of plans.

The competitive positioning approach to strategy

Strategic management thinking in the 1980s was dominated by the work of Michael Porter at the Harvard Business School whose *five forces, generic strategy and value chain* frameworks (1980 and 1985) added considerably to the tools available to the business strategist. In essence, Porter's approach to strategic management begins with analysis of the competitive environment using the five-forces framework. This serves two major purposes. It indicates the potential profitability of the industry and assists in identifying the appropriate generic strategy for acquiring competitive advantage. External analysis is followed by value chain analysis, which examines the value-adding activities of the organization and the linkages between them. The final stage is selection of a generic strategy, supported by the appropriate configuration of value-adding activities. This, Porter argued, will position the business in its competitive environment in such a way that it achieves competitive advantage. McKiernan (1997) suggested that this approach can be termed *outside-in* as the initial focus is on the competitive environment rather than the resources of the organization.

Porter's approach has been criticized on the grounds that:

- it is prescriptive and static;

- differences in industry profitability do not necessarily determine the profitability of the organizations within them (Rumelt, 1991);
- it highlights (and presupposes) competition rather than collaboration;
- it emphasizes the environment rather than the competences of the corporation.

Despite these criticisms, Porter's work provides tools that are invaluable to managers seeking to make sense of complex environments and activities.

The resource, competence and capability approach to strategy

Just as the 1980s were dominated by the competitive positioning school of thought, the 1990s saw the rise of resource-based theories of strategic management. These emphasized the importance not of the organization's position in relation to its industry but rather the way in which it manages its resource inputs in developing *core competences and distinctive capabilities* (Prahalad and Hamel, 1990; Stalk et al., 1992; Kay, 1993; Heene and Sanchez, 1997). Research in the late 1980s and early 1990s (Rumelt, 1991; Baden-Fuller and Stopford, 1992) suggests that choice of industry is not a major factor in determining business profitability. The core competence of the organization is of greater importance. This indicates an 'inside-out' approach to strategic management based on the premise that competitive advantage depends on the behaviour of the organization rather than its competitive environment.

Competence-based theories are not new; they came to prominence in the 1990s. Prahalad and Hamel (1990) argued that an organization must identify and build on its core competence:

Core competencies are the collective learning of the organisation, especially how to co-ordinate diverse production skills and integrate multiple streams of technologies.

The organization may then exploit these competences in a wide variety of markets. The emphasis on organizational learning as a source of competitive advantage has resulted in renewed interest in knowledge as an organizational competence (Quinn, 1992; Demarest, 1997; Grant, 1997; Sanchez and Heene, 1997). The resource-based approach also emphasizes the potential advantages of collaboration between organizations whose competences are mutually complementary (Sanchez and Heene, 1997).

To give an example of collaboration, let us consider the UK retailer Marks & Spencer whose core competences have traditionally lain in retailing and related activities and not in manufacturing. For this reason the manufacturing of the products sold in Marks & Spencer stores is outsourced to chosen manufacturers. Marks & Spencer collaborate with such manufacturers at home and abroad in the design and manufacture of the clothing, furniture and food products sold in the stores. There are advantages to both sides in such relationships. For Marks & Spencer there are advantages in terms of quality and cost control, input to the design process, freedom to concentrate on marketing and retailing activities. For the collaborating manufacturers there are the advantages of the St Michael brand name, access to a large number of retail outlets, long-term supply agreements, etc. Both sides benefit from collaboration by being able to concentrate on their respective areas of core competence. Furthermore, collaborative relationships are much more difficult for competitors to emulate. In this way, the ability of both Marks & Spencer and its suppliers to compete with other retailers and manufacturers is enhanced by the collaborative relationships. The recent recovery of Marks & Spencer after a difficult period has been highly dependent on a refocusing of its core competences and the development of new global strategic relationships with suppliers.

Developments in information and communications technology have transformed collaborative relationships so that co-operating organizations can be characterized as what have become known as 'virtual' corporations (Davidow and Malone, 1992; Alexander, 1997). It is therefore no longer sufficient to analyse the strategies of individual organizations. The dynamics of linked organizations and their strategies must be examined.

Despite the insight that the competence-based approach provides, two criticisms can be levelled at it:

1. It suffers from a lack of well-developed analytical frameworks – McKiernan (1997) pointed out that it is ironic that it is Michael Porter who 'developed one of the most useful tools for internal resource analysis in the value chain' when the major focus of the resource-based view is on internal activities.

2. It tends to overlook and even neglect the importance of the competitive environment – research by McGahan and Porter (1997) revived the

view that industry is an important determinant of profitability as well as the business itself.

An increasing body of evidence (Hamel and Prahalad, 1994; Narver and Slater, 1990; Greenley and Oktemgil, 1996) suggests that business must be market-driven and sensitive to customer needs. The organization must therefore analyse those markets in which its competences can be exploited. It is evident that the competence-based approach is far from being a complete methodology of strategic management in these respects.

The knowledge-based approach to strategy

Increasingly in the field of strategic management, *knowledge* is viewed as being the only sustainable source of competitive advantage. Organizational knowledge can be defined as *a shared collection of principles, facts, skills, and rules which inform organisational decision-making, behaviour and actions forming the basis of core competences* (Stonehouse and Pemberton, 1999). Knowledge can be categorized as:

- *know-how* (practical knowledge);
- *know-why* (theoretical knowledge);
- *know-what* (strategic knowledge).

For an organization to gain competitive advantage through knowledge it is necessary to create new knowledge through processes of *organizational learning* and manage and utilize existing knowledge through processes of *knowledge management*, so that organizational knowledge is embodied in the firm's core competences and value-adding activities. In many ways, the knowledge-based approach to strategic management is a natural development from the learning and core competence-based approaches. It is the approach to strategy that is largely adopted in this book. Organizations must seek to create new knowledge that is grounded in organizational learning and that underpins core competences and value-adding activities, through which competitive advantage is achieved.

The approach to global strategy in this book

The framework for global strategic management adopted by this book is derived from each of the schools of thought in the field of strategic management discussed in the previous sections. In reviewing the foregoing discussion, we propose the following conclusions:

1. competitive advantage is based on superior organizational knowledge embodied in core competences and value-adding activities;
2. knowledge is created through the process of organizational learning – organizations must seek to learn and create new knowledge more quickly than their rivals;
3. strategy will inevitably be both planned and emergent;
4. competitive advantage can result from both competitive and collaborative behaviour;
5. the complexity and unpredictability of change in both the business environment and in businesses themselves means that businesses must be intelligent or 'learning' organizations.

The implications of these conclusions shape the approach to global strategy adopted in this book.

Assumption 1 *Competitive advantage arises from new and superior knowledge*

Knowledge is the basis of competitive advantage and it is new knowledge that allows organizations to outperform their competitors.

Assumption 2 *Organizational learning and knowledge management are vital to creating and sustaining competitive advantage*

Chaos and complexity require that businesses are flexible and responsive. Such flexibility and responsiveness are critically linked to the ability of organizations to learn. Organizational learning both increases responsiveness and improves competitive performance through the creation of new knowledge. Equally, organizations must manage their knowledge assets effectively to create superior performance.

Assumption 3 *Strategy is both planned and emergent*

We base our discussion of strategy on the working premise that both prescriptive and emergent understandings of strategy are valid in part and that it is possible to construct a model which includes elements of both.

Some *planning* of strategy is necessary so as to:

- set objectives and targets against which performance can be measured;
- organize activities in a meaningful way based on prespecified objectives;
- guide actions and ensure consistency of behaviour.

Equally, a strategy will always be *adapted* (and hence continually emerged) when:

- there are major or minor unanticipated changes in the global business environment;
- goals and targets are not being met (and hence must be continually redefined);
- there are changes in the resources or competences of the organization.

The pace and unpredictability of change means that strategy must be flexible. It is essential that strategic management is not viewed as a one-off planning activity but as a continuous series of iterations constituting organizational learning and the subsequent adaptation of strategy. Such learning must be focused on the core competences of the organization and the changes taking place in its environment. This book attempts to reflect the need for both planning and adaptation of strategy.

Assumption 4 *Competitive advantage results from both internal knowledge-based core competence development and from changing conditions in the business environment*

The implication of this assumption is that both external analysis of the business environment and internal analysis of business competences, resources, activities, etc. are essential to organizational learning. The sequencing of external and internal analyses are not viewed as critical and, in reality, both types of analysis are likely to be undertaken simultaneously. Learning must be viewed as a holistic and continuous process and it is critical, however, that both analyses are undertaken on a continuous basis through external scanning of the environment and through constant monitoring of business performance, activities and competences. Equally, it is critical that the results of internal and external analysis are linked together as they will define the critical strategic issues facing the business at any point in time.

Assumption 5 *It is important to distinguish between industries and markets*

Industries and markets are separate but linked concepts. Whereas industries are defined in terms of competences, technologies and products, markets are defined in terms of customers and customer needs. It is necessary to understand both the concepts and the relationships between them as they will affect strategy. The nature of the industry will affect both the competence development and organization of value-adding activities. Similarly, market and customer needs will determine the ultimate success of any strategy.

Assumption 6 *Competitive advantage results from both competitive and collaborative behaviour*

There is ample evidence that competitive advantage results from the way that individual businesses leverage, develop and deploy their resources and competences. Equally, there is evidence that competitive advantage can be enhanced by the development of collaborative business networks that are often difficult for competitors to emulate. The potential for such collaboration has been increased by developments in information and communications technology that have resulted in the potential for formation of a virtual corporation.

A summary of the frameworks

The frameworks employed in this book have been developed by a number of different researchers and are drawn from each of the schools of strategic management. The frameworks employed are summarized in Figure 1.1.

The global and transnational strategic management process

The management process matrix

The process of global strategic management is best represented as a series of learning loops which constantly iterate. The function of these 'learning loops' is to augment organizational learning so as to continuously develop and improve the transnational strategy of the organization. There is a strategic process that is both formal and informal, planned and emergent.

Figure 1.1 Global/transnational strategy and management – a conceptual summary
STEP = sociological, technological, economic, political; SWOT = strength, weaknesses, opportunities, threats

The process is both 'inside-out' and 'outside-in' as strategy is inevitably shaped by both the environment and by the resources, competences and capabilities of the organization. The global strategic management process therefore forms a matrix that is indicative of the complex series of relationships between the various elements of the framework employed in this book (Figure 1.2).

The major elements in the process matrix

Each chapter of this book examines one or more elements of the process matrix. The order in which the elements occur is not necessarily indicative of the order of analysis. For example, analysis of the global business, its resources, competences and capabilities is covered before analysis of the global business environment, even though in reality the two key stages (internal and external analyses) are usually carried out concurrently. The elements are briefly outlined below and then explored in detail in the remainder of the book.

Globalization and the need for a global mission and objectives
Globalization means that managers must adopt a global strategy underpinned by a global vision and global objectives.

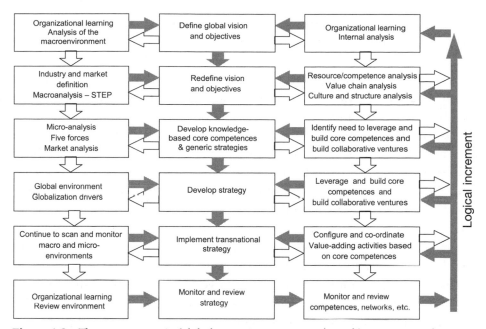

Figure 1.2 The process matrix (global strategic management) used in transnational strategy
STEP = sociological, technical, economic, political

The overall strategic vision or mission of the company must be based on the resources and competences of the organization and the extent of industry and market globalization. Globalization to a large extent is a business philosophy or way of thinking that emphasizes the similarities between national markets rather than the differences. The philosophy also highlights the potential for globalization of organizational activities whether through geographical concentration or dispersion. A transnational strategy will be based on a global vision, but will also involve appropriate local variations.

Organizational learning – analysis of global resources, competences and value-adding activities

Analysis of the business (internal analysis) is concerned with identification of its current and potential strengths and weaknesses in terms of its resources, competences and global activities. Globalization necessitates changes in the way that the value-adding activities of the business are organized, changes in working practices and therefore changes in an organization's structure and culture. Such analysis is aimed at identifying the nature and extent of the changes that are required to support a strategy which is both global and transnational. It will help to determine the global configuration and co-ordination of value-adding activities.

Organizational learning – analysis of the global business environment
Environmental analysis is concerned with understanding the macro and microenvironments in which the business operates (external analysis). Its aim is to establish the key influences on the present and future well-being of the organization and therefore on the choice of strategy. These influences include environmental threats and opportunities. It is to be emphasized that strategy is determined by *both* the competences of the organization and its environment.

In global business there are three particularly important aspects of environmental analysis. First, analysis of the global business environment enables identification of global opportunities and threats. Second, it increases understanding of the competitive environment in the form of the industry and associated markets so that critical success factors can be identified. Third, it establishes the nature and extent of sectoral globalization. The outcome of this analysis is essential in determining the precise nature of the global or transnational strategy of the organization.

Developing knowledge-based global and transnational competences and strategies
This element is concerned with the generation of global strategic options. Such options will be dependent on the development and leveraging of those core competences and distinctive capabilities that support global and transnational strategies.

Various typologies of international business strategy have been developed (Porter, 1986; Bartlett and Ghoshal, 1989; Yip, 1992) that address the issues of global configuration and co-ordination, local responsiveness and differentiated organizational structure. These are blended with recent developments in mainstream strategic management thinking relating to core competences, collaboration and organizational learning. This chapter should be viewed as central to the rest of the book since the type of strategy adopted will have major implications for the global and transnational management, organization and control examined in subsequent chapters. The type of global strategy adopted will also have major implications for strategy at the level of overseas subsidiaries, with Chapter 7 examining the link between subsidiary and corporate strategy in global business.

Global and transnational management is concerned with the implementation of the chosen strategy in the context of a global organization. Issues relating to organizational structure and culture, marketing, finance, logistics, resource allocation, management of technology, location of value-adding activities and human resource management within global businesses are explored.

Conclusion

The rapid growth of international business over the last few decades and the increasing globalization of many industries has led to a proliferation of publications on the subject. The purpose of this book is to provide a review of the work of leading authors in the field and to present this within the context of an integrative framework that establishes clear linkages between global strategy, global management and global competitiveness.

This book is intended as a core text for courses in international and global business at advanced undergraduate, postgraduate and executive levels. It can be differentiated from the competition in at least three main ways. First, many of the currently available texts are intended as basic introductions to international business. This book, in contrast, is both comprehensive and up to date in its coverage of both strategic management and the major issues of global business. Second, this book has a much clearer focus on global and transnational business (strategy and management) than its competitors. Third, the book can be differentiated from the competition in the high level of integration of global and transnational strategy, management and competitiveness throughout the text.

Review and discussion questions

1. Distinguish between globalization and internationalization.
2. Identify and discuss the major stages in the development of international and global strategy.
3. Do you agree with the view that a global strategy implies standardization of products, services, advertising and brand names?
4. Why are the activities involved in strategic management best represented as a matrix?
5. What are the major similarities and differences between the positioning and resource-based schools of strategic management? What are the major limitations of each approach?

6. Discuss the view that strategies cannot be planned because of the complexity and turbulence of the global business environment.

7. Why must strategies be both global and transnational?

References and further reading

Alexander, M. (1997) 'Getting to grips with the virtual organisation'. *Long Range Planning*, **30**(4), February.

Andrews, K. (1987) *The Concept of Corporate Strategy*. Homewood, IL: Irwin.

Ansoff, H.I. (1965) *Corporate Strategy: An Analytical Approach to Business Policy for Growth and Expansion*. New York: McGraw-Hill.

Ansoff, H.I. (1991) 'Critique of Henry Mintzberg's the "Design School" reconsidering the basic premises of strategic management'. *Strategic Management Journal*, September, 449–461.

Argenti, J. (1974) *Systematic Corporate Planning*. Sunbury-on-Thames, UK: Nelson.

Baden-Fuller, C. and Stopford, J. (1992) *Rejuvenating the Mature Business*. London: Routledge.

Bartlett, C.A. and Ghoshal, S. (1989) *Managing Across Borders: The Transnational Solution*. Boston: Harvard Business School Press.

Campbell, D., Stonehouse, G. and Houston, B. (1999) *Business Strategy: An Introduction*. Oxford: Butterworth-Heinemann.

Contractor, F. and Lorange, P. (1988) 'Why should firms co-operate?' *Co-operative Strategies in International Business*. Lexington, NY: Lexington Books.

Cravens, D.W., Greenley, G., Piercy, N.F. and Slater, S. (1997) 'Integrating contemporary strategic management perspectives'. *Long Range Planning*, **30**(4).

Davidow, W.H. and Malone, M.S. (1992) *Structuring and Revitalising the Corporation for the 21st Century – The Virtual Corporation*. London: Harper Business.

Demarest, M. (1997) 'Understanding knowledge management'. *Long Range Planning*, **30**(3), 374–384.

Douglas, S.P. and Wind, Y. (1987) 'The myth of globalization'. *Columbia Journal of World Business*, Winter, 19–29.

Doz, Y. (1986) *Strategic Management in Multinational Companies*. New York: Pergamon Press.

Gamble, P.R. (1992) 'The virtual corporation: An IT challenge'. *Logistics Information Management*, **5**(4), 34–37.

Grant, R.M. (1997) 'The knowledge-based view of the firm: Implications for management practice'. *Long Range Planning*, **30**(3), 450–454.

Greenley, G.E. and Oktemgil, J. (1996) 'A development of the domain of marketing planning'. *Journal of Marketing Management*, **12**.

Hamel, G. and Prahalad, C.K. (1985) 'Do you really have a global strategy?' *Harvard Business Review*, July/August.

Hamel, G. and Prahalad, C.K. (1994) *Competing for the Future*. Boston: Harvard Business School.

Hamel, G., Doz, Y. and Prahalad, C.K. (1989) 'Collaborate with your competitors and win'. *Harvard Business Review*, January/February.

Heene, A. and Sanchez, R. (1997) *Competence-based Strategic Management*. New York: John Wiley & Sons.

Hood, N. and Young, S. (1982) *Multinationals in Retreat: The Scottish Experience*. Edinburgh: Edinburgh University Press.

Jatusripitak, S., Fahey, L. and Kotler, P. (1985) 'Strategic global marketing: Lessons from the Japanese'. *Columbia Journal of World Business*, **20**(1), Spring.

Johanson, J. and Mattson, L.G. (1992) 'Network positions and strategic action'. In: B. Axelsson and G. Easton (eds), *Industrial Networks: A New View of Reality.* London: Routledge.

Johnson, G. and Scholes, K. (1997) *Exploring Corporate Strategy: Text and Cases.* Hemel Hempstead, UK: Prentice Hall.

Kashani, K. (1990) 'Why does global marketing work – or not work?' *European Management Journal,* **8**(2), June.

Kay, J. (1993) *Foundations of Corporate Success.* Oxford, UK: Oxford University Press.

Learned, E.P., Christensen, C.R., Andrews, K.R. and Guth, W.D. (1965) *Business Policy: Text and Cases.* Homewood, IL: Irwin.

Levitt, T. (1983) 'The globalization of markets'. *Harvard Business Review,* May/June.

Lindblom, C.E. (1959) 'The science of muddling through'. *Public Administration Review,* **19**.

McGahan, A.M. and Porter, M.E. (1997) 'How much does industry matter, really?'. *Strategic Management Journal,* **18** (Summer Special Issue), 15–30.

McKiernan, P. (1997) 'Strategy past; strategy futures'. *Long Range Planning,* **30**(5), October.

Mintzberg, H. (1990) 'The design school: Reconsidering the basic premises of strategic management'. *Strategic Management Journal,* March.

Mintzberg, H. and Waters, J.A. (1985) 'Of strategies deliberate and emergent'. *Strategic Management Journal,* **6**.

Mintzberg, H., Quinn, J.B. and Ghoshal, S. (1995) *The Strategy Process: Concepts, Contexts and Cases, European Edition.* Englewood Cliffs, NJ: Prentice Hall.

Narver, J. and Slater, J.C. (1990) 'The effect of market orientation on business profitability'. *Journal of Marketing,* **54**, October.

Nonaka, I., Toyama, R., and Konno, N. (2000) 'SECI, Ba and leadership: A unified model of dynamic knowledge creation'. *Long Range Planning,* **33**(1), 5–34.

Ohmae, K. (1989) 'Managing in a borderless world'. *Harvard Business Review,* May/June, 152–161.

Porter, M.E. (1980) *Competitive Strategy: Techniques for Analysing Industries and Competitors.* New York: Free Press.

Porter, M.E. (1985) *Competitive Advantage.* New York: Free Press.

Porter, M.E. (1986) *Competition in Global Industries.* Boston: Harvard Business School Press.

Porter, M.E. (1990) *The Competitive Advantage of Nations.* New York: Free Press.

Prahalad, C.K. and Doz, Y.L. (1987) *The Multinational Mission: Balancing Local Demands and Global Vision.* New York: Free Press.

Prahalad, C.K. and Hamel, G. (1990) 'The core competence of the corporation'. *Harvard Business Review,* May/June.

Quinn, J.B. (1978) 'Strategic change: "Logic Incrementalism"'. *Strategic Management Journal,* **10**.

Quinn, J.B. (1992) *Intelligent Enterprise: A Knowledge and Service Based Paradigm for Industry.* New York: Free Press.

Quinn, J.B., Dooley, T. and Paquette, P. (1990) 'Technology in services: Rethinking strategic focus'. *Sloan Management Review,* Winter.

Reve, T. (1990) 'The firm as a nexus of internal and external contracts'. In: M. Aoki, M. Gustafsson and O.E. Williamson (eds), *The Firm as a Nexus of Treaties.* London: Sage Publications.

Rumelt, R. (1991) 'How much does industry matter?'. *Strategic Management Journal,* March.

Sanchez, R. and Heene, A. (1997) *Strategic Learning and Knowledge Management.* New York: John Wiley & Sons.

Stalk, G., Evans, P., and Shulmann, L. E. (1992) 'Competing on capabilities: The new rules of corporate strategy'. *Harvard Business Review,* March/April, 57–69.

Stonehouse, G.H. and Pemberton, J.D. (1999) 'Learning and knowledge management in the intelligent organisation'. *Participation and Empowerment: An International Journal,* **7**(5), 131–144.

Yip, G.S. (1992) *Total Global Strategy – Managing for Worldwide Competitive Advantage.* Englewood Cliffs, NJ: Prentice Hall.

PART

FROM NATIONAL CULTURE TO GLOBAL VISION

Learning objectives

After studying this chapter students should be able to:

- understand the causes and nature of globalization;
- describe the effects that increased environmental turbulence has had on globalization;
- define and distinguish between global mission, objectives and strategy;
- understand the nature of culture at national and organizational levels;
- distinguish the forces that influence and characterize culture;
- recognize and understand the influence of culture transnational business strategy and operations;
- identify and apply techniques for managing in different cultural contexts.

Introduction

This chapter explores the relationships between globalization and culture in terms of their impact on the strategy and management of transnational organizations. It may seem paradoxical to devote detailed attention to the implications of national cultural differences for business and management in a book that has globalization as a central theme. Indeed, there are those who have argued that globalization is associated with the development of a business context in which culture is effectively ignored. Such a view, however, is simplistic and to adopt an approach based on this assumption could result in the development of seriously flawed strategy. Although global trends can be identified in many aspects of business, there are also important limitations to the extent of globalization. Similarly, the degree of globalization varies considerably both between and within industries and markets. Even within markets where there are readily identifiable leading global players, important differences exist in both customer needs and local competition that are rooted in still strongly prevalent cultural differences.

McDonald's, for example (perhaps the business most often thought of as being global), adapts its products to local differences and local competition: in some parts of Europe it offers salad dishes and beer; in Greece it offers the 'Greek Mac' (similar to a Big Mac but served in pitta bread with yoghurt replacing mayonnaise); and in China it serves chicken on the bone. All of these variations in offerings are based on differences in culture and taste and on the nature of local competition. Similarly, no manager in a transnational enterprise can afford to ignore the impact of cultural differences on working practices, industrial relations, relationships between managers and employees and so on. Furthermore, cultural differences arise within national cultures based on regional factors and within individual business organizations based on factors like the nature of their business, leadership and country of origin. For all these reasons it is essential that transnational strategy takes account of cultural similarities and differences.

At the same time, the trend toward globalization necessitates that organizations adopt a global vision. It is important to note that a global vision and strategy can, and should, recognize and embrace local cultural and other differences where appropriate. This chapter therefore considers the causes and nature of globalization, the nature of culture and cultural differences, and the need for, and nature of, global vision.

The concept of globalization

Industries and markets

What are industries and markets?
'Globalization' is a frequently used term that is almost as frequently misused. This misuse probably arises from attempts to oversimplify what is, in reality, a complex concept. It is important to distinguish between the globalization of markets and the globalization of industries, as each of these

forms of globalization has different implications for different aspects of business strategy and activity. It is also important to understand the linkages between global industries and markets as the nature of a global and transnational strategy will be influenced by industry and market characteristics.

At their simplest, we can understand the concepts of industry and market by considering them as the two sides of any economic system of exchange. Industries *supply* and markets *demand*. Such a simple definition, however, should not lead us to think that understanding industries and markets in an international setting is as straightforward.

Globalization of markets

Markets are defined by customers and their needs. The extent to which a market is global will depend on the extent to which customer needs for a product are similar throughout the world (a product may consist of a tangible *good*, an intangible *service* or a combination of both). It may well be true that customer needs are becoming increasingly homogeneous with respect to certain products. American jeans have become ubiquitous as have many other items of fashion clothing. Yet there are also many products for which markets remain nationally or regionally differentiated. In most countries of the world there is a customer need for bread, so it might be supposed that a global market for bread exists. In one sense there is, as the market for bread is worldwide. On the other hand, customer preferences for bread differ significantly between countries. For example, the French prefer the baguette, the Indians the chapatti or nan bread, the Greeks pitta bread and so on throughout the world. The market is not global in the sense that customer needs are different in each country. There is evidence that the market is becoming more global in that in many countries it is possible to obtain types of bread associated with other countries. Supermarkets in the UK typically supply all the types of bread listed above, in addition to traditional British white and wholemeal sliced breads. Despite this trend the market is far from global and, even as it becomes more global, there is unlikely to be the standardization of products that Levitt (1983) predicted. In fact, customers are likely to demand an increased variety of products (those previously associated with a variety of countries).

This demand for variety is a consequence of the fact that globalization has made customer needs more informed and sophisticated. They demand more varied and complex products rather than the standardized offerings that some predicted would become the norm. It was also predicted that global customers would be more price-conscious. This may be the case, but in many countries they are often more conscious of quality, technical features and design than price. In serving seemingly global markets, therefore, the business must not only be alert to the similarities in customer needs but also to the differences and to the increasing complexity of their requirements.

Globalization of industries

The globalization of industries is linked, but different in nature, to the globalization of markets. Whereas market globalization is centred on customer needs, industry globalization centres on the ability of businesses to configure and co-ordinate their productive or value-adding activities globally and across national boundaries. A business can choose to disperse all its activities around the world or to disperse some activities and concentrate others in locations that possess specific advantages. For example, Benetton outsources much of its manufacturing to a group of producers concentrated in a particular region of Italy because there is a high density of skilled workers in that area. At the same time as manufacturing activities are concentrated, Benetton retail outlets are dispersed so as to reach customers in different parts of the world. Globalized industries are characterized by worldwide competition, opportunities for economies of scale and scope, rapid technological change, common technical standards and favourable trading conditions.

A global industry is capable of serving fragmented markets by producing products that are adapted to meet local requirements. In most cases, however, global industries serve markets that are themselves increasingly global.

Causes of market and industry globalization

Overview

The causes of globalization are, like their effects, complex. Although globalization is itself regarded as a relatively recent phenomenon, its roots can be traced back to many of the forces causing the internationalization of business activity. There are many excellent accounts of this process (e.g., see Dicken, 1998) and only a summary is presented here. International business can be traced back to many of the earliest civilizations: the

Figure 2.1 Forces leading to globalization

Egyptians, Phoenicians, Greeks and Romans were all heavily involved in trade across national boundaries. Yet the roots of globalization as we understand it today lie in the 18th, 19th and 20th centuries. It is major technological, economic, social and political forces, some recent and others more distant, that have caused businesses to become internationalized and then globalized. All of these forces are closely linked to each other and are largely interdependent (Figure 2.1).

Technological forces

Industrial development

The technological origins of globalization lie in the Industrial Revolution, beginning in the late 18th century and continuing into the 19th and 20th centuries. *Industrialization* marked the beginning of the factory system and mass production of goods. It marked the beginning of 'a new pattern of geographical specialisation' (Dicken, 1998). The continued development of mass production techniques underlies the globalization of industries and the concentration of activities in certain locations, but this has also been dependent on other global forces. Mass production also contributed to the development of mass markets and, ultimately, to global markets. As mass production forced prices down, the global attractiveness of certain products increased.

Improved transportation

Development in transportation is the second technological force without which globalization could not have taken place. The development of railway networks throughout the world and the impact of steam and diesel power on shipping provided the means for moving materials and finished goods around the world. This, in turn, opened national markets to international products on a previously unknown scale at the same time as reinforcing the benefits of concentrated manufacturing. Similarly, air travel has played a major role in the globalization of businesses both by allowing managers to travel quickly anywhere in the world and by allowing consumers to travel widely, giving them experience of products and services that were previously denied to them.

Improved information management

The most recent technological development, which arguably completes the jigsaw of globalization, is that of what has been called the 'information revolution'. Developments in information and communications technology have had major impacts directly on the advance of globalization itself and on its underlying forces. Global communication technologies, like the telephone, the fax, the Internet and electronic mail, have made it possible for businesses to co-ordinate their activities throughout the world. Global communications like satellite television have also played a role in creating global customer needs, increasing awareness of products and brands across the globe.

As well as directly contributing to the globalization of industries and markets, all three groups of technological developments have played a major role in bringing about the economic, political and social changes that have also contributed to globalization.

Social forces

Rising real levels of income coupled with a rise in consumer credit in recent years have contributed to worldwide consumerism. Demand for consumer goods and services has increased beyond recognition in comparison with, say, the postwar years. This has been most evident in the case of motor vehicles, consumer electronics products like televisions, hi-fis, video recorders, telephones and home computers, and white goods like washing machines and refrigerators.

Such products are closely associated with increasing affluence and with converging consumer tastes and wants. Improvements in education and training have also contributed to technological progress and to rising levels of productivity throughout the world that have, in turn, helped to give rise to the globalization of production.

Political and legal forces

Another cause of increasing world trade and globalization has been the gradual reduction in barriers to international trade. Under the provisions of the World Trade Organisation (WTO) and its predecessor GATT (the General Agreement on Tariffs and Trade), barriers to trade have fallen substantially in postwar years, although progress has been uneven. Trading blocs (sometimes called *customs unions*), like the EU and the North American Free Trade Area (NAFTA), have also played a major role in fostering the inter-country trade that is the forerunner of global business.

The increasing legal recognition of intellectual property rights in most countries of the world has played a major part in protecting global products and brands. There have been similar moves to secure acceptance of similar technical standards throughout the world that are particularly important to the development of global consumer electronics products.

Many governments have taken steps to reduce their levels of intervention in economic matters. Privatization has become commonplace alongside gradual real term reductions in overall taxation and government spending. In Eastern Europe the collapse of communism in the late 1980s and early 1990s has opened up markets that were previously closed to international trade. This increasing prevalence of market forces over government regulation has helped to reduce the political barriers to globalization.

Economic forces

Competition in many industries and markets has become increasingly global as the role of governments diminishes and free market forces are allowed to play a more significant role. In addition, the increasing volume of world trade has gone hand in hand with rising real term income levels in the major developed economies. Both are interdependent and closely associated with technological and political developments. Increasing levels of income have greatly stimulated the demand for global products and services. Finally, the finance for world trade has been made available through the development of world financial markets between which transactions charges have been made effectively insignificant by technological developments.

The extent of globalization

From the previous discussion it might seem that the world has already become a global economy and that its industries and markets are already fully globalized. This is far from being the case. Different countries have been affected to differing extents by global trends. World trade remains dominated by the 'Triad' regions of Western Europe, North America, and the Pacific Rim countries of Asia. These three areas account for 80% of the world's output and only 20% of its population and are at the heart of global business. The Triad regions' dominance is based on technological and economic superiority. Other parts of the world like Eastern Europe, Africa and South America are both economically and technologically disadvantaged. As a consequence, the spread of global business is far from geographically complete. Similarly, there are many markets and industries that remain largely localized, and even within global industries there are businesses that operate successfully either only locally or regionally.

For Yip (1992) the debate was not about whether industries and markets were global but rather the *extent* of globalization in an industry and the impact that this has on business strategy. Yip's *globalization driver framework* is developed in Chapter 4 as a tool for analysing the extent of industry and market globalization. The remainder of this chapter, however, is concerned with the forces at work in the global macroenvironment that stimulate globalization rather than the techniques which are used to analyse them. We describe the context in which global managers must make their decisions before the subsequent chapters introduce the techniques available to support the making of such decisions.

Despite many important exceptions, the overall trend is still toward the increased globalization of business. The benefits of globalization are, however, accompanied by some difficulties.

Globalization and environmental turbulence

The example of the South Korean economy

Alongside the forces driving many industries and markets toward global-ization, the business environment is becoming increasingly turbulent, complex and interdependent. The impact of overseas debt and the falling value of the 'won' (the South Korean unit of currency) in 1997–98 on Korean business is an illustration of these unpredictable forces. In the 1990s the Korean economy was growing at a rate averaging almost 9% and Korean corporations like Samsung were investing heavily overseas. Then the country, along with many other South East Asian economies, was hit by a mounting financial crisis as currency values plummeted in the mid-1990s. Despite the positive impact that this might have had on Korean exports, its impact on foreign debt and investment plans was devastating. No one could have predicted such a rapid economic collapse nor that it could affect so many countries.

There are many changes taking place in the global environment with long and short-term implications. The GATT and the WTO have had a significant impact on increasing the volume of world trade since World War II, although progress slowed in the 1990s as the USA and EU wrangled over further reductions in cross-border tariffs. The development of the single European market has significantly affected trade within Europe and between Europe and other regions. At the global level, the opening of Eastern Europe, the Gulf War, the entry of China to the WTO and the growing importance of 'green' issues have all affected global business activity.

Tariffs and quotas

The most used types of governmental restrictions on international trade – the reduction and eventual removal of tariffs and quotas – is one of the stated aims of the WTO. Tariffs are a form of indirect taxation and are levied upon some goods and services on importation into a country. Sometimes referred to as excise duties, tariffs are in-tended partly to raise taxation revenues but mainly to protect domestic production by placing a cost disadvantage on imports. Quotas are limits placed on the volumes of imports and are also intended as a protectionist measure. Quotas can be expressed either in absolute terms (e.g., 1 million tonnes a year) or as a proportion, where, for example, a government may specify that no more than a certain proportion of all units sold (cars, e.g.) can come from a certain foreign country or region.

Currents and cross-currents

Porter (1986a), in discussing these globalization trends, made a distinction between *currents* and *cross-currents* of change.

Currents are the broad forces that have led to the widespread globalization of business since World War II (1939–45) including:

- the growing similarity of countries in many important areas of demand;
- increased fluidity in global capital markets;
- falling tariff barriers;
- technological restructuring and improvement;
- the integrating role of technology;
- the emergence of new global competitors.

Cross-currents are those factors that have made the patterns of international competition different and more complex since the 1960s and 1970s. These include:

- slowing rates of economic growth in some countries that push businesses to internationalize;
- eroding types of competitive advantage (e.g., labour costs that upset the traditional competitive balance between countries);
- new types of government inducements to attract inward investment;
- the proliferation of coalitions between companies and countries;
- the growing ability to tailor products to local demand conditions.

The major cross-currents of global business in the last decade or so are examined later in this chapter. Prior to this, it is necessary to introduce an analytical framework for examining global trends. Changes in the *macro* or *far environment* are major causes of the globalisation of industries and markets. Chapter 5 gives an analysis of the macroenvironment in terms of changes and trends in *social* and *cultural, demographic, political, legal, technological, economic* and *financial* factors, and their effects on international industries and markets – and the businesses that compete within them. These classifications are employed in subsequent sections of this chapter to assist in understanding the nature of changes in the global macroenvironment.

All of these changes in businesses and in the macroenvironment are likely to have a serious impact on the nature and structure of global industries and markets. If international businesses are to cope and thrive in the face of these changes, then they must adopt a more global outlook.

Global mission, objectives and strategy

Globalization implies that managers must develop perspectives that are both global and transnational. They must evolve a global philosophy and culture within their business that underpins a transnational approach to organization and strategy.

Strategy, purpose and objectives

It is not only an organization's competences, strategy and operations that distinguish it from its competitors. Sanchez et al. (1996) argued that 'firms are distinguished by their distinctive sets of goals, as well as by their individual approaches to achieving those goals.' As objectives set out the purpose of the organization, its priorities and standards of performance, it is essential that they are also reviewed as part of the analysis process. Objectives shape global strategy as they set out both the broad and specific intentions of the organization. Objectives define:

- the purpose and *raison d'être* of the organization;
- long and short-term aims and goals of the organization;
- the decision-making framework of the organization;
- anticipated outcomes of its plans and actions.

The objectives of any organization will be determined by:

- the nature of its business activities;
- the resources at its disposal;
- its culture;
- its stakeholders and their influence;
- the environment in which it operates.

A major purpose of the analysis of objectives is to ensure that they continue to be relevant in such a rapidly changing environment. Objectives should lead rather than lag behind organizational change. The need to develop a global vision as the strategic intent guiding a global strategy is an excellent example of this.

Global vision

The highest and broadest level of business objective is the *vision* of the organization. This is a statement of broad aspiration. It deals with where an organization hopes to be in the future. The vision is concerned with the *strategic intent* of the organization (Hamel and Prahalad, 1989, 1994). It is an attempt by managers to identify the gap between where the organization currently is and where it expects to be in the future. Hamel and Prahalad argued that the vision of the organization must relate to its core competences and to its future environment.

A *global vision* is an essential prerequisite to global and transnational strategy. This implies that the whole world is treated as a potential market, competition is viewed as global, that activities are configured to exploit global advantages, that activities are globally co-ordinated and, perhaps most importantly, that the organization has a global philosophy, ethos and outlook. Examples of global vision statements (Pitts and Lei, 1996) are:

CNN – to be the best and most reliable news source on any topic, anywhere, anytime.

Coca-Cola – to ensure that 'a Coke is in arm's reach' of any potential customer anywhere in the world.

McDonald's – to be the leading provider of quality food to anyone, anywhere.

Vision, philosophy and global strategy

Hamill (1992) suggested that a global strategy is, to a large extent, 'a business philosophy or way of thinking.' It is therefore important to understand how far a business is globally oriented. Perlmutter (1969) argued that the value system of the company, its history and development, its methods and practices, its vision and corporate culture will shape managerial outlook toward global strategy.

One useful framework for categorizing organizational philosophy is known as the EPRG matrix. Company philosophy can fall into one of four categories:

- An *ethnocentric* philosophy is one where there is a predisposition toward the home country based on a belief that the home industry is superior.
- A *polycentric* philosophy is oriented toward the host country (or foreign market), but emphasizes adaptation to local conditions in other locations.
- A *regiocentric* philosophy is an approach that emphasizes an orientation toward a regional grouping of countries, such as Europe, North America or the Far East.
- A *geocentric* philosophy implies a global approach to business.

Each philosophy has implications for the likely strategy of the business adopting it. Ethnocentricity implies that foreign markets are seen as inferior to the home market and the strategy adopted will be the same as that in the home market with the same product offering. Polycentricity results in a multidomestic strategy adapting fully to the requirements of each national market. Regiocentricity implies regional co-ordination of strategy but not global. Geocentricity suggests that strategy is developed on a global basis and is not determined by home or host country factors. Managers must assess the underlying philosophy of the business and determine the extent to which it is to be geared to support and encourage *a transnational approach* to business.

Nokia's global vision

In recent years some of the best examples of a global vision have been provided by the telecommuncations industry where companies such as Nokia and Vodafone have risen from fairly modest beginnings to establish strong positions in the global marketplace by pursuing bold and highly focused strategies.

Nokia, based not as might be expected in California's Silicon Valley but next to the Nokia River in rural Finland, has grown to emerge as the largest manufacturer of mobile phones in the world. Its origins, however, can be traced back to the 1860s when the company was founded as a paper mill. In the 1960s and 1970s the company added other interests, such as plastic and metal products, but the key strategic change in direction occurred in the early 1980s when the company began producing cellular phones and progressively focused on their production.

The domestic (Finnish) market was small but highly sophisticated, which had two implications for Nokia. The company had, first, to be innovative to survive in its domestic market and, second, had to export from day 1 in order to achieve its challenging growth objectives, which foresaw a 25% global market share by 1995. Thus the company turned decisively from producing low-value-added commodity products toward an emerging rapidly growing technology with few entry barriers other than technical standards and requirements for capital investment.

How then did a company from a small Nordic country rise to become internationally successful. It is difficult to be precise since there are undoubtedly a number of reasons and they are complex. However, undoubtedly the clear vision of managers in refocusing the company and setting global objectives was important. Other key factors included the priority the company placed on design, the attention given to building the awareness of the brand, fast development of new products that were attractive to customers, building numerous alliances with distributors (such as Tandy in the USA) and flexible production methods. Nokia avoided the potential pitfalls of a vertically integrated structure through outsourcing the manufacture of most essential electronic components (although they were often produced to Nokia designs). Nokia, however, assembles both cellular infrastructure and handsets in order to be able to offer complete packages to operators.

Culture and global business

Levels of culture

Culture – the way that people think, feel and act – differs between countries, industries and organizations. Each of these levels of culture interacts with, and helps to shape, the others. For example, while each advertising agency will have its own distinct and identifiable culture, there will be certain cultural characteristics like creativity and innovation common to all such agencies. At the same time, while all advertising agencies worldwide share certain cultural characteristics, there will be differences between, say, Japanese and American agencies, which are based on national cultural differences. This chapter examines the relationships between national culture, business culture and organizational culture and the requirements of management of transnationals in diverse cultural contexts. While globalization may mean that certain aspects of culture have converged across national boundaries, there are still enormous differences that impact on approaches to leadership and management, and on consumer behaviour. A transnational strategy must be based on a vision that encompasses both cultural similarity and diversity.

For example, the organizational culture of Microsoft places a high value on individual and organizational learning, so that the sharing of knowledge and information is encouraged throughout the organization. Within Japanese culture a high value is placed on age and experience so that senior managers are often older people. Younger managers are expected to defer to the decisions of their seniors. In contrast, within Western organizations promotion to senior positions is often based on merit and performance rather than age.

From a business perspective, it is useful to think of culture as existing at four different levels, those of the nation, business, industry and organization.

National culture consists of the distinctive shared values, attitudes, assumptions, beliefs and norms of the inhabitants of a nation which guide their behaviour. For example, the British place a high value on personal freedom and have resisted attempts to introduce identity cards which are seen as representing a threat to such freedom. In contrast, identity cards are widely accepted in many other countries.

Business culture (within a nation) comprises the shared values, attitudes, assumptions, beliefs and norms of the inhabitants of a country which guide business activity in that country. Aspects of business culture affect consumer, manager, investor and government behaviour, business ethics and so on. In certain countries, showing favouritism toward friends and family in business activities is both accepted and expected. In other countries such behaviour would be regarded as unethical.

Industry culture can be defined as the values, attitudes, assumptions, beliefs and norms that influence the ways in which the firms in a particular industry conduct their business. For example, universities throughout the world share certain cultural features like a belief in academic independence, irrespective of different national cultures. There will of course be some differences between the cultures of universities in different countries which arise from differences in national cultures.

Organizational (corporate) culture consists of the values, attitudes, assumptions, beliefs and norms that influence the ways in which the people in an organization behave and the way that its activities are conducted. This will depend on factors like national culture, business culture and industry culture. Of course, this is even more complicated in the case of a transnational enterprise where conducting business across national boundaries will involve an organization in dealing with many different national and business cultural differences. Managing a transnational business thus requires taking several types of cultural factor into account, such as cultural differences in consumer behaviour, attitudes to work and authority and ethical considerations.

Each of these levels of culture will interact with and affect the others. For example, an organization's culture will depend on factors that will include national culture, the business culture of the nation, the culture of the industry of which the firm is a part and organization-specific factors, like the size and nature of the business, the style of leadership and the structure.

EuroDisney – a European or American cultural identity?

The popularity of Europe as a tourist destination, the number of European visitors to Disney in the USA and the success of the Disney theme park in Japan were all factors suggesting that a similar venture would be immediately successful in Europe. The site chosen for EuroDisney (now Disneyland Paris) was Marne-la-Vallée, near Paris in northern France. The site was chosen because Paris, as well as being Europe's leading tourist destination, is also one of its best served cities in terms of road, rail and air linkages to the remainder of the continent. The transport infrastructure was also further strengthened by the development of direct road and rail linkages to EuroDisney from Paris itself and from Roissy, the major airport of Paris.

The theme park itself is equal in splendour to its American and Japanese counterparts located on a site one-fifth the size of Paris, with the trademark Disney castle, a wide array of state-of-the-art rides and attractions, and a range of hotels and restaurants designed to cater for all tastes and pockets.

Despite the meticulous planning, splendid location and magnificent attractions, the park struggled to attract visitors after its opening on 12 April 1992. It only attracted 3 million visitors in its first year of operation against a target of 11 million, leading to losses of US$920 million, which had risen to US$1.2 billion by the end of 1994.

There were many reasons for the park's initial failure. The theme park encountered severe criticism from influential sections of French society who held the view that it posed a threat to French culture which had spawned great philosophers, artists and composers. Consequently, the park's opening was shunned by leading members of French society and by the French public. This was despite the fact that, after extensive market research, many of the attractions had been given French names like *Le Chateau de la Belle au Bois Dormant* (the Enchanted Castle) and *La Cabane des Robinson* (The Swiss Family Treehouse), restaurants and cafes adopted European features like table service and continental breakfasts. There were also industrial relations problems with strict discipline and American training methods proving particularly unpopular.

In recent years there has been something of a turnaround in the park's fortunes (although only after significant amounts of loss were written off). By 2000 Disneyland Europe was attracting over 12 million visitors a year, many of whom were French. There are many reasons for this turnaround including increasing 'Americanization' with attractions being given their original American names and fast food restaurants, together with price reductions.

Characteristics of culture

Despite the intangible nature of culture, several researchers and authors have produced frameworks that make cultural comparisons between nations, industries and organizations possible. Such comparisons and categorizations are particularly important for organizations undertaking international business activities as they may well have to adapt activities because of cultural differences. Cultural differences may well affect consumer behaviour and employee working practices which will, in turn, affect the ways that international businesses organize, manage and structure their activities as well as the nature of the products they offer and the strategies that they pursue. In the same way, there are elements of similarity between human needs and wants which must be taken into account in transnational strategy. To make matters even more complex, culture is not a static phenomenon but changes irregularly over time.

There are several frameworks available to managers that can be utilized in comparing the characteristics and dimensions of culture. Two of the major frameworks are explained and compared in the next sections of this chapter – those suggested by Hofstede and by Trompenaars.

Hofstede's cultural dimensions framework

Elements of Hofstede's framework

The best known of these frameworks is that devised by Hofstede (1980, 1983, 1986, 1991, 1995). It was based initially on research in an American multinational enterprise and its subsidiaries. Hofstede identified four dimensions (later five) that could be used for comparing cultural similarities and differences. These five dimensions are:

- *power distance*;
- *uncertainty avoidance*;
- *individualism/collectivism*;
- *masculinity/femininity*;
- *long-term orientation.*

Power distance

Power distance concerns the extent to which people accept that power in society and organizations is distributed unevenly. When people are willing to accept that power is distributed unevenly, power distance is regarded as high. Low power distance is where people do not readily accept an uneven distribution of power.

Typically, within European and American cultures there is low tolerance of power distance, while in many Asian cultures there is acceptance of high power distance. Such differences will affect the nature of leadership and management, as well as decision making and structure within organizations. Within European organizations there is often an expectation that a participative style of decision making will be the norm, while in Asian organizations employees are more willing to accept decisions made by their leaders with little consultation.

Uncertainty avoidance

The cultural dimension of uncertainty avoidance relates to the lengths to which an organization or society will go to escape uncertainty. It thus describes the attitude to risk. An organization or society with a high level of uncertainty avoidance will attempt to reduce uncertainty through rules and laws, and will have a low tolerance of risk and non-conformity. On the other hand, an organization or society with low uncertainty avoidance will be characterized by an acceptance of risk taking, informality and a degree of non-conformity. A highly entrepreneurial organization like Nike embodies low uncertainty avoidance, encourages risk taking and embraces non-conformity among its customers and employees. The need for uncertainty avoidance is often higher in poorer, less developed countries, where non-conformity is often discouraged, while in richer, developed countries high degrees of non-conformity are readily accepted and even encouraged.

Individualism/collectivism

The dimension of individualism versus collectivism is based on the extent to which people stress individual or group needs. An organization or society which emphasizes individualism is characterized by self-interest, self-reliance and individual effort. American culture and many of its businesses embody highly individualistic cultures. Collectivism stresses the need for group harmony and the expectation that the group will take care of its members. This is traditionally characteristic of many Asian cultures and organizations, and is exemplified by the importance of saving 'face' in business dealings in this part of the world. At meetings Asians will often say 'yes' when they might mean 'no', so as not to give offence to their visitors, thus avoiding situations where there is a danger of either side losing face.

Masculinity/femininity

Masculinity/femininity centres on the extent to which a society or organization values assertiveness and materialism versus harmony and supportiveness. A culture is masculine when a high value is placed on assertiveness and materialism. When a high value is placed on harmony and partnership, the culture is characterized as feminine. Again contrasts can be made between largely masculine Western cultures and the femininity of eastern cultures.

Long-term orientation

Long-term orientation is the extent to which a culture emphasizes long or short-term goals. A culture with a long-term orientation is based on stability, persistence, order and thrift. On the other hand, a culture with a short-term orientation will expect immediate returns and will focus on the satisfaction of immediate needs and wants rather than on long-term investments. The success of Japanese companies in the 1970s, 1980s and early 1990s has often been attributed to their focus on long-term investment, commitment to their workers and the building of relationships with their customers. American and British companies are often criticized for their focus on short-term goals because of the need to satisfy their shareholders and thus maintain share prices.

Figures 2.2 and 2.3 show comparisons between various countries in terms of Hofstede's cultural dimensions.

To summarize, Hofstede's framework allows managers to analyse national and organizational cultures in terms of the dimensions of *power distance, uncertainty avoidance, individualism/collectivism, masculinity/*

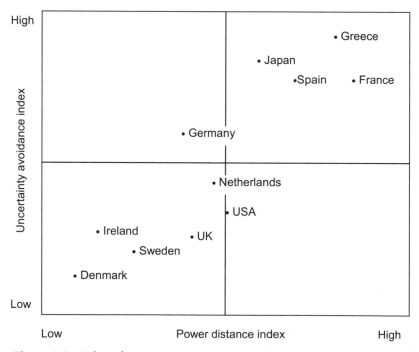

Figure 2.2 Selected countries: uncertainty avoidance versus power distance
Adapted from Mercado et al. (2001)

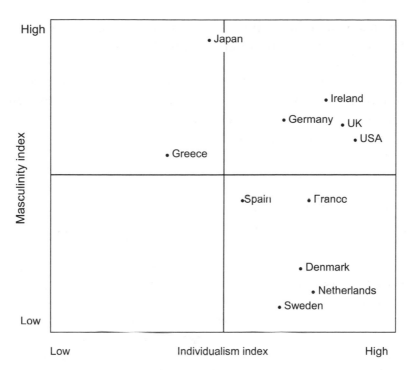

Figure 2.3 Selected countries: masculinity index versus individualism index
Adapted from Mercado et al. (2001)

femininity and *long-term orientation*. This will allow cultural similarities and differences to be considered when formulating a transnational strategy in terms of consumer preferences, management style, etc.

Trompenaars' dimensions of culture framework

Elements of Trompenaars' framework

Trompenaars (1993) and Trompenaars and Hampden-Turner (1997) devised an alternative model that can be used in the analysis of culture. It comprises three groupings of cultural factors:

- relationships with people;
- time;
- relating to nature (the natural environment).

Relationships with people can be considered in five subdivisions of: *universalism versus particularism; individualism versus communitarianism; affective versus neutral cultures; specific versus diffuse relationships;* and *achieving versus ascribing status.* Thus, in total, Trompenaars identifies seven dimensions along which culture can be compared. The first five come under the general heading of *relationships with people* and the remaining two are *time* and *relating to nature.*

Relationships with people

This dimension concerns how people relate to each other within a culture.

Universalism versus particularism

Universalism versus particularism focuses on the importance of rules, as opposed to relationships, in determining behaviour. There are two variants. A universalist culture is one within which rules determine behaviour and the favouring of friends or relations is not accepted. A particularist culture, on the other hand, is one where obligations to friends and relatives are important and must be observed in business. In Chinese culture, for example, the concept of *guanxi* (friendship) underlies many business relationships and activities. For the Chinese, friendship is a vital component of business relationships. Friends must always be favoured in business dealings. For this reason, the building of relationships is essential to successful business in China, a fact often overlooked by Western business people who are used to a universalist culture. In Western cultures, favouring friends and relatives is often opposed on the grounds of inequality of opportunity. In employment, for example, it is expected that people will be given equality of opportunity and will be appointed to posts on merit not on the basis of friendship or kinship.

Individualism versus communitarianism (collectivism)

This dimension corresponds to Hofstede's individualism versus collectivism and relates to the extent to which people stress individual or group needs. An individualistic culture is one within which self-interest, self-reliance and individual effort are predominant. Communitarianism, conversely, stresses the need for group harmony and the expectation that the group will take care of its members.

Affective versus neutral cultures
This dimension concerns the extent to which people may show emotions in communications. In an affective culture people are expected to show their emotions whereas in a neutral culture emotions must be controlled and subdued. In Japanese and Chinese cultures public displays of emotion are rare and are found embarrassing, so that these cultures can be regarded as neutral. Southern European cultures are, in contrast, far more affective whereas Northern European cultures are more neutral, but are nevertheless more affective than the Chinese and Japanese cultures.

Specific versus diffuse relationships
The extent to which people have relationships in more than one area of life is described as either specific or diffuse. A culture where relationships are only in specific areas of life (e.g., work) is known as specific. A diffuse culture is one within which relationships exist in multiple areas of life (e.g., they can span work and leisure).

Achieving versus ascribing status
This dimension centres on how far status is accorded on the basis of achievement or ascribed on the basis of age or seniority. An achieving culture is one where status is based on a person's achievements, while in an ascribing culture status is based on seniority, age or class. American culture is usually considered to be an achieving culture whereas Chinese and Japanese cultures are more ascribing in nature.

Time

This relates to time and structuring which affect planning and management. In a *sequential* culture the focus is on time moving forward and the focus is on efficiency. In a *synchronic* culture time is regarded as cyclical and repetitive, and there is more focus on effectiveness rather than efficiency. Southern European culture can therefore be regarded as synchronic as there is less importance attached to punctuality and efficiency while Northern European cultures are far more synchronic, placing much greater emphasis on efficiency.

Relating to nature

This concerns perceptions of the relationship to the natural environment and the ability to control nature. In *inner directed* or *internalist* cultures there is a common belief that nature can be controlled and manipulated. In *outer directed* or *externalist* cultures there is a shared view that people and organizations are part of nature which cannot be mechanically controlled. People in an externalist culture are far more fatalistic and accept natural benefits and disasters equally philosophically. Developed countries are far more internalist, believing that natural events can be controlled, by and large, whereas in developing countries the culture is more often externalist.

Tayeb – major cultural characteristics observed in various nations

Tayeb (2000) devised a comprehensive framework to allow cultural comparisons in terms of: *individual; relationships with others; relationship with environment; relationships with society and the state; expectations from companies; political views and activities; economic views and activities* (Table 2.1).

The importance and determinants of culture in transnational business

The importance of culture

Culture is important to transnational organizations in several respects including consumer behaviour and management.

Consumer behaviour
Culture is an important influence on consumer behaviour, consumption patterns, preferences and expenditure patterns. Certainly, global trends have affected fashions in clothing, fragrances and have influenced the design of many products. At the same time there remain important cultural differences affecting the acceptability and popularity of products, and in different parts of the world. Culture has a similar affect on the appeal and acceptability of different types of advertisement in different countries. Humour, an important ingredient of many Western advertisements, does not always translate across linguistic and cultural boundaries. As a consequence transnational businesses must pay careful attention to culture in product design and in their marketing and promotional strategies.

Table 2.1 Tayeb – major cultural characteristics observed in various nations

Individual	• Honesty, truthfulness, trustworthiness	• Independence of mind	• Control of emotions
	• Assertiveness, ambition, achievement orientation	• Ability to cope with uncertainty, ambiguity, anxiety and stress	• Care for quality of life
	• Competitiveness	• Resilence	• Hard-working, work ethic
	• Easy-going, laid-back	• Modesty, arrogance, self-confidence	
Relationships with others	• Interpersonal trust	• Co-operation and competition	• Respect for people in senior positions
	• Fear of the powerful	• Expect equality, acceptance of inequality	• Kindness, generosity, politeness
	• Appreciation of favours	• Acceptance of responsibility	• Caring
	• Group orientation, collectivism	• Self-orientation, individualism	• Small in-group, large in-group
	• Family ties, kinship	• Keeping promises	• Punctuality
	• Respect for others' viewpoints	• Conflict, harmony	• High context communication
	• Low context communication		
Relationship with environment	• Submission to failure, fatalism	• Mastery over the environment	• Living in harmony with the environment
	• Nature is a resource for us to exploit	• Nature belongs to our children, we have it on loan	
Relationships with society and the state	• Law abiding, law breaking	• Community orientation, family orientation	• Welfare state, social net
	• Statism, individual responsibility	• Big government, small government	• National health service
	• Universal education	• Private insurance	
Expectations from companies	• Active role in the community (hospitals, schools)	• Active interest in employees' private life and well-being	• Separation of private and company life
	• Care for the environment	• Contribution to charities	• Sponsorship of sporting and cultural events
Political views and activities	• Republicanism, monarchism	• Participation, indifference, revolution	• Attitudes to women's and minority rights, etc.
Economic views and activities	• Entrepreneurial spirit	• Capitalism versus socialism	• Market, mixed, state-controlled economy

Adapted from Tayeb (2000)

Transnational organizations and their management
The dimensions of culture identified by Hofstede and Trompenaars will affect the approach to management adopted within a transnational organization. Management in a transnational will inevitably have to take account of cultural differences like the importance attached to time, the need for formality in work relationships, the importance of ability versus seniority and so on.

Culture will also have an important effect on the attitudes to work of employees, aspects of motivation, loyalty to the business, personal initiative and collective responsibility. Whereas the success of Western enterprises is often attributed to personal initiative and entrepreneurship, the success of Asian-based business is often associated with aspects of culture, like a strong work ethic and company loyalty.

In a transnational, senior management can adopt a variety of approaches to managing cultural diversity (see Chapter 9). It is important to stress that cultural diversity must be viewed as a source of potential strength to an organization, as well as being a potential source of conflict. Cultural differences can cause friction and difficulties, but, equally, diversity can be an important source of the creativity required by businesses in the rapidly changing business environment of the 21st century.

Culture and the success of mergers in the automobile industry

The world automobile industry has been subject to increasing globalization, particularly since the 1980s. Globalization has been accompanied by increasing competition as well as increasing worldwide opportunities. The last decade has seen several major mergers and the development of a number of strategic alliances, partly in response to competition and partly in response to new market opportunities. The long-standing alliance between Honda and Rover (from 1979 to 1994) was mutually beneficial. Rover benefited from the technology and reputation of Honda, while Rover's UK base provided access to European markets for Honda. The alliance was brought to an end by the sale of Rover by its parent company to the German luxury car manufacturer BMW. BMW believed that by taking over Rover they could gain access to new segments of the market, particularly those for four-wheel drive sports utility vehicles (SUVs) and Minis. Despite the seeming logic of the merger, it was to become one of the 70% of international mergers that fail.

While there were business reasons for the collapse of the merger and the subsequent buyout of Rover, cultural factors, both national and organizational, were important contributory factors. One of the first actions of the BMW directors was to replace the British management of the company with its own German managers. This was seen as a condemnation of Rover's management, who had actually done much to improve the reputation, quality and reliability of the company's vehicles during the years immediately preceding the merger. This action was perceived as culturally insensitive and confirmed many cultural stereotypes of German approaches to management in the minds of the British managers. The subsequent approach to managing the company was viewed by many as autocratic. The consequence was that British managers viewed their German counterparts with suspicion. At the same time BMW's management held the view that the more laid-back approach to management of their British colleagues was a contributory factor to Rover's poor performance which had to be eliminated. The perceptions of both sides of each other were hardly conducive to the development of an inclusive team spirit. It is hardly surprising that the merger was to fail and that BMW and Rover were soon to go their separate ways.

Organizational culture

Each organization will have its own distinctive culture or way of working. In the case of a transnational this culture will be determined by the culture of its home nation, the cultures of the nations in which it operates and factors like the nature of its industry and business, its size, its history, its leadership and its structure.

Culture is therefore an aspect of transnational organizations which requires considerable management attention. Management will seek to shape the culture of an organization into a form that effectively supports its objectives, strategies and operations. The intangible nature of culture makes cultural change difficult to manage.

The *culture of an organization* (sometimes known as its corporate culture) is made up of the distinctive values, attitudes, beliefs and norms which influence the ways in which it conducts its business. Charles Handy's description of culture as '*the way we do things round here*' is a helpful one. In some ways it is the 'feel' or the 'smell' of an organization. In their famous book *In Search of Excellence* (1982), Peters and Waterman found that organizational culture was related to performance in that:

- dominance and coherence of culture was an essential feature of 'excellent' companies;
- a handful of guiding values was more powerful than manuals, rule books and controls;
- if companies do not have strong notions of themselves as reflected in their values, stories, myths and legends, the only security that employees have comes from their positions on the organization chart.

Determinants of organizational culture

It is as complex to describe the determinants of a given organizational culture as it is to describe the determinants of a human personality. In both cases a number of interdependent factors will be relevant. For an organization, we have seen earlier in this chapter that major influences will include the national culture (of the country or region in which the organization mainly operates or is based) and its industry culture, but in addition its history, size, management style and the type of employees that work within an organization will also strongly influence its culture. A schematic of these respective influences is shown in Figure 2.4. The different factors are described in Table 2.2.

Analysing organizational culture – the cultural web

Like national culture, organizational culture is impossible to measure. It is possible, however, to identify facets and characteristics of culture which can be described qualitatively. It is possible to use Hofstede's and Trompenaars' frameworks to analyse the culture of an organization, but the cultural web framework (Figure 2.5), developed by Johnson and Scholes (1992, 2001) is probably more suitable for analysing culture at the micro-level of the organization rather than the macro-level of the nation.

The cultural web is a representation of the manifestations of the culture of an organization. The central paradigm or world view – the centre of the culture – is shown and explained by the six factors described around it in

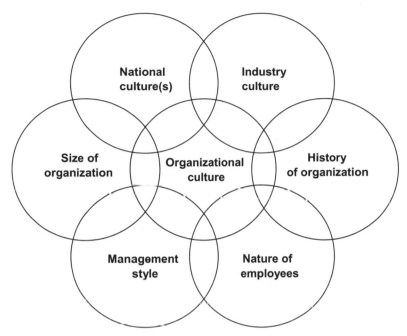

Figure 2.4 Determinants of organizational culture

Table 2.2 A description of the influences on organizational culture

National culture	Home and host country cultures will play an important role in shaping organization culture. American and Japanese organization cultures tend to be heavily based on their home country culture.
Industry culture	Businesses in the same industry will also have cultural similarities that cross national boundaries. All advertising agencies will tend to have cultures emphasizing creativity rather than formality. Of course, there will still be differences in culture between each individual organization in an industry.
Size of the organization	Culture differs between large and small organizations. Culture will tend to be less formal and more centred around an individual leader in a small organization. In a large organization culture will be far more complex and formalized.
Organization history	As culture evolves over time the culture of an organization will be associated with its history and the changes it has experienced.
Management and leadership style	The leaders and senior managers of an organization play a vital role in shaping the 'feel' of an organization. Jack Welch played a vital role in creating the innovative and entrepreneurial culture of GE.
Nature of the employees	The background of employees and the nature of their work, education and training is also important in forming an organization's culture. For example, professionals who are well educated will expect a culture where there is a high value placed on individual autonomy and where the management style is participative.

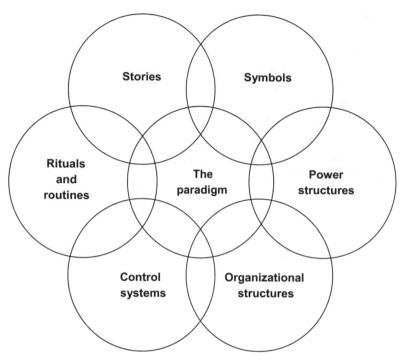

Figure 2.5 The cultural web
Reproduced from Johnson and Scholes (2001)

Figure 2.5. Organizational culture is a vital source of core competence and hence competitive advantage, as well as being vital to the coherent operation of the organization. The cultural web represents the culture of an organization in terms of the stories, symbols, rituals and routines, control systems, organizational and power structures which define its purpose and existence. Table 2.3 describes the nature of each facet of the cultural web.

Culture, at any level, develops from the interaction of people over time. The process through which culture develops and is passed on is described as *socialization*. Culture is passed on through agents of socialization which include:

- leaders and authority figures (managers, parents, politicians, religious leaders, teachers, etc.);
- peers, friends, colleagues and relatives;
- the media.

It is individuals' interaction with agents which will shape their values, attitudes, norms and behaviours within the nation, group and organizations

Table 2.3 The elements of the cultural web

Paradigm	Assumptions that constitute the culture of an organization. The central world view or set of irreducible assumptions made by the culture.
Stories	Told by members of the organization internally and externally to signal the history of the organization and its underlying values, successes and failures, and the personalities who have had a significant effect on the development of the organization.
Symbols	Logos, buildings, offices, cars, language used, etc. representing the nature of the organization, symbolizing success, power, hierarchy, etc.
Rituals and routines	Exmplify the way that things are done within the organization both formally and informally.
Control systems	Measurement and rewards systems which exist within the organization, indicative of the nature of its culture, emphasizing teamwork or individuality, organizational priorities and so on.
Organizational structures	Formalization of power structures, indicative of factors like power distance.
Power structures	Where power lies in the organization – may be based on seniority, merit or organizational history.

Based on Johnson and Scholes (2001)

of which they are part. Naturally, the context within which people live and work will also play a role in shaping culture so that geography and climatic factors, history, politics, religion, economics, etc. will all help determine culture within nations, organizations and other social groupings.

Sources of culture – an example of the influences on a country's culture

History

Several factors in a nation's history will contribute to the way that its culture develops. Empires, wars, being conquered, industrial and economic developments, emigration and immigration, and the development of political systems will all play a role in how a culture is shaped. The fact that a country has possessed an empire in its past may well give its people confidence long after it has disappeared. People from a similar country that has had no empire may not possess such confidence. Economic development also affects the confidence which a nation's people feel.

Religion

In some societies, religion is very important and highly valued, but, even in societies where religion does not appear to be highly valued today, it has still played and continues to play a significant role in shaping values and the way that people behave. Tayeb (2000) pointed out that some of the contrasting features of Eastern and Western cultures can be traced back to religious differences. For example, the individualism that characterizes many Western cultures can be traced back to the Protestant branch of Christianity which placed a high value on individuals taking personal responsibility for their lives and gaining rewards for their own hard work. In contrast the group orientation, respect for age and hierarchy, and avoidance of conflict and competition which characterizes many oriental societies can be attributed to Confucianism.

Geographic and climatic factors

Geography (including terrain and natural resources) and climate will also play an important role in shaping and sustaining national culture. A country with difficult geographical conditions (mountains and lack of natural resources) and a hostile climate will tend to produce a culture where people are hard-working, patient and resilient. According to Misumi (1994) the fact that the Japanese are hard-working can be attributed, in part, to the fact that Japan is poor in natural resources, so that people have always had to work hard to survive.

Review and discussion questions

1. Outline the major trends in the macroenvironment which have brought about the increasing globalization of (a) markets and (b) industries.
2. Why is the global environment becoming more turbulent?
3. What is the relationship between strategic intent and global vision?
4. Discuss the impact of culture on the way that a transnational business conducts its activities.
5. Explain how culture can be evaluated and compared.

References and further reading

Dicken, P. (1998) *Global Shift – Transforming the World Economy.* London: Paul Chapman.

Ginter, P. and Duncan, J. (1990) 'Macroenvironmental analysis'. *Long Range Planning*, December.

Hamel, G. and Prahalad, C.K. (1989) 'Strategic intent'. *Harvard Business Review*, **67**(3).

Hamel, G. and Prahalad, C.K. (1994) *Competing for the Future.* Boston: Harvard Business School Press.

Hamill, J. (1992) 'Global marketing'. In: M.J. Baker (ed.), *Perspectives on Marketing Management* (Vol. 2). Englewood Cliffs, NJ: Prentice Hall.

Heene, A. and Sanchez, R. (1997) *Competence-based Strategic Management*. New York: John Wiley & Sons.

Helms, M.M. and Wright, P. (1992) 'External considerations: Their influence on future strategic planning'. *Management Decision*, **30**(8), 4–11.

Hofstede, G. (1980) *Culture's Consequences: International Differences in Work Related Values*. Newbury Park, CA: Sage Publications.

Hofstede, G. (1983) 'National cultures in four dimensions: A research theory of cultural differences among nations'. *International Studies of Management and Organisation*, **13**.

Hofstede, G. (1986) 'Cultural differences in teaching and learning'. *International Journal of Intercultural Relations*, **10**, 301–320.

Hofstede, G. (1991) *Cultures and Organisations: Software of the Mind*. New York: McGraw-Hill.

Hofstede, G. (1995) 'Managerial values: The business of international business in culture'. In: T. Jackson (ed.), *Cross-Cultural Management*. Oxford, UK: Butterworth-Heinemann.

Johnson, G. and Scholes, K. (1992) *Exploring Corporate Strategy*. Englewood Cliffs, NJ: Prentice Hall.

Johnson, G. and Scholes, K. (2001) *Exploring Corporate Strategy*. Englewood Cliffs, NJ: Prentice Hall.

Levitt, T. (1983) 'The globalization of markets'. *Harvard Business Review*, May/June.

Mercado, S., Welford, R. and Prescott, K. (2001) *European Business* (Chapter 10). Financial Times/ Prentice Hall.

Mintzberg, H. (1995) *The Strategy Process – Concepts, Contexts, Cases*. Englewood Cliffs, NJ: Prentice Hall.

Misumi, J. (1994) 'The Japanese meaning of work and small-group activities in Japanese industrial organisations'. In: H S R Kao et al. (eds), *Effective Organisations and Social Values*. Newbury Park, CA: Sage Publications.

Naisbitt, J. and Aburdene, P. (1990) *Megatrends 2000*. New York: Morrow.

Negandhi, A.R. (1987) *International Management*. Boston: Allyn & Bacon.

Perlmutter, H.V. (1969) 'The tortuous evolution of the multinational corporation'. *Columbia Journal of World Business*, January/February.

Peters, T. and Waterman, R. (1982) *In Search of Excellence*. New York: Harper & Row.

Pitts, R.A. and Lei, D. (1996) *Strategic Management – Building and Sustaining Competitive Advantage*. St Paul, MN: West Publishing Company.

Porter, M.E. (1980) *Competitive Strategy: Techniques for Analysing Industries and Competitors*. New York: Free Press.

Porter, M.E. (1985) *Competitive Advantage*. New York: Free Press.

Porter, M.E. (1986a) *Competition in Global Business*. Boston: Harvard University Press.

Porter, M.E. (1986b) 'Changing patterns of international competition'. *California Management Review*, **28**(2), Winter, 9–40.

Porter, M.E. (1990) *The Competitive Advantage of Nations*. London: Macmillan.

Prahalad, C.K. and Doz, Y.L. (1986) *The Multinational Mission: Balancing Local Demands and Global Vision*. New York: Free Press.

Prahalad, C.K. and Hamel, G. (1989) 'Strategic intent'. *Harvard Business Review*, 63–76.

Prahalad, C.K. and Hamel, G. (1990) 'The core competence of the corporation'. *Harvard Business Review*, 79–91.

Prahalad, C.K. and Hamel, G. (1993) 'Strategy as stretch and leverage'. *Harvard Business Review*, March/April.

Sanchez, R., Heene, A. and Thomas, H. (eds) (1996) 'Towards the theory and practice of competence-based competition'. *Dynamics of Competence-based Competition: Theory and Practice in the New Strategic Management*. Oxford, UK: Elsevier.

Strebel, P. (1992) *Breakpoints*. Boston: Harvard Business School Press.

Smith, D. (1997) 'Wrinklies timebomb waiting to explode'. *Sunday Times*, 23 February.

Tayeb, M. (2000) *International Business – Theories, Policies and Practices* (Chapters 13 and 19). London: Financial Times/Prentice Hall.

Trompenaars, F. (1993) *Riding the Waves of Culture: Understanding Cultural Diversity in Business.* The Economist Books, London.

Trompenaars, F. and Hampden-Turner, P. (1997) *Riding the Waves of Culture: Understanding Cultural Diversity in Business* (2nd edn). London: Nicholas Brealey.

Turner, I. (1996) 'Working with chaos'. *Financial Times*, 4 October.

Yip, G.S. (1992) *Total Global Strategy*. Englewood Cliffs, NJ: Prentice Hall.

Web links

For information on different cultures   http://www.webofculture.com

Doing business in different cultures   http://www.getcustoms.com

Trompenaars Consulting   http://www.7d-culture.com

ANALYSIS OF THE GLOBAL BUSINESS

Learning objectives

After studying this chapter students should be able to:

- explain the components of an internal analysis;
- define and distinguish between an organization's competences, resources and capabilities;
- describe the value chain framework and understand its components;
- explain how value chains differ in global organizations;
- define and distinguish between configuration and co-ordination as the terms apply to global value adding activities;
- describe the importance of organizational culture and structure as they affect the strategy of global businesses;
- explain how to analyse an organization's products, portfolio and performance.

Introduction

Strategic analysis of any business enterprise involves two stages: internal analysis is the systematic evaluation of the key internal features of an organization (we address this in this chapter); and external analysis, which is covered in Chapters 4 and 5.

Internal analysis enables managers to gain a picture of their organization. Such information is essential when deciding on strategic options or on adjusting global strategy to provide optimum performance. Superior performance (i.e., returning higher profitability than the industry average) depends on management's ability to employ their resource inputs into core competences more effectively than competitors. This, in turn, depends on how well configured the organization's value-adding activities are and how it configures and co-ordinates its value-adding activities in the various parts of the world.

Product analysis is important in internal analysis because the product is the final expression of value added and the output of the whole organizational process. The extent to which products are balanced in a portfolio or are adjusted to suit regional preferences can be a vital factor in the success or failure of a global strategy.

Analysis of the global organization

Internal analysis

When considering the internal analysis of any organization, four broad areas need to be considered. They are the analysis of:

1. The organization's resources, capabilities and competences.
2. The way in which the organization configures and co-ordinates its key value-adding activities.
3. The structure of the organization and the characteristics of its culture.
4. The performance of the organization as measured by the strength of its products. This, in turn, is largely determined by the three aforementioned factors (see Figure 3.1).

These categories of enquiry form the basis of the structure of this chapter.

Competences, resources and capabilities

Understanding global competences

Many researchers in strategy including Prahalad and Hamel (1990), Kay (1993) and Heene and Sanchez (1997) have made the case that internal factors (resources, capabilities and competences) are more important in acquiring and sustaining competitive advantage than the organization's position in relation to its competitive environment. In other words, the major sources of global competitive advantage are business, rather than

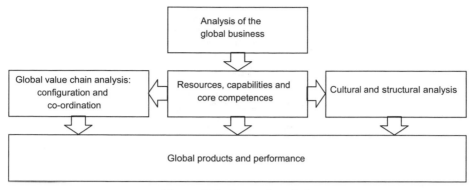

Figure 3.1 Internal analysis

industry, specific. It is therefore important to understand what constitutes core competence or distinctive capability as they form the basis of successful strategy. These concepts are also explored further in Chapter 6 which deals with the 'sources' of global and transnational strategy.

This understanding of strategy (sometimes called the 'resource-based' approach) can be traced back to the work of Penrose (1959). It is only recently, however, that researchers have begun to develop the conceptual frameworks that allow this approach to make a valuable contribution to global strategic analysis.

Definitions of resources, capabilities and competences

Although core competences are widely acknowledged as important sources of competitive advantage, there is no precise and universally agreed definition of the term. As a result, according to Kay (1995), 'Core competence is one of the most used and abused phrases in business strategy.' Accordingly, the terms *resource, capability, core competence* and *distinctive capability* are often used imprecisely in the literature. It is therefore necessary to define each of the concepts, explain their major characteristics and the relationships between them.

Prahalad and Hamel (1990) defined core competence as 'the collective learning in the organisation, especially how to co-ordinate diverse production skills and integrated multiple streams of technologies.' This definition does little, however, to reduce the ambiguity. Instead, definitions based on those proposed by Kay (1993, 1996), Gorman and Thomas (1997), Petts (1997) and Sanchez and Heene (1997) are developed and illustrated in Figure 3.2.

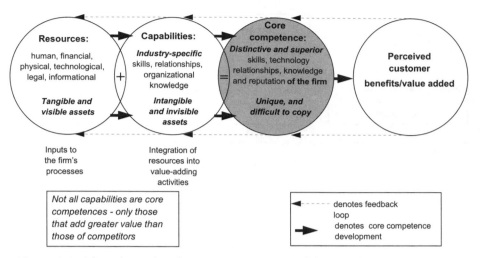

Figure 3.2 The relationships between resources, capabilities and core competences

There are significant difficulties in identifying and analysing core competences. This is because they tend to be complex bundles of resources and capabilities which are invisible and intangible, and are, therefore, difficult to describe precisely and are equally difficult to evaluate.

Despite these limitations, however, we suggest that analysis of core competences is possible by examining the factors that go to create them – resources and general competences.

Resources

Resources are assets that are employed in the activities and processes of the organization. Such assets can be either tangible or intangible. They can be obtained externally from suppliers in resource markets or can be internally generated. Internally generated resources are *organization-specific*, while externally obtained resources are *organization-addressable* (Sanchez and Heene, 1997). Resources can be highly *specific* or *non-specific*. Specific resources can only be used for highly specialized purposes and are very important to the organization in adding value to goods and services. Assets that are less specific are less important in adding value, but are usually more flexible.

Resources fall within several categories: human, financial, physical, technological or informational. An audit of resources would be likely to include an evaluation of resources in terms of availability, quantity and quality, extent of employment, sources, control systems and performance. The audit would also be likely to employ benchmarking techniques including internal and external comparisons:

- Against objectives and strategies – are the resources adequate to achieve organizational objectives?
- Against benchmarks like competitors – is the organization in question stronger or weaker?
- Against performance indicators over time – has the organization matched, exceeded or fallen short of the key indicators?

Table 3.1 illustrates some of the resource audits that may be carried out within a global organization.

General competences/capabilities

These are assets like *industry-specific skills, relationships* and *organizational knowledge* which are largely *intangible and invisible assets.* Competences and capabilities will often be internally generated, but may be obtained by collaboration with other organizations. In other words, competences may be shared or created across organizational boundaries. They are often shared between the organization and one or more of its suppliers, distributors or customers.

Certain competences are likely to be common to competing businesses within a global industry or strategic group. These competences relate to the critical success factors in the industry or market. Most competitors in the brewing industry, for example, will possess certain competences or capabilities which are essential to the production and selling of beer. Such competences are not distinctive, however, and do not account for distinctive or superior performance. They simply mean that the business in question has sufficient competence to produce and distribute beer.

Core competences/distinctive capabilities

Core competences or distinctive capabilities are combinations of resources and capabilities which are unique to a specific organization and which are responsible for generating its competitive advantage. Core competences only create competitive advantage when they are applied in markets, thus creating benefits that are perceived by customers as adding value

Table 3.1 Content of a resources audit

Human	Physical	Financial	Technological	Informational
Numbers of staff, deployment, age distribution, education, skills, training (including linguistic skills), motivation, attitudes and cultural awareness, flexibility, productivity, job specifications, recruitment, industrial relations, remuneration.	*Buildings and equipment*: locations, age, repair, flexibility, configuration, expansion potential, capacity, utilization. *Materials*: sources, quality, costs, availability.	Global sources and availability of finance, global accounts, global assets and liabilities, control systems, international accounting systems, taxation systems.	Technology – 'know how', patents, R&D facilities, IT and communication systems (internal and external), production systems.	Customer information, supplier information, competitor information, internal process information, agreements with suppliers, customers, distributors. *Note*: the information resource is generated both within the business as a result of its activities and outside the business.

over and above those of competitors. Core competences often have the potential to produce competitive advantage in more than one market.

Kay (1993) identified four potential sources of distinctive capability: reputation, architecture (i.e., internal and external relationships), innovation and strategic assets.

Core competences or distinctive capabilities may well be based on unique external relationships with other organizations or with customers. Benetton's competitive advantage, for example, rests in large part on its reputation, its knowledge of the fashion clothing industry and markets, and its unique network of relationships with manufacturers and retailers.

Core competences must be perceived *by customers* as providing benefits if they are to create competitive advantage. Thus reputation is vitally important to businesses like Porsche, Nike and Tommy Hilfiger, in achieving global competitive advantage, because customers place a high value on the reputations of such companies when purchasing their products.

Core competence development depends on the distinctive way that the organization combines, co-ordinates and deploys its resources and capabilities (Sanchez and Heene, 1997), as well as on the resources and capabilities themselves. Core competences can be evaluated against a set of criteria:

- *Complexity* – how elaborate is the bundle of resources and capabilities which comprise the core competence?
- *Identifiability* – how difficult is it to identify?
- *Imitability* – how difficult is it to imitate?
- *Durability* – how long does it endure?
- *Substitutability* – how easily can it be replaced by an alternative competence?
- *Superiority* – is it clearly superior to the competences of other organizations?
- *Adaptability* – how easily can the competence be leveraged or adapted?
- *Customer orientation* – how is the competence perceived by customers and how far is it linked to their needs?

(Adapted from Petts, 1997)

By evaluating core competences against these criteria, managers can gain a valuable insight into their ability or likelihood to bring about any sustained advantage. The strengths and weaknesses of existing competences can be assessed and any opportunities or needs for competence building and leveraging can be identified. These opportunities and needs may refer to resource markets, the industry, competing industries or product markets. Resources, capabilities and competences are both critical to, and inter-dependent with, the value-adding activities of the business. Value-adding activities are therefore analysed in the following section of this chapter.

Global value chain analysis

Organizations as systems

Sanchez and Heene (1997) described an organization as 'an open system of asset stocks and flows including tangible assets like production equipment and intangible assets like capabilities and cognitions.' This system converts inputs (resources) into outputs (goods and services). A major objective of the system is to add value to the inputs so that the value of the outputs exceeds the value of the resources used in their creation. Competitive advantage depends on the ability of the organization to organize its resources and value-adding activities in a way that is superior to its competitors, thus enabling more value to be added and more quickly. Value chain analysis is a technique developed by Porter (1985) for under-standing an organization's value-adding activities and the relationships between them. Value can be added in two ways:

1. by producing products at a lower cost than competitors;
2. by producing products of greater perceived value than those of competitors.

The analysis of value-adding activities allows managers to identify where value is currently added and where there is potential to add further value in the future by reconfiguration of activities. Porter extended value chain analysis to the value system so that, as well as internal activities, the technique also includes analysis of the relationships between the organiza-tion, its suppliers, distribution channels and customers.

The value chain

The value chain is the chain of activities which results in the final value of a business's product. Value added, or margin, is indicated by sales revenue (units sold multiplied by price) minus total costs (variable costs like

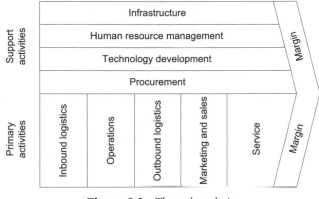

Figure 3.3 The value chain
Adapted from Porter (1985)

materials, wages, etc. plus fixed costs of capital equipment, rents, etc.). In other words, 'the margin is the difference between the total value and collective cost of performing the value activities' (Porter, 1985).

In Porter's framework, value is added as a result of value-adding activities and the linkages between them. Porter divided the internal parts of the organization into primary and support activities as indicated in Figure 3.3. *Primary activities* (inbound logistics, operations, outbound logistics, marketing and sales, and service) are those that directly contribute to the production of the good or services and the organization's provision to the customer. *Support activities* (the firm's infrastructure, human resource management, technology development and procurement) are those that aid primary activities, but do not themselves add value. Certain activities or combinations of activities are likely to relate closely to the organization's core competences. Logically, these can be termed *core activities*. They are those activities that:

- add the greatest value,
- add more value than the same activities in competitors' value chains;
- relate to and reinforce core competences.

Other value chain activities relate to capabilities, but do not add greater value than competitors and therefore do not relate to core competence (because they do not contribute toward competitive advantage).

Value chain analysis involves analysis of all the company's activities, and its internal and external linkages, in order to determine how the company's activities are currently organized and how they can be can be better organized so that competitive advantage can be achieved. The activities in the company's value chain must be organized in such a way as to support its corporate strategy. A value chain analysis will therefore include:

- a breakdown and analysis of all the activities of the organization;
- an examination of the match between configuration and current strategy (e.g., cost or differentiation-based strategy);
- identification of internal and external *linkages* between activities that result in additional added value;
- identification of *blockages* that reduce the organization's competitive advantage.

Primary and support activities can be broken down into several elements for analysis.

Primary activities

Inbound logistics
These are activities concerned with the receipt and storage of materials (inputs), stock control and distribution of inputs to those areas of the business concerned with operations.

Operations
Operations transforms inputs into final products or services. It may be concerned with manufacturing processes, assembly, testing, etc.

Outbound logistics
This function is responsible for storage and distribution of finished goods to customers. It includes warehousing, order processing, transport and distribution.

Marketing and sales
This includes activities that are concerned with analysis of markets and customers, persuading customers to buy the product, and making the product accessible to customers via appropriate channels.

Service
This consists of activities concerned with installation of the product and after-sales service.

Support activities

Procurement

This is concerned with purchasing the resource inputs used in the organization's activities (other than those that directly add value, which are part of inbound logistics). Certain purchasing functions may be centralized so as to obtain economies and control the quality of inputs. Other purchasing activities may be decentralized. Purchasing has a clear impact on value added both in terms of controlling costs and in terms of controlling the quality of inputs and therefore of final products.

Technology development

All activities within the business employ technology both in the production and distribution of physical products and in terms of producing information and services. Technology development is concerned with product, process and resource development, and improvement. It includes the research and development function if the organization has one.

Human resource management

Human resource management is concerned with obtaining, training and motivating appropriate employees. It therefore involves recruitment, selection, training, rewards and motivation. Again, human resources are employed throughout the organization's value chain. The quality and 'appropriateness' of human resources is closely associated with its ability to add value.

Firm infrastructure

The firm's infrastructure includes management systems, planning, finance, accounting, information systems and quality management. The infrastructure is vital to the success of the business and its global corporate strategy.

Using the value chain framework

All the primary and support activities described contribute to the final value of the product to the consumer, so the organization must analyse each activity and the linkages between the activities to see if any improvements can be made which will increase the final value of the product or decrease the costs of making it.

Just as important as the internal activities are the external linkages – with suppliers of inputs and services, and linkages with distribution channels and customers. The value of the product may depend on linkages with retailers, for example. Similarly, linkages with suppliers may be critical to competitive success if the business operates a just-in-time (JIT) operational philosophy.

Every different type of organization will have a very different value chain. Adidas, for example, is not generally involved in the retailing of its product, but is heavily involved in the design and marketing activities. Nissan is involved in design and manufacturing, and has involvement in the distribution of its products. Other businesses' value chains may be centred on manufacturing with no design, little marketing and no retailing. The businesses who manufacture the products sold under the Nike or Marks & Spencer brand names would fall into this category.

This analysis helps us to add to our picture of the organization's strengths and weaknesses. It may be possible to compare one value chain with that of organizations in similar sectors so as to make comparisons of performance.

The value chain of an individual organization, however, provides an incomplete picture of its ability to add value, as many value-adding activities are shared between organizations often in the form of a collaborative network. As organizations identify and concentrate on their core competences and core activities, they increasingly outsource activities to other businesses for whom such activities are core. For example, Marks & Spencer, the UK retailer, would regard its core competence as being based on its skills in design and retailing which have established its reputation for quality. Marks & Spencer has no expertise or core competence in manufacturing and, therefore, it obtains its products from a network of suppliers, for whom manufacturing is a core competence and activity. The ability to add value is enhanced for all members of the network as they benefit from each other's core competences. Marks & Spencer benefit from the core competences of its suppliers in manufacturing quality products, while the suppliers benefit form Marks & Spencer's retailing skills and reputation.

It is therefore necessary to analyse the *value system* of the business so as to establish the effectiveness of its external linkages.

The value system

The value system is the chain of activities from supply of resources through to final consumption of a product (Figure 3.4).

The total value system, in addition to the organization's own value chain, can consist of *upstream* linkages with suppliers and *downstream* linkages

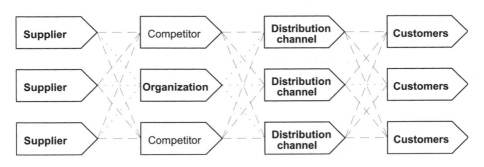

Figure 3.4 The value system
Adapted from Porter (1985) by permission of Free Press

with distributors and customers. A single organization can form any part or the whole of the value system for a product or service. The value system is a similar concept to that of the *supply chain* and illustrates the interactions between an organization, its suppliers, distribution channels and customers. It also illustrates the fact that such relationships may also be common to its competitors. Managing these external relationships can be equally as important to competitive advantage as the management of internal activities and linkages.

Co-ordinating activities and linkages

Competitive advantage arises from an organization's core competences and core activities. Businesses make themselves distinctive by the way in which they configure and co-ordinate their competences and value-adding activities. Competitive advantage is also enhanced by the distinctive network of relationships that a business has with its suppliers, distribution channels and customers. Inter-company relationships must be co-ordinated and integrated with those competences and activities which are core to the business itself. There may well be synergies between the core competences of an organization and those of linked organizations. Certainly, the linking of core competences increases the range of competences which can be deployed competitively and, at the same time, they can create a more complex source of competitive advantage which is more difficult for competitors to emulate.

At the same time, effective management of complex, linked activities can further extend advantage. To summarize, managing internal and external linkages between competences and activities is just as important as the management of the individual primary and support activities which make up the value chain. An important aspect of strategic analysis is therefore the examination of internal and external relationships between competences and activities.

The 'global' value chain

A more complex value chain

Globalization offers new opportunities and new challenges for the configuration and co-ordination of value-adding activities (Porter, 1986, 1990). The configuration of an organization's activities relates to where and in how many nations each activity in the value chain is performed. Global businesses can configure their activities to take advantage of both global and localized advantages. Co-ordination is concerned with the management of dispersed international activities and the linkages between them. Co-ordination of globally dispersed activities is, of course, a complex matter, but it is because of this complexity that it offers considerable potential for achieving competitive advantage. Managers must therefore examine the current configuration of value-adding activities and the extent and methods of co-ordination as part of their strategic analysis. This analysis makes it possible to determine possibilities for reconfiguration or improved co-ordination.

In understanding the complexity of global value chain management, two concepts are important – configuration of activities and co-ordination between them.

Configuration

In terms of each value-adding activity a global business has two broad choices of configuration:

1. *Concentration* of the activity in a limited number of locations to take advantage of benefits offered by those locations (such benefits may relate to availability of materials or labour, to cost advantages, demand conditions, markets, government incentives, etc.).
2. *Dispersion* of the activity to a large number of locations (when transport costs are high, when national markets differ significantly, etc.).

Changes in the business environment (e.g., technological change) may well lead to changes over time in the configuration that gives greatest competitive advantage. Businesses must therefore constantly monitor their current configuration in conjunction with the environment in order to identify opportunities to reconfigure their global activities to take advantage of changing conditions.

Co-ordination

Competitive edge can also be increased by more effectively co-ordinating those diverse activities that are located in a number of different nations. Co-ordination is essentially about overseeing the complexity of the organization's configuration such that all value-adding parts of the business act in concert with each other to facilitate an effective overall synergy. The more complex the configuration becomes (and some global businesses can have very complex configurations) then the greater the difficulties will be in retaining control over each value-adding part.

Those businesses that overcome the potential difficulties of co-ordination are those that sustain the greatest competitive advantage. New technology and organizational structures offer new possibilities for co-ordinating diverse activities. The increasing ability to co-ordinate activities more effectively also expands the range of alternative configurations accessible to global business.

Analysis of configuration and methods of co-ordination assists in the process of understanding current competences and identifying the potential for strengthening and adding to them. Core competences are closely related to value-adding activities. Configuring the value chain globally offers further opportunities to develop competences that are both distinctive and difficult to emulate. Figure 3.5 illustrates the issues that must be considered in relation to analysing the management of a business's value system.

Global organizational culture and structure

The importance of culture and structure

A global business must have a culture and structure which allow it to carry out its global activities. Culture and structure are investigated in more detail in Chapter 13, but they are examined briefly here as part of the process of internal business analysis.

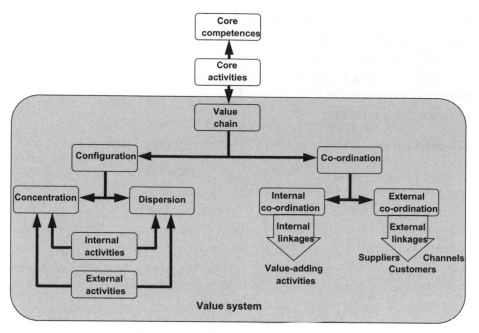

Figure 3.5 Managing the value system

In attempting to answer the question why an organization has a particular culture and structure, we find a complicated range of explanations (see, e.g., Campbell et al., 1999).

We encountered the idea that culture has a number of influences in Chapter 2. The structure of an organization is also the result of a number of factors including:

- its history;
- its size;
- the nature of its product and production processes;
- the nature of its business environment, markets and industry;
- its country of origin and areas of operation;
- the nature of its strategy;
- the philosophy of key members of the organization.

Structure

Major problems can arise when either structure or culture is not adapted in response to changes in strategy, size, the environment, processes or philosophy. As organizations grow they must restructure to continue to co-ordinate and control their activities. More clearly defined roles, responsibilities and channels of communication are required than the informal arrangements that exist in small businesses.

Some large businesses with very rigid and hierarchical structures have difficulty in responding to changes in the environment. As the environment becomes more turbulent and as activities globalize it becomes increasingly difficult to reconcile the need for flexibility with that for control and co-ordination. Similarly, different strategies require different structures. As the pace of environmental change increases, there is the potential for misalignment between an organization's structure and its strategy. Analysis of structure on an ongoing basis is therefore necessary to ensure it is the most appropriate, given its ephemeral environmental conditions. The aspects of structure that require analysis include:

- grouping of activities and functions;
- roles and responsibilities;
- communication channels;
- lines of authority;
- rules and regulations.

The structure of the business must allow it to accomplish its objectives as effectively and as efficiently as possible. The larger and more diverse the activities of an organization the more complex its structure will usually need to be.

BP Amoco and global structure

BP Amoco, the British-based energy company, is one of the world's largest companies and was one of the world's first 'truly' global businesses. The factors that drove BP Amoco's globalization in the middle years of the 20th century are those common to other players in the petrochemicals industry. The resource markets and products markets relevant to petrochemicals companies are both global, and the scale economies required for competitive advantage in the sector necessitate a capital intensiveness of very large proportions.

The fact that oil and gas are primary products means that parts of BP Amoco need to be located, with substantial investment, wherever reserves are to be found. In practice, this means that BP sources oil and gas from all six continents. Similarly, because demand for energy products is global, BP Amoco's participation in products markets means it operates in most regions of the world.

The company is primarily structured according to its major activities: exploration and production; gas, power and renewables; refining and marketing; and chemicals. In order to enable each activity to operate as autonomously as possible, each 'division' is a separate 'stand-alone' company, and the name BP Amoco refers to the parent holding company.

Each of the four activity areas is responsible for its own performance against targets and has the autonomy to operate in order to ensure that performance targets are met. The different nature of the four areas means that the extent of globalization and international presence differs between them. Exploration and production tends to be global but concentrated around oil and gas fields and so has a strong presence in such areas as South America and the Caspian region of Eastern Europe. Marketing activities, by contrast, tend to be geographically focused around the locations of the company's key product markets – predominantly the developed countries and regions where the concentration of customers make such activities economically worthwhile.

Culture

What is culture?
One of the best definitions of culture was offered by Stacey (1996):

> *The culture of any group of people is that set of beliefs, customs, practices and ways of thinking that they have come to share with each other through being and working together. It is a set of assumptions people simply accept without question as they interact with each other. At the visible level the culture of a group of people takes the form of ritual behaviour, symbols, myths, stories, sounds and artefacts.*

Hence, the culture of any organization consists of the shared values, attitudes, assumptions and beliefs of the managers and employees of the organization which shape their behaviour and actions. The culture of an organization shapes its style and 'feel'. It will govern attitudes to work and dictate how people think things ought to be done. Culture will be an important determinant of how effectively the organization operates and has important implications for employee motivation.

Culture and success

Although this is not a textbook designed to explore culture in any depth, we do make the following observations about the linkages between culture and successful strategy.

First, successful organizations tend to have cultures that emphasize excellence, quality and customer service. It affects interactions between people within the business and between the business and its customers, its suppliers and its other stakeholders.

Second, culture should not be seen as static – it must change as environmental conditions change. As is often the case with structure, a frequent problem for businesses is that culture does not change quickly enough to account for environmental changes. Culture is thought to change relatively over time through the process of socialization. The pace of culture change cannot always be controlled by managers. These difficulties in achieving change arise because people's long-held attitudes and beliefs do not alter unless they can be persuaded that the alterations are both justified and necessary. It is therefore important to appraise organizational culture as part of the analysis process. Yet the process of appraisal is problematic because there are difficulties inherent in 'measuring' culture. Culture cannot be readily described nor quantified.

Finally, culture is closely linked to the vision and mission of the organization. Vision and mission can help to shape organization culture and vice versa. To develop a global and transnational outlook is clearly dependent on both vision and culture (see Chapter 2).

Products, performance and portfolio analysis

The concept of portfolio

A global business exploits its resources, capabilities and competences in the production of goods and services which meet the needs of its customers. A key concept with regard to successful product or subsidiary strategy is that of portfolio.

Many, although not all global companies consist of a portfolio of businesses offering multiple products and services. Portfolio analysis is used in evaluating the balance of an organization's range of products. Successful product management relies on maintaining a portfolio of products that increase the organization's ability to withstand and exploit opportunities and threats in the environment. In this regard, the key advantage of a broad portfolio is that risk can be spread across more than one market. Offsetting this is the fact that a narrower portfolio can mean that the organization becomes more specialized in its knowledge of fewer products and markets – its expertise is less 'diluted'.

Several matrices have been developed to allow analysis of an organization's products and markets. Probably the best known of these is the Boston Consulting Group (BCG) growth-share matrix. The matrix is most often used by organizations in multiproduct and multimarket situations. It considers products in terms of their market share and the growth rate of the market in which they are sold.

The BCG matrix

The Boston Consulting Group matrix offers a way of examining and making sense of a company's portfolio of product and market interests. It is a relatively sophisticated approach, based on the idea that market share in mature markets is highly correlated with profitability and that it is relatively less expensive and less risky to attempt to win share in the growth stage of the market, when there will be many new customers making a first purchase. This is the approach taken by the BCG matrix. It is used to analyse the product range with a view to aiding decisions on how the products should be treated in an internal strategic analysis. Figure 3.6 shows the essential features of the Boston matrix.

The market share measure
The horizontal axis is based on a very particular measure of market share. That measure is share relative to the largest competitor. A product with a share of 20% of the market, where the next biggest competitor had a share of 10% would have a relative share of 2, whereas a product with a market share of 20% and the biggest competitor also had 20%, would have a relative share of 1. The cut-off point between high and low share is 1, so high market share products in this analysis are market leaders. This arrangement of scale is sometimes described as being *logarithmic* in nature.

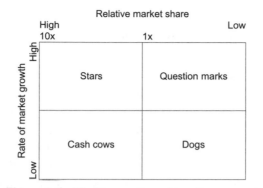

Figure 3.6 The Boston Consulting Group matrix

The market growth measure
The vertical axis is the rate of market growth, with the most relevant definition of the market being served. A popular point used to divide high and low growth in the market is 10% year-on-year growth, but the authors have found it useful in practical situations to use growth that is faster than the rate of growth in the economy as a whole, which, after inflation in most Western countries, is usually between 1 and 2.5% a year.

Using the BCG matrix

Cash cows
A product with a high market share in a low-growth market is normally both profitable and a generator of cash. Profits from this product can be used to support other products that are in their development phase. Standard strategy would be to manage conservatively, but to defend strongly against competitors. Such a product is called a *cash cow* because profits from the product can be 'milked' on an ongoing basis. This should not be used as a justification for neglect.

Dogs
A product that has a low market share in a low-growth market is termed a *dog* in that it is typically not very profitable. To cultivate the product to increase its market share would incur cost and risk, not least because the market it is in has a low rate of growth. Accordingly, once a dog has been identified as part of a portfolio, it is often discontinued or disposed of.

More creatively, opportunities might be found to differentiate the dog and obtain a strong position for it in a niche market. A small share product can be used to price aggressively against a very large competitor as it is expensive for the large competitor to follow suit.

The matrix does not have an intermediate market share category, but there are large numbers of products that have large market share, but are not market leaders. They may be the biggest profit earners for the companies that own them. They usually compete against the market leader at a disadvantage that is slight, but real. Management need to make very efficient use of marketing expenditure for such products and to try to differentiate from the leader. They should not normally compete head on, especially on price, but should attempt to make gains if the market changes in a way that the leader is slow to exploit.

Stars
Stars have a high share of a rapidly growing market and therefore rapidly growing sales. They may be the sales manager's dream, but they could be the accountant's nightmare, since they are likely to absorb large amounts of cash, even if they are highly profitable. It is often necessary to spend heavily on advertising and product improvements, so that when the market slows these products become cash cows. If market share is lost, the product will eventually become a 'dog' when the market stops growing.

Question marks
Question marks are aptly named as they create a dilemma. They already have a foothold in a growing market, but if market share cannot be improved they will become dogs. Resources need to be devoted to winning market share, which requires bravery for a product that may not yet have large sales, or the product may be sold to an organization in a better position to exploit the market.

Limitations of the BCG matrix

Accurate measurement and careful definition of the market are essential to avoid misdiagnosis when using the matrix. Critics, perhaps unfairly, point out that there are many relevant aspects relating to products that are not taken into account, but it was never claimed by the Boston Consulting Group that the process was a panacea and covered all aspects of strategy. Above all, the matrix helps to identify *which* products to push or drop, and *when*. It helps in the recognition of windows of opportunity and can provide strong evidence against simple rules of thumb for allocating resources to products.

The matrix has also been criticized for the imprecise nature of its four categories and because of the difficulties inherent in predicting future market growth. There are alternatives to the BCG matrix which indicate competitive position and market development (Hofer and Schendel, 1979), but these share similar limitations. Despite these limitations, evaluating the performance and potential performance of products is a necessary part of the process of analysis.

Global activity may add an extra dimension to the process of portfolio analysis. The market for a global product may be at different stages of development in different countries. Similarly, the market share which a given product commands may differ from country to country. Global portfolio analysis must take these factors into account.

BAT in the 1970s and 1980s – managing an international portfolio

BAT, the Anglo-American tobacco group, underwent a number of changes in the period from the 1970s to the 1990s and is a good example of the way that both product and geographical interests can be spread to maximize robustness. The tobacco part of BAT's portfolio began in the 1890s in the USA, and the company structure in 1950 was the result of a number of mergers and acquisitions over the intervening decades.

In the 1950s the realization that there was a link between tobacco consumption and ill health drove the company to look to diversify in order to reduce its dependency on tobacco. Throughout the 1960s and early 1970s, BAT made substantial investments by acquisition in several sectors other than tobacco. Its acquisitions in tobacco tended to concentrate on developing its international portfolio.

BAT in the 1970s

By 1976, BAT had developed its business to the point that, although tobacco still formed the majority of product output, it had substantial interests in retailing, paper and pulp, cosmetics and some other minor sectors.

In tobacco, the company boasted over 300 brands of cigarettes, operating 90 factories in 37 countries together with a number of affiliated (part rather than wholly owned) companies in another 38 countries. This grew to the point where BAT had interests in a total of 47 countries based around principal subsidiaries in the UK, Europe, Latin America, the Caribbean, Asia and Africa.

In addition to BAT tobacco brands it also owned Brown and Williamson (USA) – manufacturers of Kool, Raleigh and Viceroy brands; Interversa (Germany) – main brands included HB, Kim and Krone; and Souza Cruz (Brazil) – main brands included Minister, Hollywood and Continental.

Its major retail subsidiaries included International Stores (UK) – a chain of 694 supermarkets and self-service stores in England and Wales; Gimbel Brothers (USA) – 38 department stores in the New York, Philadelphia, Pittsburgh and Milwaukee areas; Kohl Corporation (USA) – 92 supermarkets in Wisconsin and Illinois; Saks Fifth Avenue (USA) – 30 high-fashion stores in major metropolitan locations throughout the USA; Supermercados Peg-Pag SA (Brazil) – 39 stores in or near the major cities of São Paolo and Rio de Janeiro. BAT purchased Argos in 1979. The relatively new concept of catalogue shopping on the high street was thought to have significant growth potential, and on acquisition Argos had 91 stores in England and Wales.

The Group's paper interests included industrial and printing papers. Subsidiaries in the paper and pulping business (mainly mills and factories) were situated in the UK, Europe, Brazil, India and Africa. In 1979 the company acquired Mardon Packaging International from Imperial Group (Mardon had packing and printing operations in Canada, the USA, France, Germany, Republic of Ireland and Zimbabwe).

The company's fourth major division – cosmetics – produced perfumes, cosmetics, toiletries and skin care products. Manufacturing of cosmetics took place in 41 countries and the products were sold in 143 stores. The main brands in the cosmetics division included the Houses of Yardley, Lenthéric, Cyclax, Juvena and Morny.

BAT in the 1980s

By 1982 over 80% of total assets by value were outside the UK. The chairman, Patrick Sheehy, described the company's approach to its international coverage:

> *Geographically, we are well represented in the industrialised parts of the world and also in the more volatile regions where there are greater inherent risks, but where good growth prospects can be discerned. Both types of area have a place in the Group's development and we will continue to strengthen our businesses and to extend them into new markets.*

In his second statement as chairman (in 1983), Sheehy set out his perspective on the company's activities:

> *Although tobacco profits were significantly affected by difficulties in a number of markets [i.e. in different national markets], the balance was more than made good by the substantial profit increase achieved by our newer businesses.*

These 'newer businesses' referred to in 1983 mainly comprised its major acquisitions of the previous year. Other financial services business – Farmers (USA) and Allied Dunbar (UK) – were later added to the group.

Global products and services

Yip (1992) argued that 'The benefits of global products (or services) can be achieved by standardising the core product or large parts of it, while customising the peripheral or other parts of the product.' Analysis of an organization's products must identify those features of a product which appeal to customers on a worldwide basis and those features that must be adapted to meet local preferences. A global product will have core features that will appeal to all customers. For example, most of Sony's consumer electronics products are generally standardized, but some parts are adapted to meet national electrical standards (Yip, 1992). Similarly, McDonald's offerings are largely standardized, but there are minor variations from country to country in terms of the products offered and in their presentation.

There are several benefits to be obtained from offering global products: reduced costs, enhanced quality, increased consumer preference, competitive leverage (Yip, 1992). The analysis of global products must be closely related to analysis of the global competitive environment (see Chapter 4).

Performance analysis

Strategic analysis of the global organization must also include appraisal of past and present performance. Current performance can be evaluated against:

- stated objectives and targets;
- past performance;
- competitors' performances;
- external and internal benchmarks.

In addition, the performance of different divisions within the same organization can be compared. The measures of performance can include the following areas:

- finance – accounting information including profits, return on investment, sales, etc.;
- products – price, quality, value for money, functionality, design, etc.;
- customer interfaces – delivery times, after-sales service, etc.;
- marketing – market share, etc.;
- production – productivity, quality standards, etc.

Establishing objectives, targets and performance standards can be extremely effective in improving organizational performance, but it is important that standards are prioritized and related to critical success factors. They should also relate to areas of core competence which generate competitive advantage.

Benchmarking

A benchmark is the value of some parameter that is used as a reference point in comparisons (e.g., the top speed of a car or the number of pages per minute from the leading laser printer). The benchmark may also be the performance of a business (e.g., ROCE, profit/employee or customer satisfaction). Benchmarking is used to compare the effectiveness of the various *processes* within a business with those in other organizations and, using this information, to help improve the original processes. Benchmarking can be:

- internal, using other businesses owned by the parent company;

- external, using divisions of multinationals or companies in different sectors;
- best practice – identifying the *leader* in whatever sector they operate.

Note that unlike conventional comparative analysis, the benchmark for any given process may be selected from businesses of different size and in different sectors – often the best solutions are to be found in businesses that are not competitors. To summarize, benchmarking is:

- a continuous process of evaluating and developing products, services and practices by comparison with the *best* that can be recognized globally;
- an integral part of total quality management;
- essential for continuous improvement of products and performance.

Successful benchmarking must be based on:

- commitment from the managers of the organization;
- acceptance of the need for improvement;
- willingness to take on other people's ideas;
- a supportive vision, mission and clear objectives;
- subsequent development of competences;
- a supportive culture.

Performance measures, although imprecise and potentially misleading, provide important indications of past and current performance. They help in identifying strengths and weaknesses which form the basis of future developments in global strategy.

Outside in or inside out?

In understanding internal analysis, we need to understand the two 'sources' of strategy and how they relate to this part of the strategic process.

'Outside in' strategy

The positioning school implies an approach to strategic analysis which is 'outside in'. That is to say, the strategic process begins with analysis of the environment in order to establish which industries are potentially the most profitable. Global strategy is then determined by adopting a strategy that best matches industry conditions. In other words, the business looks for a 'strategic fit' between its resources and strategies so as to exploit opportunities and reduce threats in the global environment.

'Inside out' strategy

The resource-based school emphasizes the importance of organization-specific resources, capabilities and competences in acquiring competitive edge. The approach is therefore 'inside out'. Analysis begins inside the organization to identify core competences and how new competences can be built or existing competences can be leveraged in new markets.

The two approaches and internal analysis

Despite the different starting points there is more common ground than is apparent at first glance. The positioning school accepts the importance of organization-specific factors in gaining competitive advantage as part of a generic strategy. In fact, value chain analysis (Porter, 1985) is a fundamental part of its methodology, just as the way that a business's value-adding activities are configured and co-ordinated will determine its strategy and therefore its competitiveness.

   Similarly, the resource-based approach, although focused on the organization, accepts the necessity to analyse the environment so as to identify the potential for competence-building and leveraging opportunities. The reality is that no business can ignore its environment and that competitive advantage depends on the competences of the organization and the way that it deploys them. In practice, the rapidly changing environment indicates that both external analysis and the analysis of competences and activities must both be continuous and therefore simultaneous. The purpose of strategic analysis remains, as it has always been, to determine the organization's strengths and weaknesses, to identify opportunities and threats in the environment prior to developing a strategy, based on core competences, which produces and sustains competitive advantage.

Review and discussion questions

1. Distinguish and explain the relationships between resources, capabilities and core competences.

2. Evaluate the role of core competences in delivering sustainable competitive advantage.

3. Choose a transnational business that you know of, identify its core competences and assess the competences against the criteria specified in the chapter.

4. Using the same business as in the previous question, identify and evaluate the key activities and relationships in its value chain and value system.

5. Using the same company again, explore the relationships between its core competences and key value-adding activities.

6. Obtain the annual company report of an international business and gather any other relevant materials that you can, covering a recent period of as many years as you can. Using the appropriate measures, evaluate its performance.

References and further reading

Bogner, W.C., Thomas, H. and McGee, J. (1996) 'A longitudinal study of the competitive positions and entry paths of European firms in the US pharmaceutical industry'. *Strategic Management Journal*, **17**, 85–107.

Campbell, A. (1997) 'Mission statements'. *Long Range Planning*, **30**(4), August, 931–932.

Campbell, D., Stonehouse, G. and Houston, B. (1999). *Business Strategy – An Introduction*. Oxford: Butterworth-Heinemann. See especially p. 44ff. on culture and p. 171ff. on structure.

Collis, D.J. and Montgomery, C.A. (1995) 'Competing on resources: Strategy in the 1990s'. *Harvard Business Review*, July/August, 199–128.

Cravens, D.W., Greenley, G., Piercy, N.F. and Slater S. (1997) 'Integrating contemporary strategic management perspectives'. *Long Range Planning*, **30**(4), August, 493–506.

Day, G.S. (1994) 'The capabilities of market-driven organizations'. *Journal of Marketing*, **38**, October, 37–52.

Gorman, P. and Thomas, H. (1997) 'The theory and practice of competence-based competition'. *Long Range Planning*, **30**(4), August, 615–620.

Hamel, G. and Prahalad, C.K. (1994) *Competing for the Future*. Boston: Harvard Business School Press.

Hamill, J. (1992) 'Global marketing'. In M.J. Baker (ed.), *Perspectives on Marketing Management*, Vol. 2. Englewood Cliffs, NJ: Prentice Hall.

Heene, A. and Sanchez, R. (eds) (1997) *Competence-based Strategic Management*. New York: John Wiley & Sons.

Hofer, C. and Schendel, D. (1979) *Strategy Formulation: Analytical Concepts*. St Paul, MN: West Publishing.

Kay, J. (1993) *Foundations of Corporate Success*. Oxford: Oxford University Press.

Kay, J. (1995) 'Learning to define the core business'. *Financial Times*, 1 December.

Penrose, E. (1959) *The Theory of the Growth of the Firm*. Oxford: Oxford University Press.

Perlmutter, H.V. (1969) 'The tortuous evolution of the multinational corporation'. *Columbia Journal of World Business*, January/February.

Petts, N. (1997) 'Building growth on core competences – a practical approach'. *Long Range Planning*, **30**(4), August, 551–561.

Pitts, R.A. and Lei, D. (1996) *Strategic Management – Building and Sustaining Competitive Advantage*. St Paul, MN: West Publishing.

Porter, M.E. (1985) *Competitive Advantage*. New York: Free Press.

Porter, M.E. (1986) *Competition in Global Industries*. Boston: Harvard Business School Press.

Porter, M.E. (1990) *The Competitive Advantage of Nations*. London: Macmillan.

Prahalad, C.K. and Hamel, G. (1990) 'The core competence of the corporation'. *Harvard Business Review*, May/June, 79–91.

Sanchez, R. and Heene, A. (1997) *Strategic Learning and Knowledge Management*. New York: John Wiley & Sons.

Sanchez, R., Heene, A. and Thomas, H. (eds) (1996) 'Towards the theory and practice of competence-based competition'. *Dynamics of Competence-based Competition: Theory and Practice in the New Strategic Management*. Oxford: Elsevier.

Stacey, R. (1996) *Strategic Management and Organisational Dynamics* (2nd edn). London: Pitman.

Stalk, G., Evans, P., and Shulmann, L. E. (1992) 'Competing on capabilities: The new rules of corporate strategy', *Harvard Business Review*, March/April, 57–69.

Yip, G.S. (1992) *Total Global Strategy*. Englewood Cliffs, NJ: Prentice Hall.

ANALYSIS OF THE COMPETITIVE ENVIRONMENT

Learning objectives

After studying this chapter students should be able to:

- define and distinguish between the micro and macroenvironments;
- define and distinguish between industries and markets;
- explain and apply Porter's five-forces framework for analysing industries and markets;
- explain and apply Yip's framework for international business drivers;
- explain the importance of strategic groupings in competitive strategy.

Introduction

The strategy of any organization will be shaped in part by its own capabilities and competences, and in part by its competitive environment. The micro or competitive environment consists of the industry and markets in which the organization carries out its business. Industries are concerned with the production of goods and services, while markets are concerned with the demand side of the economic 'equation'.

In this chapter we introduce Yip's globalization driver framework to explain the factors in the environment that stimulate the increased globalization of industries and markets. This is important when seeking to understand why some competitive situations are globalized, while others are more regional or localized in nature.

Two key frameworks for understanding competition in industries are then explained. First, Michael Porter's five-forces framework can be used to understand the competitive forces at work in industries. The five-forces framework suggests that competitive advantage depends on how strongly an organization is positioned with regard to the five competitive forces. Second, the resource-based view school of thought is introduced. This suggests that competitive advantage rests more on how well the organization captures and develops resources into competences which can then be exploited in markets. The features of markets as they influence competitive behaviour are discussed.

Finally, the importance of strategic groupings is discussed. Competition in any industry will be at its most intense between the competitors in such a group and we discuss what factors come together to form such a grouping.

The nature of the business environment

The importance of environmental analysis

Analysis of the external business environment is a major factor in determining the strategy adopted by a business. For businesses that are international, this stage in strategic analysis is even more important.

Factors in the environment, the industry and the market will drive the enterprise toward one type of international strategy – either one that is fully global or one that makes concessions to localized customer needs. Environmental analysis is therefore a key element of the strategic process, yet it is probably the stage of the process about which there is greatest ambiguity. This ambiguity arises from the problem of gaining external information that is reliable and based on which the business can make decisions about its strategic future.

One way of conceptualizing the external environment is as a network of macro and microenvironments, all of which are related to each other. Every international enterprise operates within one or more industries and one or more markets which are found in more than one country. National and global industries and markets all interact with each other and are interdependent to varying degrees. Similarly, industries and markets exist in the context of global and national macrobusiness environments that also interact with each other. These global and national macrobusiness environments are important in shaping individual industry and market characteristics at both national and global levels. Changes in the macroenvironment at both global and national levels cause changes in customer needs, products and production techniques, competition, and industry and market structures. Managers must therefore be aware of both the global and national contexts in which their business operates and the complex network of relationships between each of these environments.

The macroenvironment

The macroenvironment (sometimes called the *far* or *remote* environment) consists of the forces at work in the general business environment which will shape the industries and markets in which an organization competes. Analysis of the macroenvironment is concerned with changes and trends in *social and cultural, demographic, political, legal, technological, economic and financial factors.* The effects of such changes on international industries and markets is assessed and on the businesses who compete within them.

The macroenvironment can be further subdivided into both global and local (or national) elements:

● the global macroenvironment – this is concerned with global trends;
● the national macroenvironment – this is concerned with trends and changes at the level of the individual country.

The forces at work in these two subdivisions fall into the same categories and are often linked. Their magnitude and direction may well differ at the global and national levels.

The microenvironment

The microenvironment (sometimes called the *near* environment) is the competitive environment facing a business. It consists of the industries and markets in which the organization conducts its business. The microenvironment can also be subdivided:

● the global microenvironment – concerned with global industry and market trends;

- the national or regional microenvironment – concerned with national industry and market trends.

The microenvironment will be largely shaped by the forces at work in the global and national macroenvironments. The near environment is the part of the environment over which the business is likely to be able to exercise some direct influence and control through its corporate strategies.

There are several techniques available for analysing the microenvironment. Porter's 'five-forces' model (Porter, 1980, 1985) is the most widely used in strategic management texts, but Yip's globalization drivers (Yip, 1992) is a useful model in the context of studying global businesses. This chapter will consider both of these models, but we begin with exploring the key concepts of industries and markets – the two major components of the microenvironment.

Industries and markets

Identifying industries and markets

Some strategic management texts wrongly use the terms 'industry' and 'market' interchangeably. Kay (1995) pointed out that to confuse the two concepts can result in flawed analysis of the competitive environment and, hence, in flawed strategy. Matters are sometimes complicated because many businesses operate in one or more industries and in one or more markets. Each will have its own distinctive structure and characteristics which will have particular implications for the formulation of corporate strategy. Kay (1993) also pointed out that a distinctive capability, or core competence, 'becomes a competitive advantage only when it is applied in a market or markets.' Industries are centred on the supply of a product, while markets are concerned with demand. It is essential, therefore, to understand and analyse both industry and market when undertaking microenvironmental analysis.

The industry

An industry consists of a group of businesses producing similar outputs (goods or services). Although there is no precise way of defining an industry, all of the businesses in a particular industry might be expected to share the following related features:

- skills and competences;
- technology;
- processes and value-adding activities;
- materials (especially input stocks);
- supplier channels;
- distribution channels;
- products.

Analysis of these features of an industry will inform the process of strategy formulation. The players in a given industry may produce products for more than one market (e.g., businesses in the 'white goods' industry produce both washing machines and refrigerators). The materials, technology, skills and processes employed in the manufacture of both products are very similar. The materials used are obtained from similar suppliers and the products are sold to consumers through the same distributors. There is therefore clearly a 'white goods' industry. Yet both products (washing machines and refrigerators) satisfy very different customer needs, are used for entirely different purposes and are therefore sold in separate markets. One make of washing machine competes with another, while one make of refrigerator competes with another.

The market

We generally think of a market as comprising the demand side of an economic system (the industry is the supply side). Unlike an industry, a market is defined in terms of shared:

- products or services;
- customers;
- customer requirements;
- distribution channels;
- competitors.

Thus a market centres on products or services which meet a specific set of consumer requirements. Given that their needs are met, the skills involved in the production of the product or service are generally of little consequence to consumers. It is important to note that businesses operate within two distinct groups of markets: those where they sell their products and services and those where they acquire their resource inputs. In addition, markets for substitute products and services will have an important bearing on the attractiveness of a particular market. Whereas understanding the industry is concerned with skills, technology and so on, understanding the market is centred on awareness of customers and their needs.

The importance of the distinction between industry and market

Businesses gain competitive advantage by developing core competences within an industry which are then deployed in markets to satisfy customer demands. An industry may well produce more than one product and may serve more than one market or group of customers (e.g., the players in the chemical industry can produce a variety of products like pharmaceuticals, fertilizers, paints, etc.). These are then sold in completely separate markets.

Similarly, a market may be served by more than one industry (e.g., the transport needs of commuters are met by the automobile industry, the railways and bus companies). While there is a world automobile industry, there are still several distinct markets for automobiles. Despite the fact that consumer needs have converged in recent years, their preferences in the North American market remain significantly different from those of their European counterparts.

The distinction between industry and market is important to make, as the success of a business will depend on its competitive position in both areas of operation – as a supplier of outputs and as a buyer of inputs.

Understanding the nature of the industry and markets in which a business conducts, or may potentially conduct its business, allows its managers to determine the most effective ways to exploit its resources, competences and technology in the context of existing and potential markets. The ability of a business to achieve competitive advantage depends on the development of company-specific competences and capabilities, and the identification of those markets to which they may give access. Such awareness is provided by internal and external analysis of the business and its environment. Internal analysis helps to identify the core competences of the business, while external analysis, particularly of the microenvironment, assists in identifying those industries and markets where the competences can be applied.

Globalization of industries and markets

Industries and markets differ vastly in the extent to which they are globalized. The consumer electronics industry and its markets are largely globalized. On the other hand, both the market for personal banking and the associated industry providing banking services are still largely localized (in that they operate in limited geographical regions). Yet, as deregulation of financial services develops throughout the world, both banking industry and market are becoming increasingly globalized.

The dynamic nature of the business environment means that the trend toward globalization is gaining momentum both in terms of the number of industries and markets which are becoming global and the extent to which they are globalized. There are a number of notable examples, however, where industries are largely globalized, but whose markets remain locally differentiated in terms of customer needs, product specifications, legal requirements, branding, advertising and other factors. In the paint industry, for example, the processes of making paint and the products of the paint industry are almost completely standardized, but the packaging, advertising and brand names are often adapted for both linguistic and cultural reasons.

Yip's globalization drivers

The four categories of drivers

Yip (1992) provided the most widely used framework for assessing the extent of, and potential for, industry and market globalization. Yip's research suggested that there are four categories of drivers (market, cost, government and competitive) which must be analysed in order to determine the degree of globalization within an industry. The strength of each of these drivers will vary from industry to industry and from market to market. It is important not to regard any industry or market as being either entirely global or local. In the case of a specific industry, certain drivers may be strongly indicative of globalization and the others more suggestive of localization. In such a situation it is appropriate for a transnational strategy that incorporates both global and local features matched to the industry drivers.

There is a strong relationship between the factors at work in the macroenvironment and the globalization drivers. This relationship is illustrated in Figure 4.1. Changes in the macroenvironment will affect both the general extent of globalization and the degree of globalization in specific industries.

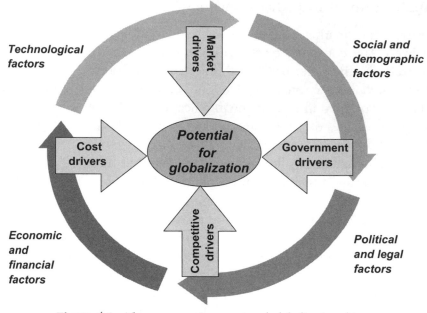

Figure 4.1 The macroenvironment and globalization drivers
Adapted from Yip (1992)

For example, cultural convergence and developments in transport and communications technology have been important factors in increasing the strength of the market, cost and competitive drivers that push toward globalization in a number of industries. Yip's framework therefore establishes linkages between the macro and microenvironments and the extent to which changes in the macroenvironment cause globalization of the microenvironment.

Each of the drivers must be analysed in detail in order to assess the extent of the pressures on an industry and market for globalization or localization. Table 4.1 shows aspects of the drivers which are indicative of globalization or localization potential. By such detailed analysis it is possible to match transnational strategy to each of the drivers. Equally, the transnational strategy of a business will seek to modify the drivers so that they match its core competences and distinctive capabilities.

Market globalization drivers

The extent to which customers, customer needs, distribution channels and marketing strategy are global will together determine the extent of market

Table 4.1   The globalization drivers

Driver		Pressure for globalization	Pressure for localization
Market	Customers	Global customers	Local customers
	Channels	Global channels	Local channels
	Marketing	Transferable marketing	Differentiated marketing
	Countries	Lead countries	No obvious lead countries
Cost	Economies of scale	High fixed costs	Low fixed costs
	Experience curve	Steep learning curve	Shallow learning curve
	Sourcing	Centralized purchasing	Decentralized purchasing
	Logistics	Low transport costs, perishable products, no need to locate near customers	High transport costs, perishable products, need to locate near customers
	Country costs	Differences in costs	Similarities in costs
	Product development costs	High	Low
	Technological change	Rapid	Slow
Government	Trade policies	Low trade barriers	High trade barriers
	Technical standards	Compatible	Incompatible
	Marketing regulations	Common	Different
	Government ownership	Government-owned Competitors present	Government-owned Competitors absent
	Host government concerns	Policies that favour global businesses	Policies that hinder global businesses
Competitive	Volume of exports and imports	High exports and imports	Low exports and imports
	Competitors	Competitors from different continents Competitors globalize	Local competitors
	Interdependence of countries	Countries largely interdependent	Countries largely independent

globalization or localization. The role of 'lead' countries in promoting the globalization of industries and markets is also an important determinant.

Customer needs
Similarities and differences in customer needs for a product or service will depend on similarities and differences in culture, economic development, climate, physical environment and whether countries are at the same stage in the product's life cycle. Cultural and economic convergence are causing customer needs to converge in many markets (Levitt, 1983).

Customers and channels
Some customers – often global organizations themselves – purchase goods and services on a global basis. They seek those suppliers who can offer the best worldwide product, service and price package. These businesses often

demand inputs that are globally standardized. The leading motor vehicle manufacturers, for example, source components globally. The world's largest motor manufacturer, General Motors, spends about UK£44 billion (US$70 billion) per annum on components. These are sourced globally from a smaller and smaller number of larger and larger suppliers, so as to ensure both lower costs and consistent quality. The increasing number of global businesses, of course, has increased the number of global customers, as such businesses increasingly co-ordinate their activities globally including purchasing decisions.

Although global distributors who buy on a global basis are less common, they exist on a regional basis in large numbers. Major supermarket chains in Europe co-ordinate their purchasing largely within the EU, but they demand uniform product standards.

Marketing

In an increasing number of markets, like fashion clothing, global brand names and marketing mixes have been established. In others, product names and advertising are varied locally. For example, the Ford Mondeo, as it is known in Europe, is badged as the Ford Contour and the Mercury Mystique in the USA. Similarly, the advertising campaign for the Renault Clio in the UK featuring 'Nicole and Papa' was not used in France. In those markets where standardized marketing is possible, it clearly indicates the existence of a global market.

Lead countries

Certain countries take the lead in product innovation in certain industries, and it is essential that global competitors compete in such lead countries. It is Japan that leads in consumer electronics, the USA in computer software and Italy in ceramic tiles (Porter, 1990). Such countries tend to set global standards for the products and services in which they are leaders, creating global markets.

To summarize, globalization is stimulated by common customer needs, global customers, the presence of lead countries and transferable marketing messages.

Cost globalization drivers

Those industries where fixed costs are high will tend to be global, so that such costs can be diluted by higher sales volumes. Higher sales volumes reduce unit fixed costs as the organization benefits from greater scale economies.

Economies of scale and scope

When a national market is not large enough for the players in an industry to achieve economies of scale, then they will be driven to enter global markets. Similarly, the desire to obtain economies of scope (advantages gained by providing two or more distinct goods or services together rather than providing them separately) has pushed industries toward globalization.

Scope economies often arise because products share the same distribution outlets or because consumers require a group of goods to be packaged together. For example, many travel agents provide currency exchange *and* insurance services alongside their normal travel services. This is thought to attract customers requiring the full range of travel-related services rather than because they possess any particular competitive advantage in the provision of such goods. Indeed, global economies of scope drive an industry toward globalization. Yip (1992) gave the example of household products like detergent and toothpaste whose manufacture gives little scope for economies of scale. In spite of this, the industries that produce these things are dominated by global companies like Unilever, Procter & Gamble, and Colgate-Palmolive. This suggests that global economies of scope derived from marketing, consumer needs and research are the drivers toward globalization rather than economies of scale.

Experience curve

If there are substantial learning and experience effects in an industry, then global operation is likely to produce substantial competitive advantages.

Sourcing

There may be cost and quality advantages to be obtained by centralizing the acquisition of supplies and services on a global basis. Global customers like Ford and other large motor manufacturers source components so as to reduce costs and 'Such cost advantages are often multiplied by the fact that big component specialists supply more than one carmaker giving them greater economies of scale' (Simonian, 1996). Global sourcing will drive an industry toward globalization.

Logistics
If transport costs are low and products are non-urgent and non-perishable, then there are advantages to be gained from global concentration of production.

Country costs, productivity and skills
Countries differ considerably in terms of production costs, productivity levels, infrastructure and availability of skilled labour. There are sometimes global cost advantages to be obtained by concentrating activities in countries where productivity is high and costs are relatively low.

Product life cycles and product development costs
The speed with which new products are required is increasing and, at the same time, the development costs of new products are high. In order to cover these costs it is necessary to sell such products in global markets because national markets are not sufficiently large to provide the necessary returns (again, especially if the business has relatively high fixed costs).

Government globalization drivers

Government policies, legislation and regulation can also drive an industry toward globalization.

Trade policies
The increasing liberalization of world trade (with falling barriers to trade) has greatly increased the potential for globalization, even though in some countries there are still substantial government-imposed trade barriers.

Technical standards
If technical standards for a product are common between countries, then this will drive an industry toward globalization, while incompatible standards will tend to fragment the market. In the 1970s, technical standards for telecommunications tended to be different from country to country, although the digitization of the 1990s increased compatibility. The resultant compatibility was one of the most important stimulants behind global communications media, such as the Internet.

Marketing regulations
Marketing regulations like those governing advertising tend to vary from country to country, which can sometimes inhibit the use of global advertis-

ing. Yet, even in this case there is a tendency toward global standards. As a consequence, major companies like Nike and Coca-Cola have been able to design advertising campaigns that meet advertising standards across the world such that the advert's ability to offend in some cultures is minimized.

Government-owned competitors

Yip argued that the existence of government-owned competitors in an industry can spur an industry toward globalization. Government subsidies and protection of home markets encourages such businesses to seek foreign customers, and this can increase global competition.

Government-owned customers

Government-owned customers tend to reduce globalization potential as they often tend to favour domestic suppliers for local political reasons.

Host government concerns

Global businesses will seek those countries where national conditions are the most favourable. Governments can advance globalization business by policies that encourage global businesses to locate value-adding activities within their national boundaries.

Competitive globalization drivers

The existence of global competitors from several countries, high levels of exports and imports, and interdependence between countries are all indicators of global competition.

Exports and imports

The level of exports and imports will indicate the extent of globalization of an industry. The higher their levels the greater the potential for the industries and markets to become globalized.

Competitors

The greater the number of competitors from different countries and continents the greater will be the level of global competition. A business that faces global competitors making use of global strategies will, almost inevitably, be forced to compete globally itself. If competitors are largely domestic, then a business will not be forced to adopt a global strategy and can continue to operate within its national boundaries.

Interdependence of countries

If there is a high level of interdependence in an industry between countries, then this will also stimulate global competition. In most industrial sectors, both markets and industries are becoming increasingly interdependent.

A summary of the drivers

Analysis of the extent of globalization in industries and markets will require examination of the strength of Yip's four drivers: market, cost, government and competitive drivers. There are several advantages to be gained by using Yip's framework:

1. it allows identification of those drivers that are global and those that are local, so that the attributes of transnational strategy can be tailored to match the drivers;
2. it can be used to analyse both industry and market;
3. it can be mapped onto Porter's five forces;
4. changes in the drivers can be indicated by macroenvironmental analysis;
5. it assists in the identification of the critical success factors of a global industry and market.

The influence of government globalization drivers in the airline industry

Economic restructuring through the philosophy of 'economic disengagement' by governments in many parts of the world has had a major impact on many industries including the airline industry over the last two decades. This philosophy influenced by the widespread adoption of the 'theory of contestable markets' (which advocated the removal of restrictive market entry barriers) from the early 1980s (Baumol, 1982; Baumol et al., 1982) manifested itself as deregulation and privatization. The Chicago Convention of 1944 established the bilateral system of air service agreements (between pairs of national governments) which have since governed international air transport. The international market that developed was characterized by national airlines from each country serving routes, airlines charging the same fares, and often sharing markets and revenues. Some bilateral agreements also stipulate conditions governing responsibility for such matters as ground handling. The terms of the bilateral agreements reflected the negotiating power and current aviation policies of the countries involved, and the resulting productivity was often low and costs high.

Deregulation of domestic services occurred in the USA in 1978, followed by Canada, the UK, Australia and New Zealand in the 1980s and the completion of deregulation within the EU in April 1997. However, parallel liberalization in international air services has taken place much more slowly. Notwithstanding the change that has occurred in some markets, even the liberalized structures are often restrictive in terms of market entry. Requirements for designated airlines to be owned by nationals of the states involved are common and airport congestion and allocation of take-off and landing slots often further impede effective market entry.

Another, and linked, aspect of 'economic disengagement' is the worldwide movement toward the privatization of state-owned airlines. However, despite this gradual process many international airlines remain publicly owned or have major government shareholdings. Controls on foreign ownership remain in most markets, but some foreign ownership now exists and with planned privatizations this will increase.

The EU's third air transport package (implemented from April 1997), for instance, sets no limit on the stake an EU national or EU airline can hold in an airline registered in another EU state. With limited exceptions, however, non-EU investors cannot hold a majority stake in any EU airline. In the USA, foreign shareholdings of up to 49% of equity under certain circumstances and 25% of voting stock is possible, although the US government also imposes an *ad hoc* control test to determine whether the foreign shareholder would substantially influence decision making irrespective of equity held.

Liberalization, privatization, foreign ownership and transnational mergers have had a major impact on the structure of the airline industry (and will continue to do so), but many regulatory and ownership barriers remain in force worldwide. As a result alternative methods of strategic development (namely, internally generated growth and mergers and acquisitions) are often precluded as viable growth strategies for international airlines, and consequently the formation of strategic alliances is, in many cases, the only available form of market entry.

Industry analysis

Industry analysis aims at establishing the intensity and nature of competition in an industry and the competitive position of the individual business with it. Industry dynamics are, in turn, affected by changes in the macroenvironment. For example, ageing populations in many developed countries have significantly affected the need to develop drugs suitable for treating the ailments of older people. There is a danger that industry analysis will be treated as a one-off activity, but, on the contrary, it is usually important that it is given a dynamic perspective and repeated on a regular basis. The framework developed by Porter (1980) is the most widely used in industry analysis. It is explained in this section.

Porter's five-forces framework

According to Porter (1979):

> *Every industry has an underlying structure, or set of fundamental economic and technical characteristics that gives rise to ... competitive forces. The strategist wanting ... to influence that environment in the company's favour, must learn what makes the environment tick. The state of competition in an industry depends on five basic forces, the collective strength of which determines the ultimate profit potential of the industry.*

The competitive forces in question are (Figure 4.2):

1. threat of new entrants to the industry (i.e., the height of barriers to entry);
2. threat of substitute products;
3. bargaining power of customers;
4. bargaining power of suppliers;
5. rivalry among current competitors in the industry.

Porter (1980) argued that it is the strength of these forces in an industry which determines its potential for profitability and which strongly influences its structure.

This view was challenged by Baden-Fuller and Stopford (1992) who observed that 'There is little difference in the profitability of one industry

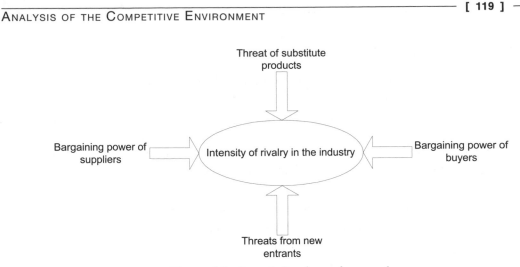

Figure 4.2 Porter's five-forces framework
Adapted from Porter (1979), (1980) and (1985)

versus another.' Their argument is based on the research of Rumelt (1991) which suggested that company-specific factors like preferred strategy were of much greater importance in determining the profitability of a business rather than its competitive environment.

There are two reasons why Rumelt's argument should not deter managers from undertaking industry and market analysis. First, whether or not industry structure determines profitability, managers must understand the environment in which they operate to assist in the choice of strategy. Second, McGahan and Porter (1997a) carried out a broader and more rigorous study than that of Rumelt and concluded that industry structure influences profitability alongside company-specific factors.

The strength of each of the five forces will differ within an industry over time and between different industries. Equally, it is true that each of the forces will be of different strengths. In fact, it is likely that just one or two of the forces will be of critical importance within a particular industry at a given point in time. The analysis of an industry will therefore seek to identify the nature and relative strength of each of the forces over time. Analysis must begin with an explanation of the nature of each of the forces and will culminate in an assessment of:

- the relative strength of each force;
- any changes likely to occur in the future.

The analysis of each of the five forces is now considered in detail.

Force 1: the threat of new entrants

The more easily new competitors can enter an industry the greater will be the level of competition. The threat from new entrants will depend on the 'height' of the barriers to entry to an industry. Barriers to entry consist of:

- the economies of scale which existing businesses in the industry already enjoy which give them a cost advantage over new entrants;
- product differentiation and brand loyalty which make it difficult for new players to attract customers from existing competitors;
- the start-up capital required to enter the industry;
- switching costs incurred by customers which deter them from buying from new entrants;
- difficulty in accessing supply or distribution channels which may make it difficult for new entrants to gain key inputs or to provide their products to the customer;
- government policy which may restrict entry;
- the resistance offered by existing players like price cuts and advertising campaigns which may deter customers from switching to new entrants.

The greater the height of the entry barriers for a particular industry the fewer competitors will be in the industry and, hence, the higher the potential profits available to the businesses within it. As a consequence, one objective of corporate strategy will be to create and increase barriers to entry.

Force 2: the threat of substitute products

A substitute is the product of (usually) another industry which meets very similar customer needs to those of the product of the industry in question. The threat from substitutes will depend on the number available and how readily they can be substituted for the product in question (i.e., what the switching costs are). For example, butter, margarine and low-fat spreads are all produced in different ways but satisfy the same customer needs. They are very close substitutes for each other, so resulting in a high level of competition between them. When there are few close substitutes for a product the level of competition will be reduced (such as for patented medicines). The degree of competition from substitutes will depend on:

- how effectively they meet the specific customer need;

- their relative price and performance;
- the cost of switching to the product for buyers;
- the willingness of buyers to substitute.

A business can reduce the competition from substitutes by taking action to differentiate its product, to enhance its performance and to increase switching costs for consumers.

Force 3: the bargaining power of buyers (customers)

The customers purchasing a product can include manufacturers, service businesses, retailers, wholesalers and distributors as well as retail consumers. Such customers have, to varying degrees, the power to bargain with the players in an industry over price, product features, availability, etc. The extent of buyer or customer power will depend on factors such as:

- the number of large and powerful customers that there are for a product;
- the ease with which customers can switch to substitute products;
- the ability of the customer to threaten to take over any of the businesses supplying the particular product by backward integration;
- the skills of the customer in negotiating price with the suppliers in the industry;
- the ability of customers to act collectively when dealing with the industry;
- the availability of information to customers.

In short, customers are powerful if individually they are large purchasers of the industry's product, switching costs are low or they pose a credible threat of backward integration, etc. The businesses in an industry will obviously try to reduce the power of their customers by differentiating their products and taking other action to increase actual or perceived switching costs.

Force 4: the bargaining power of suppliers

The suppliers to an industry include providers of raw materials, components, labour, energy, plant and equipment, finance, etc. Their power will depend on:

- the size and power of individual suppliers compared with the size and power of the businesses in the industry (who, in this case, are the buyers);

- the importance of suppliers' products to the businesses in the industry;
- the costs for the players in the industry of switching to alternative suppliers;
- the importance of the buyers in the industry as customers of the suppliers;
- the threat of forward integration by the suppliers.

Supplier power will be greatest when they are few in number and large in size, their products or services are important to the industry, when switching costs are high, when the industry is unimportant as a customer and when there is a threat of forward integration by suppliers. There are several ways in which supplier power can be reduced, such as by locating alternative sources of supply.

Force 5: the rivalry among existing competitors in the industry

Rivalry among the players in an industry can take several forms. The most common are price competition, product development, product differentiation, promotion and advertising. The intensity of rivalry can be related to a number of factors:

- the number of competitors in the industry;
- similarity of the size of the competitors;
- the overall rate of industry growth;
- the extent of differentiation and brand loyalty among consumers;
- the costs to competitors of exiting the industry (exit costs).

Rivalry will be greatest when there are a large number of roughly evenly sized businesses, when industry growth is limited, when brand loyalty is low and when exit costs are high.

Such competition may have both positive and negative effects on the industry. If competition results in enhanced innovation, it may cause the industry to expand. It is just as possible, however, that competition may result in reduced levels of profit.

Use of the five-forces framework

The five-forces framework can be used as either a tool for understanding industry structure and dynamics or as a means of identifying and understanding the key forces at work in the industry (or both).

Some criticisms can be made of the five-forces framework as an analytical tool. There seems to be an assumption that the threat of substitutes, the power of buyers and the power of suppliers will be equally important to *all* of the competitors in an industry. In reality, some of the players in an industry may be able to manage the effects of the forces more effectively than others.

Managers must seek to establish the strength of the five forces in relation to their business as well as for the industry as a whole. This analysis will help in determining how the business's strategy can modify competitive forces in its favour without providing similar benefits to the competitors in the industry. Finally, the framework has been criticized as being static when, in reality, environmental analysis must be undertaken on an ongoing basis.

Globalization drivers and the five forces

Synthesizing the two frameworks

The strength of the globalization drivers can affect the strength of the competitive forces at work within an industry. The potential relationships are illustrated in Table 4.2.

Although the effect of the drivers will differ from industry to industry, it is evident that globalization will increase competition in almost all cases. At the same time, however, there is also potential for the growth of global businesses who can compete with smaller businesses who are locally and nationally based. The smaller businesses usually suffer in such a competitive situation – often to the point of going out of existence.

Ulcer treatments and the international development of Glaxo

In the late 1970s a number of breakthroughs were made in the treatment of stomach and duodenal ulcers. The company then called SmithKline French developed cimetidine (trade name: Tagamet) which worked by encouraging ulcers to heal by reducing the level of acidity in the stomach. This became widely used, but it was the development a few years later of a similar but improved medicine called ranitidine (trade name: Zantac) by Glaxo that was to signal a period of sustained international growth – especially for Glaxo.

In the late 1970s Glaxo was a relatively successful but not very internationalized British pharmaceuticals company. The development of Zantac thrust Glaxo onto the international stage because of a number of interrelated factors. First, Glaxo was able to protect its new innovation (in this case a molecular formula) by patent – a legal instrument enforceable in almost all countries in the world. The £100 million it took to develop Zantac (it takes a great deal more than that figure to develop a new medicine today) could be recovered and a profit made, because Glaxo knew it could protect its new drug from would-be generic producers because of the patent protection. The patent did not expire until 1997. Substitution was thus legally forbidden for almost 20 years.

Second, Zantac had a clinical superiority over its rival ulcer treatments. With fewer side effects than Tagamet and more effective than other treatments then on the market, Zantac's therapeutic effect required that patients took the medicine every day if the ulcers were to be certain not to return. The effect of this was that a Zantac patient tended to remain a Zantac patient (i.e., customer) for life. 'Loyalty' to the product among its users was thus very high.

Third, the drug could be assumed to have more or less globally homogeneous demand. While the distribution of ulcer patients was not globally equal (many diseases have higher and lower incidences in different parts of the world), the effectiveness of Zantac as an ulcer treatment where ulcers were discovered was equal. This is simply because human physiology is the same regardless of race, nationality or region of residence. The fact that regional adjustment was not necessary meant that Glaxo could enjoy global scale economies on the product.

These factors combined to make Zantac the best selling prescription drug of all time and helped to make Glaxo the worldwide company it became. At its height in the late 1990s, worldwide sales of Zantac exceeded £2.5 billion. It is difficult to overstate the importance of Zantac for Glaxo. That one product alone accounted for 70% of Glaxo's profits, and using the revenue flows from it Glaxo was able to establish itself as a global player with many new innovative products including anti-AIDS products and treatments for asthma and migraines. It helped to place Glaxo in a position to be able to finance the

> merger with Wellcome plc in the mid-1990s and later the merger with SmithKline Beecham to form Glaxo SmithKline plc which, in 2003, was the largest pharmaceuticals company in the world.

Table 4.2 Globalization drivers and Porter's five forces.

Competitive force	Globalization driver impact
Threat of entry	Common customer needs increase threat of entry. Global economies of scale reduce threat of entry. Global marketing reduces threat of entry. High product development costs reduce threat of entry. Global competition increases threat of entry to national markets from global competitors.
Threat of substitutes	Threat of substitutes is increased by presence of lead nations. Threat of substitutes is increased by research and development of global businesses who use innovation as means of competition.
Power of buyers and suppliers	Existence of global customers can weaken supplier power. Existence of global suppliers can counteract the power of global customers.
Competitive rivalry	Common customer needs make it difficult for businesses to differentiate themselves which increases competition. Global customers increase competition as businesses compete to supply them. Economies of scope increase competitive rivalry. Global sourcing increases competitive rivalry. Compatible technical standards and favourable trade policies increase competitive rivalry. Increased number of businesses operating across national boundaries increases competition.

Market analysis

Market identification

Besides developing an appreciation of the forces at work within their industry, strategic decision makers must also develop an understanding of the markets in which they sell their products. Unless they can sell the organization's products at a profit the business cannot succeed.

Kay (1993) pointed out that it is only when core competences or distinctive capabilities are applied in the context of one or more markets that they become sources of competitive advantage. Markets are based on customer needs, so that success in the marketplace is largely dependent on a business being customer-driven. In addition to meeting existing customer needs, this implies that a business must also seek to create new ones. Sony, for example, created a customer need for the personal hi-fi when it launched the Walkman concept. An organization can attempt to shape the needs of its customers through new product development and advertising. Similarly, market research attempts to identify and test out ideas for new products. It is evident that the major aim of market analysis is an increased understanding of customers and their needs. Equally, markets are defined in terms of competitors and distribution channels, so that analysis also endeavours to increase understanding of these facets of the market.

Customers and their needs

Customer analysis attempts to develop knowledge of customer groupings (segmentation analysis), customer motivations and the unmet needs of customers (Aaker, 1992). We consider each of these below.

Market segmentation analysis

This analysis seeks to identify the largest and most profitable customers and to group them according to shared characteristics. Such shared characteristics will cause specific customer groups to have different needs and to act and behave differently to other customer groups. Fundamentally, segmentation means subdividing a market into customer subgroupings, each with its own distinctive attributes and needs. Customer groups are commonly segmented according to factors like age, sex, occupation, socio-economic grouping, race, lifestyle, buying habits, geography (i.e., where they live), etc. Where the customers are other businesses, they can be grouped by the nature of their business, organization type and by their size. Each segment is then analysed for its size and potential profitability, for customer needs and for potential demand, based on ability and willingness to buy. Segmentation analysis assists in the formulation of strategy by identifying particular segments and consumer characteristics which can be targeted. Computer games, for example, are largely targeted at young males between the ages of 11 and 25. This is not to say that other groups and individuals do not play computer games, but the segment identified is easily the largest and most profitable.

Customer motivations

Once market segments have been identified they must be analysed to reveal the factors that influence customers to buy or not to buy products. It is particularly important to understand factors affecting customer motivations. These include:

- sensitivity to price;
- sensitivity to quality;
- the extent of brand loyalty.

Differences in customer motivations between market segments can be illustrated by reference to the market for air travel. The market can be segmented into business and leisure travel. Customers in each group have very different characteristics and needs. Business travellers are not particularly price-conscious but are sensitive to standards of service, to scheduling and to the availability of connections. Leisure travellers are generally much more price rather than service-conscious and are less sensitive to scheduling and connections. Market research has an important role in building understanding of customer needs so that they can be targeted by appropriate product or service features.

Unmet needs

Aaker (1992) defined an unmet need as 'a customer need that is not now being met by the existing product offerings.' There are many relevant examples in markets for pharmaceutical products. There are many illnesses for which there is no current cure and often, when a cure exists, treatment has undesirable side effects. Cancer, for example, is often incurable and even where a cure is possible, it sometimes involves a number of unpleasant side effects. Clearly, a cure which was successful in a greater number of cases, and which eliminated harmful side effects, would both meet patient needs and, as a result, be potentially very profitable. The identification of unmet customer needs, as a basis for future product development, is a vital function of market research.

In addition to analysis of market segmentation, customer motivations and unmet customer needs, Porter's five-forces framework 'can also be applied to a market or submarket within an industry' (Aaker, 1992). Although the framework is designed primarily for industry analysis, it can also be useful in the analysis of competition within an organization's markets.

Strategic group and competitor analysis

What are strategic groups?

Although businesses compete within industries and markets, they face the strongest competition from businesses possessing similar core competences, pursuing similar strategies and satisfying similar customer demands. Strategic group analysis (Porter, 1980) attempts to compare an organization with the group of businesses which are its closest competitors. A strategic group consists of organizations that:

- possess similar core competences;
- pursue similar strategies;
- serve a similar customer group and similar market segments;
- employ similar technology;
- utilize similar distribution channels;
- produce similar products or services of comparable quality.

The importance of each of these attributes in circumscribing the strategic group will differ from industry to industry. It is necessary to decide which attributes are the most significant for the industry under analysis in defining its strategic groupings. In the motor industry, for example, businesses like Porsche, Ferrari, Aston Martin and Lotus fall into the same strategic group for which technology, quality and customer group are probably the most definitive characteristics. In the brewing industry, businesses like Heineken, Carlsberg and Kronenberg fall into the same group which is best characterized by their similarity of product range and distribution channels.

While the similarities between the businesses are used to define the group, it is the purpose of strategic group analysis to facilitate analysis of direct competitors and to highlight differences as well as similarities. In other words, the businesses that constitute a particular strategic group can then be compared in terms of a range of indicators which include:

- shared or similar objectives;
- core competences;
- strategies;
- markets and segments served;
- market share;
- profitability;
- cost structure;

- price structure;
- access to finance;
- product quality;
- customer loyalty;
- approach to marketing;
- organization of value-adding activities;
- suppliers and distribution channels;
- organizational culture;
- research, development and innovation.

Information on competitors can be obtained from several sources including:

- company accounts and annual reports;
- market research reports;
- suppliers;
- the government and other regulators;
- the press.

Strategic group and competitor analysis make it possible for the managers of an organization to better understand their own position and that of their competitors, in the context of both industry and market. Such knowledge is essential because it:

- identifies and focuses on an organization's closest competitors;
- assists in assessing competitive potential;
- highlights opportunities for development;
- provides external performance benchmarks;
- helps to identify critical success factors.

Globalization trends in the pharmaceuticals industry

The pharmaceutical industry, previously considered to be only a part of the chemical manufacturing sector, emerged into a defined industry sector in the middle years of the 20th century. The development of many medicine types marked milestones in the human fight against disease and in the development of the modern way of life. It is difficult to overstate the importance of the pharmaceutical industry's contribution to modern society. The top pharmaceutical companies are among the largest businesses in the world by market value and are driven by their respective ranges of high value, research-driven products.

Although highly regulated, pharmaceuticals was always a profitable industry and returns on sales are rarely lower than 20%, and can be as high as 35%. Throughout the 1970s and 1980s, pharmaceutical companies enjoyed rising sales and high profit margins. Profitability was based on a consistent and straightforward research-based strategy.

Since the beginning of the 1990s, health care cost containment has become a key issue within the industry as the need to control rapidly spiralling national health care costs became apparent, especially to national governments that ended up with increasing medicine bills in their respective health services.

Irrespective of the vast market size for pharmaceutical products, no single company has ever dominated it, although there is evidence of increased supply side concentration – the top 10 companies account for 50% of global industry sales. To maximize shareholder value, pharmaceutical companies needed to achieve a critical mass in their operations. What followed was pharmaceutical consolidation in the form of multiple mergers and acquisitions, particularly after 1990.

In terms of the international growth of the pharmaceuticals industry, a number of important trends were relevant.

From a demographic point of view, in both absolute and relative terms, the elderly population has been growing significantly and is set to continue doing so. While in 1990 the over-60s constituted approximately 18% of the combined EU, Japanese and US populations, by 2020 they are forecast to account for as much as 27%. While the ageing population does offer some economic advantages for some countries as working lifetimes are lengthened, the incidence of diseases associated with old age are expected to increase.

The apparently continual emergence of new and varied forms of disease offers another opportunity for pharmaceutical companies. Prior to 1980, HIV and AIDS, for example, were unheard of, but these conditions and others have triggered massive R&D efforts, while at the same time yielding substantial returns on investment for pharmaceutical companies. The internationalization of the industry has in part been driven by the fact that many new and variant diseases have arisen in the Far East and Africa.

Customers have become increasingly informed with regard to the usage and types of drug treatments. This has led to a partial shift in the balance of power in the pharmaceutical marketplace toward the purchaser and away from the manufacturer.

This has intensified the need for cost containment on the part of the companies in the industry, owing to the fast introduction of new products, thus shortening the life cycle of some products. Increased competition among the leading R&D-driven companies has meant that the time available for the recovery of the massive development costs of each new product have been greatly reduced. This, in turn, has placed a greater and greater emphasis on truly global coverage for a company. Achieving product roll-out in as many markets as possible in as short a time as possible has become strategically vital for the success of any new product launch.

Other factors that drove globalization have arisen from within the industry itself. Technology has affected supply chain relationships through the use of networks for the electronic exchange of research, compliance and product information, and integration with manufacturer, packaging supplier and backwards supplier systems. Customer relationships for over the counter products have been altered due to increased market understanding of medicines and their purposes. Relationships with doctors, pharmacists and patient groups have changed since the introduction of *e-detailing*.

The approximate annual growth rate of 8% of the world pharmaceuticals market suggests that sales could amount to $400 billion by 2005. This growth rate is significantly higher than the 2% underlying growth rate in most developed countries. It is partly because of this growth rate and partly because the industry is so profitable that most countries welcome investment by pharmaceuticals companies. The trend toward globalization of the pharmaceuticals industry is expected to continue.

A resource-based approach to environmental analysis

Limitations of traditional frameworks

This chapter has concentrated on explaining the traditional strategic management frameworks employed in analysis of the competitive environment. The resource-based approach to strategic management, which emphasizes the importance of core competence in achieving competitive advantage, employs a different approach to analysis of the competitive environment. We suggest that there are several limitations to existing frameworks:

- they do not integrate external and internal analysis (Sanchez and Heene, 1997);
- they emphasize the competitive and not the collaborative behaviour of businesses;
- they emphasize product and service markets rather than those where organizations obtain resources;
- they do not adequately recognize the fact that businesses themselves may alter their own competitive environments by their competence leveraging and building activities;
- they do not adequately recognize that organizations currently outside of an organization's industry and market may pose a significant competitive threat, if they possess similar core competences and distinctive capabilities;
- similarly, they do not recognize that the leveraging of existing competences and the building of new ones may enable businesses to compete outside their current competitive arenas.

Understanding the framework

A resource-based framework for analysis of the business and its competitive environment is shown in Figure 4.3. Analysis is divided into five interlinked areas:

1. the organization itself;
2. the industry;
3. product markets;
4. resource markets;
5. competing industries.

The organization itself
The internal features of the organization itself as it relates to the resource-based view is discussed in Chapter 3. To introduce these themes again here would be unnecessary duplication.

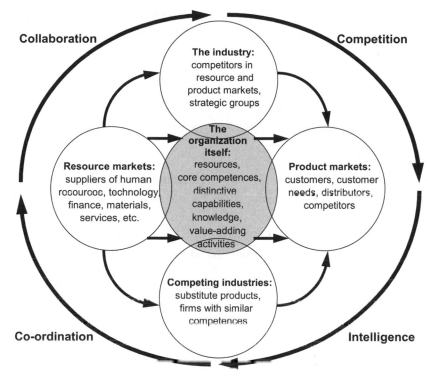

Figure 4.3 The competence-based competitive environment

The industry

The industry consists of a group of businesses producing similar products, employing similar capabilities and technology. Analysis of the industry therefore examines over time:

- the skills and competences of the companies in the industry;
- the organization of their value-adding activities;
- the technology that they employ;
- the number of competitors in the industry;
- ease of entry to and exit from the industry;
- strategic groupings.

Product markets

Product markets are those in which businesses sell their products. A business may operate in one or more product markets. Each of these markets will have its own characteristics and each market will typically be analysed in terms of:

- the number of businesses in the market and their relative market shares;
- the number of customers and their relative purchasing power;
- segments and their profitability;
- customer motivations;
- unmet customer needs;
- access to distribution channels;
- potential for collaboration with customers.

Resource markets

Resource markets are those where organizations obtain finance, human resources, materials, equipment, services, etc. It is evident that businesses will normally operate in several such markets, each with its own characteristics, depending on the company-addressable resources that they require. Resource markets need to be analysed in terms of:

- the resource requirements of businesses;
- the number of actual and potential resource suppliers;
- size of suppliers;
- supplier capabilities and competences;
- potential for collaboration with resource suppliers;
- access by competitors to suppliers.

Competing industries

Competing industries are those that produce substitute products or services. These must be analysed for:

- substitutability of the product – how close the substitute is to satisfying the same consumer demands as the original product or service;
- key competences of the businesses in the industry;
- the number and size of the businesses in the industry.

Critical success factors (CSFs) and core competences

What are CSFs?

Analysis of the industry, market and competitive position provide the means for managers to identify CSFs. CSFs are those factors that are fundamental to the success of all businesses in a particular industry and associated markets. CSFs will dictate the skills which a business must possess to ensure survival in the context of its competitive environment. Competitive advantage, however, depends on the possession of company-specific attributes that are superior to and distinctive from those of competitors. These are known as core competences and distinctive capabilities.

CSFs will differ from industry to industry and from market to market. For example, in the financial services industry, a reputation for reliability, attractive interest rates and an extensive salesforce are essential, while in the motor vehicle industry research and development of new models, efficient and cheap supply of components, extensive dealer networks and heavy advertising are essential.

CSFs are not only shaped by the competitive environment in which the organizations operate but are also influenced by the way in which individual businesses develop their core competences. They are heavily influenced by customer demands and by the actions of competitors. It is therefore essential to understand the competitive environment and its effect on CSFs.

Review and discussion questions

1. Define and distinguish between the following: industry; product market; resource market; strategic group.
2. Discuss the extent to which the personal computer market is globalized using Yip's framework.
3. Discuss the extent to which the profitability of a business is due to industry-dependent or business-specific factors.
4. Why is analysis of the competitive environment so important?
5. Explain the major forces that may cause the competitive environment to change.
6. Discuss the major similarities and differences between the traditional and resource-based approaches to analysis of the competitive environment?
7. Define and distinguish between CSFs and core competences.

References and further reading

Aaker, D.A. (1992) *Strategic Market Management.* New York: John Wiley & Sons.

Abell, D.F. (1980) *Defining the Business: the Starting Point of Strategic Planning.* Englewood Cliffs, NJ: Prentice Hall.

Arthur, W.B. (1996) 'Increasing returns and the new world of business'. *Harvard Business Review*, **74**, July/August.

Baden-Fuller, C. and Stopford, J. (1992) *Rejuvenating the Mature Business*. London: Routledge.

Baumol, W.J. (1982) 'Contestable markets: An uprising in the theory of industry structure'. *American Economic Review*, **72**(1), 1–15.

Baumol, W.J., Panzar, J.C. and Willig, R.D. (1982) *Contestable Markets and the Theory of Industry Structure*. New York: Harcourt Brace Jovanovich.

Boettcher, R. and Welge, M.K. (1994) 'Strategic information diagnosis in the global organisation'. *Management International Review*, 1st Quarter.

Chakravarthy, B. (1997) 'A new strategy framework for coping with turbulence'. *Sloan Management Review*, Winter, 69–82.

Chakravarthy, B.S. and Perlmutter, H.V. (1985) 'Strategic planning for a global business'. *Columbia Journal of World Business*, Summer.

D'Aveni, R.A. (1994) *Hypercompetition: Managing the Dynamics of Strategic Manoeuvring*. New York: Free Press.

Fahey, L. and Narayanan, V.K. (1994) 'Global environmental analysis'. In: S. Segal-Horn (ed.), *The Challenge of International Business*. London: Kogan Page.

Ginter, P. and Duncan, J. (1990) 'Macroenvironmental analysis'. *Long Range Planning*, December.

Hamel, G. and Prahalad, C.K. (1989) 'Strategic intent'. *Harvard Business Review*, **67**(3).

Hamel, G. and Prahalad, C.K. (1994) *Competing for the Future*. Boston: Harvard Business School Press.

Heene, A. and Sanchez, R. (1997) Competence-based Strategic Management. New York: John Wiley & Sons.

Helms, M.M. and Wright, P. (1992) 'External considerations: Their influence on future strategic planning'. *Management Decision*, **30**(8).

Henzler, H. and Rall, W. (1986) 'Facing up to the globalization challenge'. *McKinsey Quarterly*, Winter.

Kay, J. (1993) *Foundations of Corporate Success*. Oxford, UK: Oxford University Press.

Kay, J. (1995) 'Learning to define the core business'. *Financial Times*, 1 December.

Klugt, C.J. Van der (1986) 'Japan's global challenge in electronics – the Philips' response'. *European Management Journal*, **4**(1).

Levitt, T. (1983) 'The globalisation of markets'. *Harvard Business Review*, May/June.

Lindsay, W.K. and Rue, L.W. (1980) 'Impact of organisation environment on the long range planning process'. *Academy of Management Journal*, **23**.

Mascarenhas, B. (1982) 'Coping with uncertainty in international business'. *Journal of International Business Studies*.

McGahan, A.M. and Porter, M.E. (1997a) 'How much does industry matter, really?'. *Strategic Management Journal*, **18** (Summer Special Issue), 15–30.

McGahan, A.M. and Porter, M.E. (1997b) 'The persistence of profitability: Comparing the market-structure and Chicago views'. Manuscript, Harvard Business School.

Porter, M.E. (1979) 'How competitive forces shape strategy'. *Harvard Business Review*, March/April.

Porter, M.E. (1980) *Competitive Strategy: Techniques for Analysing Industries and Competitors*. New York: Free Press.

Porter, M.E. (1985) *Competitive Advantage*. New York: Free Press.

Porter, M.E. (1990) *The Competitive Advantage of Nations*. London: Macmillan.

Prahalad, C.K. and Hamel, G. (1990) 'The core competence of the corporation'. *Harvard Business Review*, 79–91.

Rumelt, R. (1987) 'Theory, strategy and entrepreneurship'. In: D.J. Teece (ed.), *The Competitive Challenge*. Cambridge, MA: Ballinger Publishing.

Rumelt, R.P. (1991) 'How much does industry matter?'. *Strategic Management Journal*, **12**(3).

Sanchez, R. (1995) 'Strategic flexibility in product competition'. *Strategic Management Journal*, **16**, Summer.

Sanchez, R. (1995) 'Strategic flexibility, firm organisation, and managerial work in dynamic markets: A strategic options perspective'. *Advances in Strategic Management*, **9**, 251–291.

Sanchez, R. and Heene, A. (1997) *Strategic Learning and Knowledge Management*. New York: John Wiley & Sons.

Simonian, H. (1996) 'Star parts for bit players'. *Financial Times*, 28 October.

Strebel, P. (1992) *Breakpoints*. Boston: Harvard Business School Press.

Turner, I. (1996) 'Working with chaos'. *Financial Times*, 4 October.

Yip, G.S. (1992) *Total Global Strategy*. Englewood Cliffs, NJ: Prentice Hall.

Yip, G.S., Loewe, P.M. and Yoshino, M.Y. (1988) 'How to take your company to the global market'. *Columbia Journal of World Business*, Winter.

ANALYSIS OF THE GLOBAL MACROENVIRONMENT

Learning objectives

After studying this chapter students should be able to:

- describe the nature of the macroenvironment;
- define and distinguish between continuities and discontinuities in the business environment;
- explain each of the factors to be analysed in a STEP analysis;
- describe why macroenvironmental analysis is more complex for international businesses;
- explain how national circumstances can affect global strategy;
- describe the stages in carrying out a STEP analysis.

Introduction

Strategic planning is made more difficult by the rate of change, complexity and associated uncertainty in the environment. Sanchez and Heene (1997) stated that 'In dynamic environments, building and leveraging competences requires flexibility in acquiring and deploying new resources effectively in changing circumstances.' It is evident therefore that successful strategy and associated competence development must be informed by a detailed understanding of the business environment.

In Chapter 4 we examined the importance of industry analysis. In this chapter we look outside of the industry to learn about those forces at work that are outside an organization's control and with which the business must usually learn to 'cope'. A thorough macroenvironmental analysis is an ambitious task for a non-internationalized business, but for a global company the task is made all the more complex because of the number of industries, markets and countries in which it may operate.

Change in the business environment

The nature of environmental change

The global business environment may be described as possessing three important characteristics:

- it is *dynamic* – this describes the rate of change (environmental factors tend to change with increasing dynamism as time passes);
- it is *complex* – the forces at work in the environment are numerous, difficult to understand individually and the relationships between them are increasingly intricate;
- it is *turbulent* – the changes taking place are variable in direction, uneven in magnitude and do not always conform to a recognizable or predictable pattern.

Change in the network of business environments can be regarded as either continuous or discontinuous:

- continuous change is a series of minor developments in technology, the world economy, political alignments and societies which is constantly taking place;
- discontinuous change describes major developments in the global business environment which arise almost at random and which may cause major alterations in the way that business is conducted. They tend to be 'one-off' occurrences, but they can precipitate significant change in business strategies.

The effects of discontinuities on governments and businesses can bring about changes in the balance of power in society, such is their potential influence. The oil crisis of 1974 brought about a large increase in the price of crude oil in Western economies. The effect of this was recession, very high inflation and numerous business failures. Similarly, the demise of communism in Eastern Europe (an example of a political change) opened up these countries, their markets and their industries to the rest of the world. In Europe, the creation of the Single European Market in 1992 eliminated many of the barriers to trade between member countries.

Discontinuities can also result from 'industry breakpoints' (Strebel, 1992; Turner, 1996) which can be 'caused by a revolutionary product or by fundamental changes in process or distribution channels.' Strebel identified the major indicators of breakpoints as falling demand for standardized products, availability of new sources of supplies or technologies, the breaking down of traditional customer segment groups and convergence of separate industries.

Organizations must respond to continuous and discontinuous changes in their environment if they are to compete and survive. It may be tempting to assume that it is impossible to make sense of the chaos which sometimes comprises the modern business environment, but such a negative approach is unlikely to result in commercial success. It may be impossible to predict some discontinuities, but awareness and understanding of the environmental forces at work increase the likelihood of prompt and appropriate organizational responses.

Change and prescriptive strategy

For the planning or prescriptive school of strategists, environmental analysis is supposed to allow the prediction of future events so that strategic plans can be formulated accordingly. The fact that the complexity and turbulence of the environment make accurate prediction problematic may suggest that environmental analysis is of little value. However, even the incrementalists (Lindblom, 1959) and the logical incrementalists (Quinn, 1980; Mintzberg and Waters, 1985) acknowledged the need for business to anticipate and respond to changes in the environment. Chakravarthy (1997) and D'Aveni (1994) argued that businesses should actively seek to modify their environment, constantly challenging and changing the rules of the game. Analysis of the environment is therefore vital, whether it is to act as the basis of a long-term plan, to inform incremental modifications to strategy or to increase understanding of those 'rules' that the business may wish to change.

The complex and chaotic nature of the global business environment rules out (in most cases) a rigidly planned approach to strategic management. Complexity theory, however, advocates that organizations foster cultures that are flexible and experimental, and that place an emphasis on learning (Turner, 1996). Both individual and organizational learning imply the acquisition of information and knowledge. In consequence, monitoring and analysis of the business environment can be regarded as fundamental to organizational learning within the global enterprise.

The complexity of the global environmental means that the process of analysis must attempt to structure, simplify and summarize events so as to facilitate their evaluation prior to management decision making. The dynamics of the environment and the pace of change mean that external analysis must be a continuous process. The frameworks employed in environmental analysis provide the means to order and relate seemingly random and isolated events in a format that is understandable to the managers of international enterprises. Managers must, however, continue to recognize the imperfections of the analytical frameworks that they employ and the often incomplete and inaccurate nature of the information on which they base their decisions. Environmental analysis can never remove risk from business activities, but it provides a means of understanding the nature and extent of the risks involved. The next section of this chapter explores the major forces at work in the macroenvironment (in contrast to the microenvironment which was considered in Chapter 4).

The macroenvironment

STEP analysis

The macro (or 'far') environment is the part of the environment over which the business can rarely exert any direct influence but to which it must respond. Conventionally, it is analysed by categorizing environmental influences at the macro-level into broad groupings. In this context the most commonly used framework is STEP (sociological, technological, economic and political factors). This chapter uses an alternative categorization of forces which is more appropriate for global analysis. The forces at work in the macroenvironment are grouped under the headings of social and cultural, demographic, political, legal, technological, economic and financial. Each of these forces must be considered at both global and national levels. Global trends in these forces will significantly affect national trends, but there will frequently be differences in magnitude and direction at the global and national levels. For example, the information revolution has transformed global business activities, but its effects on individual countries have been uneven.

Table 5.1 Macroenvironmental forces

Social and cultural
values, attitudes and beliefs;
lifestyle and tastes;
ethics;
working practices and attitudes;
levels of education and training;
language;
ecological and environmental concern;
religion and moral dispositions;
health and related issues;·
openness (to international products and new
    technology);
individualism versus collectivism (in national
    culture).

Legal (vary between countries)
contract law;
employment law;
trade union law;
monopoly and restrictive practices legislation;
consumer protection legislation;
tax law;
company law;
corruption law;
international law.

Demographic
size and growth of population (birth and death
    rates);
composition of population (age, sex, ethnic
    mix);
geographic distribution and population
    movements (internal migration, emigration
    and immigration).

Technological
research and development;
information technology and communications
    systems;
communications systems;
transport systems and infrastructures;
production technologies;
design technologies and new products;
levels of technology, adoption rates and
    availability of technology.

Political
constitutional issues in the country;
national parties and groupings;
stability (or lack of);
international groupings and trading blocks;
government economic intervention;
levels of taxation;
availability of government subsidies;
levels of trade protectionism.

Economic and financial
economic systems – market, centrally planned,
    mixed;
size of economies (usually measured by GDP),
    structures and structural changes;
cyclical changes – recessions, booms, etc.;
growth rates and levels of economic development;
levels and distribution of income;
price/inflation levels;
cost levels (labour, energy, transport, materials);
employment levels;
currency and exchange values;
interest rates;
levels of investment and capital markets;
international groupings;
banking systems

Table 5.1 shows the major groupings of forces at work in the macro-environment and the variables associated with them. It is essential that information on these forces and associated variables is gathered continuously both globally and within each country of operation. The information must then be assessed for relevance to industry and markets.

Global and national macroenvironments

The process of analysis of the global macroenvironment is concerned with global movements in culture and society, demography, politics, international law, economics and technology. It is such movements that can create the conditions for breakpoints (Strebel, 1992) which may, in turn, drastically alter competitive conditions either in favour of, or against, countries, industries and organizations.

International enterprises operate within several national environments. Each country in which a business operates presents a different set of environmental influences at the macro, industry and market levels. It is therefore necessary to monitor the macroenvironmental situation in each country of operation, as national trends will differ from those taking place in the global environment in terms of pace, size and direction. Again the national macroenvironment must be analysed in terms of the social, cultural, demographic, political, legal, technological, economic and financial forces at work.

The relationship between global and national macroenvironments

The global macroenvironment will influence the development of individual national conditions, but each nation will have its own unique set of macroenvironmental conditions related to its history and development. Trends in the global macroenvironment will play a major part in shaping the global industry and market for particular products. Similarly, the national macroenvironment will substantially shape national industry and market conditions.

A major purpose of macroenvironmental analysis is to identify both the similarities and differences that exist between countries. Levitt (1983) emphasized the advantage that can be gained by concentrating on national similarities. There are two dangers, however, in overemphasizing similarities between countries as a source of competitive advantage. First, while there are benefits to be gained by concentrating on similarities in global customer requirements, there are also advantages to be gained by remaining responsive to differences in customer needs (Prahalad and Doz, 1986). Such thinking is at the heart of transnational strategy. Second, exploitation of national differences in relation to core business activities can be important as a source of competitive advantage. Porter (1990) stressed the role of national circumstances in fostering competitive advantage. Differences in wage and price levels, availability of skilled labour and the availability of government assistance can all be important sources of competitive advantage. The ability to exploit both national similarities and differences is central to international competitive advantage. Analysis of international business environments makes it possible to identify where potential sources of competitive advantage can be found both in terms of actual and potential markets, and the location of value-adding activities.

The role of national circumstances in international business

Porter (1990) argued that global competitive advantage 'results from an effective combination of national circumstances and company strategy.' It is therefore useful to examine those factors that are likely to make a country attractive as a market and as a base for value-adding activities. In other words, national circumstances may be important in determining the success of a business that chooses to locate certain of its activities in a country. It is therefore important to consider what factors constitute the major determinants of national competitive advantage.

Determinants of national competitive advantage

Porter (1990) identified four sets of circumstances (represented in Porter's Diamond – see Figure 5.1) which are crucial in determining national competitive advantage.

(a) Factor conditions

Factor conditions refer to the quality and availability of the key inputs to a business's processes. Typically, this includes an analysis of the quality and quantity of the nation's human, physical, knowledge, capital technological and capital resources, and the national infrastructure. The stock of factors is important in determining national competitiveness, but more important still is the rate at which the factors are created, upgraded and made more specialized in particular industries. As well as the role of businesses in factor creation and improvement, the government can also have an important role to play via its policies on education, training and industry.

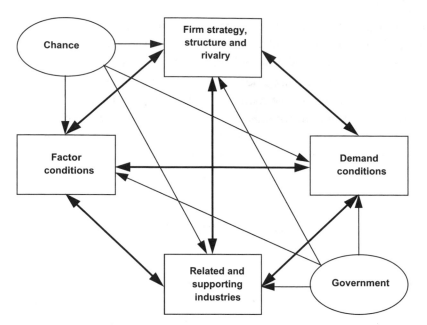

Figure 5.1 Determinants of national competitive advantage – Porter's diamond
Adapted from Porter (1990)

(b) Demand conditions

The quantity and quality of home demand for an industry's product will also help to determine national advantage in that industry. If domestic buyers are sophisticated and demanding, and if domestic demand is internationalized, this will stimulate competitive advantage as domestic businesses will be forced to innovate faster and will be more accustomed to catering for international preferences.

(c) Related and supporting industries

Supporting industries refer to suppliers or downstream buyers, while related industries describe those industries that interlink with the industry in question such that there is some degree of reciprocal advantage. If these industries are stronger in some countries than others, then such regions will tend to have more competitive industry. For example, many Japanese car companies benefit from the fact that Japanese component manufacturers (a supporting industry) are extremely competitive in international markets.

(d) The business's strategy, structure and rivalry

The context in which businesses are established, organized and managed as well as the nature of domestic rivalry will also help to determine national competitive advantage in specific industries. Factors like attitudes to risk taking and commitment to goals are important. Similarly, vigorous domestic rivalry, both price and non-price, produces companies that are likely to be able to compete in international markets. Technological rivalry is also important as it will help to create technological superiority.

As well as these four factors there are two others that can play an important role in national competitive advantage: *chance* and *government*.

(e) The role of chance

Chance can also affect national competitive advantage. Events like major technological discontinuities, wars, political decisions by foreign governments, significant shifts in world financial markets or exchange rates can all create or destroy national advantages. The problem with chance events is their inherent unpredictability.

(f) The role of government

Porter argued that government can affect national competitiveness by influencing the other four factors. Factor conditions are affected by government subsidies, policies toward education, capital markets, the setting of product standards, etc. Governments provide the framework within which businesses compete and formulate their structures and strategies, hence playing a significant role in determining national advantage.

Prudential: factor conditions in Reading, UK and Bombay, India

In September 2002 the UK-based insurance giant, Prudential, announced plans to cut 850 UK jobs as part of a move to create a new call centre operation in India. The new Bombay call centre would result in staff numbers at Reading, UK being reduced by 850 to around 1,400. Prudential expected to save £16 million a year from the switch, which will see Indian graduates paid an estimated one-tenth of the salary of their UK counterparts.

A prominent trade union, Amicus, pledged to fight the proposals. Its general secretary Roger Lyons said: 'This is a despicable act by Prudential. Selling 850 UK call centre jobs to India is disgraceful. The only reason being given is an 80% saving on wages, but no thought has been given to customer impact or the devastation this will cause to those affected.'

> Prudential's chief executive, Mark Wood said that staff in India would be well paid by local standards and trained to a high degree. He went on to explain that the labour market was one reason for the change: 'The UK market for trained, experienced financial services staff is very competitive. There's a much larger pool of graduate staff in India, and in Bombay, than in the UK.' Salaries for Indian graduates can start at only £2,500 – at least £10,000 less than the equivalent in Britain and firms do not have to pay national insurance or pension contributions.

Porter's Diamond

Porter's Diamond is a way of conceptualizing the six circumstantial influences that are relevant in determining national competitiveness. These determinants, individually and collectively, create the context in which a country's businesses are born and compete. The factors and the relationships between them are illustrated in Figure 5.1. Nations are most likely to succeed in industries or segments where the combination of factors is most favourable. Similarly, from the perspective of the individual business, those countries with the most favourable combination of circumstances are likely to be chosen as markets and as locations for value-adding activities by global businesses.

The analytical process

Stages in the process

At each stage of analysis of the macro and microenvironments a number of activities are carried out. Ginter and Duncan (1990) argued that environmental analysis 'consists of four interrelated activities – scanning, monitoring, forecasting and assessing.' The process of analysis, which must be applied to all the global and national environments in which the organization conducts business, may alternatively be conceived as comprising three stages.

1. *information gathering* – identification of sources of information and obtaining relevant information from those sources;
2. *information processing* – organization of information into a manage-

able and meaningful format that identifies indicators of change, trends and patterns;

3. *knowledge generation* – the assessment of information to identify and prioritize those external events that are critical to the success of the organization, the creation of models and scenarios that are used to evaluate different possibilities so as to augment organizational learning and inform strategic decision making.

We will now consider each of these stages in turn.

Information gathering

Data and information about the environment can be obtained from a variety of sources which must be constantly scanned and monitored for changes that may affect markets, competition and industry structures. Two major problems exist with regard to information gathering.

The number and variety of sources
There are so many diverse sources of data and information that it is extremely difficult to monitor them all, so that it may be necessary to be selective. This carries the danger of missing some vital information.

The accuracy, relevance and reliability of sources
It is very difficult to gauge the accuracy, relevance and reliability of sources, particularly as much of the information may be speculative in nature. In both cases experience and judgement are essential to the selection process.

Information processing

Once the information has been gathered it must be processed into a usable format. There are many methods of processing the data once gathered (Table 5.2). These will often require the use of information technology (IT) to manipulate, summarize, tabulate, model and graph data. Database and spreadsheet software is helpful, but in recent years developments in decision support systems, expert systems and intelligent databases have transformed the ability of managers to generate the quality of information required to support decision making.

Table 5.2 Data sources in international strategic analysis

Type of data source	Examples
World organizations (reports and statistics)	OECD, World Bank, IMF, UN
Computerized sources	Internet, commercial databases both online and on CD-ROM (e.g., Datastream, Mintel, Extel, FAME)
Government sources	National government reports and statistics
General and academic publications	Quality newspapers and magazines (e.g., *The Economist* and associated publications, *Financial Times*, etc.), international academic journals
Business publications	Market research reports (Neilsen's, etc., *The Economist*, banks, trade journals, *Financial Times*, national and international market research agencies, commercial bank reports)
Directories	*International Directory of Marketing Research Agencies*, Market Research Society, London and *International Directory of Marketing Research Houses and Services*, American Marketing Association, Chicago.

Knowledge generation

The more rapid the pace of change the greater is the need for accelerated learning by both the individual and the organization. In such a dynamic environment, it is those organizations that learn rapidly and generate organizational knowledge which survive and outperform their rivals. The boundaries between information processing and knowledge generation have become increasingly blurred as a result of the major developments that have taken place in IT. IT greatly assists knowledge generation by allowing the development of sophisticated models and the ability to simulate a range of situations.

Turbulence in the environment makes the process of knowledge generation uncertain, but scenario analysis, game theory and computer simulations make it possible to explore a range of possibilities in terms of both change in the environment and appropriate organizational responses. As Boettcher and Welge (1994) put it, 'the diagnosis of strategic information by globally dispersed organizations has been identified as a largely neglected but extremely relevant field of inquiry.'

Summary – analysis of the global macroenvironment

The links between the micro and macroenvironments

Analysis of the macroenvironment is a fundamental prerequisite to the formulation of global strategy. The macroenvironment plays a vital role in shaping industry and market structures. Consequently, the process of analysis must begin with definition of the industry and markets in which the business operates, so that analysis of the macroenvironment is focused and the dynamic relationships between the macro and microenvironments are highlighted.

As has been shown, changes in social, demographic, political, legal, technological, economic and financial factors can create new industries and markets and can drastically alter existing ones. Additionally, it is important to understand the interaction between global and national business environments at the micro and macro-levels. Global trends may affect each country, industry and market differently, thus changing the balance of competitive forces between different nations and creating a complex set of opportunities and threats for global business organizations.

The process of analysis seeks to gather information and to process it in such a way as to enhance organizational learning and knowledge, thus adding to the organization's stock of strategic assets. Although such knowledge is inevitably imperfect because of the complexity and turbulence of the environment, it is invaluable in the process of managing risk. Sanchez (1995) and Heene and Sanchez (1997) argued that 'in dynamic environments, creating "higher order" capabilities like organisational learning that improve the strategic flexibility of an organisation becomes critical to building, leveraging, and maintaining competences.' Such competence development and flexibility are essential to successful global strategy in a complex and rapidly changing environment.

In Chapter 4 we discussed the links between the micro and macroenvironments with particular emphasis on globalization drivers. We can also develop a framework that shows how changes in the macroenvironment affect the five forces in Porter's model of the competitive environment. This enables us to predict how trends in the macroenvironment will change industry profitability.

An example of such a link is the trend toward reduction of tariff and nontariff trading barriers between trading nations. This reduces the barriers to entry into formerly protected national or regional industries and hence the threat of new entrants into such industries is increased. The increased threat, in turn, is likely to apply a downward pressure on the prices charged by the industry and thus lower the profitability of the industry as a whole.

Review of the key stages

Despite the emphasis in the literature on competences and capabilities as internal sources of competitive advantage, environmental analysis is still of vital importance to strategy formulation. Organizations must assess both their current and potential capabilities, and the competitive, and sometimes collaborative, global context in which they must conduct their business.

In terms of specific stages, we suggest that a thorough environmental analysis for an international business will involve the following:

- definition of industry and market, and identification of their chief characteristics;
- analysis of the macroenvironment at both global and national levels;
- an understanding of the role of nations in competitive advantage;
- analysis of the globalization drivers affecting the industry and market;
- analysis of industry and market structures (product and resource);
- identification and analysis of strategic groupings;
- identification of critical success factors.

The main output of the analysis is identification of the opportunities and threats facing the business and the factors that are critical to success in the business environment. It is important to remember that such analysis must be undertaken on a continuous basis because of the dynamic and turbulent nature of the business environment. Similarly, such analysis must be recognized as inherently imprecise. Nevertheless, knowledge of the environment in which it operates is essential to the learning process of an intelligent organization.

External analysis also forms the basis of the assessment of how well the capabilities of a business are matched to its environment. It may demonstrate that there are opportunities, or requirements, for an organization to develop new competences or leverage existing ones, if it is to succeed in the future.

Discussion and review questions

1. Explain the importance of the macroenvironment in shaping competition and global strategies.
2. Discuss the major trends that are forcing the globalization of industries and markets. Illustrate your answer with examples.
3. Explain the difference between an industry and a market.
4. Discuss the effects of changes in the macroenvironment in an industry you know about (such as in the fast food industry).

References and further reading

Abell, D.F. (1980) *Defining the Business: The Starting Point of Strategic Planning.* Englewood Cliffs, NJ: Prentice Hall.

Boettcher, R. and Welge, M.K. (1994) 'Strategic information diagnosis in the global organisation'. *Management International Review,* 1st Quarter.

Chakravarthy, B. (1997) 'A new strategy framework for coping with turbulence'. *Sloan Management Review,* Winter, 69–82.

Chakravarthy, B.S. and Perlmutter, H.V. (1985) 'Strategic planning for a global business'. *Columbia Journal of World Business,* Summer.

D'Aveni, R.A. (1994) *Hypercompetition: Managing the Dynamics of Strategic Manoeuvring.* Free Press, New York.

Elenkov, D.E. (1997) 'Strategic uncertainty and environmental scanning: The case for institutional influences on scanning behaviour'. *Strategic Management Journal,* **18**(4), 287–302.

Fahey, L. and Narayanan, V.K. (1994) 'Global environmental analysis'. In: S. Segal-Horn (ed.), *The Challenge of International Business.* London: Kogan Page.

Ginter, P. and Duncan, J. (1990) 'Macroenvironmental analysis'. *Long Range Planning,* December.

Hamel, G. and Prahalad, C.K. (1989) 'Strategic intent'. *Harvard Business Review,* **67**(3).

Hamel, G. and Prahalad, C.K. (1994) *Competing for the Future.* Boston: Harvard Business School Press.

Heene, A. and Sanchez, R. (1997) *Competence-based Strategic Management.* New York: John Wiley & Sons.

Helms, M.M. and Wright, P. (1992) 'External considerations: Their influence on future strategic planning'. *Management Decision,* **30**(8), 4–11.

Henzler, H. and Rall, W. (1986) 'Facing up to the globalization challenge'. *McKinsey Quarterly,* Winter.

Kay, J. (1993) *Foundations of Corporate Success.* Oxford, UK: Oxford University Press.

Kay, J. (1995) 'Learning to define the core business'. *Financial Times,* 1 December.

Klugt, C.J. Van der (1986) 'Japan's global challenge in electronics – the Philips' response'. *European Management Journal,* **4**(1), 4–9.

Levitt, T. (1983) 'The globalization of markets'. *Harvard Business Review,* May/June.

Lindblom, C.E. (1959) 'The science of muddling through'. *Public Administration Review,* **19**.

Lindsay, W.K. and Rue, L.W. (1980) 'Impact of organisation environment on the long range planning process'. *Academy of Management Journal,* **23**.

Mascarenhas, B. (1982) 'Coping with uncertainty in international business'. *Journal of International Business Studies,* **13**(2), 87–99.

Mintzberg, H. (1973) 'Strategy-making in three modes'. *California Management Review*, **16**.

Mintzberg, H. (1991) *The Strategy Process – Concepts, Contexts, Cases*. Englewood Cliffs, NJ: Prentice Hall.

Mintzberg, H. and Waters, J.A. (1985) 'Of strategies deliberate and emergent'. *Strategic Management Journal*, **6**.

Negandhi, A.R. (1987) *International Management*. Boston: Allyn & Bacon.

Phatak, A.V. (1963) *International Dimensions of Management*. Boston: Kent.

Porter, M.E. (1980) *Competitive Strategy: Techniques for Analysing Industries and Competitors*. New York: Free Press.

Porter, M.E. (1985) *Competitive Advantage*. New York: Free Press.

Porter, M.E. (1986a) *Competition in Global Business*. Boston: Harvard University Press.

Porter, M.E. (1986b) 'Changing patterns of international competition'. *California Management Review*, **28**(2), Winter, 9–40.

Porter, M.E. (1990) *The Competitive Advantage of Nations*. London: Macmillan.

Prahalad, C.K. and Doz, Y.L. (1986) *The Multinational Mission: Balancing Local Demands and Global Vision*. New York: Free Press.

Prahalad, C.K. and Hamel, G. (1989) 'Strategic intent'. *Harvard Business Review*, 63–76.

Prahalad, C.K. and Hamel, G. (1990) 'The core competence of the corporation'. *Harvard Business Review*, 79–91.

Prahalad, C.K. and Hamel, G. (1993) 'Strategy as stretch and leverage'. *Harvard Business Review*, March/April.

Prahalad, C.K. and Hamel, G. (1995) *Competing for the Future*. Boston: Harvard Business School Press.

Quinn, J.B. (1978) 'Strategic change: "Logic incrementalism"'. *Strategic Management Journal*, **10**.

Sanchez, R. (1995) 'Strategic flexibility in product competition'. *Strategic Management Journal*, **16**, Summer, 135–159.

Sanchez, R. (1995) 'Strategic flexibility, firm organisation, and managerial work in dynamic markets: A strategic options perspective'. *Advances in Strategic Management*, **9**, 251–291.

Sanchez, R. and Heene, A. (1997) *Strategic Learning and Knowledge Management*. New York: John Wiley & Sons.

Segal-Horn, S. (1992) 'Global markets, regional trading blocs and international consumers'. *Journal of Global Marketing*, **5**(3).

Smith, D. (1997) 'Wrinklies timebomb waiting to explode'. *Sunday Times*, 23 February.

Stalk, G., Evans, P., and Shulmann, L.E. (1992) 'Competing on capabilities: The new rules of corporate strategy'. *Harvard Business Review*, March/April.

Strebel, P. (1992) *Breakpoints*. Boston: Harvard Business School Press.

Turner, I. (1996) 'Working with chaos'. *Financial Times*, 4 October.

Yip, G.S. (1992) *Total Global Strategy*. Englewood Cliffs, NJ: Prentice Hall.

Yip, G.S., Loewe, P.M. and Yoshino, M.Y. (1988) 'How to take your company to the global market'. *Columbia Journal of World Business*, Winter, 37–48.

PART III

GLOBAL AND TRANSNATIONAL STRATEGY

Introduction

In many ways this chapter is the core of the book. It links with subsequent chapters on international and global business management and links back to Chapters 2–5 which examined the most important influences on global strategy (namely, core competences, industry/market characteristics – especially the extent of globalization) and the global vision and philosophy of the business.

This chapter focuses on the competitive strategies of global businesses and is pivotal to the rest of the book, drawing together analysis of the global business and its environment with global management. Global and transnational strategies are developed on the basis of analysis of global knowledge-based competences, activities and the global environment. The choice of strategy is by no means simple. Industries and markets cannot be classified as either entirely global or entirely multidomestic. Yip's research (1992) showed that an industry or market may simultaneously possess both global and local characteristics, based on the relative strength of each element of each of the four types of globalization driver. It is likely that most industries and markets will be both global and local in some respects. On this basis, a global and transnational strategy must be 'a flexible combination of many elements' (Yip, 1992). That is to say, the strategy of a global business must be tailored to match each element of each globalization driver, being in part global and in part adapted to local requirements, as conditions dictate. The use of the term 'global strategy' could be seen as slightly misleading when describing a complex strategy that combines global and local components. For this reason, we use the term 'transnational strategy' to describe a worldwide strategy based on core competences, integrating both global and local elements.

Transnational strategies and global competitiveness

Sustainability and competitive advantage

One of the key objectives of any business strategy is to achieve competitive advantage that is sustainable. This implies two things: first, it implies that a strategy will lead to superior performance in an industry; and, second, that the superior performance can be sustained over time (i.e., not just for a limited period of time).

Competitive advantage
The strategy literature makes a number of observations with regard to competitive advantage. It tends to be explained in terms of a number of interlinked concepts:

- *superior performance* – there is no precise measure, but this is often measured in terms of above average profit returns against sales or investment, higher unit revenue, lower unit costs, higher market share, etc.;

- *strategy* – the plan or course of action by which the business hopes to achieve competitive advantage;
- *core competences/distinctive capabilities* – the distinctive knowledge, skills and organization of activities which make the corporation different and superior to its competitors, acting as the basis of its generic strategy;
- *innovation* – the pace of change in the global business environment means that firms must constantly seek to develop new knowledge and core competences, so as to innovate more quickly than competitors;
- *configuration/architecture* – the way in which the value-adding activities of the organization are configured on an international or global basis (they may be geographically concentrated or dispersed);
- *co-ordination/integration* – how the value-adding activities are co-ordinated on a transnational or global basis;
- *responsiveness* – the ability of the organization to respond to local needs (at another level this may also imply responsiveness to a rapidly changing environment).

Sustainability
This is best considered as the time period over which superior performance is maintained. The extent to which competitive advantage is sustainable will usually depend on a number of organizational features:

- its ability to build and leverage knowledge-based core competences, build an architecture and develop strategies that are superior to those of competitors and that are difficult to emulate;
- its ability to co-ordinate and integrate its worldwide activities more effectively than its competitors;
- its ability to continuously innovate and improve strategies, knowledge, competences, architecture and co-ordination.

Sustainability will also depend on the ability of competitors (or lack of ability) to imitate or surpass a business that has achieved a superior level of performance. Finally, it will depend on changes in the business environment, like technological change, which may be beyond the control of the leading competitor and which may enhance or reduce its competitive advantage.

Transnational, global and international business strategies

A successful international strategy must create and then sustain competitive advantage across national boundaries whether on a regional or worldwide basis. Global, regional and multidomestic strategies were once perceived as the only international strategic alternatives. A key concept to emerge in the late 1990s, however, was that of *transnational* strategy. This is a concept that combines the efficiency gains of a global strategy (with its scale economies) with the advantages of local responsiveness.

The next section considers the various theories that seek to explain how competitive advantage is created and sustained. Figure 6.1 is illustrative of the process of formulating a transnational strategy. It incorporates the various approaches to global strategic management. The approach is both 'inside out' and 'outside in' (see Chapter 3), in that the importance of simultaneous, continuous and iterative internal and external analysis of the business and its environment are recognized as inseparable from the process of developing core competences, generic and transnational strategy.

Note: core competences are entirely dependent on organizational knowledge.

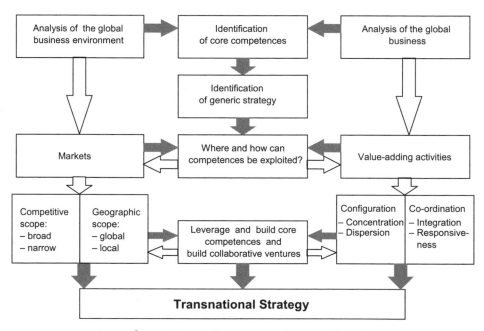

Figure 6.1 Global and transnational strategy formulation

Strategies – the choice

Various authors have developed typologies of global strategy which provide the focus of this section. Broadly speaking, the various typologies can be divided into three main categories:

1. those that centre on the organization's generic strategies and its competitive positioning as the sources of competitive advantage;
2. those that focus on knowledge, resources, capabilities and competences as sources of sustained superior performance;
3. those that emphasize the co-ordination and integration of geographically dispersed operations in the pursuit of global competitiveness.

This chapter integrates all three approaches into a framework for evaluating the transnational strategies of global organizations.

There are three well-established frameworks that explain the ways in which sustainable competitive advantage can be achieved. These approaches are summarized in the next three subsections.

Competitive positioning

This approach is based largely on the work of Porter (1980, 1985) on industry analysis, value chain analysis and generic strategy (see Chapters 3 and 4). Industries are assessed for their potential profitability, value-adding activities are assessed for their effectiveness and efficiency and a generic strategy is developed which creates a strategic fit between the opportunities and threats in the environment and the strengths and weaknesses of the business itself. According to the competitive-positioning school of thought, it is the ability of the business to select the appropriate generic strategy for its industry, and to configure its value-adding activities in support of it, which will generate competitive advantage.

Knowledge and competence-based strategy

The core competence approach is based on the work of theorists including Penrose (1959), Prahalad and Hamel (1990), Stalk et al. (1992), Kay (1993) and Sanchez and Heene (1997). In this model of strategy, businesses are viewed as open systems interacting with their environments to acquire resources and deliver outputs (products). According to this school of thought, superior performance is based on the ability of the business to develop core competences that are not possessed by its competitors and that create perceived benefits for consumers. Existing core competences can be leveraged, and new competences can be built in order to generate competitive advantage in both new and current markets. Additionally, competitive advantage can result from collaboration with suppliers, customers and even competitors. For Prahalad and Hamel (1990) core competences are based on the collective learning (or knowledge) of the organization.

More recently, attention has focused on *knowledge* as the key element of core competences (Grant, 1997; Stonehouse and Pemberton, 1999; Nonaka et al., 2000; Stonehouse et al., 2001). Knowledge, in an organizational context, can be regarded as 'principles, facts, skills, and rules which inform organizational decision-making, behaviour and actions' (Stonehouse and Pemberton, 1999). This knowledge will form the basis of all the organization's activities, competences, products and services. Competitive advantage depends on the ability of the organization to develop new knowledge, and hence core competences, more quickly or effectively than its competitors.

Global strategy

Writers on global strategy, including Porter (1986a, b and 1990), Bartlett and Ghoshal (1987, 1988 and 1989), Prahalad and Doz (1986) and Yip (1992) argued that in international business there are significant advantages to be gained from the global scope, configuration and co-ordination of a firm's international activities. Yip argues that global strategy must be tailored to match each of the globalization drivers in an industry.

Although they are often seen as alternative approaches, the competitive positioning and resource-based approaches are viewed as being complementary to each other in this book. By drawing on all three approaches it is possible to develop a comprehensive overview of all the strategic alternatives available to a global business.

In the remainder of this chapter we discuss each of these schools of thought in more detail.

Knowledge and competence-based strategy

The emphasis on the organization itself

We introduced the ideas behind competences when we discussed internal analysis in Chapter 3. In this chapter we consider the competence-based idea of strategy as it relates to competitive success.

The knowledge and resource-based approach to strategy focuses on the business itself, rather than the industry, as the primary source of competitive advantage (in contrast to the competitive positioning school). Within any global industry or market, those businesses that perform exceptionally do so because they possess qualities that make them both distinctive from, and superior to, their competitors. These qualities are known as *core competences* (Prahalad and Hamel, 1990) or *distinctive capabilities* (Kay, 1993) and are based on superior knowledge (Stonehouse and Pemberton, 2001). This section explains what constitutes a core competence or distinctive capability, the knowledge on which they are based, how knowledge can be created and managed, and, finally, how such competences can be deployed as the essence of a successful transnational strategy.

In Chapter 3 we learned that to distinguish between competences and core competences was an important starting point in understanding this approach. While competences are abilities possessed by all competitors in an industry, core competences are possessed only by those who achieve superior performance.

Prahalad and Hamel (1990) argued that a core competence might:

- provide potential access to a wide variety of markets;
- make a significant contribution to the perceived consumer benefits of the end product;
- be difficult for competitors to emulate.

The components of core competences

Core competences have three essential components: resources, capabilities and perceived consumer benefits. This make-up of a core competence is illustrated in Figure 3.2.

Resources
The first two of these, resources and general competences, were introduced in Chapter 3. Resources – the inputs into an organization's

processes – include human, financial, physical, technological, legal and informational resources. They can be both tangible and intangible, but are much easier to identify and evaluate than capabilities and competences, which may be invisible. The quality, cost and availability of resources to a business will affect its ability to compete, but the same or similar resources can often be acquired by competitors. Accordingly, resources alone are unlikely to create a core competence or sustainable competitive advantage. Nevertheless, resources contribute to core competences.

Human resources in particular are important in forming core competences. In addition, human resources can significantly affect an organization's ability to co-ordinate its activities and to learn from its experiences. Thus, according to Prahalad and Hamel (1990) 'the value of human capital in the development and use of capabilities and core competencies cannot be overstated.'

In a dynamic environment, businesses must be flexible and 'a firm's strategic flexibility can be increased by acquiring resources that are flexible (i.e., can be switched among a range of different uses quickly and at low cost)' (Sanchez and Heene, 1997). Resources are valuable in creating core competences when they are superior to those of competitors, when they are not accessible to competitors, when they cannot be substituted and when they cannot be copied. Resources are both generated within the business and are obtained from external suppliers. The importance of a resource to the development of a core competence 'depends on the way a firm combines, co-ordinates, and deploys that resource with other firm-specific and firm-addressable resources' (Sanchez and Heene, 1997).

General competences and capabilities
Competences or capabilities are assets that are essential to the operation of the competitors within an industry. Capabilities are specific skills, relationships, organizational knowledge and reputation. Capabilities are much less tangible and visible than resources. A capability may or may not be 'core'. This will depend on the extent to that it is a capability that is possessed by competitors. In other words, all core competences stem from an organization's capabilities, but not all capabilities are core competences. A core competence will be a capability that is unique to the individual business and that adds value to its products. A capability must therefore meet certain criteria before it is regarded as a core competence (see below).

Core competences and distinctive capabilities

'Owning' core competences
Core competences, or distinctive capabilities, are a combination of re-sources and capabilities which are unique to a specific business and which generate its competitive advantage.

Resources and capabilities form core competences when they create sustainable competitive advantage for a business. This will arise when a combination of resources and capabilities:

1. *adds to perceived customer value of the product* – the product is perceived as possessing advantages over those of competitors;
2. *is superior* – it adds greater value than capabilities possessed by competitors;
3. *is complex, difficult to imitate and durable* – this will prevent com-petitors from identifying the characteristics of the capability and copying it;
4. *is unique* – it is not available to competitors;
5. *is non-substitutable* – it cannot be substituted by other resources and capabilities;
6. *is adaptable* – it can be leveraged to give competitive advantage in other markets.

A business will create a core competence when it combines its resources and capabilities in such a way that the competence produced meets the criteria above.

Core competences and collaboration
Core competences are also often based on unique external and/or collab-orative relationships. Marks & Spencer's competitive advantage is, in part, due to its unique relationships with its manufacturers and suppliers who contribute to its core competence as a retailer. This is largely based on its reputation for high quality and reliability. Collaboration can add to com-petitive advantage by:

- combining the core competences of two different organizations to add greater value and to increase complexity, so reducing the danger of imitation;
- allowing the partners to specialize on a smaller number of competences;

- denying access to resources for competitors;
- increasing strategic flexibility.

Cravens et al. (1997) demonstrated the benefits of collaboration in producing competitive advantage through the example of the sportswear company Tommy Hilfiger:

> *A network organisation linked with independent global suppliers and marketers, Hilfiger designs its own products and licences its name to other organisations for products such as fragrances and jeanswear. Innovative versions of traditional casual wear clothing, high quality products and efficient production enables Hilfiger to appeal to the price segment between Polo and The Gap. Sales and net product growth have been impressive. Remarkably, the company has less than 500 employees, generating about $1 million in sales per employee compared with only $55,000 per employee for a leading competitor* (Cravens et al., 1997).

Prahalad and Hamel (1990) cited numerous examples of core competence producing competitive advantage. Philips' development of optical media, notably the laser disc, has spawned a whole new range of products. Honda's engine technology has led to advantage in car, motorcycle, lawn-mower and generator businesses. Canon's mastery of optics, imaging and microprocessor controls has allowed it to compete in diverse markets including copiers, laser printers, cameras and image scanners.

Prahalad and Hamel (1990) went on to argue that global leadership in a market is likely to be based on no more than five or six competences. These competences will allow an organization's management to produce new and unanticipated products and to be responsive to changing opportunities because of production skills and the harnessing of technology. Given the turbulence of the global business environment, such adaptability is essential if competitive advantage is to be built and sustained.

Knowledge, core competences and global competitive advantage

Knowledge is the sole source of core competence and hence sustainable competitive advantage. It is Sony's knowledge of consumer electronic technology, Nike's knowledge of consumer attitudes, marketing and supply chain management which give rise to their respective core competences. As a consequence of the pace of change in the business environment, competitive advantage can only be achieved and sustained by the creation of new knowledge at a faster rate than competitors. Knowledge creation involves individual and organizational learning, so that organizations must develop behaviours, systems and structures (a *social architecture* or *organizational context*) which will enable them to create and manage knowledge more effectively than their competitors (Senge, 1990; Stonehouse and Pemberton, 1999; Nonaka et al., 2000).

Knowledge

As indicated earlier, organizational knowledge can be defined as 'a shared collection of principles, facts, skills, and rules which inform organisational decision-making, behaviour and actions' (Stonehouse and Pemberton, 1999). Organizational knowledge concerns any aspect of its *activities* (e.g., R&D, sourcing, production, marketing, distribution) and is also *embodied* in its core competences, processes, technology, products and services, so as to deliver superior performance. It is new knowledge that produces improved behaviours and performance, and thus competitive advantage. Knowledge can be considered as *explicit* or *tacit*. *Explicit knowledge* is knowledge whose meaning is clearly understood and its details can be readily recorded and stored. This explicit knowledge is articulated in the procedures and processes which allow an organization to function efficiently and effectively. Examples of explicit knowledge include accounting procedures, business manuals, training manuals and so on. *Tacit knowledge*, on the other hand, is expert knowledge, derived from experience. It is by nature difficult to record and store, but, equally, it can be an essential source of competitive edge. Table 6.1 gives a comparison of the main features of explicit and tacit knowledge.

Both explicit and tacit knowledge contribute to competitive advantage through their interaction, but tacit knowledge is of greater value at one level as it gives rise to sources of competitive advantage that are intangible and difficult for competitors to emulate. Paradoxically, it is this same intangibility which makes it difficult for organizations to convert it from individual knowledge into organizational knowledge.

Table 6.1 Explicit and implicit knowledge

	Explicit	Tacit (implicit)
Format	Codified (tangible)	Uncodified (intangible)
Recording	Recorded in documents, procedure, processes	Stored in the memory of an individual
Objectivity	Objective (independent of the individual)	Subjective (dependent on the individual)
Context	Context-free, widely accepted	Context-specific, not widely understood
Communication	Through written, spoken, multimedia formats	Difficult, depends on experience
Emulation/Imitation	Easily emulated, copied	Difficult to emulate
Contribution to business operation/competitive advantage	Essential to the operation of the business, interacts with tacit knowledge	Often the essence of competitive advantage

Knowledge creation and management

Knowledge creation and management require an organization to become 'knowledge-centric' by creating an 'organizational context' (Stonehouse and Pemberton, 1999) or 'social architecture' (Senge, 1990) which facilitates the rapid development of new knowledge. This organizational context, or social architecture, comprises the organization's leadership, culture, structure and infrastructure (technology and systems).

The organizational context in a knowledge-centric organization is likely to display the following characteristics:

- *leadership* – a vision and leadership style which facilitate learning and innovation and which foster an organizational culture, structure and infrastructure conducive to individual and organizational learning;
- *culture (organizational)* – fosters experimentation and the sharing of ideas, and values learning and knowledge highly;
- *structure* – encourages the sharing of ideas by concentrating expertise together and at the same time has substructures and systems which allow ideas to be shared across the whole organization (network or matrix structures, project teams and task groups);
- *infrastructure* – the configuration and use of information and communications technology and systems to store and share knowledge.

The ability to transform individual knowledge into organizational knowledge is vital to competitive advantage in a changing environment because 'knowledge is . . . one of the few assets that grows most – usually exponentially – when shared' (Quinn, 1992).

Sharp Corporation – a knowledge-centric organization
Adapted from Nonaka and Takeuchi (1995) among many others

Sharp Corporation is a large and very successful producer of electronics products. Its founder was an inventor named Tokuji Hayakawa who gradually moved into the manufacture of radios and in postwar years became one of the first and leading manufacturers of television sets. The business has always recognized the importance of knowledge as the essence of its business success. In fact, Hayakawa had told his employees from the beginning: 'Don't imitate. Make something that others want to imitate' (Nonaka and Takeuchi, 1995). He thus fully recognized the need for knowledge creation as the basis of competitive advantage from the outset of the business.

Since the 1980s the organization has sought to institutionalize the creation of knowledge through its culture, structure and systems. The 'Corporate R&D Group' is responsible for long-term technology and product development, the 'Business Group' deals with medium-term developments and the 'Business Division Laboratories Group' deals with short-term developments. The Corporate R&D Group develops concepts and prototypes, the Business Group and Business Division Laboratories Group are responsible for commercializing the ideas. The Business Division Laboratories Group brings together engineering, production and marketing functions to share knowledge and ensure that new products are commercially viable. Regular conferences are held throughout the organization to both co-ordinate knowledge creation and to ensure that knowledge is shared effectively. In addition, an 'Urgent Project System' brings together multidisciplinary project teams to develop strategic projects when developments are required without delay.

Organizational learning

Organizational learning can be categorized as 'single loop' (adaptive) or 'double loop' (generative) (Argyris, 1977, 1992; Senge, 1990). Single loop or adaptive learning is concerned with organizations adapting behaviour in response to changes in their environment. Double loop or generative learning, on the other hand, is concerned with both building new knowledge, so as to do business in new ways, and with modifying the organization, so that it is truly knowledge-centric. As Quinn (1992) put it, 'By concentrating on key elements of the learning process companies can leverage intellect enormously.'

Knowledge creation and management in transnationals

Transnational business activity brings an extra dimension to knowledge creation and management. On the one hand, differences in language, culture, political and economic conditions can complicate knowledge-based processes, but at the same time transnational operation provides greater opportunities for knowledge-creating synergies.

Transnationals often concentrate their value-adding activities in certain locations on the basis of availability of highly specific knowledge. For example, Silicon Valley in the USA is a focus for expertise in computing while fashion design centres on Milan, Paris, London and New York.

Quinn (1992) also points out that knowledge grows exponentially when it is shared. Such knowledge sharing can take place within and between organizations, and within and across national boundaries. It is the synergies created through knowledge sharing which give rise to the exponential growth of knowledge identified by Quinn. In short, the major benefits of knowledge sharing are faster creation of knowledge through its exponential growth, prolonged competitive advantage through the creation of core competences that are difficult to emulate and knowledge synergies.

Competence building and leveraging

Key to the success of organizations possessing knowledge-based core competences is the extent to which they can build new ones to account for changes in their environments and the extent to which they can be leveraged to establish an advantage in another market. When international markets are concerned, this ability can be one of the most crucial of all:

- *competence building* is the development of new competences through organizational learning which are required to compete either in an existing market that is changing or in a new market;

- *competence leveraging* is the application of existing competences in a new market.

Entry to a new market will often require both competence leveraging and competence building. Similarly, collaboration between organizations may well provide access to new markets by combining the core competences of different businesses.

Global organizations must develop core competences that provide the organization with the ability to access a range of global markets. Many of the leading fashion design houses like Ralph Lauren and Calvin Klein have exploited their core competence in fashion by entering the global market for fragrances.

The process of gaining competitive advantage through global competences involves the organization in:

1. identification of its resources, capabilities and competences;
2. identification of the need for competence leveraging and building within existing markets to preserve or enhance competitive position;
3. identifying industries and markets where core competences may give competitive advantage;
4. identifying the need for competence leveraging and competence building to enter new markets.

Implicit in the processes of competence building and leveraging is analysis of the environment (macroenvironment, industry, market, competitors and strategic group) to identify the need or opportunity for competence development (leveraging or building). In particular, organizations seeking to leverage competences and actually seeking the opportunities that the strategic analysis throws up.

Globalization of business activities provides several opportunities that relate to a business's core competences:

1. core competences can be exploited globally in a large number of countries and markets;
2. new sources of resources can be identified and exploited, making use of localized advantages to potentially strengthen core competences;
3. value-adding activities can be reconfigured to enhance core competences.

Summary of knowledge and competence-based strategy

In overview, competence-based (or resource-based) strategic management emphasizes the importance of an 'inside out' approach to the development of transnational strategy. A transnational strategy must be based on core competences that provide access to global markets. Adopting a transnational approach also provides opportunities for competence strengthening, building and leveraging. A number of factors can contribute to a global core competence. Each one needs to be distinctive and unique in order to achieve competitive advantage:

- products and relationships to distributors and customers;
- resources and relationships to suppliers;
- company-specific information, knowledge and organizational learning;
- collaboration with businesses with complementary core competences;
- configuration or architecture of global internal and external activities;
- methods of co-ordinating global activities;
- culture of the organization;
- technology and the way that it is employed.

Alternative approaches to resource-based strategy

Stalk et al. (1992) advanced similar ideas on what they called 'capabilities-based competition'. They suggested four basic principles on which such competition should be based. By focusing on these four factors, they argued that these would, in turn, enhance the organization's ability to achieve a superior performance:

1. corporate strategy consists of a focus on business processes rather than products and markets (superior processes will, in turn, result in superior products);
2. competitive success depends on transforming a company's key processes into strategic capabilities that consistently provide superior value to the customer;
3. companies create these capabilities by making strategic investments in a support infrastructure that links together and transcends traditional strategic business units and functions;
4. because capabilities necessarily cross functions, the champion of a capabilities-based strategy is the CEO.

A capability, in the context of Stalk et al.'s meaning of the term, is a set of business processes whose strategic importance has been understood. In other words, organizations must identify which of their processes are of strategic importance and must focus on them.

Distinctive capabilities

Kay (1993) developed the concept of capability and that of the value chain a stage further. He argued that the achievement of competitive advantage relies on *distinctive capability*. This idea of distinctive capability is similar to that of core competence. In both cases the organization acquires competitive advantage by possession of attributes that make it superior to its competitors. These attributes may be features of products or services, or may result from the way that activities are organized. According to Kay (1993), distinctive capability depends on:

1. architecture – the networks of relationships both within and outside a business which are critical to determining its success;
2. reputation – this is based on product quality and characteristics, but equally as important is how effectively the information is conveyed to consumers;
3. innovation – the ability to successfully develop and market new products;
4. strategic assets – these are advantages based on dominance or market position and include natural monopoly, cost advantages and market restrictions like licensing.

Although resource-based strategy can be viewed as an alternative to the generic strategy or competitive positioning approach, there are advantages in viewing strategy from both perspectives in seeking to identify sources of competitive advantage.

Manchester United and superior performance

One of the most successful football clubs of all time is Manchester United. With a turnover (total sales) in 2003 of over £150 million, Manchester United was also the biggest football club, in business terms, in the world. Many rival managers and fans have long looked to Manchester United for clues as to what has been the source of its continued success, but as with all successful businesses the sources of its superior performance are complex.

The club was first formed in 1878, under the name Newton Heath LYR (Lancashire and Yorkshire Railway). When the football league was first formed in 1888, Newton Heath did not consider itself good enough to become a founder member alongside the likes of Blackburn Rovers and Preston North End. How things were to change in later years.

It won its first domestic championship title in 1908 (the old first division), its first FA challenge cup in the following year and, since those early successes, went on to win the domestic championship (first division and premiership) a total of 15 times. This is in addition to 10 FA Cup wins, two European Champions' Cup wins and a handful of other honours. Since the Premiership was formed in 1992, Manchester United have won it seven times.

As with many other football clubs in its 'league', Manchester United has the key resources of a good quality stadium, a squad of players, a loyal support base and a number of sources of revenue with which to build and strengthen the team. For those seeking to understand the club's continued success, however, other internal factors need to be explored. Observers have long noticed that the club seems not only to be able to attract the best players to the club through the transfer system but it has also brought some of the best players in the world up through its youth network. The reputation of the club as one of the most successful teams in Europe means that top players are keen to play for the team, and the strong revenue flows through the loyal fan base, the club-owned television station and many club shops mean that the club is one of the richest when it comes to affording transfer fees. Its stadium, Old Trafford, is thought to be one of the best in Europe and is capable of accommodating over 67,000 fans.

Since Sir Matt Busby built a top Manchester United team in the 1950s and 1960s (capable of winning its first European Cup in 1968), the club has continued to enjoy success, with one or two short exceptional seasons, partly because of its succession of successful managers. The club's ability to select and develop managers has been noted by rival clubs and the appointment of Alex (later Sir Alex) Ferguson in 1986 brought about the most sustained period of success in the club's history.

One doesn't need to be a fan of the club to observe and understand the reasons for its continued success. Other clubs have, to varying degrees of success, sought to emulate parts of its winning strategy, and in most respects such activities are about obtaining and developing resources to help achieve competitive success. Its knowledge gap advantage is more difficult to describe, but may lie partly in networks, contacts, ability to recruit and retain fans and its understanding of strategy and tactics in both managing players and in playing the game itself.

Competitive positioning – Porter's generic strategies

The generic strategy framework

The competitive-positioning school of thought is the second major way in which competitive advantage is explained. Porter (1985) argued that competitive advantage depends on selection of the most appropriate *generic strategy* for achieving business objectives in the context of the competitive environment. This generic strategy can be one of, or a combination of, three types – cost leadership, differentiation and focus (Figure 6.2).

Although we introduce these strategies here, the global and international variants are explored later in this chapter. Although Porter's work has been criticized (Cronshaw et al., 1990; Kay, 1993; Sanchez and Heene, 1997), it is still a very widely used model of competitive behaviour.

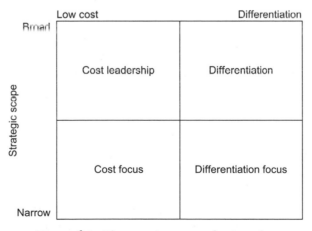

Figure 6.2 The generic strategy framework
Adapted from Porter (1985)

Cost leadership strategy

A cost leadership strategy implies that a business endeavours to be the lowest cost producer within an industry. The main advantages of such a strategy to a business are twofold. First, there is the potential to earn profits above the industry standard while charging a price comparable with the average for the industry. Second, the strategy places the business in a position where it is able to compete effectively on the basis of price, both with existing competitors and with potential new entrants to the industry. Value chain analysis (see Chapter 3) is central to identification of where cost savings can be made at various stages in the value chain and its internal and external linkages.

To establish a position as cost leader depends on the organization of value chain activities so as to:

- advertise and promote the product to achieve large volume sales;
- achieve economies of scale in the production process;
- invest in and utilize the latest production technology, thus lowering production costs;
- achieve the highest levels of productivity, thus reducing labour costs;
- copy designs rather than producing originals;
- acquire cheaper raw materials (as measured on a unit cost basis);
- reduce distribution costs;
- obtain locational cost advantages;
- secure government assistance;
- exploit organizational knowledge and experience.

A cost leadership strategy will normally entail charging a price equal to or slightly lower than competitors so as to increase sales, although the real aim is to charge a price roughly equivalent to the industry norm, selling a similar volume to competitors but earning higher than normal profits because unit costs are lower. Such a strategy can be most effective in a situation where price elasticity of demand for the product is high. In this situation a slightly lower price than competitors will result in a more than proportionate gain in sales.

It is often used as the strategy for entering a new market. For example, some of the major Japanese car and motorcycle manufacturers initially entered overseas markets on the basis of low-cost and low-price strategies (see 'Hybrid strategies' below), often coupled to focus on a particular market segment (see 'Focus strategies' below). Similarly, international markets provide the opportunity for the large-volume sales that are essential to the success of a cost leadership strategy.

Differentiation strategy

A differentiation strategy seeks to distinguish a company and its products from its competitors by establishing characteristics for the company and its products which are perceived as both unique and desirable by customers. The aim is to reduce the price elasticity of demand for the company's product so that higher prices can be charged without significant reductions in demand (because consumers perceive the product as superior to those of competitors).

Differentiation can be achieved in a variety of ways including creating distinctiveness in brand name, technical superiority, quality, packaging, distribution, image or after-sales service. A business can create differentiation by organizing activities so as to:

- provide superior service relative to price;
- innovate continually providing the technical superiority to stay ahead;
- make customers perceive and believe that the product is superior by branding and advertising of products and services.

The differences between a company's product and those of its competitors may be real (e.g., in design) or perceived (they may be created by advertising and brand image). Levi jeans, for example, may be of high quality, but the ability of Levi's to charge a premium price may well be more to do with the perception of consumers that they are also a fashionable brand name. Consumer perceptions are the decisive influence in such a situation.

Focus strategy

In some situations, businesses choose to target only certain segments of the market in which they operate. This is termed a focus strategy. This can imply focus on a specific geographical segment or concentration on a particular group of buyers within the market. To compete with other companies within the chosen market segment, businesses may employ a cost focus strategy that is essentially cost leadership confined to one market segment. Alternatively, they may utilize a differentiation focus strategy whereby they seek to differentiate themselves and their product from other products within the chosen market segment.

A good example of differentiation focus is that of Porsche, the German sports car manufacturer. It focuses on the performance car segment of the automobile market and does not produce cars for other segments of the market. Its cars are sold on the basis of brand name, based on consumer perceptions that its products are technically superior to those of competitors, are better designed, have superior performance and are more reliable than those of their competitors.

Focus strategy is based on identification of a market segment with distinct characteristics and selecting a strategy that matches those characteristics. There are two possibilities for strategy based on segmentation:

- focus – on a single segment;
- multifocus – focus on a number of segments (a variation of the same generic strategy will be used in each segment of the market to match its characteristics).

A focus strategy is most suitable for a business that is not large enough to target the whole market, so that targeting only one segment is the most viable possibility. It is also appropriate in markets where distinct segments can be clearly identified. This makes it possible to minimize costs and/or to achieve differentiation.

Hybrid strategies

Porter argued that to acquire sustainable competitive advantage a business must select one of the generic strategies. To attempt to be cost leader and to differentiate simultaneously will (he argued) result in the organization being 'stuck in the middle'. This, according to Porter, is unlikely to result in competitive advantage that is sustainable.

Both the underlying assumptions of the generic strategies and the idea of being 'stuck in the middle' have been criticized. In the case of cost leadership, low cost itself does not establish competitive advantage, as it does nothing to promote sales of a product. Low price may, however, encourage sales. Thus the combination of low cost and low price may jointly produce competitive advantage. In the case of differentiation, Porter emphasized that it allows the company to charge a premium price. Differentiation, however, also presents the alternative of charging a price comparable with that of competitors so as to increase sales volume and augment market share. Equally, there is evidence to support the view that many companies pursue a strategy that combines very low costs with differentiation to produce competitive edge. The Japanese automobile manufacturer Nissan is a good example of a business broadly adopting such a strategy.

A strategy that combines elements of low cost, price and differentiation is known as a *hybrid* strategy (Johnson and Scholes, 1993). The extent of each of these elements in the strategy will depend on the nature of the market in which the business is operating. In markets where consumers show a preference for quality the emphasis will then be less on price and costs, while in markets where demand is price-sensitive the emphasis will be on keeping both price and costs as low as possible. A hybrid strategy can be successful but only where it is a conscious decision. Being stuck in the middle because of lack of awareness is usually a recipe for failure. Mintzberg (1991) made the point that, 'price can be viewed as simply another way of differentiating a product.' A business that uses price as a major element of its strategy must also concentrate on keeping costs low.

The generic and hybrid strategy frameworks provide an alternative explanation of the sources of competitive advantage to those provided by competence theory. It must be accepted that there is a difference of emphasis between the two approaches, but there are also linkages. The success of the generic strategy adopted by a business is dependent on its ability to configure its value-adding activities in a way that appropriately supports the strategy. Similarly, there are strong relationships between resources, capabilities, core competences and configuration and co-ordination of value-adding activities. In this way the two approaches provide different but complementary perspectives on the various sources of competitive advantage.

Knowledge, core competence and generic strategy – a synthesis

Drawing the threads together

Different strategies require different configurations of value chain activities and are associated with different areas of core competence. For example, a differentiation strategy is likely to place a strong emphasis on design and

Table 6.2 Generic strategies and core competences

Generic strategy	Associated value chain activities	Associated areas of knowledge and core competence
Differentiation	Design	Innovation to deliver improved product quality, new products and new product features.
	Marketing	Strong brand identity created through reputation, advertising and promotion, and design features.
	Distribution	Product available to target consumer groups. Distributors add value to the product.
	Service	Superior service adds to product differentiation.
Cost leadership/price-based	Production	Lowering of production costs through use of latest technology.
	Marketing	Market on basis of price to achieve economies of scale. Knowledge of customer's price preferences.
	Purchasing	Purchase in volume and use cheaper materials. Collaborative relationships with suppliers.

marketing activities. Core competences in these areas are likely to be distinctive from those of competitors. In this way the value chain provides the bridge between generic strategy and core competence. Porsche pursues a focus differentiation strategy. Its core competences in design, technology development and marketing underpin its brand name, which is the basis of its differentiation. Its value-adding activities emphasize design, technology development and marketing, so as to enhance its reputation. Thus Porsche's core competences are rooted in its value-adding activities. The relationship between generic strategies, core competences and value-adding activities is illustrated in Table 6.2.

Grant (1991) presented a similar line of argument stating that 'capabilities are developed in functional areas.' Table 6.3 illustrates the capabilities associated with the functional areas of several businesses.

Clearly, differentiation strategies will rely on knowledge and core competences centred around design, marketing and distribution, while cost or price-based strategies will be more dependent on production, purchasing and marketing. Having reviewed the strategy alternatives generally available to all businesses it is now necessary to explore those specific to transnational businesses.

Table 6.3 Capability development in functional areas

Functional area	Capabilities	Examples
MISs	Data-processing skills	American Airlines
Marketing	Promoting brand name	Nike
R&D	Innovation	Honda
Manufacturing	Rapid change in product lines. Miniaturization of components and products	Benetton Sony

Adapted from Grant (1991). MIS = management information systems

Global and transnational strategy

Domestic and global strategies have much in common. They are both based on core competences, generic strategies and the way in which value-adding activities are organized. Equally, however, global strategy differs from domestic strategy in the following respects:

- the scale and scope of activities are greater;
- there are far more alternatives for the configuration of value-adding activities;
- there are not only greater difficulties in co-ordinating global activities but also greater scope for competitive advantage if activities are effectively co-ordinated;
- the strategy must take account of cultural and linguistic similarities and differences;
- national economic and factor conditions differ and can be harnessed to give competitive advantage.

Porter's work (1986a, b, 1990) focused on global generic strategies and the possibilities for global configuration and co-ordination of activities. Prahalad and Doz (1986) examined the importance of integration and responsiveness in global strategy. Yip (1992) and Bartlett and Ghoshal (1987, 1989) presented the models for global strategy and transnational organization from which the model of transnational strategy in this book is drawn.

Porter's model of global strategy – the value system

Porter (1986a) proposed a model of international global strategy based on the generic strategy framework. He argued that the generic cost leadership or differentiation strategies can be operated on a global scale as either *global cost leadership* or *global differentiation* – targeting either an entire global market or a particular global segment. In other words, the scope of the strategy can be either broad or narrow but on a global scale. The success of such global strategies will depend on the market being global. When global market conditions do not exist a *country-centred strategy* can be implemented based on responsiveness to local needs.

Of much greater significance is Porter's work (1986a, b, 1990) that advanced two unique options, based on the value chain concept, which are available to enhance corporate strategy in global markets. These choices are:

- *configuration* – where and in how many nations each activity in the value chain is performed;
- *co-ordination* – how dispersed international activities are co-ordinated.

The decisions of the business relating to these two choices are the key to international competitive advantage.

Configuration

The way in which a business configures its upstream, downstream and internal value-adding activities presents several alternatives. A business may choose to concentrate its manufacturing activities in one nation and to export and market in a range of countries. Alternatively, a global business may decide to disperse its value-adding activities to several nations. In both cases the advantages of alternative locations for each activity will influence the architecture of value chain activities which is finally selected. It is important to note that changes in technology may well lead to changes over time in the configuration that gives greatest competitive advantage. Organizations must constantly strive for the optimal configuration of their international operations showing flexibility in dynamic conditions.

There are two broad directions of configuration of value-adding activities – concentration or dispersal.

(1) Concentrating activities

In some industries there are advantages to be obtained from concentrating activities in a small number of nations and exporting to foreign markets. This is true when locational factors are important and regional advantages may be gained.

(2) Dispersing activities

Competitive advantage may arise from dispersing activities in several nations. Dispersed activities involve foreign direct investment (FDI). It is best to disperse activities when:

- transportation, communication or storage costs are high;
- factors like exchange rates and political risk are important;
- national markets differ because of culture;
- governments exert influence via tariffs, subsidies and nationalistic purchasing (governments tend to favour location of the whole value chain in their country).

Dispersed global strategies involving FDI are typical in such industries as services, health care, telecommunications, etc.

Co-ordination

In addition to adopting the optimum configuration, competitive edge can be gained by the efficient and effective co-ordination of diverse activities that are located in a number of different nations. According to Porter (1990), 'Co-ordination involves sharing information, allocating responsibility, and aligning efforts.' It is differing linguistic, cultural, political, legal, techno-logical and economic factors, coupled to geography and distance, which pose the problems that beset multinational co ordination. It is the global businesses that overcome these problems most effectively who will gain the greatest competitive advantage from a global strategy.

Figure 6.3 shows the various alternatives that exist for global organiza-tions from a country-based strategy with widely dispersed activities, requiring minimal co-ordination to what Porter called purest global strategy. In this purest global strategy, activities are concentrated and extensive co-ordination is in evidence. The configuration chosen, and the extent of global co-ordination of activities, will depend on the nature of the industry and markets in which the business operates.

High co-ordination of activities	High foreign investment in dispersed activities with a high degree of co-ordination among subsidiaries	Purest global strategy (with extensive co-ordination and concentration)
Low co-ordination of activities	Country-centred strategy for company with several national subsidiaries, each operating in only one country	Strategy based on exporting of product/service with decentralized marketing in each host country

Geographically dispersed   Geographically concentrated

Configuration of activities

Figure 6.3   Configuration and co-ordination for international strategy
Adapted from Porter (1986)

Integration and responsiveness

Prahalad and Doz (1986) reached conclusions that are in some respects similar to those of Porter (1986a, b, 1990). Prahalad and Doz identified three major characteristics of global management.

(1) Global integration of activities
This is the centralized management of geographically dispersed activities which is necessary to reduce costs and optimize investment. In striving to reduce costs, corporations may use low-wage labour in South East Asia, shipping products to well-developed markets in Europe and America. Thus there is a need to manage across national boundaries.

(2) Global strategic co-ordination
This is the strategic management of resources across national boundaries. It includes co-ordination of R&D, pricing and technology transfer to subsidiaries. Prahalad and Doz argued that 'The goal of strategic co-ordination is to recognise, build and defend long-term competitive advantages.'

(3) Local responsiveness
This requires that decisions be taken locally by subsidiaries where local market conditions dictate the need for local responsiveness. Such markets are not global in nature.

To summarize, Prahalad and Doz (1986) suggested that corporate success at an international level is dependent on the ability of the business to co-ordinate and integrate global activities, while at the same time retaining responsiveness to the demands of local markets and changing circumstances when necessary.

Pressures for and against increased global co-ordination

Stimulating forces
Pressures for global strategic co-ordination include:

- importance of multinational customers – dependence on customers on a worldwide basis make it necessary to co-ordinate activities globally;
- presence of multinational competitors – global competition demands global co-ordination;
- investment intensity – where investment costs are high (e.g., R&D costs), the need to recoup investment costs increases the need for global co-ordination;
- technology intensity – where technology encourages businesses to manufacture in only a few locations to control quality and product development;
- pressure for cost reduction – often stimulates global integration of activities to intensify scale economies;
- universal consumer needs – lead to standard global products requiring integration;
- access to raw materials and cheap energy – often means that manufacturing has to be concentrated in a single area remote from other activities, thus necessitating integration and co-ordination.

Restraining forces
While the above forces work in favour of increased global co-ordination of value-adding activities, some factors act to partly offset them. These are factors that stimulate local responsiveness and include:

- differences in customer needs – when these differ between countries, local responsiveness is required;
- differences in distribution channels – when such differences exist between countries, local responsiveness is required in relation to differences in pricing, promotion and product positioning;
- availability of local substitutes – if local substitutes with different specifications exist, then there is a need to adapt products in order to compete;

Figure 6.4 The integration responsiveness matrix
Adapted from Prahalad and Doz (1986)

- market structure – where local competitors are important and there is a high concentration, then businesses must respond locally;
- host government demands – when such governments promote self-sufficiency a business may be forced to be more locally responsive.

Prahalad and Doz (1986) represented the relationships between these factors on an integration responsiveness matrix (see Figure 6.4).

The conclusions reached by Prahalad and Doz's research are remarkably similar to those of Porter. Both emphasize the need for global co-ordination and integration of activities when a global strategy is adopted and the need for local responsiveness when conditions dictate.

Regional strategies

Under certain circumstances a business may elect to adopt an international regional strategy as opposed to a multidomestic, global or transnational strategy. A regional strategy focuses on one or more geographical regions of the world rather than on an entire world market. Prahalad and Doz (1986) argued that, although businesses must be multimarket competitors, they may benefit from choosing to operate in certain 'critical markets'. These are markets that, at the minimum:

- are reliable 'profit sanctuaries' of the key competitors in that market;
- provide volume and include state-of-the-art customers;

- have a competitive intensity that allows suppliers to achieve reasonable margins.

International businesses may therefore choose to adopt a regional strategy for a variety of reasons. These reasons include:

- the existence of critical markets (as described above) which make regional operation viable;
- the removal of barriers that have inhibited cross border trade within a region. Such customs unions as the EU and NAFTA (North American Free Trade Area) have assisted in this;
- the size and importance of certain regional markets (which tend to be those where trade barriers have been reduced);
- the limited importance of cultural differences within a particular regional market in comparison with the more important differences that exist between certain regions;
- limited business resources and objectives which confine the operations of the business to a regional scale.

Within a region the organization faces several strategic alternatives. The regional strategy may be little more than a multidomestic strategy. This will be the case when there are one or more of the following distinctions between the national markets within the region: political, cultural, linguistic or legal. Such distinctions will inhibit the possibilities for standardization and increased economies of scale. On the other hand, the less such distinctions exist within a region the greater the opportunities for standardization, co-ordination and integration of strategies, products and operations.

Total global strategy

Development of total global strategy

For Levitt (1983) globalization implied that the focus of a global strategy ought to be standardization of products and marketing. In reality, globalization is far more complex than this and requires the development of more complex strategies to reflect this. Yip (1992) argued that an industry may be more or less global in several respects, according to the strength of each of its globalization drivers. Chapter 4 shows how the extent of globalization of an industry can be assessed by analysis of the extent to which its market, cost, competitive and government drivers are global. Global strategy must then be tailored to match each of the drivers. Yip's concept of total global strategy is, therefore, not rooted in the idea of global standardization but rather in the idea that global strategy must be flexible.

Yip (1992) stated that a total global strategy has three separate components or stages:

1. *developing the core strategy* – this is the basis of the organization's global competitive advantage;
2. *internationalizing the core strategy* – the international expansion of activities and the adaptation of the core strategy;
3. *globalizing the international strategy* – integrating the strategy across countries.

Yip's three stages are considered below.

Stage 1
The *core business strategy* is viewed as consisting of several elements:

- types of products or services that the business offers;
- types of customers that the business serves;
- geographic markets served;
- major sources of competitive advantage;
- functional strategy for each of the most important value-adding activities;
- competitive posture, including the selection of competitors to target;
- investment strategy.

Stage 2
Internationalizing the core business involves:

- selecting the geographic markets in which to compete;
- adapting products.

Stage 3
Globalizing the core business requires:

- identification of the areas of strategy to be globalized (based on the globalization drivers);
- integration of activities.

Global strategy levers

The business must then identify its 'global strategy levers' that determine the way in which the global strategy is used. They are:

- global market participation (which markets and countries in which to participate);
- global products (standardized products);
- global location of activities;
- global marketing;
- global competitive moves.

The extent to which each of these aspects of strategy is global will depend on the relative strength of the globalization drivers. A global strategy can give benefits in terms of reduced costs, improved quality, enhanced customer preference and competitive leverage.

Transnational organizations

There is a further dimension to global management – that of transnational strategy. These are strategies that, although global in nature, incorporating a global configuration and a high degree of co-ordination, allow the business to retain local responsiveness. Bartlett and Ghoshal (1987, 1988, 1989) found that managers often oversimplified the choices available to them. They found such erroneous management attitudes as a belief that it had to be:

- global strategy versus local responsiveness;
- centralized versus decentralized key resources;
- strong central control versus subsidiary autonomy.

They went on to argue that the transnational business strategy ought to incorporate the following features:

- strong geographical management to allow responsiveness to local markets based on sensitivity to local needs;
- strong business management based on global product responsibilities so as to achieve global efficiency and integration through product standardization, manufacturing rationalization and low-cost global sourcing;
- strong worldwide functional management to develop and transfer its core competences via organizational learning.

Bartlett and Ghoshal (1989) argued that strong geographical management, business management and worldwide functional management incorporating a differentiated organization with extensive co-ordination would enable the business to develop multiple strategic capabilities to adapt to local and global needs. Such an organization can be said to have *transnational capability* – an essential ingredient of a transnational strategy that is at the same time global and locally responsive. In fact, there is much in common between Yip's approach and that advocated by Bartlett and Ghoshal.

Global and localized elements of transnational strategy

A transnational strategy combines the benefits of global scope, configuration and co-ordination with local responsiveness (Figure 6.5). Certain components of the strategy will be essentially global while others will be more or less global according to the pressures for globalization or localization. These pressures are assessed through the normal procedures of macroenvironmental analysis and an analysis of how the globalization drivers affect the business.

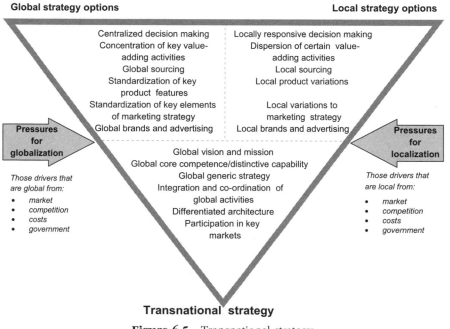

Figure 6.5 Transnational strategy

Globalized components of transnational strategy
The following elements of a transnational strategy are always likely to be global:

- *global vision* – this determines the outlook of the business which will always be to take a global perspective on business activities;
- *global knowledge-based core competences* – these are core competences that can be built, enhanced and leveraged to enter global markets;
- *global generic strategy* – the generic strategy, based on core competences, will be applied globally;
- *global co-ordination* – global value-adding activities will be co-ordinated on a worldwide basis;
- *differentiated architecture* – activities will be structured so as to maximize global advantages, but this is likely to mean that some activities are concentrated while others are dispersed (structures will be adapted to accommodate this);
- *participation in key markets* – the transnational organization will always view the whole world as a potential market but may choose only to target key markets.

Activities that can be global or localized components in transnational strategy
Certain components of transnational strategy can be globalized or localized according to changes in the macroenvironment and to the globalization drivers:

- *decision making* – conditions may dictate that decisions are made centrally or are devolved when local responsiveness is required;
- *value-adding activities* – may be dispersed or concentrated, or some combination of the two, according to locational advantages;
- *products* – may be standardized or adapted when conditions dictate;
- *marketing strategy* – may be global or local according to consumer and product characteristics;
- *branding* – may be global or local according to consumer and product characteristics;
- *sourcing* – resources may be globally or locally sourced according to locational advantages.

McDonald's Inc. – an example of transnational strategy

In recent years McDonald's has adopted the global vision of becoming the world's largest and best fast food restaurant chain. Some of McDonald's key objectives emphasize global standardization, as in the statement: 'Expand our global mindset by sharing best practices and leveraging our best people resources around the world.'

McDonald's restaurants are a mix of company owned and independently owned franchised restaurants that sell McDonald's products (almost) exclusively. The extensive use of franchising lowers expansion costs and keeps owners motivated to provide high-quality service so as to earn high profits. McDonald's itself owns many of the restaurants with city centre locations. This allows the company direct control over quality and keeps control of the most profitable locations.

McDonald's strategy is based on achieving low costs and prices along with reliable quality and value for money, based on the McDonald's brand. The company's strategy is based on knowledge of modern lifestyles, young people's tastes, food production processes and service levels. Coupled with this is constant product innovation and effective marketing tools including the twin arches logo and constant new promotional campaigns. Aspects of McDonald's global strategy emphasize standardization in terms of key products and product features, food production systems, staff training, service levels and so on. McDonald's entry to new national markets is always preceded by an exercise to identify local suppliers who can meet the company's stringent quality standards. Such suppliers are expected to comply fully with McDonald's recipes and procedures.

The recent restructuring of McDonald's into five geographical divisions, while continuing to support the company's quality and service standards, has been accompanied by a reduction in central control, greater local autonomy and by greater variations in product and service offerings in different parts of the world. For example, salads and beer are offered in restaurants in continental Europe, chicken is served on the bone in China and in Greece they have recently introduced the 'Greek Mac', a burger accompanied by Greek salad, served in pitta bread. As well as indicating McDonald's recognition to adapt to the needs of local markets, this strategy represents the company's attempt to transform itself through innovation. McDonald's intends to innovate through new product offerings and restaurant designs. The development of McCafes, following the global trend for coffee shops, is an example of recent strategic innovation.

Discussion and review questions

1. Explain what is meant by sustainable competitive advantage.
2. Explain the factors that determine the choice of a global or locally responsive strategy.
3. What will determine the competitive scope of the strategy of a global business?
4. Explain and critically evaluate Porter's generic strategy framework. What does the concept of the hybrid strategy add to the debate?
5. What are the major differences between domestic and international strategies?
6. Provide an example of a global business, in each of the three categories (at least in part of its activities), that:
   o adopts a differentiation strategy;
   o adopts a cost leadership strategy;
   o adopts a cost focus strategy;
   o adopts a differentiation focus strategy;
   o adopts a hybrid strategy.
7. Explain the significance of each of the following to a transnational business:
   o knowledge;
   o core competence/distinctive capability;
   o configuration/architecture;
   o co-ordination/integration;
   o responsiveness.
8. Discuss the nature of the relationships between:
   o generic strategy, knowledge and core competence;
   o core competence and configuration/architecture;
   o configuration/architecture and co-ordination/integration.
9. Explain the similarities and differences between regional, global and transnational strategies.

References and further reading

Argyris, C. (1977) 'Double loop learning in organizations'. *Harvard Business Review*, September/ October, 115–125.

Argyris, C. (1992) *On Organizational Learning*. Cambridge, MA: Basil Blackwell.

Argyris, C. and Schon, D. (1978) *Organization Learning: A Theory of Action Perspective*. Reading, MA: Addison-Wesley.

Arthur, W.B. (1996) 'Increasing returns and the new world of business', *Harvard Business Review*, **74**, July/August.

Barney, J.B. (1991) 'Firm resources and sustained competitive advantage'. *Journal of Management*, **17**(1), 99–120.

Bartlett, C. and Ghoshal, S. (1987) 'Managing across borders: New organizational responses'. *Sloan Management Review*, Fall, 45–53.

Bartlett, C. and Ghoshal, S. (1988) 'Organizing for a worldwide effectiveness. The transnational solution'. *California Management Review*, **30**, 54–74.

Bartlett, C. and Ghoshal, S. (1989) *Managing Across Borders: The Transnational Solution*. Boston: Harvard Business School Press.

Chakravarthy, B. (1997) 'A new strategy framework for coping with turbulence'. *Sloan Management Review*, Winter, 69–82.

Chakravarthy, B.S. and Perlmutter, H.V. (1985) 'Strategic planning for a global business'. *Columbia Journal of World Business*, Summer, 3–10.

Collis, D.J. and Montgomery, C.A. (1995) 'Competing on resources: Strategy in the 1990s'. *Harvard Business Review*, July/August, 199–128.

Cravens, D.W., Greenley, G., Piercy, N.F. and Slater, S. (1997) 'Integrating contemporary strategic management perspectives'. *Long Range Planning*, **30**(4), August, 493–506.

Cronshaw, M., Davis, E. and Kay, J. (1990) *On Being Stuck in the Middle or Good Food Costs Less at Sainsburys* (Working paper). London: Centre for Business Strategy, London School of Business.

D'Aveni, R.A. (1994) *Hypercompetition: Managing the Dynamics of Strategic Manoeuvring*. New York: Free Press.

Day, G.S. (1994) 'The capabilities of market-driven organisations'. *Journal of Marketing*, **38**, October, 37–52.

Demarest, M. (1997) 'Understanding knowledge management'. *Long Range Planning*, **30**(3), 374–384.

Doz, Y. (1986) *Strategic Management in Multinational Companies*. New York: Pergamon Press.

Fayerweather, J. (1981) 'Four winning strategies for the international corporation'. *Journal of Business Strategy*, **1**(2), Fall.

Gorman, P. and Thomas, H. (1997) 'The theory and practice of competence-based competition'. *Long Range Planning*, **30**(4), August, 615–620.

Grant, R.M. (1991) 'The resource-based theory of competitive advantage: Implications for strategy formulation'. *California Management Review*, **33**, Spring, 114–135.

Grant, R.M. (1997) 'The knowledge-based view of the firm: Implications for management practice'. *Long Range Planning*, **30**(3), 450–454.

Hamel, G. and Prahalad, C.K. (1985) 'Do you really have a global strategy'. *Harvard Business Review*, July/August.

Hamel, G. and Prahalad, C.K. (1994) *Competing for the Future*. Boston: Harvard Business School Press.

Heene, A. and Sanchez, R. (1997) *Competence-based Strategic Management*. New York: John Wiley & Sons.

Helms, M.M. and Wright, P. (1992) 'External considerations: Their influence on future strategic planning'. *Management Decision*, **30**(8), 4–11.

Henzler, H. and Rall, W. (1986) 'Facing up to the globalisation challenge'. *McKinsey Quarterly*, Winter.

Hitt, M.A. and Ireland, R.D. (1985) 'Corporate distinctive competence, strategy, industry and performance'. *Strategic Management Journal*, **6**(3), 273–293.

Johnson, G. and Scholes, K. (1997) *Exploring Corporate Strategy*. Englewood Cliffs, NJ: Prentice Hall.

Katz, D. (1993) 'Triumph of the Swoosh'. *Sports Illustrated*, 16 August, 1993.

Kay, J. (1993) *Foundations of Corporate Success*. Oxford, UK: Oxford University Press.

Klugt, C.J. Van der (1986) 'Japan's global challenge in electronics – the Philips' response'. *European Management Journal*, **4**(1), 4–9.

Kogut, B. (1985a) 'Designing global strategies: Comparative and competitive value-added claims'. *Sloan Management Review*, Summer, 15–27.

Kogut, B. (1985b) 'Designing global strategies: Profiting from operational flexibility'. *Sloan Management Review*, Fall, 28–38.

Leontiades, J.C. (1985) *Multinational Corporate Strategy: Planning for the World Markets*. Lexington, MD: Lexington Books.

Levitt, T. (1983) 'The globalization of markets'. *Harvard Business Review*, May/June.

Miller, D. (1992) 'The generic strategy trap'. *Journal of Business Strategy*, **13**(1), 37–42.

Mintzberg, H. (1991) *The Strategy Process – Concepts, Contexts, Cases*. Englewood Cliffs, NJ: Prentice Hall.

Nonaka, I. and Takeuchi, H. (1995) *The Knowledge-creating Company*. Oxford, UK: Oxford University Press.

Nonaka, I., Toyama, R. and Konno, N. (2000) 'SECI, *Ba* and leadership: A unified model of dynamic knowledge creation'. *Long Range Planning*, **33**(1), 5–34.

Penrose, E. (1959) *The Theory of the Growth of the Firm*. Oxford, UK: Oxford University Press.

Perlmutter, H.V. (1969) 'The tortuous evolution of the multinational corporation'. *Columbia Journal of World Business*, January/February.

Petts, N. (1997) 'Building growth on core competences – a practical approach'. *Long Range Planning*, **30**(4), August, 551–561.

Porter, M.E. (1980) *Competitive Strategy: Techniques for Analysing Industries and Competitors*. New York: Free Press.

Porter, M.E. (1985) *Competitive Advantage*. New York: Free Press.

Porter, M.E. (1986a) *Competition in Global Business*. Boston: Harvard University Press.

Porter, M.E. (1986b) 'Changing patterns of international competition'. *California Management Review*, **28**(2), Winter, 9–40.

Porter, M.E. (1990) *The Competitive Advantage of Nations*. New York: Free Press.

Prahalad, C.K. and Doz, Y.L. (1986) *The Multinational Mission: Balancing Local Demands and Global Vision*. New York: Free Press.

Prahalad, C.K. and Hamel, G. (1989) 'Strategic intent'. *Harvard Business Review*, 63–76.

Prahalad, C.K. and Hamel, G. (1990) 'The core competence of the corporation'. *Harvard Business Review*, 79–91.

Quinn, J.B. (1992) *The Intelligent Enterprise*. New York: Free Press.

Sanchez, R. and Heene, A. (1997) *Strategic Learning and Knowledge Management*. New York: John Wiley & Sons.

Senge, P. (1990) 'The leader's new work: Building learning organizations'. *Sloan Management Review*, Fall.

Stalk, G., Evans, P. and Shulmann, L. E. (1992) 'Competing on capabilities: The new rules of corporate strategy'. *Harvard Business Review*, March/April, 57–69.

Stonehouse, G.H. and Pemberton, J.D. (1999) 'Learning and knowledge management in the intelligent organisation'. *Participation and Empowerment: An International Journal*, **7**(5), 131–144.

Stonehouse, G.H., Pemberton, J.D. and Barber, C.E. (2001) 'The role of knowledge facilitators and inhibitors: Lessons from airline reservations systems'. *Long Range Planning*, **34**, 115–138.

Yip, G.S. (1992) *Total Global Strategy – Managing for Worldwide Competitive Advantage*. Englewood Cliffs, NJ: Prentice Hall.

GLOBAL AND TRANSNATIONAL MARKET-SERVICING STRATEGIES

Introduction

An important element of the global strategy of a transnational organization is its market-servicing strategy. This is the method of entry and operation chosen by a business for a particular overseas market. A business can select from a wide range of alternative strategies for servicing foreign markets. Possible strategies include exporting, licensing, joint ventures, wholly owned subsidiaries, etc. Each alternative may be suitable under particular circumstances, but each is subject to limitations. The choice of strategy from the alternatives available has been described as a 'frontier issue' in international business. This is because the method of market servicing is one of the most important factors influencing company performance in foreign markets.

Given its importance, it is not surprising to learn that the issue of foreign-market-servicing strategies has been extensively covered in the international marketing literature (see Brooke, 1986; Root, 1987; Young et al., 1989). Literature on the subject of foreign market-servicing strategies concentrates on methods for selecting the most efficient alternative for a particular market. Choice of servicing strategy will depend on the characteristics of the market and on the global strategy of the organization.

Alternative foreign market-servicing strategies

What is market servicing?

Foreign market-servicing strategies can be regarded as one of a series of linked decisions which any company must make in the process of internationalization and globalization. In an 'ideal' international marketing plan (as shown in Table 7.1 and in the simplified schematic in Figure 7.1), businesses would first of all decide the strategic reasons for internationalization. Environmental scanning would then take place to identify external threats and opportunities, and internal strengths and weaknesses. Following this, international marketing opportunities would then be identified, taking into account product suitability for foreign markets and country market choice. Once the firm has decided 'which product in which foreign market', it would then need to examine the best way of entering

Table 7.1 An 'ideal' international marketing plan

Stage	Focus
1	Deciding to go abroad: reasons for internationalization
2	Scanning the international marketing environment (opportunities/threats, strengths/weaknesses)
3	Product suitability and choice of products for foreign markets
4	Country market choice
5	Choosing the foreign market entry and development strategy
6	Designing the international marketing mix
7	Financing international operations

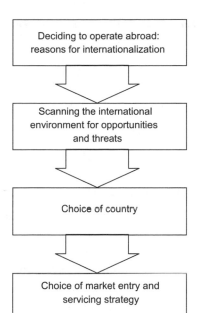

Figure 7.1 Stages in the market servicing and entry decision

and developing that market. This final stage, that of deciding on the mode of market entry, is the essence of market-servicing analysis.

Market-servicing options

An organization seeking to develop activities in international markets has a number of options open to it. We consider each one in turn (see Young, Hamill, et al., 1989).

(1) Direct exporting

Exporting normally begins as domestic sales of a product begin to slow down due to home market saturation. Exporting usually begins by simply shipping a product on receipt of payment, but as sales expand an export office may be set up in the domestic office, then sales offices may be set up overseas. At its simplest the product is manufactured in the home country and then marketed abroad.

The costs of exporting may be reduced by 'piggyback' distribution (i.e., by using an already established distribution network in the overseas country like a chain of stores).

Table 7.2 Pros and cons of exporting

Advantages of exporting	Disadvantages/Potential problems
Least expensive	Remote from customers
Least complicated	Lack of market knowledge
Profits do not have to be shared	Difficult to control remotely
Risk is limited to the value of the shipment	Distribution arrangements can be complex

Direct exporting may be carried out using a local agency. This has the benefit of exploiting local knowledge and links, but will mean that a commission has to be paid which will reduce profitability (Table 7.2).

(2) Contractual agreement type 1: licensing

Licensing involves a producer renting out certain intellectual property rights to a licensee. Payment is made to the licensor (the licence holder) on the basis of an agreed licensing contract, possibly on the basis of pro rata with profits earned on the use of the intellectual property or against sales. For the licensor this can be a low-cost but effective way of setting up an operation overseas while retaining control over the product. It protects the technology and know-how of the licensor and can also help to circumvent protectionist measures imposed by host governments. There may, however, be problems including the danger that the licensee may become a competitor when the license expires. Licensing is used in industries where branding is important (such as food FMCGs [fast-moving consumer goods] like soft drinks), in scientific industries (such as pharmaceuticals) and in brewing (Table 7.3).

(3) Contractual agreement type 2: patents

Patenting is a method of safeguarding an innovation against illegal copying by competitors. It involves patenting the exporting company's product in the domestic home and in the foreign countries in which it hopes to do

Table 7.3 Pros and cons of licensing

Advantages for licensor	Disadvantages/Potential problems
Little capital outlay	Limited contact with customers
Some control of operations	No direct control of operations
Risks are shared and limited	Profits must be shared with licensee
Licensee has local knowledge	

Table 7.4   Pros and cons of patenting

Advantages of patenting	Disadvantages/Potential problems
Prevents copying	Different laws in different countries
Protects product standards	Laws not enforced in some countries
Protects profits	
Protects technology	

business. Patent rights are protected by the Patent Co-operation Treaty, the European Patent Convention and the European Community Patent Convention. These can help to protect the products of an exporter from competition, but there are many less developed countries where the patent laws do not apply. It is used in industries where competitors are technically able to copy, but must be prevented from doing so (such as in pharmaceuticals) (Table 7.4).

(4) Contractual agreement type 3: franchising

Franchising is similar in concept to licensing. In licensing the licensor allows the licensee to use a piece of intellectual property, such as a brand name, a formulation, recipe or similar. In franchising the franchisor allows a franchisee, possibly in a foreign country, to use an entire business idea, including a brand, an 'image' (if appropriate) and a set of procedures and systems that have proven themselves to have worked previously by the franchiser.

In most franchise situations, the franchisee is encouraged to maintain the same business format as the franchiser. It becomes a rather more complicated situation if the franchisee deems it to be necessary to make some modifications to the franchise idea in order to accommodate national or regional differences in lifestyles, tastes, socio-cultural factors and legal requirements.

Franchising tends to work best in retailing industries and is widely used in multiple chains, such as fast food, hotels, specialist chains and car hire (Table 7.5).

International expansion through franchising – Holiday Inn

Franchising is one of the most popular methods of growth, especially in the service industries. It is a growth method involving two parties: the franchisor and the franchisee. In return for gaining access to the image, marketing and other support (such as procurement, training and systems) from the franchisor, the franchisee usually takes a substantial portion of the financial risk and pays ongoing fees to the franchisor.

Franchising has facilitated the rapid international growth of many well-known brands (such as McDonald's and KFC [fast food] and Avis and Hertz [car rental]) and many international hotel companies (such as Radisson and Marriott). Such companies are able to use the strength of their brand attributes to expand while the investment capital is provided and the associated risk is borne by another party (i.e., the franchisee). Since growth is less restrained by having limited access to capital resources, many companies adopting franchising for international growth have been able to expand very quickly as they roll out a tried and tested product across new territories.

The international hotel brand, Holiday Inn, has expanded rapidly around the world in the last few decades largely through franchising. An American entrepeneur, Kemmons Wilson, opened the first Holiday Inn hotel in 1952 in Memphis, Tennessee, after he returned from a family holiday discouraged over the lack of family and value-oriented lodging. At the Holiday Inn children stayed free and the hotel offered a swimming pool, air conditioning and restaurant on the property. Telephones, ice, and free parking were standard as well. Although commonplace today, these services were revolutionary at the time and set a standard for the hotel industry.

The company became a pioneer of franchising and rapidly expanded the Holiday Inn system, primarily through utilizing this method of strategic growth. The brand was almost literally rolled out across the USA, following the US interstate highway system's growth across the country. On the heels of this domestic success, the brand soon found investor interest in Europe and Asia, becoming the largest single hotel brand in the world. By the late 1980s the Holiday Inn brand could be found in many parts of the world.

In 1990 the InterContinental Hotel Group plc, which has its corporate headquarters in London (part of what was the then known as Bass plc), acquired Holiday Inn and moved the hotel headquarters from Memphis to Atlanta. Atlanta offered the corporate infrastructure, worldwide transportation access and international presence Bass felt was necessary for the company to succeed as a global business. Holiday Inn, together with its complementary brands (which include Holiday Inn

Express, Crowne Plaza and Intercontinental Hotels) now operate approximately 3,100 hotels, accounting for about 500,000 rooms. Approximately, 2,700 of the hotels are franchised.

The franchise strategy pursued by Holiday Inn was later emulated by other hotel companies. However, franchising is not without risk for the franchisor. In managing franchise relationships, especially in an international context, it can be extremely difficult to ensure that consistent standards are maintained when managers are having to cope with various languages, cultures and regulatory environments and having to communicate across time zones. One way of trying to ensure consistent standards are maintained is to standardize the product as much as possible, so that it becomes easier to manage and business problems are predictable. However, in standardizing the product there is a risk that the product fails to adapt to local conditions and cultural environments.

In the case of the hotel industry, many visitors travel in order to experience diversity and want the hotel to reflect local climate, traditions and culture. In recent years companies such as Holiday Inn – in attempting to deliver consistency of standards across a global network – have been accused of being dull and predictable, which may be reassuring to many business travellers, but may fail to attract more discerning leisure travellers who seek a diversity of product offerings, reflecting local conditions.

Table 7.5 Pros and cons of franchising

Advantages for the franchisor	Disadvantages/Potential problems
Little capital outlay	Limited contact with customers
Some control of operations	No direct control of operations
Risks are shared and limited	Profits must be shared with franchisee
Franchisee has local knowledge	

(5) Contractual agreement type 4: contract manufacturing

This involves a business entering a foreign market by contracting local organizations in the foreign country to produce all or some portion of a product. This reduces the amount of direct investment required, but still allows the business to retain control of its product and technology.

(6) Contractual agreement type 5: management contract
Under this arrangement a business provides the management functions for
another. Many major airlines including PanAm, BA, etc. supply mainten-
ance and technical services to smaller airlines in this way. The same is true
of civil engineering and construction management consultancies which
manage construction projects abroad, such as dams and bridges.

(7) Contractual agreement type 6: turnkey operations
This arrangement involves a foreign business constructing an entire production facility, such as a chemical plant, in a host country. On completion
the facility is duly handed over to the recipient who then operates it. The
majority of recipients of turnkey operations are governments of developing
countries. Because of the high costs involved, payments are made in
instalments with the last payment being made on satisfactory completion.

(8) Local assembly
The components are imported to the host country and are assembled into
the finished product which is then marketed and distributed in the host
country (i.e., the foreign country), and perhaps in other markets in that
region (Table 7.6).

(9) Local manufacture
The product is manufactured, either partly or wholly in the host country
and sold in the host country, and perhaps in other markets. It is the next
stage in terms of commitment after local assembly (Table 7.7).

(10) Co-production
A domestic and a foreign business may enter into an arrangement to produce a certain product using both domestic and foreign components. The
advantages of this are economies of scale, use of specialist technologies,

Table 7.6 Pros and cons of local assembly

Advantages	Disadvantages/Potential problems
Possibility of lower labour costs	May be difficult to obtain skilled labour
Reduced transport costs	Difficult to control quality standards
Creates local jobs	More expensive to set up than some other options due to transport costs
May avoid import restrictions in host country	

Table 7.7 Pros and cons of local manufacture

Advantages	Disadvantages/Potential problems
Possibility of lower labour costs	Difficult to obtain skilled labour
Reduces transport costs	Difficult to control quality standards
Creates local jobs	
May avoid import restrictions in host country	

Table 7.8 Pros and cons of foreign subsidiaries

Advantages	Disadvantages/Potential problems
Retain central control	Possible opposition from host government
Provides sensitivity to local conditions	Possible labour relations problems
Creates local jobs	May be conflict between HQ and local managers
May avoid import restrictions in host country	

local materials and experience. The development of the Eurofighter in the 1990s was an example of co-production, with different parts of the aircraft being built by various companies throughout Europe.

(11) Establishing foreign subsidiaries

This is the case when a parent company has total control of its overseas operations, decision making and profits. Wholly owned subsidiaries may however give rise to opposition from the foreign government and there may also be labour relations problems (Table 7.8).

(12) Joint ventures and strategic alliances

The joining of two or more separate businesses for a mutually beneficial project is a relatively common arrangement in domestic business. When it is used in international business, cultural and political differences can partly offset the opportunities it presents.

Two or more companies from different countries contribute resources to carry out certain activities without forming a new company. Each partner contributes a specialized resource or skill. We consider this arrangement in some detail in Chapter 14 (Table 7.9).

(13) Mergers and acquisitions

In a merger, two companies join to form a new business entity. In an acquisition, one company purchases a controlling interest in another. Both are used in international business (the two parties in the arrangement

Table 7.9 Pros and cons of international joint ventures and strategic alliances

Advantages	Disadvantages/Potential problems
Synergy	Conflicts of interest
Shared knowledge, expertise and skills	Some partners gain more than others
Shared technology	Difficult to sustain in long run
Shared costs and benefits	Competitive instincts prevail
Mutual profits	Decision making is slower
Knowledge of local markets	
Existing business contacts can be used	
Reduces political risks	
Less costly than a merger	

Table 7.10 Pros and cons of foreign mergers and acquisitions

Advantages of mergers and acquisitions	Disadvantages/Potential problems
Synergy between the two parties	Costs are higher than most other modes of entry
Shared knowledge, expertise and skills	May create resentment in host country
Shared technology	May take over a business with poor local reputation
Full operational control can be gained in an acquisition (less so in a merger)	May take over a business whose image does not match
Control of quality	May take over a business with problems
Knowledge of local markets	Financial exposure is much higher than for exporting, licensing, etc. as an investment is made abroad which may be lost
Existing business contacts can be used	
Reduces political risks as partner company will aleady be established	
Locally known trading name	

are from different countries). Again, we consider this matter in detail in Chapter 14 (Table 7.10).

(14) Global business

Many large companies configure their business in such a way as to spread their activities around the world so as to maximize the locational advantages to be obtained from each of their activities.

The sportswear producer Nike is an example of a global business in this regard. The company bases its design and development in the USA. Manufacturing is concentrated primarily in the Far East to meet high-quality

Table 7.11 Costs and benefits of alternative modes of entry (4 is highest, 1 is lowest)

Criteria	Exporting	Contractual agreements (e.g., licensing)	Joint ventures and alliances	Wholly owned subsidiary
Cost of capital	2	1	3	4
Potential revenue	3	1	2	4
Political risk	2	1	3	4
Revenue stability	?	4	?	?
Corporate control	2	1	3	4

standards while maintaining low unit costs (especially for labour). Marketing and distribution is spread around the world to allow maximum flexibility and responsiveness to local markets.

A summary of the modes of entry

Companies should consider the costs and benefits of the above strategies in relation to the foreign market to select the most appropriate. Table 7.11 is an example of how this might be done.

The range of alternative foreign-market-servicing strategies available is summarized in Appendix 7.1 at the end of this chapter. Various attempts have been made to classify these alternatives. Brooke (1986), for example, distinguished between exporting, knowledge agreements and foreign investment as shown in Figure 7.2.

Root (1987) adopted a similar classification that distinguished between:

a. export entry modes including indirect exporting, direct exporting through agents and distributors, and direct branch/branch subsidiary exports;

b. contractual entry modes including licensing, franchising, technical agreements, service contracts, management contracts, construction/turnkey contracts, contract manufacturing, co-production agreements; and

c. investment entry modes including new plants, acquisitions and joint ventures.

Luostarinen's (1979) classification (see Figure 7.3) distinguished foreign-market-servicing strategies according to three main dimensions, namely:

• the location of production whether domestic or overseas (e.g., domestic production in exporting, overseas production in licensing, foreign direct investment [FDI], etc.);

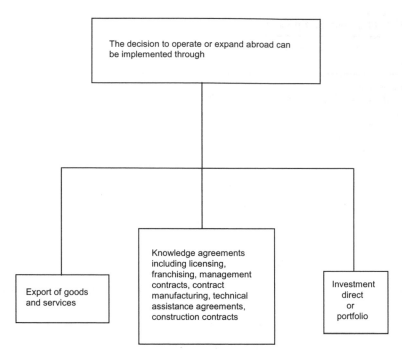

Figure 7.2 International business options
According to Brooke (1986)

Production in home market		Production overseas	
Non-direct investment marketing operations	Direct investment marketing operations	Non-direct investment marketing operations	Direct investment marketing operations
• Indirect goods exports	• Sales promotion subsidiaries	• Licensing	• Assembly ⎱ Wholly owned ⎰ joint ventures ⎰ Minority holding
• Direct goods exports	• Warehousing units	• Franchising	• Manufacture ⎱ 'Fade-out' ⎰ agreements
• Service exports	• Service units	• Contract manufacturing/ international subcontracting[a]	
• Know-how exports	• Sales subsidiaries	• Turnkey operations	
• Partial project exports			

Figure 7.3 Luostarinen's (1980) forms of international market entry and development[b]
Reproduced from *Acta Academica Oeconomicae Helsingiensis*. [a]Assuming that international subcontracting takes place between independent companies in home and overseas markets. [b]Excludes industrial co-operation agreements and the range of forms of contractual joint ventures because of their variety.

- whether FDI occurs or not (i.e., direct investment versus non-direct investment operations); and
- the type of activity undertaken, whether manufacturing, marketing or the transfer of know-how.

Selection of mode of entry

Choosing the most appropriate mode of entry

A range of factors will influence the choice between these alternative modes of entry. Particularly important will be the costs, risks and control considerations of each option. The various modes can be considered to exist on a continuum ranging from low cost, low risk, low control (such as indirect exporting) to high cost, high risk, high-control modes, such as FDI.

Other factors influencing strategic choice regarding market entry and development modes include the following.

The nature of the product provided
Certain entry and development modes are more appropriate for certain products or services than others. Thus, exporting would not be an appropriate supply mode for products where transportation costs are high as a proportion of value added. Similarly, subcontracting arrangements are more appropriate in labour-intensive products, such as in the textile industry and certain parts of the electronics industry. For technology intensive products the business may wish to retain control over access to know-how, thus favouring a higher control option, such as a foreign wholly owned subsidiary.

Management commitment
For small to medium-sized companies the range of alternative supply modes may be limited because of restrictions to managerial time and resources.

Host country legislation
Depending on the political leanings of host governments, some countries make impositions, such as import controls, restrictions on profit and royalty payments, controls on technology transfer through licensing, incentives and disincentives for foreign investors.

Marketing objectives
Supply mode choice will vary depending on the organization's objectives in the foreign market. Where market share is important, more direct forms of entry may be desirable. Alternatively, a company that wishes to skim a number of foreign markets may prefer less direct modes, such as franchising, etc.

Culture
More direct forms of involvement may be encouraged where there are cultural similarities between the foreign and domestic markets, since this reduces the risk of cultural clashes.

Criteria for choosing mode of entry

Various models have been developed to assist companies in choosing between alternative foreign market entry and development strategies. These can be classified into three different approaches.

The economic approach
This emphasizes the rate of return or profitability of different entry and development modes. After considering the return profile of each option, the one offering the highest return is chosen regardless of any other considerations.

The stage of development approach
This approach relates the entry and development mode decision to the internationalization process. Different entry/development modes are 'best suited' at different stages of internationalization (exporting, for example, is typically the first foray that a business makes into international business).

The business strategy approach
This approach relates the entry and development mode to the strategic motivations to be achieved and to the internal environmental and external environmental factors influencing the decision (see Figure 7.4).

Global market-servicing strategies

Literature summary

While there is an extensive literature on foreign market entry mode choice, there has been little attempt to incorporate such decisions into the wider context of global strategy. The existing literature tends to view market-servicing decisions as specific to each new market entered. They largely ignore the interdependencies that may exist between operations across borders. This is a major weakness in the literature from the perspective

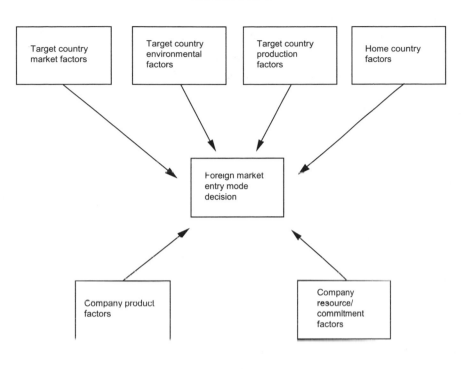

Figure 7.4 Factors in the entry mode decision
Adapted from Root (1987)

of this book with its emphasis on the co-ordination and integration of geographically dispersed operations. Thus, it may reasonably be expected that the overall global strategy of a business may be an important determinant of the choice of foreign market-servicing mode. Decisions regarding the mode of entry must be consistent with and support the overall strategic development of the business in global industries.

The importance of global strategic considerations in the choice of market-servicing modes is only beginning to be recognized in the literature. Kim Hwang (1992), Porter (1986a), Yip (1992) and Young et al. (1989) extended the traditional approach to market entry choice (as discussed in the previous section) to include aspects of global strategy. In addition to the environmental and transaction-specific variables extensively covered in the previously cited literature, entry mode decisions are influenced by three global strategic variables: global concentration, global synergies and global strategic motivations.

Three key variables

Global concentration

Many global industries have become highly concentrated with a high level of competitive or oligopolistic interdependence. In other words, the actions taken by one company in one national market will have repercussions in other national markets. This leads to the hypothesis that, when the global industry is highly concentrated, companies will favour high-control entry modes.

Global synergies

This refers to the synergies that can arise from the shared utilization of core competences among strategic business units (such as Honda's transfer of advanced engine technology from motorcycles to automobiles). The achievement of such synergy requires a degree of hierarchical control. This, in turn, leads to the hypothesis that businesses will demand higher levels of control over foreign operations as the extent of potential global synergies between the subsidiary and other sister business units increases.

Global strategic motivations

Companies entering or developing a particular foreign market may have strategic motivations that are wider than simply choosing the most efficient entry mode. These global strategic motivations are set at corporate level for the purpose of overall corporate efficiency maximization rather than efficiency of individual national markets. Foreign business units, for example, may be established as a strategic outpost for future global expansion, as global sourcing or to attack a competitor. To successfully achieve these global strategic motivations requires tight co-ordination across global business units. This leads to the hypothesis that businesses exercising global strategic motivations will favour high-control entry modes.

Collaborative arrangements

Collaboration rather than competition

Collaborative networks or strategic alliances are arrangements between businesses to co-operate with the express purpose of gaining competitive advantage. The conventional model of business behaviour is that of competition, but collaborative relationships have become increasingly important as a means of acquiring competitive advantage for the businesses who are members of the collaborative network. The basis of collaborative behaviour can be related to conventional theories explaining sources of competitive advantage.

Porter (1986a, b, 1990) stressed the importance of *configuration* of business activities and their *co-ordination* as a means of achieving competitive advantage.

Kay (1993) identified *distinctive capability* as the source of competitive edge. Distinctive capabilities rest on architecture, reputation, innovation and strategic assets (see Chapter 6).

Prahalad and Hamel (1990) argued that an international business must identify and build on its *core competences*. Core competences are '*the collective learning in the organisation, especially how to co-ordinate diverse production skills and integrate multiple streams of technologies*' (Prahalad and Hamel, 1990). Three criteria can be applied in identifying a core competence:

- it provides potential access to a wide variety of markets;
- it should make a significant contribution to the perceived consumer benefits of the end product;
- it should be difficult for competitors to emulate.

Core competence should lead to core products that in turn should lead to competitive advantage

A study by Prahalad and Doz (1987) of a number of multinationals, spanning a decade, reached similar conclusions to those of Porter (1986a, b, 1990). They found that corporate success at an international level was dependent on the ability of the multinational to *co-ordinate and integrate* global activities, while at the same time retaining *responsiveness* to the demands of local markets and changing circumstances. Achieving competitive advantage will therefore require:

- identification of the core competences of the organization;
- identification and focus on activities that are critical to the core competence of the organization and outsourcing those that are not;
- achieving the internal and external linkages in the value/supply chain which are necessary for effective co-ordination of activities and which permit responsiveness.

The literature has for many years stressed the competitive elements of the behaviour of organizations in achieving competitive advantage. More recently research has pointed to collaboration between companies as a potential source of competitive edge.

The nature and rationale of collaboration

Partners for collaboration
Collaboration may take place between an organization and any of the following:

- suppliers;
- customers;
- financiers;
- competitors;
- governments and other public organizations.

Taken to one extreme, collaboration may lead to mergers and acquisitions (see our discussion of this in Chapter 14). More often it can take place between businesses who retain their separate identities but who collaborate in a network on a short or long-term basis.

Reasons for collaboration
Contractor and Lorange (1988a) identified several rationales for collaboration:

- risk reduction (e.g., of investment exposure);
- the sharing of different but linked core competencies;
- economies of scale and/or rationalization;
- complementary technologies and patents;
- blocking competition;
- overcoming government-mandated investment or trade barriers;
- initial international expansion;
- vertical quasi-integration – access to materials, technology, labour, capital, distribution channels, buyers, regulatory permits.

In addition, we suggest that collaboration can enable each party to bring unique core competences to the alliance. By combining their core competences, partners can enjoy synergy. In this regard, collaboration can provide similar benefits to a business to outsourcing – taking advantage of another business's core competences to add value more effectively than could be accomplished in-house.

Reve (1990) identified two explanations of what holds alliances together:

1. The economic approach which states that alliances exist between businesses because the parties involved see the possibility of increased profits. Such relationships depend on safeguards to protect the interests of the participants, and the relationship is therefore 'impersonal and unstable'.
2. The behavioural approach which says that there is value attached to the relationship between the parties involved, social ties are built, there is trust and integrity and personal contacts are important. Such alliances are usually longer lasting and more stable.

Potential problems
There are, however, problems associated with collaboration:

- the initial rationale for collaboration may shift over time (e.g., technology changes or one partner has a reduced need for the other);
- language problems;
- cultural differences (differences in values and norms);
- incompatibilities between management styles and systems;
- co-ordination and integration problems;
- an increase in competitive pressures, which changes the competitive environment for one or both parties;
- changes in the market.

Horizontal and vertical collaboration

Horizontal relationships
Horizontal collaboration is an arrangement involving two or more companies at the same stage in the supply chain. It usually takes place between competitors (although rarely on anything other than a limited scale). They can serve to strengthen the participating companies against outside competition, possibly an aggressive (and larger) competitor.

The nature of collaboration necessitates sharing between the partners. This can be shared technology, skills, costs (say, of an overseas investment) or risks. It can also increase scale economy benefits to both parties, thus giving vertical advantage over suppliers.

Vertical relationships

These can be upstream in the supply chain (toward suppliers) or downstream (toward distributors and customers). Collaboration in either direction can enable a business to gain cost or price advantage against its competitors. If the upstream or downstream partner is in another country, the arrangement can be used to circumvent local import or export restrictions.

Benefits

Both horizontal and vertical relationships offer benefits:

- improved responsiveness;
- each partner in the alliance can concentrate on its core competences and thus add greater value at lower cost;
- create barriers to entry (the two act in concert and thus are effectively one when attacked by a would-be new entrant);
- produce logistical economies of scale;
- superior information on activities at all stages of the supply chain;
- ties in suppliers and customers to the focal business;
- the creation of synergy between partners and a lowering of unit costs.

Alliances

An alliance is one type of collaborative arrangement (see Chapter 14 for a detailed discussion of this topic). With regard to considering alliances as a market-servicing strategy, the participants must consider a number of issues:

- deciding which activities and assets are core and should therefore be carried out by the business itself (configuration);
- deciding which activities are of medium specificity and should be obtained via alliances and outsourcing (configuration);
- deciding which activities are of low specificity and should be obtained through the market (configuration);
- integration of core and alliance activities (co-ordination);
- management and operation of the alliances (co-ordination).

Summary – advantages of collaborative arrangements as modes of entry

Collaborative networks have the potential to deliver sustainable competitive advantage by:

- enhancing core competence and distinctive capability;
- making possible and improving organizational architecture;
- creating new organizational assets;
- creating synergy;
- reducing unit costs;
- increasing efficiency;
- increasing flexibility.

The survival and prosperity of a collaborative relationship depends on:

- its ability to co-ordinate intra-organizational activities;
- its ability to integrate business strategies;
- external contracts and motivations to foster the alliance;
- its ability to adapt to a changing environment and changing network relationships.

Appendix 7.1   Some additional notes on foreign-market-servicing strategies

Adapted from Young et al. (1989)

Firms can choose from a wide range of alternative strategies when entering and developing foreign markets. These include (a) export entry and development modes; (b) contractual entry and development modes; and (c) modes of entry and development involving direct investment abroad.

Exporting

This involves the transfer of goods and/or services across national boundaries from a domestic production base. Exporting may be either indirect (which involves little effort on the part of the firm itself) or direct (which involves a greater internal commitment). The main forms of indirect and direct exporting include:

- *Indirect exporting*
- Export houses
- Confirming houses
- Trading companies
- Piggybacking

- *Direct exporting*
- Agents
- Distributors
- Company export salesmen
- Overseas sales subsidiaries

Contractual agreements

This covers a wide range of alternatives, as outlined in the following seven subsections.

Licensing
Contracts in which the licensor provides licensees abroad with access to one or a set of technologies or know-how in return for financial compensation. Typically, the licensee has rights to produce and market a product within an agreed area in return for royalties.

Franchising
Contracts in which the franchisor provides the franchisee with a 'package', including not only trademarks and know-how but also local exclusivity and management, and financial assistance and joint advertising. Management fees are payable.

Management contracts
An arrangement under which operational control of an enterprise, which would otherwise be exercised by a board of directors or managers elected and appointed by its owners, is vested by contract in a separate enterprise which performs the necessary management functions in return for a fee.

Turnkey agreements
A contractor has responsibility for establishing a complete production unit or infrastructure project in a host country – up to the stage of the commissioning of total plant facilities. Payment may be in a variety of forms including countertrading. 'Turnkey plus' contracts include product in hand and market in hand contracts.

Contract manufacturing or international subcontracting
A company (the principal) in one country places an order, with specifications as to conditions of sale and products required, with a firm in another

country. Typically, the contract would be limited to production, with marketing being handled by the principal.

Industrial co-operation agreements
Conventionally applied to arrangements between Western companies and government agencies or enterprises in the Eastern Bloc, including licensing, technical assistance agreements, turnkey projects and contract manufacturing, as well as contractual joint ventures and tripartite ventures.

Contractual joint ventures
Formed for a particular project of limited duration or for a longer term co-operative effort, with the contractual relationship commonly terminating once the project is complete. May relate to *co-production, co-R&D, co-development, co-marketing* plus *co-publishing* and *consortium ventures* by banks to finance large loans, etc.

Foreign direct investment

The three main types of foreign-market-servicing strategy involving direct investment abroad are:

- the establishment of wholly owned, greenfield subsidiaries;
- cross-border acquisitions;
- equity joint ventures.

Toyota – FDI greenfield development in the UK

Toyota is Japan's largest motor manufacture and it occupies the third position (by volume) in the world. Toyota's worldwide output amounts to almost 5 million vehicles a year. Operating in 150 countries, the company has 29 manufacturing plants in 22 countries, sells its vehicles through over 7,000 dealerships and employs more than 100,000 people.

In the early 1960s Toyota made its first incursions into the European market by exporting cars to Denmark. Its growth in the EU since then has been substantial. By 1992 Toyota was selling vehicles in 22 European countries through 3,500 dealerships.

The market potential for sales in the EU, as one of the legs of the 'triad' (the Far East, North America and Europe), proved too tempting an opportunity to miss for Toyota, and in 1989 it announced plans to make a direct investment in a manufacturing plant in the EU. After much discussion the company chose two sites in the UK and one in Belgium. Toyota's initial investments in the UK – at Burnaston in Derbyshire and at Deesside, North Wales – amounted to £840 million. Its investment at Diest, Belgium, was in a European parts centre and came to £26 million. Construction of the two UK plants commenced in 1990 and the first British Toyotas left the production line in December 1992.

Unlike other Japanese motor companies that have invested in the UK, Toyota did not develop a single 'super-site'. The plant in North Wales is dedicated to the production of engines, while the company's plant in Derbyshire produces passenger cars for the European market using Deesside-produced engines.

In common with other manufacturers who have made sizeable inward investments into the EU, one of Toyota's key objectives in its direct investment manoeuvre was to overcome the import restrictions that the EU places on imports from outside its borders. By producing from within the EU, the cars produced were British as far as sales to other EU states were concerned – not Japanese. Of course, direct investment also means that transport costs to other EU states from the UK are significantly less than they would be from Japan.

Philip Morris – foreign acquisitions in the former communist states of central and eastern Europe

Philip Morris Inc. is the largest cigarette manufacturer in the world and the world's third largest brewer. Its tobacco brands occupy 47% of the USA's 500 billion cigarettes per year market and 30% of the EU's total cigarette consumption. The company's 3,000 brands also include a wide range of food products. It is the largest worldwide producer of consumer-packaged goods and one of the world's largest trading companies. Its best known brands include Marlboro, L&M and Chesterfield cigarettes, Miller beers and a wide range of food products including Post cereals, Kraft foods (e.g., Philadelphia, Maxwell House, etc.) and the confectionery brands Toblerone, Suchard and Terry's of York.

The company is based in the USA and sells its products in over 170 countries, employing around 155,000 people in its worldwide operations. European, Middle Eastern and African operations are controlled from the Philip Morris offices in Lausanne, Switzerland.

During the 1990s Philip Morris pursued a strategy of direct investment in the tobacco industries of the former communist countries of central and eastern Europe. Central Europe's cigarette consumption is around 600 billion cigarettes per year, which, unlike demand in some parts of the world, is relatively stable (i.e., it is not in decline). The decentralization of the economies in these states has provided investment opportunities for Western companies who, for such reasons as above, wish to gain a market presence in these parts of the world. Philip Morris has had links, through licensing agreements, with companies in central and eastern Europe for over 20 years, so the demise of communism in these countries offered a unique opportunity for expansion (by means of FDI) into these national markets.

Some of its major acquisitions include:

Foreign interest	Date	Country	Value	Shareholding
Tabak A.S.	1992	Czech Republic	$400 million	Majority (>77%)
Newly built factory in St Petersburg	1992	Russia	Undisclosed	Majority
Klaipeda State Tobacco Company	1993	Lithuania	$50 million	62.5% (including a newly built factory)
Krasnodar Tobacco Factory	1993	Russia	$60 million	Majority
Almaty Tobacco Kombinat	1993	Kazakhstan	$200 million	Majority
Kharkov Tobacco Factory	1994	Ukraine	Undisclosed	Majority

Review and discussion questions

1. Why do organizations seek to develop markets abroad?
2. What are the market entry options open to a business seeking to service foreign markets?
3. Which market entry option carries the highest risk?
4. Summarize the criteria for selecting a market entry strategy.
5. Why might an organization seek to develop a collaborative arrangement as a mode of foreign market entry?
6. Distinguish between vertical and horizontal relationships.

References and further reading

Borys, B. and Jemison, D.B. (1988) *Hybrid Organizations as Strategic Alliances: Theoretical Issues in Organizational Combinations.* Palo Alto, CA: Stanford University.

Bowerson, D.J. (1990) 'The strategic benefits of logistics alliances'. *Harvard Business Review*, **90**(4), 36–47.

Brooke, M.Z. (1986) *International Management: A Review of Strategies and Operations*. London: Hutchinson.

Buckley, P.J. and Casson, M. (1976) *The Future of the Multinational Enterprise*. London: Macmillan.

Buckley, P.J. and Casson, M. (1981) 'The optimal timing of a foreign direct investment'. *Economic Journal*, **92**(361), 75–87. (Reprinted in Buckley, P.J. and Casson, M. (1985) *The Economic Theory of the Multinational Enterprise*. London: Macmillan.)

Buckley, P.J. and Casson, M. (1988) 'A theory of co-operation in international business'. In: F.J. Contractor and P. Lorange (eds), *Competitive Strategies in International Business*. Lexington, MD: Lexington Books.

Buckley, P.J., Pass, C.L. and Prescott, K. (1990) 'Foreign market servicing by multinationals – An integrated treatment'. *International Marketing Review*, **7**(4), 25–40.

Buckley, P.J., Pass, C.L. and Prescott, K. (1992) 'Foreign market servicing strategies of UK retail financial service firms in continental Europe'. In: S. Young and J. Hamill (eds), *Europe and the Multinationals: Issues and Responses for the 1990s*. Aldershot, UK: Edward Elgar.

Contractor, F.J. and Lorange, P. (1988a) 'Why should firms co-operate?' *Co-operative Strategies in International Business*. Lexington, MD: Lexington Books.

Contractor, F.J. and Lorange, P. (1988b) 'Competition vs. co-operation: A benefit/cost framework for choosing between fully-owned investments and co-operative relationships'. *Management International Review*, **28**, Special issue 88.

Cooke, T.E. (1986) *Mergers and Acquisitions*. Oxford, UK: Basil Blackwell.

Cooke, T.E. (1988) *International Mergers and Acquisitions*. Oxford, UK: Basil Blackwell.

Davidow, W.H. and Malone, M.S. (1992) *Structuring and Revitalising the Corporation for the 21st Century – The Virtual Corporation*. London: Harper Business.

Davidson, K.M. (1990) 'Mergers and acquisitions: Anatomy of the fall'. *Journal of Business Strategy*, **11**(5), 48–51.

Davidson, K.M. (1991) 'Mergers and acquisitions: Innovation and corporate mergers'. *Journal of Business Strategy*, **12**(1), 42–45.

De Noble, A.F., Gustafson, L.T. and Hergert, M. (1988) 'Planning for post-merger integration – Eight lessons for merger success'. *Long Range Planning*, **21**(110), 82–86.

Devlin, G. and Bleackley, M. (1988) 'Strategic alliances – Guidelines for success'. *Long Range Planning*, **21**(5), 18–23.

Douglas, S.P. and Craig, C.S. (1989) 'Evolution of global marketing strategy: Scale, scope and synergy'. *Columbia Journal of World Business*, Fall, 47–59.

Doz, Y.L., Hamel, G. and Prahalad, C.K. (1986) 'Strategic partnerships: Success or surrender? The challenge of competitive collaboration'. Paper presented at *Joint Academy of International Business/European International Business Association Conference, London, November*.

Gall, E.A. (1991) 'Strategies for merger success'. *Journal of Business Strategy*, **12**(2), 26–30.

Gamble, P.R. (1992) 'The virtual corporation: An IT challenge'. *Logistics Information Management*, **5**(4), 34–37.

Ghoshal, S. and Bartlett, A. (1990) 'The multinational corporation as an interorganisational network'. *Academy of Management Review*, **15**, 603–625.

Gilbert, X. and Stebel, P. (1989) 'From innovation to outpacing'. *Business Quarterly*, **54**(1), 19–22, Summer.

Gogler, P. (1992) 'Building transnational alliances to create competitive advantage'. *Long Range Planning*, **25**(1), 90–99.

Goldberg, W.H. (1983) *Mergers – Motives, Modes, Methods*. Aldershot, UK: Gower Press.

Goodnow, J.D. and Hanz, J.E. (1972) 'Environmental determinants of overseas market entry strategies'. *Journal of International Business Studies*, Spring, 33–50.

Hamel, G., Doz, Y. and Prahalad, C.K. (1989) 'Collaborate with your competitors and win'. *Harvard Business Review*, January/February.

Hamel, G., Doz, Y.L. and Prahalad, C.K. (1989) 'Collaborate with your competitors – and win'. *Harvard Business Review*, January/February, 133–139.

Hamill, J. (1988) 'British acquisitions in the US'. *National Westminster Bank Quarterly Review*, August.

Hamill, J. (1988) 'US acquisitions and the internationalisation of British industry'. *Acquisitions Monthly*, November.

Hamill, J. (1991) 'Strategic restructuring through international acquisitions and divestments'. *Journal of General Management*, **17**(1), Autumn.

Hamill, J. (1991) 'Changing patterns of international business: Crossborder mergers, acquisitions and alliances'. Paper presented at *UK Region, Academy of International Business Conference, London*, April.

Hamill, J. (1992) 'Crossborder mergers, acquisitions and strategic alliances in Europe'. In: S. Young and J. Hamill (eds) *Europe and the Multinationals: Issues and Responses for the 1990s*. Aldeshot, UK: Edward Elgar.

Hamill, J. and Crosbie, J. (1989) 'Acquiring in the US food and drink industry'. *Acquisitions Monthly*, May.

Hamill, J. and El-Hajjar, S. (1990) 'Defending competitiveness'. *Acquisitions Monthly*, April, 36–39.

Harrigan, K.R. (1984) 'Joint ventures and global strategies'. *Columbia Journal of World Business*, Summer.

Harrigan, K.R. (1985) *Strategies for Joint Ventures*. Lexington, MD: Lexington Books.

Harrigan, K.R. (1988) 'Joint ventures and competitive strategy'. *Strategic Management Journal*, **9**.

Harrigan, K.R. (1988) 'Restructuring industries through strategic alliances'. *Strategic Management Journal*, **9**.

Helms, M.M. and Wright, P. (1992) 'External considerations: Their influence on future strategic planning'. *Management Decision*, **30**(8), 4–11.

Jain, S.C. (1987) 'Perspectives on international strategic alliances'. *Advances in International Marketing* (pp. 103–120). Greenwich, CT: JAI Press.

Jarillo, J.C. and Stevenson, H.H. (1991) 'Co-operative strategies – The payoffs and pitfalls'. *Long Range Planning*, **24**(1), 64–70.

Jemison, D.B. and Sitkin, S.M. (1986) 'Acquisitions: The process can be a problem'. *Harvard Business Review*, March.

Johanson, J. and Mattson, L.G. (1992) 'Network positions and strategic action'. In: B. Axelsson and G. Easton (eds), *Industrial Networks: A New View of Reality*. London: Routledge.

Kay, J. (1993) *Foundations of Corporate Success*. Oxford, UK: Oxford University Press.

Keenan, M. and White, L.J. (1982) *Mergers and Acquisitions*. Lexington, MD: Lexington Books.

Kobayashi, N. (1988) 'Strategic alliances with Japanese firms'. *Long Range Planning*, **21**(108), 29–34.

Kohn, R.L. (1990) 'Japanese–US alliances: Resolving economic conflict'. *Journal of Business Strategy*, **11**(4), 48–50.

Lorange, P. (1988) *Co-operative Strategies: Planning and Control Considerations* (WP-512). Philadelphia: Centre for International Management Studies.

Lorange, P. and Roos, J. (1991) 'Why some strategic alliances succeed and others fail'. *Journal of Business Strategy*, **12**(1), 25–31.

Lorange, P. and Roos, J. (1992) *Strategic Alliances: Formation, Implementation and Evolution*. Oxford, UK: Basil Blackwell.

Love, J.H. and Scouller, J. (1990) 'Growth by acquisition: The lessons of experience'. *Journal of General Management*, **15**(3), Spring.

Luostarinen, R. (1979) *The Internationalisation of the Firm*. Helsinki: Acta Academica Oeconomicae Helsingiensis.

Lyons, M.P. (1991) 'Joint ventures as strategic choice – A literature review'. *Long Range Planning*, **24**(4), 130–144.

Malekzadeh, A.R. and Nahavindi, A. (1990) 'Making mergers work by managing cultures'. *Journal of Business Strategy*, **11**(3), 55–58.

Morgan, N.A. (1988) 'Successful growth by acquisition'. *Journal of General Management*, **14**(2), Winter.

Morris, D. and Hergert, M. (1987) 'Trends in international collaborative agreements'. *Columbia Journal of World Business*, Summer.

Ohmae, K. (1989) 'The global logic of strategic alliances'. *Harvard Business Review*, March/April.

Oman, C. (1984) *New Forms of International Investment in Developing Countries*. Paris: OECD.

Payne, A.F. (1987) 'Approaching acquisitions strategically'. *Journal of General Management*, **13**(2), Winter.

Perlmutter, H.V. and Heenan, D.H. (1986) 'Cooperate to compete globally'. *Harvard Business Review*, March/April.

Porter, M.E. (1985) *Competitive Advantage*. New York: Free Press.

Porter, M.E. (ed.) (1986a) *Competition in Global Industries*. Boston: Harvard Business School Press.

Porter, M.E. (1986b) 'Changing patterns of international competition'. *California Management Review*, **28**(2), Winter, 9–40.

Porter, M.E. (1986c) *Competition in Global Business*. Boston: Harvard University Press.

Porter, M.E. (1990) *The Competitive Advantage of Nations*. New York: Free Press.

Porter, M.E. and Fuller, M.B. (1987) 'Coalitions and global strategy'. In: M.E. Porter (ed.), *Competition in Global Industries*. Boston: Harvard Business School Press.

Prahalad, C.K. and Doz, Y.L. (1987) *The Multinational Mission: Balancing Local Demands and Global Vision*. New York: Free Press.

Prahalad, C.K. and Hamel, G. (1989) 'Strategic intent'. *Harvard Business Review*, **67**(3), 63–76.

Prahalad, C.K. and Hamel, G. (1990) 'The core competence of the corporation'. *Harvard Business Review*, 79–91.

Quinn, J., Dooley, T. and Paquette, P. (1990) 'Technology in services: Rethinking strategic focus'. *Sloan Management Review*, Winter.

Reich, R.B. and Mankin, E.D. (1986) 'Joint ventures with Japan give away our future'. *Harvard Business Review*, March/April, 78.

Reve, T. (1990) 'The firm as a nexus of internal and external contracts'. In: M. Aoki, M. Gustafsson and O.E. Williamson (eds), *The Firm as a Nexus of Treaties*. London: Sage Publications.

Root, F.R. (1987) *Entry Strategies for International Markets*. Lexington, MD: Lexington Books and D.C. Heath & Co.

Shelton, L.M. (1988) 'Strategic business fits and corporate acquisitions: Empirical evidence'. *Strategic Management Journal*, **9**.

Stalk, G. (1988) 'Time – The next source of competitive advantage'. *Harvard Business Review*, July/August.

Steiner, P.O. (1975) *Mergers, Motives, Effects, Control*. Ann Arbor, MI: University of Michigan Press.

Teece, D.J. and Pisano, G. (1987) *Collaborative Arrangements and Technology Strategy*. Berkeley, CA: University of California.

Toyne, B. and Walters, P.G.P. (1993) *Global Marketing Management: A Strategic Perspective*. Boston: Allyn & Bacon.

UNCTC (1988) *Transnational Corporations in World Development: Trends and Prospects*. New York: UN Centre on Transnational Corporations.

Wissema, J.G. and Euser, L. (1991) 'Successful innovation through inter-company networks'. *Long Range Planning*, **24**(6), 33–39.

Yip, G. (1992) *Total Global Strategy*. Englewood Cliffs, NJ: Prentice Hall.

Young, S., Hamill, J., Wheeler, C. and Davies, J.R. (1989) *International Market Entry and Development: Strategies and Management*. Hemel Hempstead, UK: Harvester Wheatsheaf.

GLOBAL PRODUCTION AND LOGISTICS MANAGEMENT

Learning objectives

After studying this chapter students should be able to:

- explain what is meant by production and logistics in the context of international business;
- review the most relevant literature as it relates to global operations strategy;
- describe Dicken's four production strategies;
- explain the factors that influence where transnational businesses locate their production facilities;
- describe the issues surrounding procurement decisions for international businesses;
- explain how logistics is managed by multisite transnational businesses.

Introduction

The core of any global strategy is the use of a company's international scope as a key competitive weapon in global industries. This implies a degree of central co-ordination and integration of geographically dispersed operations, and involves complex decisions across a range of functional management areas. Nowhere is this more important than in the co-ordination and integration of global production and logistics management – the focus of this chapter.

Global production and sourcing is concerned with the what, where and how of worldwide production. In other words, it is concerned with global management decisions relating to the number, size and location of production facilities throughout the world; plant roles and specialization (by either products or markets); and interplant relationships. Especially important is the extent of co-ordination and integration of production facilities in different countries. Global logistics is concerned with the physical movement of final goods (and services) from producer to end-user and the flow of intermediate products, parts and components between plants (i.e., both external and internal logistics).

Production strategy and competitive advantage

The critical success factors in operations

An efficient, co-ordinated and integrated global production and logistics system can be an important source of competitive advantage in global industries. Co-ordinated global production can provide advantages in terms of costs (production and transportation), production flexibility and market responsiveness.

The major sources of value added in external logistics relate to:

1. place – the availability of a product in a location that is convenient to customers;
2. time – the availability of a product at a time that fulfils a customer's needs; and
3. information – that answers questions and communicates useful product and applications knowledge to customers (Keegan, 1995).

An efficient internal logistics network is essential to achieve the benefits of plant specialization and integration.

The overall global competitive strategy of the business will have a major impact on production and logistics management. The latter needs to be consistent with and integrated in the former. The major influence on production and logistics management in transnationals adopting country-centred strategies will be the requirement of national responsiveness. Global strategies, on the other hand, imply greater co-ordination and integration of worldwide production and logistics. Global strategies were defined by Doz (1986) as the 'specialisation of plants across countries into an integrated production and distribution network involving substantial cross border flows of components or products.' Similarly, Porter's (1986) definition of global strategy emphasized the configuration (location) and co-ordination (control) of value-added activities throughout the world. This chapter is largely concerned with configuration and co-ordination issues as they relate to global sourcing and distribution.

The issues raised in this chapter have become highly topical in recent years as a consequence of the globalization of markets and the emergence of global competition. Globalization has reduced the need for a market by market approach to sourcing and distribution, and has provided the international business with greater strategic flexibility in this area. The emergence of global competition has forced many companies to reassess their sourcing and distribution strategies aimed at greater cost-effectiveness. As a consequence of these two trends, a number of international businesses have rationalized their sourcing and distribution systems by consolidating activity into fewer, larger plants serving multicountry markets.

Global production strategies

The 'big' decisions in production strategy

This section examines global production strategies taking into account the issues involved, the alternative strategies available and the important links between global strategy and production strategy.

In designing its global production strategy, an international business needs to make decisions in a number of important areas:

1. The number and location of plants throughout the world, with plant location in turn being determined by a number of factors including costs, risks, return and government regulation.
2. Plant roles and inter-plant relationships including decisions regarding plant specialization and integration. Important issues here are whether to establish largely self-contained manufacturing plants or assembly plants which rely on a high proportion of bought-in parts and components; whether these bought-in components are from related or unrelated concerns; the product line of the plant; and markets to be supplied. The three main strategic options in terms of plant roles are:
   o to operate a number of plants each producing the same product for different markets;

    ○ to operate a number of factories each producing non-competitive products for the same market;

    ○ to have plants specializing in component manufacture with assembly being undertaken elsewhere.

3. Transnational procurement policies where three types of purchasing policy are possible – central purchasing, autonomous subsidiary purchasing and partial central purchasing.

Plant roles and inter-plant relationships

Reference has already been made in previous chapters to the different classifications of companies in international business where a distinction can be made between international, multinational and global companies (see Chapter 1). Keegan (1995) used this distinction to classify the alternative production/sourcing strategies available to global businesses. The three alternatives are described below.

'International' sourcing

This relies heavily on home country manufacturing, with foreign markets being mainly served through exports from a domestic production base. The main advantage of this strategy is that it reduces the requirement for international transfers of know-how and manufacturing capability.

'Multinational' sourcing

This establishes production operations in each foreign market. The three main advantages of this strategy are that it can overcome any barriers to market entry (e.g., import controls), it takes advantage of local factors of production and shortens supply lines, and production is more responsive to country customer needs and wants. The main disadvantage is that multiple production facilities limit the possibilities of economies of scale.

'Global' sourcing

In this strategy, production activities are located in such a way as to maximize quality and availability while minimizing costs. Global sourcing implies considerable co-ordination and integration of worldwide manufacturing and distribution.

Research in global productions strategy

The issue of global production involving cross-border co-ordination and integration of activity has attracted significant attention in the academic literature. We review the work of three of the most important thinkers in this area: Doz (1978), Starr (1984) and Dicken (1998).

Doz – opportunities from relaxations in trade restrictions

One of the earliest attempts to examine the process of manufacturing rationalization in international businesses was that by Doz (1978). Although published in the late 1970s, the study remains highly relevant, especially in the context of the development of trading blocks and customs unions (such as the European single market and NAFTA [North American Free Trade Area]).

The main argument developed by Doz was that reduction of tariffs and other trade barriers and the emergence of free trade zones in Western Europe during the 1970s provided an opportunity for international businesses to specialize and integrate their European manufacturing plants. Instead of multiproduct–multistage plants autonomously serving national markets, it had become feasible and economic to develop plants that manufacture only one model or one product line, or are involved in only certain stages of the production process for worldwide markets. This represents a shift from local for local plants (local production for local markets) to an integrated network of large-scale production-specialized plants serving world markets. The process of manufacturing rationalization is particularly important for companies with less differentiated (standardized) products; where production costs are high in relation to total costs; where major economies of scale can be derived from plant specialization; and for companies facing strong competition from strong competitor nations.

The above factors were then incorporated by Doz into a framework that helps to (a) diagnose the need for rationalization and (b) to manage the rationalization process itself. This is shown in Table 8.1.

Manufacturing rationalization is most needed in mature industries with significant price competition and where there are unexploited economies of scale (the European automobile industry is given as an example). Even when the benefits of rationalization are diagnosed clearly, there will be major problems in the implementation of rationalization strategies arising

Table 8.1 A framework for managing the rationalization process

Diagnosis	Product/market maturity; price competition; unexploited economies of scale.
Start-up	Product type inventory; co-ordination group; staff experts; co-ordinators.
Changes in the management process	Marketing co-ordination; export co-ordination and sourcing control; logistics; overall market share; production programming; technical co-ordination; funding for R&D and capital expenditure.
Corporate management actions to support rationalization	Communication of purpose; planning integration; changes in measurement, evaluation and reward systems; changes in career paths and management development.
Pitfalls	Lack of perception of new competition; autonomous subsidiary structure favours national responses rather than diagnosis of rationalization need; rationalization may be opposed by national subsidiary managers' diagnosis; too assertive co-ordinator; too little top management support of co-ordinators; co-ordinators subordinate to group of subsidiary managers; too many subsidiaries; joint ventures; wrong timing; inappropriate sequencing; poor choice of co-ordinators; lack of top management visible support; continuation of country-based evaluation and compensation schemes; poor choice of country managers.

Source: Doz (1978)

from the conflict between analytical (i.e., the diagnostic need for rationalization) and behavioural issues. The latter refer to social and political difficulties within the international business which hinder the start of rationalization.

The major pitfalls to rationalization implementation include a lack of perception of the new competitive forces, the search for local solutions by local managers and subsidiary opposition to rationalization. To overcome these difficulties, a number of guidelines are suggested (deriving from examples of successful rationalizations) for managing the rationalization process. These fall into three main groups covering start-up, implementation of changes in the management process and actions by corporate management to support rationalization. To start up the process an initial inventory of redundant product types and plants should be established. The process then shifts to gaining the co-operation of subsidiary managers to rationalization through co-ordination and strategic planning groups to facilitate social interaction. The process overall can be greatly assisted by clear communications from the corporate centre and a clear commitment to the need for rationalization. The process of manufacturing rationalization has accelerated considerably in recent years in response to the pressures of global competition.

Starr's network

Starr (1984) provided an exposition of the strategic considerations important to the development of a successful global production operation. This is defined to include global sourcing, fabrication, assembly, marketing and distribution. A global network model is developed to illustrate the alternative strategies available in this respect. The network shows the various connections (links) between suppliers, fabricators, assemblers and marketers (nodes). In most cases the network will involve complicated arrangements (and various combinations) between domestic and international nodes. According to the author, the choice of network will depend on a cost/benefit analysis of the alternatives. Important issues to consider include the costs of various suppliers, the effects of exchange rate movements, inflation rates in different countries which can affect purchasing as well as production and marketing decisions, the quality of supplies and proximity to markets.

Dicken and international value adding

The view of global production as a network of relationships was developed in more detail by Dicken (1998). Two sets of relationships are explored:

1. the internal network of relationships within the global business;
2. the network of external relationships with independent and quasi-independent businesses (large, small, transnational and domestic).

The basic building block to understand both internal and external networks is the model of the production chain shown in Figure 8.1, where the term 'production' is used in its widest sense to include the provision of services as well as physical production.

This model shows the whole range of activities (value-added activities in Porter's, 1985 terminology) performed within the production system (i.e., a chain of linked functions: see Chapter 3 on the value chain). The way in which the chain of transactions is organized and co-ordinated determines the international business's internal and external network of relationships. At one extreme, the chain of transactions can be performed entirely within the business itself (i.e., internalization). At the other extreme, each function could be the responsibility of individual, independent businesses (i.e., externalization). A wide variety of relationships may exist between these two extremes.

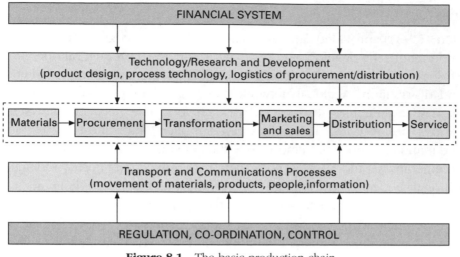

Figure 8.1 The basic production chain
Source: Dicken (1998)

In terms of the transnational business's internal production network, Dicken (1998) drew on Porter's (1986) configuration and co-ordination alternatives (see Chapter 3) to identify the alternatives available. Four main types of internal production strategy are identified, as summarized in Figure 8.2.

Dicken's four production strategies

Globally concentrated production
This is the simplest case, where the business concentrates all production in one central location and supplies world markets through its marketing and sales network. This is consistent with Porter's (1986) purest global strategy of geographically concentrated and highly co-ordinated operations.

Host market production
According to Dicken (1998) this has become a common production strategy among global businesses. It is essentially local production for local markets consistent with Porter's (1986) multidomestic strategy of geographically dispersed and unco-ordinated (autonomous) operations.

Product specialization for a global or regional market
This is a strategy of production as part of a rationalized product or process strategy (i.e., specialization of production in a few plants supplying multi-

(a) Globally concentrated production

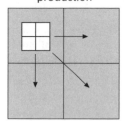

All production occurs at a single location. Products are exported to world markets

(b) Host-market production

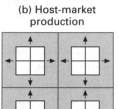

Each production unit produces a range of products and serves the national market in which it is located. No sales across national boundaries. Individual plant size limited by the size of the national market

(c) Product specialization for a global or regional market

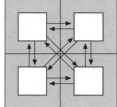

Each production unit produces only one product for sale throughout a regional market of several countries. Individual plant size very large because of scale economies offered by the large regional market

(d) Transnational vertical integration

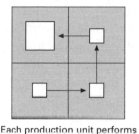

Each production unit performs a separate part of a production sequence. Units are linked across national boundaries in a 'chain like' sequence

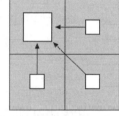

Each production unit performs a separate operation in a production process and ships its output to a final assembly plant in another country

Figure 8.2 Some major ways of organizing the geography of transnational production units
Source: Dicken (1998)

country markets). According to Dicken (1998) this strategy is becoming increasingly popular, especially in large regionally integrated markets, such as the EU.

Transnational vertical integration of production
This is a strategy of specialization by process or by semi-finished products (rather than by final products as in product specialization above) and is consistent with Porter's (1986) strategy of high FDI (foreign direct investment) with extensive co-ordination among subsidiaries. A particularly important aspect of this strategy according to Dicken (1998) is the increasing use of offshore processing as part of a vertically integrated global production network. Two main types of activities are particularly suited to offshore sourcing:

1. products at the mature stage of the product life cycle, in which technology has become standardized, long production runs are needed and semi-skilled or unskilled labour costs are very important;
2. there are certain parts of the production process of newer industries (e.g., electronics) which are labour-intensive and amenable to the employment of semi-skilled and unskilled labour, even though the industry as a whole is capital and technology-intensive.

Selecting the most appropriate strategy

The choice between Dicken's alternatives involves a balance between the economies of scale to be achieved through plant specialization against the extra costs of moving products either between plants or from plants to markets. Other factors requiring consideration are the risks associated with plant specialization, whether local manufacturing is required for product adaptation and government policy regarding investment incentives or disincentives and import regulations. The internal production network is also highly dynamic and subject to rapid change due to both changes in the organization's external environment and internal pressures that may necessitate reorganization and rationalization.

In addition to the internal network discussed above, Dicken (1998) also stressed the importance of external networks. International businesses are often engaged in many external interconnections with other businesses. The linkages can be with domestic companies (large and small) or public and private organizations as shown in Figure 8.3.

Plant location decision making

Decision criteria

For transnational companies that have decided to manufacture abroad through FDI, a complex decision on plant location must be made. Scully and Fawcett (1993), in their study of 103 US companies with international operations, found that the level of formal planning for facility location was greater than that for overall planning, production systems and logistics decisions. They suggested that this may be 'the result of the many mathematical models and software programs which exist to assist in making this decision.'

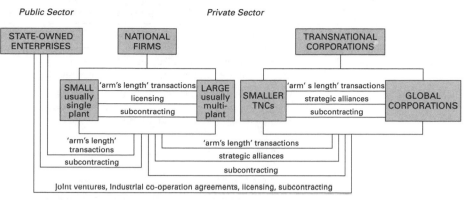

Figure 8.3 Major organization segments within a global economic system
Source: Dicken (1998)

There are a number of factors that have to be taken into consideration in making the location decision. Dunning (1980), as part of his 'eclectic' theory of international production, identified five major location-specific factors derived from FDI considerations:

1. markets – size, growth, type of products/services demanded, degree of competition;
2. resources – availability of raw materials and services, availability of a workforce with appropriate skills (or which is 'trainable'),
3. production costs – labour and productivity, raw materials, transportation, energy, currency exchange;
4. political conditions – attitude of host government to FDI (e.g., restrictions on ownership, tax rates, incentives, trade barriers, government and economic stability [the degree of risk], employment legislation);
5. cultural and linguistic affinities – product attractiveness and other marketing issues, similar ways of doing business, no need to communicate in a different language, attractiveness of host country to parent company nationals.

The perceived relative importance of these factors will not only vary from one industry to another but will also depend on the type of production that the individual business intends to use in the host country. Dunning (1993) described six types of production with the main location-specific advantages for each. These are summarized in Table 8.2.

Table 8.2 Factors affecting location decisions for each type of intentional production

Type of international production	Location advantages sought
Natural resource seeking	Possession of natural resources and related transport and communications infrastructure; tax and other incentives.
Market seeking	Material and labour costs; market size and characteristics; government policy (e.g., with respect to regulations and to import controls, investment incentives, etc.).
Efficiency seeking (a) of product (b) of processes	(a) Economies of product specialization and concentration. (b) Low labour costs; incentives to local production by host governments.
Strategic asset seeking	Any countries from the first three that offer technology, markets and other assets in which the business is deficient.
Trade and distribution (import and export merchanting)	Source of inputs and local markets; need to be near customers; after-sales servicing, etc.
Support services	Availability of markets, particularly those of 'lead' clients.

Source: adapted from Dunning (1993)

The most frequently used criteria

The majority of FDI has been for the first three types of production. Dicken (1998) discussed these in terms of market, supply and cost-oriented production.

Market-oriented production

In the first case, businesses aim to supply an overseas market by locating production within that market, often to circumvent such trade barriers as tariffs and quotas. In simple terms, the major factors to be considered are market size and growth. A crude estimate of these can be made by examining GNP per capita and how it is changing. In these terms, the USA and Western Europe are the most attractive markets. However, the picture is more complex – the type of products demanded vary with GNP per capita, with poorer countries requiring more basic goods while richer countries spend more income on 'higher order' goods and services.

Supply-oriented production

Supply-oriented production is the dominant form of production for businesses dependent on natural resources for their output, such as those in the extractive industries. However, Dicken (1998) argued that only some of the operations of such companies may be located at the source of supply; for example, some oil companies transport crude oil relatively long distances to refineries located in countries considered to be more attractive for such investment.

Cost-oriented production

Cost-oriented production has accounted for many of the global shifts in production in the last 30 years, away from the developed to the less developed countries whose labour costs were much lower. For manufacturing industries where labour inputs are a relatively high proportion of costs, there are major potential savings by locating production in low-wage areas. Dicken (1998) compared the changes in patterns of production of the textiles and clothing industries. In both cases there was been a decline in production in the industrialized countries and a growth in production in the developing countries. The shift, however, was more marked for clothing manufacture where automation has been less successful in replacing manual labour. Although variations in labour costs are well documented it is also necessary to consider variations in productivity levels, workforce adaptability and workforce 'manageability' between different countries.

Dornier et al. (1998) questioned both market and cost orientation as viable long-term reasons for locating overseas. They found that the notional advantages of proximity to market are often offset by government restrictions on domestic content, technology transfer and domestic ownership which can severely limit the control that the parent has over its subsidiary. Furthermore, wage rates change as today's newly developing countries become tomorrow's industrialized nations. In addition, the recent collapse of Far Eastern economies has created major uncertainties on future exchange rates and government policies toward FDI. Dornier et al. (1998) argued that the key to successful location overseas is a commitment to strategic planning. Once FDI has been made, the development of the facility must be guided by strategic, rather than operational thinking.

The location decision

The way in which the decision is made depends on many company-related factors, such as experience in FDI, type of production, inter-plant relationships and type of product. Many production and operations management textbooks describe analytical methods of determining optimal locations for new investment. Most of these involve the calculation of tangible costs and returns followed by a factoring in of other intangible variables through some kind of weighting. Such approaches are probably more suited to cost-oriented production than market-oriented production. One approach is to use a hierarchical screening of options, beginning with continent followed by country then actual site.

Choice of continent

For a business with a wide spread of international manufacturing plants, the choice of continent may be a significant one, as the company may have to decide between competing proposals from subsidiaries in various parts of the world. In such a case, the company should be able to compare the expected costs, returns and risks of the alternative proposals. In cases where the company has a narrow spread of international investment, some form of broad screening will be required based on the type of production required.

Choice of country

Unless the business is present in a large number of countries already, it will probably limit consideration to a few obvious candidates that either have an attractive market or offer low-cost manufacturing. However, in a major trading bloc such as the EU, a much more detailed country by country comparison may be made, particularly if different incentives are offered by host governments.

Choice of site

A much more detailed investigation is required to examine such factors as labour availability, transport infrastructure, regional incentives, other related industries and general attractiveness of the area. The analytical methods mentioned earlier may be used to rank the shortlist. Large businesses investing in the EU are likely to have a shortlist of 2–3 sites in different countries with the final decision coming down to the most attractive financial package being offered by the host government.

Procurement and transnational business

Procurement policy

Procurement policies are closely linked to the plant roles and inter-plant relationships discussed earlier in the chapter. The policies are linked to the

Table 8.3 Benefits obtained from international sourcing.
Rating is on a seven-point Likert scale with 7 = greatest benefit

Rank	Benefits from international sourcing	Rating
1	Access to lower priced goods	5.56
2	Enhanced competitive position	5.29
3	Access to higher quality goods	4.89
4	Access to worldwide technology	4.49
5	Better delivery performance	3.48
6	Better customer service	3.38
7	Increased number of suppliers	2.76
8	Helps meet countertrade obligations	2.60

Source: Birou and Fawcett (1993)

overall global strategy of the business, and the issues affecting procurement
can be discussed in terms of a number of variables:

- in-house manufacturing versus external purchasing/subcontracting;
- corporate versus third party suppliers;
- domestic versus other country purchasing;
- single versus multiple sourcing.

Birou and Fawcett (1993) in a survey of US companies identified a range of
perceived benefits of international sourcing (Table 8.3).

Types of purchasing policy

Broadly speaking, three types of purchasing policy are possible: central
purchasing, autonomous procurement and a mixture of these two
extremes.

Central purchasing

In the most extreme case, a single part of the corporation is responsible for
carrying out all purchasing for all parts of the company with the objective of
gaining economies of scale and uniformity of quality. Purchasing is carried
out on a global basis and is mainly of standard products, such as electronic
components. Subsidiaries are then required to buy from (usually through a
quasi-market or transfer-pricing arrangement) the central purchasing organization. In less extreme cases, groups of plants located in a particular region
may set up their own regional purchasing organizations.

Autonomous purchasing

Individual plants are responsible for their own procurement. This may be forced on the business because of government policies on local sourcing or it may be part of a corporate country-centred policy. The plant will still have to ensure that vendors meet the company's agreed standards of quality, cost and delivery, particularly in cases of transnational vertical integration.

In many cases a mixture of the two extremes is used with central purchasing for standard components and local procurement for more specialized components.

Global logistics

The 'flow' of materials

'Logistics' is defined (Slack et al., 1998) as activities concerned with the flow of material from supplier to production and from production to the customer. The meaning has extended, however, to include reverse flows of material (e.g., returned or faulty goods, packaging, etc.) and flows of information. This wider definition reflects the greater emphasis on logistics as part of the overall global strategy of a business. This view of logistics as linking the operations of the business is summarized in Figure 8.4.

Logistics is thus the means through which the competitive advantage sought by globalized business will be realized. Conversely, weaknesses in logistics may undermine that competitive advantage through the creation of 'blockages' in the organization's primary value-adding activities (Porter, 1985 – see our discussion on this in Chapter 3).

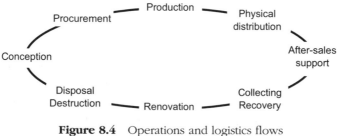

Figure 8.4   Operations and logistics flows
Source: Dornier et al. (1998)

Logistics and strategy

The type of global production strategy adopted will have important implications for logistics management. Decisions will be made concerning both internal logistics (i.e., the flow of intermediary products, parts and components between subsidiaries) and external logistics (i.e., the flow of final goods from producer to end-user).

In transnationals adopting country-centred or multi-domestic strategies, logistics management will be concerned mainly with distribution within countries since production is located in the markets being served. Companies adopting 'purest' global and export-based strategies, on the other hand, will be concerned more with international (cross-border) logistics, given that dispersed foreign markets are supplied through centralized production facilities. The most complicated arrangement arises in companies adopting strategies of high FDI with extensive co-ordination among subsidiaries. In addition to within-country and cross-border product flows, this involves the global co-ordination and integration of worldwide production and distribution into a global logistics network.

Scully and Fawcett (1993) analysed the comparative costs of production and logistics in different regions of the world for a number of US companies. They noted that, while management time tends to be concentrated on seeking production locations that offer cost advantage, there is relatively little time spent on the co-ordination of the organization's dispersed productive operations. They also found that some areas that offered very advantageous production costs also suffered from comparatively high logistics costs. The reasons for this are that areas that offer lower labour costs tend to have less well-developed infrastructures and management practices.

Scully and Fawcett also showed that, for US-based companies, any move out of the USA resulted in higher logistics costs. This can be explained by considering that over 90% of logistics costs come from documentation, stock and transport costs. Documentation costs, despite attempts to reduce them within trading blocs such as the EU and NAFTA, are invariably higher than when all operations take place in a single country. Stock costs rise because companies tend to carry more stock when distribution lines are lengthened in order to guard against delays and stock-outs. Finally, longer distances raise transport costs.

A further study by Ghosh and Cooper (1997) of the impact of NAFTA on US companies showed that, while logistics in Mexico were expected to improve as a result of NAFTA, customs inefficiencies, poor transport infrastructure and different management practices were still likely to be a significant barrier to increased trade between the USA and Mexico.

Managing logistics

The complexity of managing logistics for organizations with global operations can be immense and the potential for problems correspondingly large. Companies have identified a number of techniques to manage and reduce logistics lead times. Fawcett (1992) listed a number of examples including:

- developing partnership relationships with providers of transportation services;
- developing partnership relationships with domestic and foreign suppliers of sourced components;
- reliance on third-party transportation companies;
- use of advanced information systems such as EDI to track and/or expedite shipments.

The emphasis on partnerships and alliances, a growing feature of global business, is discussed further in Chapter 14, and the use of information systems to co-ordinate activities is discussed in Chapter 10.

Discussion and review questions

1. What are the critical success factors that enable production strategy to contribute to competitive advantage?
2. Explain how the three types of materials sourcing can help a business's strategy.
3. What features of a business's strategy would influence the choice between Dicken's four production strategies?
4. Explain the key decision criteria when deciding on plant location.
5. Define and distinguish between central and autonomous purchasing.
6. Define and distinguish between internal and external logistics.

References and further reading

Agodo, O. (1978) 'The determinants of US private manufacturing investments in Africa'. *Journal of International Business Studies*, Winter, 95–107.

Birou, L. M. and Fawcett, S. E. (1993) 'International purchasing: Benefits, requirements and challenges'. *International Journal of Operations and Production Management*, **29**(2), 27–37.

Channon, D.F. and Jalland, M. (1978) *Multinational Strategic Planning*. New York: AMACOM.

Dicken, P. (1998) *Global Shift – Transforming the World Economy*. London: Paul Chapman.

Dornier, P., Ernst, R., Fender, M. and Kouvelis, P. (1998) *Global Operations and Logistics*. New York: John Wiley & Sons.

Doz, Y.L. (1978) 'Managing manufacturing rationalisation within multinational companies'. *Columbia Journal of World Business*, **13**(3), Fall.

Doz, Y. (1986) *Strategic Management in Multinational Companies*. New York: Pergamon Press.

Dubin, M. (1975) 'Foreign acquisitions and the growth of the multinational firm'. Doctoral thesis, Harvard Business School, Cambridge, MA.

Dunning, J.H. (1973) 'The determinants of international production'. *Oxford Economic Papers*, **25**(3), 289–336.

Dunning, J.H. (1980) 'Towards an eclectic theory of international production: Some empirical tests'. *Journal of International Business Studies*, **11**, 9–31.

Dunning, J.H. (1986) *Japanese Participation in British Industry*. London: Croom Helm.

Dunning, J.H. (1993) *Multinational Enterprises and the Global Economy*. Reading, MA: Addison-Wesley.

Economist (1985) 'The Hanson Trust: Low Tech, High Profit', 20 April.

Fawcett, S. (1992) 'Strategic logistics in co-ordinated global manufacturing success'. *International Journal of Production Research*, **30**(4), 1081–1099.

Ghosh, A. and Cooper, M. (1997) 'Manager's perceptions of NAFTA'. *The International Journal of Logistics Management*, **8**(2), 33–45.

Goldar, J.D. and Jelinek, M. (1983) 'Plan for economies of scope'. *Harvard Business Review*, November/December, 141–148.

Graham, E.M. (1978) 'Transatlantic investment by multinational firms: A rivalistic phenomenon'. *Journal of Post-Keynesian Economics*, **1**(1), 82–98.

Groo, E.S. (1972) 'Choosing foreign locations: One company's experience'. *Columbia Journal of World Business*, September/October.

Guisinger, S.E. and Associates (1985) 'Investment incentives and performance requirements, patterns of international trade'. *Production and Investment*. Westport, CT: Praeger.

Hamill, J. (1988) 'British acquisitions in the US'. *National Westminster Bank Quarterly Review*, August.

Hood, N. and Young, S. (1981) *The R and D Activities of US Multinational Enterprises: A Review of the Literature* (Report to the Department of Industry). London: Department of Industry.

Hood, N. and Young, S. (1982) *Multinationals in Retreat: The Scottish Experience*. Edinburgh University Press.

Hood, N. and Young, S. (1983) *Multinational Investment Strategies in the British Isles*. London: HMSO.

Keegan, W. J. (1995) *Global Marketing Management* (5th edn). Englewood Cliffs, NJ: Prentice Hall.

Kitching, J. (1974) 'Winning and losing with European acquisitions'. *Harvard Business Review*, March/April.

Knickerbocker, F.T. (1973) *Oligopolistic Reaction and the Multinational Enterprise*. Cambridge, MA: Harvard Business School.

Malecki, E.J. (1980) 'Corporate organization of R and D and the location of technological activities'. *Regional Studies*, **14**, 219–234.

Mansfield, E. (1978) *Studies of the Relationship between International Technology Transfer and R and D Expenditure by US Firms* (Report). Arlington, VA: National Science Foundation.

Merritt, G. (1985) 'How Europe's governments are "aiding" the multinationals'. *Multinational Info*, February, 6–8.

Nigh, D. (1986) 'Political events and the foreign direct investment decision: An empirical examination'. *Managerial and Decision Economics*, **7**(2).

OECD (1980) *Impact of Multinational Enterprises on National Scientific and Technological Capacities: Analytical Report.* Paris: Organization for Economic Co-operation and Development.

OECD (1981) *Relationships of Incentives and Disincentives to International Investment Decisions.* Paris: Organization for Economic Co-operation and Development.

Porter, M.E. (1985) *Competitive Advantage.* New York: Free Press.

Porter, M.E. (1986) *Competition in Global Industries.* Boston: Harvard Business School Press.

Ricks, D.A. and Ajami, R.A. (1981) 'Motives of non-American firms investing in the United States'. *Journal of International Business Studies*, Winter, 25–34.

Ronstadt, R. (1977) *Research and Development Abroad by US Multinationals.* Westport, CT: Praeger.

Rugman, A.M., Lecraw, D.J. and Booth, L.D. (1985) *International Business, Firm and Environment.* New York: McGraw-Hill.

Scully, J. and Fawcett, S. (1993) 'Comparative logistics and production costs for global manufacturing strategy'. *International Journal of Operations and Production Management*, **13**(12), 62–78.

Slack, N., Chambers, S., Harland, C., Harrison, A. and Johnston, R. (1998) *Operations Management* (2nd edn). London: Pitman.

Starr, M.K. (1984) 'Global production and operations strategy'. *Columbia Journal of World Business*, **18**(4), Winter.

PART IV

GLOBAL LEADERSHIP AND STRATEGIC HUMAN RESOURCE MANAGEMENT

Learning objectives

After studying this chapter students should be able to:

- understand the nature of, and relationships between, leadership and management;
- recognize the issues involved in transnational leadership;
- understand the need for, and basis of, a strategic approach to human resource management (HRM);
- understand the benefits of global approach to HRM;
- identify and evaluate strategies for managing in culturally diverse transnational organizations;
- identify the link between the transnational company's value system and global strategy, and its human resource strategy.

Introduction

Human resources play a central role in determining the success of global and transnational strategy. Human resources are of singular importance because they:

- provide the leadership and management of the organization;
- play a unique part in organizational learning and competence building;
- pose particular questions in a global context, in terms of their management;
- are crucial in converting strategies into action.

Heijltjes et al. (1996) stated that, 'Human resource management (HRM) carries the promise that, if people are regarded and managed as strategic resources, it can help the firm to obtain a competitive advantage and superior performance.'

The implementation of effective leadership and management strategies within transnational business is complicated by variations in culture, value systems, language, business environment and industrial relations systems between countries. Cultural diversity and national physioeconomic differences, while presenting unquestionable challenges, also give rise to significant capability in terms of creativity, skills, aptitudes and resources. In approaching transnational human resource strategy, consideration must be given to:

- the means by which the human resource strategy is determined and the extent to which it is integrated with global and transnational strategy;
- leadership and management issues in culturally diverse and geographically dispersed organizations.

These issues are discussed in this chapter.

Leadership and management in transnationals

Definitions

Leadership and management are two distinct but related sets of behaviours and activities. The growth of globalization and the accelerating rate of change in the business environment have led to an increasing focus on the role and importance of leaders and leadership in organizations. Management is primarily concerned with planning, organizing, directing, budgeting, maintaining stability and controlling. Management activities are closely integrated into the structure and systems of the organization and are centred on its effective and efficient operation. Leadership, on the other hand, centres on the strategic development and transformation of the organization. In other words, leadership looks toward the future, creates a vision and seeks to move people and the organization toward it. Leadership involves developing a vision and strategic intent for the organization, creating shared values, developing people and the organization, creating change, and moving the organization toward the aspirations encapsulated in the vision statement. Despite these distinctions between management and leadership, leaders are often required to manage and managers to lead.

The need for leadership has emerged because the paradigm within which business operates has been transformed from an industrial age to the era of knowledge-based business. The industrial age emphasized manufacturing and production in a comparatively stable environment, characterized by competition and management control. The new era of knowledge-based business is exemplified by complexity, diversity and change, requiring continuous learning and innovation, based on people, empowerment and customer service.

The nature of leadership

There are many definitions of leadership, but in essence it is the ability of one person to influence the behaviour and actions of other people toward achieving the goals of an organization. There are also several theories that seek to explain the nature of leadership:

- *qualities or traits theories* – conceptualize leadership in terms of the traits that leaders possess;
- *functional or group theories* – consider leadership in terms of the functions that leaders carry out;
- *behavioural theories* – categorize leadership in terms of the behaviours of leaders;
- *style theories* – examine the nature of the approach adopted by leaders to their role;
- *situational approach and contingency models* – explore leadership in terms of the organizational and environmental context in which it takes place;
- *transitional or transformational theories* – examine the impact of leadership on the development of the organization.

None of these theoretical models excludes the others. In fact, they simply represent different, but equally valuable insights into the nature of leadership. It is important to consider two recent, related trends that have led to a rethinking of approaches to leadership. First, the importance of vision the leadership has gained, increasing recognition. Competitive advantage depends on the creation of new and distinctive knowledge based on a unique, demanding but achievable vision. Second, the importance of informal leadership behaviours has been recognized. In the past, leaders were considered as few in number, concerned with goal setting, directing, supervising, controlling, resolving conflicts and developing managers. Today, it is recognized that leadership is required at all levels of the organization and that they must provide vision, leading to the development of new and distinctive knowledge-based competences, which deliver competitive advantage because the people within the organization are empowered, through flatter organizational structures, to deliver customer-focused services. Leadership is concerned with the mentoring, motivation and development of subordinates, the sharing of knowledge, and the development of learning organizations that create and manage knowledge more effectively than their competitors. Leaders are, therefore, change agents who transform organizations and develop future leaders through coaching and knowledge sharing.

Leaders are not 'born', nor is there a single set of characteristics or behaviours which characterize 'good' leaders. Consider the differences in personality and behaviour between successful leaders like Bill Gates (Microsoft), Jack Welch (GE), Anita Roddick (Body Shop) and Richard Branson (Virgin). Whereas Bill Gates would characterize himself as something of a computer 'nerd', the success of his leadership is comparable with, and even surpasses that of, more flamboyant characters like Welch and Branson who might well be conceived as more typical leadership types. Leadership can be developed and will involve:

- the ability to develop an innovative and distinctive vision for the future;
- the capability to learn and develop new knowledge-based competences;
- risk taking based on judgement informed through knowledge;
- the ability to develop, empower and motivate others by communicating the vision to others;
- the capacity to combine task orientation (concern with the objectives of the organization) with people orientation (concern for the development and motivation of people);
- the development of a culture and shared values which support the leader's vision and encourage trust and sharing, risk taking, and team working.

Senge (1990) argued that leaders in a learning organization must be:

- *designers* – designing the vision, strategies, policies and structures of the organization;
- *teachers* – facilitating learning so people take a new view of reality;
- *stewards* – developing people and the organization.

GE – the new leadership paradigm

A good example of the new requirements of leadership is provided by the defence and electronics group, General Electric (GE). GE is a large, diversified transnational organization facing hypercompetitive and rapidly changing environments in all its spheres of operation. Yet, in every market in which it competes it has successfully developed and maintained a position in the top three providers and producers. While the traditional paradigm of leadership regards the CEO as the strategic leader, developing vision and strategy, and the remainder of people as doers and implementers, the approach in GE represents the new paradigm of leadership within which there are many leaders within the organization. The new paradigm presents leadership as spread throughout the organization and based on delegation, sharing, collaboration and teamwork.

The dilemma for leadership in a huge, diversified transnational like GE is combining the management necessary for control and integration with the leadership and entrepreneurship necessary for change and innovation. GE has attempted to resolve this dilemma through the creation of strategic business units (SBUs) that are long term-focused, customer-oriented and that have considerable autonomy in terms of decentralized decision making.

When Jack Welch became CEO of GE in 1981 there began an era which tried to build visionary leadership throughout the organization. Welch aimed to be a visionary, setting a clear challenging vision for the whole organization, and, coupled to this, a communicator and organizer, providing strategic thinking rather than strategic planning. Managers at lower levels throughout the organization were empowered to become entrepreneurial leaders, not bureaucrats. Welch set long-term goals for all the business units which were benchmarked to be stretching, but achievable. The emphasis was on achieving long term rather than short-term goals, through the strategic thinking and innovation of managers within the SBUs.

Leadership and cultural issues

The new leadership paradigm, which has gained widespread acceptance in Western developed economies, must be considered alongside differing national cultural characteristics. The new paradigm encapsulates a style of leadership which involves participation, consultation, mentoring and coaching, sharing of knowledge, and empowerment of individuals and groups to question ways of working and take the initiative in decision making. Such values and behaviours, however, conflict with those found in certain national cultures. For example, in many Asian cultures, respect for authority is paramount and the questioning of leadership decisions is unacceptable. Similarly, subordinates expect senior managers to make decisions with which they will comply. Attempts to consult and empower workers in such circumstances may give rise to difficulties that are rooted in national culture. Similarly, Schneider and Barsoux (2003) pointed out the conflict between Western approaches to leadership and the expectations of Russian managers for tough directive leadership, obedience of rules and compliance with job descriptions.

There is strong evidence that many organizations succeed with modes of leadership which differ from the new Western paradigm. This may be because the alternative paradigms that they adopt are more resonant with the national culture within which they are found. Equally, culture is not a static phenomenon. It evolves over time, so that leadership styles are likely to evolve in a similar manner and pattern to national culture. The message is simply that leaders in transnational organizations must be sensitive to cultural differences and may need to adapt leadership styles in different cultural settings.

Body Shop: embracing a new management 'ethos'

The case of changing leadership at Body Shop provides an example of how different management styles are sometimes appropriate at different points in an organization's development. Anita Roddick's leadership in the earlier years of the company's history included a pledge to 'campaign passionately' for the social and environmental priorities she believed in. A later change in management, however, led to the adoption of a new management ethos that embraces greater financial accountability and responsibility, instilling in its staff a strong financial performance ethic, previously given less emphasis under the leadership of the Roddicks.

Founded in Brighton in 1976 by Anita Roddick, the single store operation went on to become an international organization operating in 50 countries with almost 1,700 outlets. Mrs Roddick stepped down as chief executive in 1998 after Body Shop's financial performance slid and subsequently resigned as co-chairman in February 2002 to focus on her campaign work. She was succeeded by a new management team consisting of Peter Saunders as CEO, while Peter Ridler joined as managing director for the UK and Ireland, having held a similar role at stationery group Staples.

The revamp has included a marketing shake-up, reorganization of the supply chain and development of new products particularly in the popular Body Butter range. From the outset, Saunders was prepared to tackle some of the key themes that had made Body Shop successful in the past. In denouncing the chain's signature decor, he said that, 'the traditional Body Shop green box is tired.' The company began its journey on the road of better performance based on 'better execution and operations'. The company improved its stock control and cash flow through more efficient processes and through the installation of new computer systems in its UK business. Saunders said that these changes enabled the company to have a more effective customer service while focusing on better and more professional execution.

The move from the entrepreneurial leadership of Mrs Roddick to the more business-focused leadership of Mr Saunders appeared to pay off. The moves saw pre-tax profits surge 76% to £20.4 million for the year ending 2003, despite a drop of 1% in like for like sales. Retail analyst Richard Ratner of analysts Seymour Pierce said, 'the new management team are very good, very strategic and know exactly what has to be done and they are doing it.'

Leading and managing cultural diversity in transnational organizations

Cultural differences clearly exist at a number of levels – national, regional, industrial, organizational, etc. – and they exist within organizations. In fact, departments within the same organization may also develop distinctive subcultures. The nature of transnational business is that activities will span national boundaries and national cultural differences. Such cultural differences will pose challenges to leaders and managers, but, equally, cultural diversity can offer opportunities in terms of complementary competences and alternative approaches to business.

Tayeb (2000), drawing on the work of Perlmutter (1969), identified three alternative approaches to cultural differences available to transnational managers for dealing with cultural differences:

1. an *ethnocentric* policy – this implies imposing the culture and practices of the home country and parent organization on all its overseas subsidiaries, ignoring local cultural differences;
2. a *polycentric* policy – this implies following the culture and practices of each host country and adapting completely to local conditions (this is a multinational or multidomestic approach);
3. a *global* policy – this involves devising a global company-wide policy to shape global organizational culture, which will combine different cultural approaches.

We suggest, however, that a fourth option exists which combines an overall global approach with some local adaptations:

4. a *transnational* or *hybrid* policy – this incorporates both global integration of culture, to produce worldwide norms to guide activity toward a common set of goals, and differentiation of culture, to allow it to be adapted where necessary to local differences (Bartlett and Ghoshal, 1989; Prahalad and Doz, 1986). The optimum combination of integration and differentiation of culture and practices will vary from company to company depending on their individual circumstances.

Shaping culture in transnational organizations

Leaders will inevitably wish to create a coherent culture within their organization. The intangibility of culture makes it extremely difficult to shape and change. Successful cultural change involves the learning of new values, attitudes and behaviours within the organization which will entail:

- determining the desired values, attitudes, norms and behaviours which are to form the new organizational culture;

- unfreezing the existing culture to make members of the organization receptive to change;
- building the new culture;
- refreezing the new culture once the desired change has been achieved.

Leaders can seek to promote desired cultural change through:

- a vision that is communicated throughout the organization;
- education and training to foster organizational learning;
- new organizational and power structures which support devolved decision making;
- new reward systems that promote the behaviours desired within the organization;
- creating new stories, myths and symbols which emphasize desired values and actions.

Strategic human resource management

The importance of human resources

Probably the single most important determinant of the success of global strategy is the leadership and management of a transnational's human resources. HRM, according to Beer et al. (1984), 'involves all management decisions and actions that affect the nature of the relationship between the organisation and its employees – its human resources.' People have a crucial role to play in devising and implementing strategy, in strategic decision making and in making strategy successful. Strategic HRM has been defined as: 'a strategic and coherent approach to the management of an organisation's most valued assets: the people working there who individually and collectively contribute to the achievement of its objectives for sustainable competitive advantage.' (Armstrong, 1992). Strategic HRM is therefore concerned with making the most effective use of people in determining and operationalizing strategy. It is important to note that leadership, as distinct from management, is just as critical an issue in relation to transnational HRM.

It is also concerned with ensuring that HR strategy is fully congruent with corporate strategy. When the business is globalized, the importance of arriving at an appropriate HR strategy is very great. Global and transnational HR strategy is not only more complex but it offers more strategic alternatives. Human resources are central to achieving global competitive advantage, so they must be managed strategically by ensuring that an organization has an HRM strategy that is fully integrated with its global and transnational strategy. Walker (1992) made the following case for adopting a strategic approach to HR management:

1. it defines the opportunities for and barriers to achievement of business objectives;
2. it prompts new thinking about issues, orientates and educates participants, and provides a wider perspective;
3. it tests management commitment for actions and creates a process for allocating resources to specific programmes and activities;
4. it develops a sense of urgency and commitment to action;
5. it establishes selected long-term courses of action considered high priority over the next two to three years;
6. it provides a strategic focus for managing the business and developing management talents.

Features of HR strategy

Anthony et al. (1993) listed six key features of an HR strategy:

1. *recognition of the impact of the external environment* – need to take advantage of opportunities and to minimize the effects of threats;
2. *recognition of the impact of competition and the dynamics of the labour market* – organizations compete for employees and must recognise the forces affecting local, regional and national labour markets (labour market dynamics of wage rates, unemployment levels, working conditions, minimum wage legislation, benefit level, competitor reputation all affect or are affected by strategic HR decisions);
3. *long-range focus* – a time frame of three to five years is normal;
4. *choice and decision-making focus* – strategy implies choosing between alternatives and making major decisions about HR which commit the organization's resources toward a particular direction;
5. *consideration of all personnel* – the value of all employees from top level management to unskilled workers is seen as being important;
6. *integration with corporate strategy and functional strategies* – HR

strategy must be fully integrated with both corporate strategy and the strategies of the other functional areas of the business.

As well as these general characteristics of a strategic approach to HR, it is important to consider the impact of core competence and generic strategy on the organization's HR strategy.

HR strategy, core competences and organizational learning

Globalization, turbulence and hypercompetition in markets demand increased organizational flexibility and accelerated organizational learning. In addition, a customer focus is also an essential element of sustained competitive advantage. These twin needs for responsiveness and customer orientation have profound implications for global strategic HRM.

We learned in Chapter 6 that a global business can adopt a competence-based approach to strategic management. This, in turn, implies the adoption of an open systems perspective to human resources which looks across and beyond organizational boundaries. Furthermore, the development of core competences is often based on organizational learning and knowledge building. Organizational learning and knowledge building are based on individual knowledge and learning, which is stored and shared.

The importance of human beings in the development of both individual and organizational knowledge is as evident as it is paramount. Strategic HRM, therefore, has a pivotal role to play in knowledge management and development, and in competence building. Hagan (1996) argued that a competence-based HR strategy 'will demand major changes in the way we organise, the way we structure work, the importance we place on learning and innovation, and the way we approach the management of our employees.' Hagan proposed 12 hypotheses believed to govern a competence based approach to strategic HRM (see Table 9.1).

Integration of HRM with corporate strategy and functional strategies

The importance of congruence
A common assumption made in American models of HRM is that the corporate strategy of an organization drives its functional strategies. In other words, an organization determines its overall strategy and then sets functional strategies in order to implement it. However, the functional

Table 9.1   Strategic human resource management – implications of a core competence approach

Job design	1.	Greater technical knowledge will be required for individual jobs. Project teams and rotation of jobs will be used to foster the sharing of knowledge.
	2.	Jobs will increasingly combine thinking and doing.
Staffing issues	3.	Most challenging positions will be filled by internal transfers. Externally hired employees will be mainly at entry level.
	4.	Businesses will enter relationships with educational institutions to obtain suitably qualified employees.
	5.	Personality and attitudinal tests will be used to assess the potential of individuals.
Training and development	6.	Investment in training and development programmes will increase to facilitate personal and organizational development.
	7.	Training and development of personnel will increasingly be decentralized to operating departments.
	8.	Training and development will move away from traditional skills building to development.
	9.	Performance review will be used to assess the contribution of employees rather than to determine pay. This will be based on feedback from peers and customers rather than supervisors and subordinates.
Rewards systems	10.	A greater proportion of pay will be based on group or organizational outcomes.
	11.	Traditional hierarchical pay plans will be replaced by broader banding of jobs. Job evaluation will shift from a quantitative to a qualitative focus.
	12.	Compensation systems will become flexible.

Adapted from Hagan (1996)

strategies can also impact on corporate strategy in that senior management must consider existing functional strategies when setting corporate strategy. For example, current HR strategy and capabilities will be important considerations when developing the corporate strategy of a transnational business. Brewster (1994) suggested that, 'the development of strategy is in fact a complex, iterative and incremental process, so that it is difficult to define a point at which the corporate strategy can be finalised sufficiently to allow the HRM strategy to be created.'

Accordingly, human resource must be acutely aware of overall corporate strategy and how HR strategy aligns with it. Furthermore, they must be aware of functional strategies and endeavour to integrate HR strategy with them. In aiming to integrate HR strategies with business strategies, the HR strategy can be modelled on the business strategy and can use it

Table 9.2 Human resource implications of business strategy

Business strategy questions	Human resource implications
What industry and markets are we in?	What people do we need?
Are organizational culture, structure and value systems appropriate or inappropriate?	How do we change them?
Strategic direction	Who will we need in the future?
New businesses and new markets	What systems and procedures might be developed?
Strengths, weaknesses, opportunities, threats	To what extent are they related to existing use of human resources? Demand and supply in the labour market?
Critical success factors	To what extent do these depend on employees rather than other factors?

Table 9.3 Examples of organizational strategies and associated human resource strategies

Corporate strategy (strategic direction)	Example company	Human resource strategies
Retrenchment (cost reduction)	General Motors	Layoffs, wage reduction, productivity increases, job redesign, re-negotiated labour agreements
Growth	Intel	Aggressive recruiting and hiring, rapidly rising wages, job creation, expanding training and development
Renewal	Chrysler	Managed turnover, selective layoff, organizational development, transfer/replacement productivity increases, employee involvement.
Niche focus	Kentucky Fried Chicken	Specialized job creation, elimination of other jobs, specialized training and development.
Acquisition	General Electric	Selective layoffs, transfers/placement, job combinations, orientation and training, managing cultural transitions

Source: Anthony et al. (1993)

as a starting point. Table 9.2 illustrates some of the possible relationships, and Table 9.3 gives some examples of organizational and HR strategies.

Problems of integrating HRM with global and transnational strategies
A number of problems are commonly encountered when attempting to integrate HR strategy with transnational strategy:

1. An organization will have a number of business strategies, especially if it operates in a variety of product markets. Therefore, different

approaches to HR might be needed for each. This is particularly true of global and transnational businesses.

2. If business strategy changes, it might be difficult to change HR strategy because it involves the internal structure and culture of the organization. Softer features of organizations like culture are notoriously difficult to change to a desired state.

3. HRM is often qualitative, meaning that it is not easy to prove the relationship between HRM and the performance of the organization.

4. HRM is often long term and large scale but can easily be subverted. For example, a change in culture can be undermined by quick fix management decisions or by a management that only pays lip service to change.

Criticisms of the concept of strategic HRM

The concept of HRM and the strategic approach originated in the USA, but there has been criticism of the view that American models of HRM can be applied universally, particularly in European literature on the subject. Some of the main criticisms of the American concept are that it:

- lacks clarity and precision;
- is too prescriptive and normative;
- lacks supporting empirical evidence;
- is difficult to distinguish from traditional personnel management;
- is too derivative in its approach to HRM strategy, which is seen as being driven by corporate strategy, rather than contributing to it;
- is overly prescriptive with regard to industrial relations history and practice in Europe (and perhaps in other continents as well).

European and American approaches to HRM

Two common elements of American models of HRM are the ideas of:

- organizational independence and autonomy; and
- the integration of HRM and business strategy.

A survey of HRM policy and practice in Europe (Brewster and Hegewisch,

1994) found important differences between the USA and Europe in respect of these two elements.

(1) Organizational autonomy is more restricted in Europe because of:
- *Culture and legislation* – US culture is more individualistic and achievement-oriented. HRM in Europe is influenced and determined to a greater degree by state regulations.
- *Patterns of ownership* in the private sector vary between Europe and the USA. For example, in Germany a network of a small number of large banks owns most of the major companies. Public ownership is more extensive in Europe.
- *Trade unions and workforce communication* – Europe is more heavily unionized and union influence is still strong (in most European countries more than 70% of employers recognize trade unions for the purpose of collective bargaining).
- *The controlled labour market* – In Europe, higher levels of state support in the external labour market enable European organizations to develop both internal and external labour market strategies with a lower degree of risk (although employers are also faced with restrictions in recruitment methods, for example).

(2) HRM and business strategy
Brewster and Hegewisch (1994) argued that there is little evidence of the integration of HRM and business strategy in the USA, but there appears to be a higher degree of integration of HRM at the top levels of organizations in Europe.

A transnational model of HRM

Brewster (1994) proposed 'a model of HRM which places HR strategies firmly within, though not entirely absorbed by, the business strategy.' The model (Figure 9.1) shows that the business strategy, HR strategy and HR practice are all affected by, and interact with, an external environment of national culture, legislation, patterns of ownership, employee representation, education, etc.

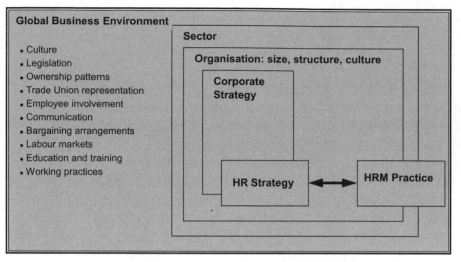

Figure 9.1 A transnational model of HRM
Adapted from Brewster (1994)

Porter's global strategy and HR strategy

Congruence between HR and corporate strategy

Several references have already been made in this chapter to the link between the global and transnational strategy of a company and its HR strategy. Porter's global strategy model can be employed to indicate various aspects of a transnational's HR strategy (Figure 9.2).

According to Porter, there are two key dimensions to a global as opposed to a domestic strategy: configuration and co-ordination. The former refers to the location of activities, the latter to the extent of co-ordination between locations. The combination of configuration and co-ordination options gives rise to Porter's four categories of international strategy (see Figure 9.2).

HRM problems will vary with the type of international strategy adopted. Thus, in country-centred businesses, the need for national responsiveness is more important than global co-ordination and direction. This implies a predominance of host country nationals in key management positions at subsidiary level and only limited cross-national transfers of personnel. Thus, country-centred businesses may have little need for well-defined expatriate or international management development policies. The need for national responsiveness also implies that industrial relations decision making will be decentralized at subsidiary level and that subsidiary indus-

High co-ordination strategies Low local responsiveness	Dispersed activities/high degree of co-ordination	Purest global strategy (with extensive co-ordination and concentration)
	HR strategy requiring high degree of co-ordination: • may necessitate the employment of home country nationals at subsidiary level; • significant cross-national exchange of personnel; • effective expatriate policies needed to ensure smooth exchange of staff; • a pool of internationally experienced executives; • extensive international management development programme; • labour problems at one location must not affect operations elsewhere; • standardization of employee benefits between subsidiaries is necessary; • significant transfer of parent country industrial relations practices to subsidiaries.	
Low co-ordination strategies High local responsiveness	Country-centred strategy Dispersed activities/little co-ordination	Strategy based on exporting of product with decentralized marketing in each host country
	HR strategy requiring local responsiveness: • predominance of host country nationals in key management positions of subsidiary level; • limited cross-national transfers of personnel; • little need for well-defined expatriate or international management development policies; • industrial relations decision making will be decentralized at subsidiary level; • subsidiary industrial relations practices will be based on host country customs and practices.	
	Geographically dispersed activities	Geographically concentrated activities

Configuration of activities

Figure 9.2 Human resource strategy and degree of co-ordination of global activities
Source: based on Porter (1986)

trial relations practices will be based on host country customs and practices. A similar approach may be expected in businesses adopting an export-based strategy of concentration and minimum co-ordination.

The opposite approach to HRM may be expected in geographically dispersed but highly co-ordinated transnationals (high foreign investment/extensive co-ordination). Here the need for global co-ordination and direction outweighs the need for national responsiveness. This may necessitate the employment of home country nationals at subsidiary level and a significant cross-national exchange of personnel. Effective expatriate policies will therefore be needed to ensure the smooth exchange of staff. The achievement of global co-ordination and direction also requires a pool of internationally experienced executives, which requires an extensive international management development programme. In the labour area, highly co-ordinated businesses must ensure that labour problems at one location do not affect operations elsewhere. Similarly, some standardization of employee benefits between subsidiaries will also be necessary. This implies active parent company involvement in subsidiary industrial relations issues and a significant transfer of parent country industrial relations practices.

Review and discussion questions

1. Discuss the reasons for and nature of the modern paradigms of leadership.
2. Explore the cultural issues that must be addressed in relation to leadership in transnational operations.
3. Explain the relationship between a business's transnational and HR strategies.
4. Describe the basis of a 'strategic' approach to global HRM.
5. Explain the relationships between a business's core competences and HR strategy, and those between generic strategy and HR strategy.
6. Explain the relationship between an organization's global strategy (using Porter's model) and its expatriate and management development policies and practices.

References and further reading

Anthony, W.P., Perrewe, P. and Kacmar, K.M. (1993) *Strategic Human Resource Management*. New York: Dryden Press/Harcourt Brace Jovanovich.

Armstrong, M. (1992) *Human Resource Management: Strategy and Action*. London: Kogan-Page.

Bartlett, C. and Ghoshal, S. (1989) *Managing Across Borders: The Transnational Solution*. Boston: Harvard Business School Press.

Beer, M., Spector, B., Lawrence, P.R., Quinn, M.D. and Walton, R.E. (1984) *Managing Human Assets*. New York: Free Press.

Brewster, C. (1994) 'European HRM: Reflection of, or challenge to, the American concept?' In: P.S. Kirkbride (ed.) *Human Resource Management in Europe*. London: Routledge.

Brewster, C. and Hegewisch, A. (eds) (1994) *Policy and Practice in European Human Resource Management: The Price Waterhouse Cranfield Survey*. London: Routledge.

Chakravarthy, B.S. and Perlmutter, H.V. (1985) 'Strategic planning for a global business'. *Columbia Journal of World Business*, Summer, 3–10.

Desatnick, R.L. and Bennett, M.L. (1977) *Human Resource Management in the Multinational Company*. Aldershot, UK: Gower Press.

Doeringer, P.B. and Piore, M.J. (1971) *Internal Labour Markets and Manpower Analysis*. Lexington, MD: D.C. Heath & Co.

Edwards, P., Ferner, A. and Sisson, K. (1996) 'The conditions for international human resource management: Two case studies'. *International Journal of Human Resource Management*, **7**(1), February, 20–40.

Fombrun, C.J., Tichy, N.M. and Devanna, M.A. (1985) *Strategic Human Resource Management*. New York: John Wiley & Sons.

Gunnigle, P. and Moore, S. (1996) 'Linking business strategy and human resource management: Issues and implications'. *Personnel Review*, **23**(1).

Hagan, C.M. (1996) 'The core competence organisation: Implications for human resource practices'. *Human Resource Management Review*, **6**(2), 147–164.

Hamill, J. (1984) 'Labour relations decision-making within multinational corporations'. *Industrial Relations Journal*, Summer.

Hamill, J. (1989) 'Expatriate policies in British multinationals'. *Journal of General Management*, **14**(4), Summer.

Harris, P. (1979) 'The unhappy world of the expatriate'. *International Management*, July.

Heijltjes, M., van Witteloostuijn, A. and Sorge, A. (1996) 'Human resource management in relation to generic strategies: A comparison of chemical food and drink companies in the Netherlands and Great Britain'. *International Journal of Human Resource Management*, **7**(2), May, 383–412.

Heller, J.E. (1980) 'Criteria for selecting an international manager'. *Personnel*, May/June.

Holmes, W. and Piker, F. (1980) 'Expatriate failure – Prevention rather than cure'. *Personnel Management*, December.

Howard, C.G. (1984) 'How relocation abroad affects expatriates' family life'. *Personnel Administration*, November.

Lanier, A. (1979) 'Selecting and preparing personnel for overseas transfers'. *Personnel Journal*, March.

Mahoney, T.A. and Deckop, J.R. (1986) 'Evolution of concept and practice in personnel administration/human resource management'. *Journal of Management*, **12**(2), Summer.

Ohmae, K. (1990) *The Borderless World*. London: Collins.

Ondrack, D.A. (1985) 'International transfers of managers in North American and European MNEs', *Journal of International Business Studies*, Fall.

Perlmutter, H.V. (1969) 'The tortuous evolution of the multinational corporation'. *Columbia Journal of World Business*, January/February.

Perlmutter, H.V. (1984) 'Building the symbolic societal enterprise: A social architecture for the future'. *World Futures*, **19**(3/4), 271–284.

Porter, M.E. (1986) *Competition in Global Industries*. Boston: Harvard Business School Press.

Prahalad, C.K. and Doz, Y.L. (1906) *The Multinational Mission. Balancing Local Demands and Global Vision*. New York: Free Press.

Reynolds, C. (1979) 'Career paths and compensation in multinational corporations'. In: S. Davis (ed.), *Managing and Organizing Multinational Corporations*. New York: Pergamon Press.

Schneider, S.C. and Barsoux, J.C. (2003) *Managing Across Cultures*. London: Financial Times/Prentice Hall.

Senge, P. (1990) 'Building learning organizations'. *Sloan Management Review*, Fall.

Tayeb, M. (2000) *International Business – Theories, Policies and Practices*. London: Financial Times/Prentice Hall.

Toyne, B. and Kuhne, R.J. (1983) 'The management of the international executive compensation and benefits process'. *Journal of International Business Studies*, Winter.

Tung, R.L. (1982) 'Selection and training procedures of US, European and Japanese multinationals'. *California Management Review*, Fall.

Tung, R.L. (1984) 'Strategic management of human resources in the multinational enterprise'. *Human Resource Management*, Summer.

Tung, R.L. (1988) *The New Expatriates: Managing Human Resources Abroad.* Cambridge, MA: Ballinger.

Van Den Bulcke, D. and Halsberghe, E. (1984) *Employment Decision-Making in Multinational Enterprises: Survey Results from Belgium.* Geneva: International Labour Organization.

Walker, J.W. (1992) *Human Resource Strategy.* London: McGraw-Hill.

Young, S., Hood, N. and Hamill, J. (1985) *Decision-Making in Foreign-Owned Multinational Subsidiaries in the United Kingdom* (ILO Working paper No. 35). Geneva: International Labour Organization.

GLOBAL TECHNOLOGY MANAGEMENT

10

Learning objectives

After studying this chapter students should be able to:

- describe the linkages between technology and strategy;
- explain how technology can be defined and employed as a strategic asset;
- describe how technology can be used to enhance competitive advantage;
- describe how technology needs to be managed to enable it to be used to enhance global competitive advantage;
- explain what ICT is, how it has stimulated globalization and how it can be used in a company's technology strategy.

Introduction

The scope of what we refer to as 'technology' is too large to be considered in detail in a single chapter of a book of this type. The many ways in which the word is used is testimony to the plethora of ways in which it can impact on business strategy. Technology can be found in electronics, chemicals, aerospace, telecommunications, design, production, logistics and many other fields – and in most cases, one technology is highly interconnected with other types. So, while we might think of technology as describing computers and robots (which it certainly does), we should not forget that the same management skills required in these sectors are also required in every other area of technology: in pharmaceuticals, petrochemicals, automobiles and in hundreds of other contexts.

This chapter seeks to explain the key themes of technology strategy as they relate to international business. Much of the literature in this field has stressed the growing influence of technology on the competitiveness of international business. Harris et al. (1984) focused on the influence of 'technology-driven events' causing a lack of competitiveness in US industry. They correctly forecast that technology would continue to trigger major market shifts. Hence, the need for transnational businesses to adroitly manage technology is difficult to overstate.

Technology and strategy

A powerful force drives the world toward a converging commonality, and that force is technology. It has proletarianized communication, transport and travel. It has made isolated places and impoverished peoples eager for modernity's allurements. Almost everyone everywhere wants all the things they have heard about, seen, or experienced via the new technologies (Levitt, 1983).

Technology is, without doubt, one of the most important contributory factors underlying the internationalization and globalization of economic activity (Dicken, 1998).

The impact of technology on strategy

Theodore Levitt's (1983) prescient paper on market homogenization captured the enormous impact that technology has and will continue to have on markets and businesses. Although other authors (e.g., Douglas and Wind, 1987) have pointed out weaknesses in Levitt's arguments, we can now look back and see how right he was to highlight the significance of technology in shaping the markets that the transnational deals with as well as the way in which the company is organized.

The effects of technology have however sometimes been different to those that Levitt discussed. For example, while communication technologies such as satellite television have continued to encourage a convergence of demand, flexible manufacturing technologies have enabled businesses to offer a much greater variety of product designs without sacrificing economies of scale. Similarly, while the dramatic improvements in information technologies have enabled businesses to operate on a global scale, they have also enabled a move away from the old style multinational corporation with central control to the transnational with information shared throughout the organization.

Technology is one of the major factors behind the increased turbulence in the environment of many business sectors. The shortening of the new product design cycle through, for example, sophisticated CADCAM (computer-aided design, computer-aided manufacture) technologies has increased the rate of product obsolescence. Businesses have less time to respond to new developments and must make strategic decisions where the future becomes less and less predictable. The emergence of new, competing technologies and the acquisition of existing technologies by competitors can also increase the complexity of the environment. This complexity is even greater for the transnational facing both global and local competitors.

The general impact of technology on the macroenvironment has already been discussed in Chapter 5. The purpose of the present chapter is to examine how the transnational can 'manage' technology as part of its corporate strategy. To do this we shall first consider the role of technology as a strategic asset and how it differs from more conventional assets; second, we shall review the elements of a technology strategy – how the business responds to the challenges and opportunities posed by new technology; finally, we shall examine the special cases of information and communication technologies (ICTs) and their impact on the strategy and operations of the transnational.

Technology as a strategic asset

Defining technology

'Technology' is a word that is often used but not often explained. In this chapter we shall use the dictionary definition of the application of science to industry or commerce. There is an important distinction here: by 'science' we mean the results of fundamental academic investigations, while by 'technology' we mean the *application* of science. This distinction is important when we consider how businesses acquire new technologies.

The importance of technology to a business lies in the fact that possession of a technology can give a competitive advantage. Technology can be therefore regarded as a strategic asset. Furthermore, we can also say that a business's ability to manage and exploit its technology can represent a core competence. There is also a close link between a company's ability to manage technology and its capacity to innovate. We shall now examine more closely how technology can give a competitive advantage through its products and production processes. The contribution that information and communication technologies can make to a business's operations will be discussed later in the chapter.

Technology and products

Technology can enhance a company's product portfolio in a number of ways:

New functions
A new product can be developed which allows the user to perform tasks that were hitherto not possible or else very difficult. An example of this is the development of the satellite telephone that allows the user to communicate from almost anywhere on the Earth's surface. Some customers are willing to pay high prices to own such a product. Such products are likely to be highly innovative requiring major investments in new technology.

New features
An existing product can be modified to make it more useful while the basic function remains the same (e.g., the development of compact satellite telephones that require almost no setting up). Companies continually seek innovations to differentiate their products from that of competitors. Although such innovations may be minor, over time these can add up to represent a significant advance in technology.

Greater reliability
As the technology becomes more mature, product reliability becomes a key factor in product differentiation. Design improvements and different assembly techniques will focus on performance and quality (e.g., increased use of specialized integrated circuits can make the product easier to assemble and more robust).

Lower costs
As the product matures, technology development focuses more on cost reduction. The use of specialized integrated circuits, mentioned above, which are expensive to design but in mass production offer huge cost advantages over discrete components offer a tremendous advantage to the businesses that can master this technology.

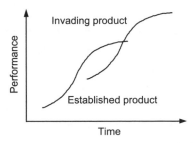

Figure 10.1 Performance of invading product compared with that of established product
Source: Abernathy and Utterback (1978)

Technology is one of the underlying reasons for the existence of a product life cycle. Product performance tends to follow an 'S'-shaped curve as shown in Figure 10.1.

When the technology is new, developments are rapid and product performance rises quickly. As the technology becomes mature, the rate of change of performance tends to level off as the technological limits are reached. At some point, a new technology may be developed and incorporated in the product. At first, product performance is lower than that of the existing technology. But as the invading technology is developed, product performance overtakes that of the current technology, and eventually the old product/technology becomes obsolete.

As an example, consider the technology in wristwatches. The basic mechanism of the wristwatch was established around 1765. By the early 20th century the watch was a sophisticated piece of precision mechanical engineering, but there was relatively little rate of improvement in accuracy. When the electronic quartz movement was developed in the 1970s, the inherent accuracy was much greater than conventional mechanical movements. Since the quartz movement was also much cheaper to mass-produce, the old mechanical technology was soon obsolete, with dramatic effect in the Swiss watch industry. The lesson here is that the invading technology can come from other industry sectors and other countries – and the time between initial launch and annihilation of the current product/technology can be quite rapid.

Technology and production

The section above has indicated that product design is a major factor in production cost. However, the technologies used in the production process itself can lead to competitive advantage.

Shorter lead times
The use of CADCAM systems has dramatically reduced lead times from initial design to full-scale production. In many industries, components can be designed on computer and a prototype generated within a few hours. After testing is complete the computer-generated design can be used directly in the manufacturing process. Design information can be electronically transferred from one location to another.

Increased quality
The use of automated assembly, with robots as a leading example, can not only increase throughput but can also reduce errors in complex, repetitive processes. Automation can also increase production flexibility; changes to a process can be introduced by reprogramming which is faster and cheaper than hardware changes.

Reduced cost
The higher throughput and increased reliability offered by new technologies can also lead to reduced unit costs. With flexible manufacturing techniques large production runs are no longer required to keep unit costs low.

An example of technological change was the development by Pilkington Brothers of the float glass process. The traditional method of manufacturing flat glass was to pass molten glass through a series of rollers until it was the correct thickness; the glass has then to be polished on both sides. In the float process the glass flows in a continuous process across a bath of molten tin and emerges as a perfectly flat sheet at the other end with no rolling or polishing required. Although the development of the new process required a huge financial outlay it revolutionized the economics of flat glass production and put Pilkington in an unassailable competitive position.

Patterns of technological innovation

The pattern of technological innovation outlined above has been shown to apply to many product types. Abernathy and Utterback (1978) described a model of innovation summarized in Figure 10.2.

In the early stages of the product's life, innovation dominates. The emphasis of technological development is on improving product performance, stimulated by information on user needs. The product design is 'fluid' with

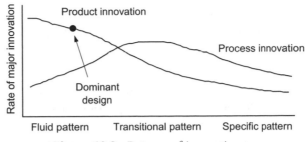

Figure 10.2 Patterns of innovation
Source: Abernathy and Utterback (1978)

frequent major changes, together with flexible and inefficient production. Organizational control tends to be informal and entrepreneurial.

At some point a 'dominant design' emerges which all manufacturers adopt as a basic standard. The emphasis moves toward process innovation with the objective of reducing costs and improving quality. Changes are incremental and cumulative, and products tend to be very similar. Production processes are efficient and capital intensive. Organizational control tends to be based on structure, goals and rules.

The significance of this for any business is that the nature of technological development and how it is managed changes greatly over the life of a product.

Differences between technology and other assets

Like other assets (except for some fixed assets), technology can be transferred from one location to another; it can be acquired and it can be considered as having value. The difference from other assets is that the *form* that the technology takes can vary. The clearest distinction is that between *tangible* and *intangible* technology. We can illustrate this difference in one way by considering how the technology appears to the user of the company's products.

Tangible technology
In the example mentioned above of the satellite telephone, the technology is embodied in the product itself and made available to the user. It would be possible for the user to 'reverse-engineer' the telephone and acquire the company's technology to design and build his or her own telephones. Of course, reverse-engineering complex integrated circuits and software is very difficult but most businesses make some attempt to examine their

competitors' products to see if any secrets can be learned. The company must therefore find some means of protecting its technology.

Intangible technology
On the other hand, the user of glass manufactured by the float process would not be able to deduce from the product itself anything about the manufacturing process. The technology is not embodied in the product; this helps the company to protect its secrets from competitors. This technology in its purest form is intangible. The knowledge of how something is made may reside in the heads of a few key employees. It is much more difficult to talk about acquiring this kind of technology and even more difficult to value it. We shall consider this later in the sections on technology transfer (pp. 278 and 280).

Technology and global competitiveness

Design technology
Many examples can be given of the link between technology and international competitiveness. In the consumer electronics industry, for example, international competitiveness depends to a significant extent on the continual introduction of new products incorporating new technology (e.g., VCRs, digital audio tapes, personal computers, electronic calculators, personal hi-fi systems, remote control and flat screen TVs). Similarly, in the pharmaceutical industry, the development and introduction of new drugs is a major determinant of transnational competitiveness – as in the case of Glaxo with its anti-ulcer drug Zantac and Hoffman-La-Roche with its anti-depressant drugs valium and librium.

Process technology
International competitiveness is also closely linked to new process developments, with one of the earliest examples being the pioneering of mass production technology by Ford. In the textile and clothing industry, producers in developed countries have responded to the flood of low-cost textile imports from developing countries by introducing increasingly automated production techniques.

Some businesses are more capable of generating a stock of proprietary information than they are of achieving commercial success. Others discover that their technology is more readily exploited by others who learn from their errors. In other cases, the company's international investment is largely motivated by the desire to acquire technology skills as a basis for a future stream of innovations.

Technology strategy

The components of a technology strategy

In order to exploit the opportunities and counter the challenges posed by technology, many transnational companies develop a technology strategy. Many businesses have some sort of 'IT strategy' that is rather limited in scope; here we suggest that this should be linked with a wider strategic approach to managing technology as a strategic asset. As with any other functional strategy (such as a human resource strategy), a technology strategy should be consistent with the overall corporate strategy and the objectives underlying that strategy. The components of the strategy will vary from one business to another but in general will include:

- technology audit;
- sourcing new technology;
- exploiting technology;
- protecting the competitive advantage.

We consider each of these components in turn.

Technology audit

This activity is similar to the general internal analysis of the business described in Chapter 3. The purpose of such an audit (also known as an *innovation* audit) is to identify the specific technological competences within the business and match these against the opportunities the business intends to pursue in its corporate strategy. The outcome of the audit should be an estimate of the potential of the business to obtain a competitive advantage from the technology in one or more of the ways described earlier in this chapter. The audit should also identify technology 'gaps' that have to be filled. This information will be used to determine the level of investment in technological development required to meet corporate objectives and where that investment should be directed.

Goodman and Lawless (1994) described three systematic approaches to carrying out an audit that, when taken together, can present a useful picture of the business.

Table 10.1 Technology categories

Category	Description	Investment level
Base	Technological foundation of business; widely available to competitors.	Needs little
Key	Technologies with the greatest impact on competitive performance.	Systematically built
Pacing	Technologies in early development which have the demonstrated potential to alter the basis of competition.	Selective investment
Emerging	Technologies with long-term promise to alter the basis of competition.	Monitored

Source: adapted from Goodman and Lawless (1994)

Technological innovation process audit

The aim of this is to construct a risk profile for existing and new projects by assessing the length and depth of the company's experience in its chosen technologies, its markets, project organization, the far environment and the industry structure. This can assist management in deciding which techno-logical areas are more likely to be successful and which should perhaps be avoided, as the risk of failure may be considered unacceptable.

Innovative comparison audit

This is an analysis of the business's innovative abilities compared with competitors. It requires an examination of the company's track record in new products, R&D staff capabilities, R&D performance, idea generation, time to commercialize (i.e., time to market), costs/benefits of R&D and relationships between R&D and other key functional areas.

Technological position audit

This reviews the technologies needed by the business and places them in one of four categories as shown in Table 10.1. For each category, the table shows a suggested level of investment that might be appropriate.

Sourcing new technology

Development or transfer?

Having identified weaknesses or gaps in its technology capabilities, man-agement has a number of options to build new capabilities. The basic decision is to develop in-house or look externally. Some authors have discussed how the decision should be made; one example is the discussion

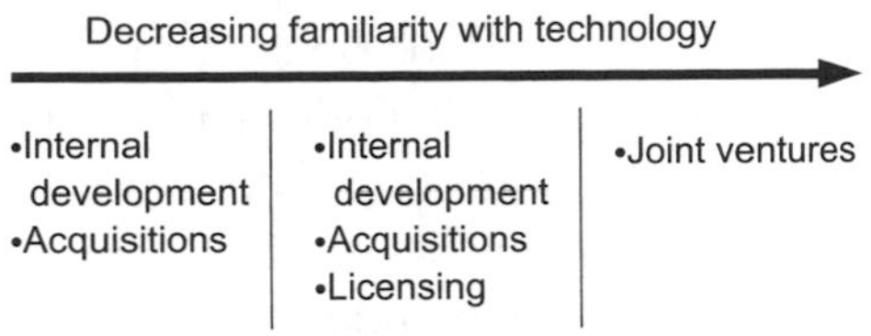

Decreasing familiarity with technology

•Internal development •Acquisitions	•Internal development •Acquisitions •Licensing	•Joint ventures

Figure 10.3   Optimum entry methods for new technologies
Source: adapted from Roberts and Berry (1985)

in Roberts and Berry (1985). The key variable is the familiarity of the company with the technology, ranging from already making some use of the technology to simply being aware of the technology but without any practical experience. Figure 10.3 summarizes the recommended approaches.

Roberts and Berry (1985) noted that joint ventures were often between a large business with an established market position and a small business with a new technology seeking entry to market. It is interesting to note that acquisition is not a recommended method when the company is unfamiliar with the technology – failure rates tend to be high in such circumstances.

For most large transnationals (especially those operating in technology-intensive industries), new technology emerges mainly from the results of internally generated R&D. It is important to be aware, however, that there are a range of alternative sources of technology available to a business where a distinction is made between internal and external sources, both domestic and foreign. While large transnationals may rely mainly on internal R&D, smaller and non-dominant transnationals may focus on external sources of technology transfer and accumulation, since these will reduce the high capital expenditures involved.

Recent years have seen a rapid growth in the use made of these alternative forms of technology acquisition and development given the pace of technology change, shortening product life cycles and the intensity of global competition. For example, foreign acquisitions of US companies have increased rapidly (in both number and value) since the late 1970s. Although motivated mainly by the need to gain access to US markets and existing distribution outlets, many US acquisitions have been motivated (at least in part) by the desire to acquire US technology (Hamill, 1988). Similarly, recent years have seen the growing importance of joint government/industry-sponsored research initiatives, mainly in the electronics industry and in various forms of international collaboration between organizations of different nationalities, including strategic alliances.

While the objectives of these various options are similar (i.e., technology development and transfer), the management implications of internal and external forms of technology acquisition differ significantly.

Some of the major management decisions that need to be taken in the case of internally generated R&D include:

- the level of R&D expenditure;
- the focus of R&D effort;
- the location of R&D (i.e., the centralization/decentralization issue);
- the nature of R&D undertaken at subsidiary level;
- the transfer and diffusion of R&D results throughout the global network.

External forms of technology involve partnerships and collaboration between unrelated concerns. The major managerial issues involved, therefore, relate to the planning, negotiation and organization of collaborative agreements (this issue is examined in more detail in Chapter 14).

Problems with technology transfer

The problems associated with the successful transfer of technology into an organization are closely related to those in any merger or acquisition and require careful management. We have already mentioned that technology can exist both as a tangible and as an intangible asset. Simply acquiring a few product samples and manufacturing drawings does little more than permit the company, at best, to manufacture a copy of the original product. If the acquiring business is unfamiliar with the technology, it is also necessary to acquire the underlying knowledge that went into the design of the product. Only then can the business expect to be able to continue the product and process innovations discussed earlier that are an essential part of achieving a sustainable competitive advantage. The business therefore needs to have available the key technologists in the source organization either as new employees of the business or on some kind of consultancy basis to educate the current employees.

Another problem can be caused by the acquiring company not having the appropriate expertise to manufacture the product in a reliable way. Once again the acquirer may have to go through a substantial learning period. The difficulties may be increased if the source company is small and entrepreneurial; as we have already seen, production processes in such companies may be inefficient and poorly documented.

A further problem in technology transfer is caused by the nature of

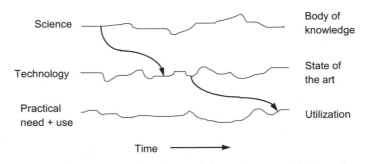

Figure 10.4 Science, technology and the utilization of their products
Source: Allen (1984)

technology itself – something between science and its practical application. The relationship is shown schematically in Figure 10.4.

The nature, location and timescales of the three types of activity can be very different. Acquisition of a technology that is still in the experimental stage is risky; there may be culture clashes between the technologists in the business and the scientists who carried out the original research. The problems are similar to the clashes that may occur between technologists in an R&D department and the engineers in a manufacturing department. All parties need to have a good understanding of each others' needs and problems for the transfer to be successful.

Exploiting new technology

The process of technology development and acquisition (discussed in the previous section) represents only the first stage in effectively managing technology within the transnational business. There are many companies who have successfully generated new proprietary technology, but who have failed to exploit such know how commercially. In order to commercially exploit new technology know how, two other stages need to be covered in the company's technology strategy.

First, effective organizational channels need to be established for transferring technology throughout the transnational network. Second, the organization needs to determine the most effective foreign market entry and development strategy for exploiting the newly acquired technology know-how. This (second point) involves an assessment of the relative merits of exporting, licensing, joint ventures, FDI (foreign direct investment), etc. (see Chapter 7).

The two key issues relating to the process of technology diffusion within the transnational are the location of R&D activity and the organizational structure.

Location of R&D activity

Most transnationals adopt a qualified policy of centralization in R&D. Where decentralization does occur, overseas R&D units tend to take the form of technology transfer units to assist in the transfer of technology from parent to foreign subsidiary (Hakanson, 1983; Ronstadt, 1977, 1978). The importance of these units is that technology can rarely be transferred without some form of modification. There is evidence (Davidson, 1980) to suggest that the speed, rate and extent of technology transfer have accelerated over time, reflecting the transnational's need to apply new technology throughout the international network almost immediately in order to obtain (even a brief) competitive advantage. In these circumstances, the transnational's competitive position is enhanced if its key subsidiaries have some development capability and can handle much of their own adaptation. As a result, this is perhaps one of the strongest motivations for a measure of R&D decentralization in recent years.

Structure and technology exploitation

The organizational structure of the transnational plays an important role in its ability to transfer technology. Davidson (1983), for example, found that the transfer performance of companies organized along matrix lines was superior to those with alternative organizational structures, especially those with global product divisions. He argued that, in this context, accumulated experience and information is better exploited in more centralized structures. Thus, global matrix companies tend to transfer new products more rapidly and more extensively to foreign subsidiaries.

Systems to support technology exploitation

There have been a number of attempts to address the question of appropriate systems for the management and transfer of technology within the business. One of the earliest and most comprehensive, by Burns and Stalker (1961), noted the need to move from mechanistic to organic models of organization of work in the transfer into new technologies. Many transnationals are frequently, if not constantly, in that change process. Gresov (1984) captured this position quite effectively for transnationals. Recognizing that the successful management of technology involves the two distinct processes of innovation and implementation, he observes two organizational dilemmas. Where the business is centralized, implementation is usually improved at the expense of innovation; with a complex organizational design the converse is true.

Similarly with an organization's culture. A homogeneous culture favours implementation at the cost of innovation, with the reverse holding true for a heterogeneous organizational culture. Gresov (1984) suggested that it may, for instance, be possible to compensate for the poorer adoptive capacity of the centralized structure by encouraging and promoting cultural hetero- geneity. Similarly, by extending aspects of homogeneous organizational culture, the implementation weaknesses of the complex structural form might be improved. The resulting trade-off may produce a solution that improves the company's overall capacity to manage its technology.

Protecting the competitive advantage

If possession and application of one or more key technologies give a business a significant competitive advantage, the business needs to con- sider how it can ensure that such technologies remain proprietary for as long as possible. We mentioned earlier that it is easier for process tech- nologies to be kept secret than for technologies that are embedded within the final product. Even so, the company would be wise to consider how it can maintain the value of its intellectual property. The business has two main courses of action: it can apply for a patent or it may choose to keep the technology as a trade secret.

Patents

If the technology and its application are considered sufficiently novel, the company may be granted a patent that gives the company exclusive rights to the benefits of the technology for a certain period (20 years in the USA). There are, however, some disadvantages in gaining a patent:

- In return for the patent, the company must publish openly a detailed explanation of the technology and its application. This information is freely available to competitors who may use it to develop alternative forms of technology that they themselves can patent. Once the patent expires no further protection is possible.
- Although 20 years may seem a long time the actual time during which the company can profit from the technology may be much less (e.g., it can

take several years after the patent is filed for new compounds developed by pharmaceutical companies to enter the market).

- If the patent is contested by another company the cost of patent litigation can be high.
- The cost of filing an application and keeping the patent in force in several countries can be high; however, for a transnational of any size this should not be a serious problem.
- Different countries have different patent systems, so each patent application may have to be adapted. This problem is being reduced by increasing co-operation between governments (e.g., only one application is necessary for protection in all the member countries of the EU).
- It is not possible to gain such protection in some countries, so competitors there are free to sell goods using the technology in such countries.

However, the benefits in owning a patent are considerable. The protection offered by the patent means that it has measurable *value*. This means that it can be used as an instrument of negotiation (e.g., the company may grant a licence to a competitor allowing it to use the technology in return for royalty payments). This was the approach used by Pilkington after it developed the float glass technology in the 1960s. The company received substantial payments from competitors throughout the world for many years without having to make substantial capital investments itself. However, this approach was later criticized as being too risk-averse (Stopford and Turner, 1985).

When patents expire

The patent on the world's best-selling drug expired in July 1997. The patent was taken out by the product's developers (British drug company Glaxo) in 1977, although because of the development time the product wasn't actually launched until 1983. The legal patent enabled Glaxo (and Glaxo in its later guises, including after 1995 Glaxo Wellcome) to enjoy sole manufacturing and distribution rights on the drug throughout the world. All forms of legal substitution were prohibited and the superior performance of Zantac against other anti-ulcer treatments made it the best-selling drug up to that point with annual sales exceeding £2.5 billion.

> Several firms attempted to challenge the patent before its expiry. Most notably, Canadian generic drug manufacturer Novopharm appealed to the legal authorities in the USA in the early 1990s to manufacture a form of the drug's basic molecule, ranitidine hydrochloride. Glaxo spent a lot of money fighting off this legal challenge and, although it was technically successful in doing so, Novopharm did begin producing its generic form several months before the final expiry of the patent. Other firms sued by Glaxo for patent infringement included Geneva Pharma (a Novartis group company), Roxane (part of Boehringer Ingelheim) and Torpharm.
>
> These four generic firms were geared up to start producing ranitidine in the summer of 1997. Because ranitidine was protected under patent, its molecular structure and pharmacokinetic mechanism were not secret – they were disclosed as part of initial patent application. When generic production started, competition was described as 'cutthroat'. As a profit earner for Glaxo, ranitidine had had its day but it was relaunched at half strength (75-mg tablets as opposed to 150-mg tablets) as a treatment for heartburn (Zantac 75).

Trade secrets

If the company believes that it can keep the technology secret for a substantial length of time, then it can obtain the benefits of the technology without the drawbacks of the patent approach. This approach is particularly useful when the company can bring the product to market rapidly, so that even if competitors can copy the technology the company still has a substantial lead. However, the company should maintain certified records to prove that it developed the technology first to prevent a competitor obtaining a patent for themselves.

Comparisons of transnational technological performance

Comparing US and Japanese performance

Transnationals have differential rates of success in maintaining technological advantage. Over recent years there has been much discussion about different levels of innovation and their influence on competitiveness.

Much of this has been motivated by the decline in US and European competitiveness in many fields and by the growth of Japanese exports. While some of the explanations for these changes lie at the macro-level, managers of transnationals are increasingly sensitive to company-specific dimensions.

On national comparisons, Johnson (1984) compared the R&D strategies of Japanese and US companies to determine whether differences in them had contributed to different competitive positions. He noted that Japanese businesses:

- invested more heavily in applied research and product development (and less in basic research projects);
- concentrate more on building pre-existing products and technologies developed by other companies in the same or related industries than on the development of new, unproven products of technologies; and
- they tended to follow the products or technologies of other businesses, rather than trying to be first.

This pattern of difference is by now well established, of course, and Johnson showed that over the period 1965–81 Japanese companies pursuing such strategies had a substantially higher private rate of return than their US counterparts. In seeking explanations for this, he emphasized the importance of differential government subsidiaries and tax incentives for R&D in the two countries. He also indicated that the US government's strict enforcement of the patent system has deterred many US companies from taking advantage of opportunities to build on the products and technologies of their foreign competitors.

Commentary on different home nation support environments for technology has become an increasingly important dimension of this debate. Daneke (1984), for example, contrasted US and Japanese policy approaches using illustrations from the biotechnology industry. Japanese businesses have benefited from their government's policy of making biotechnology a national priority, providing direct public financing for private sector R&D and the commercialization of its output, compared with the (less effective) US motivation of tax incentives. Daneke believed that US governmental policy will effectively drive a wedge between the successful and entrepreneurial aspects of biotechnology, allowing Japanese and European transnationals to take the lead.

Learning good practice

Another important aspect of comparative work has inevitably been that of the identification of lessons from practice at a corporate level. Here again there are illustrations from the literature. Maidique and Hayes (1984) examined a large sample of US high-technology companies, including many transnationals, in an endeavour to trace the origins of their successful technology management.

They found that five themes emerged, and while none of the companies showed excellence in all areas at any one time, neither was any one of them less successful in all of them.

- *Business focus.* This was clearly related to success, with the examples of IBM, Boeing, Intel (integrated circuits), Genentech (genetic engineering) being cited as among those whose sales were largely in single or clearly related product groups.
- *Adaptability.* Having a long-term focus, but also with the capability for rapid change. Not strategically immobile.
- *Organizational cohesion.* Widely regarded as critical in successful high-technology companies. Reflected for example, in Hewlett-Packard's 50 divisions; Texas Instruments with some 30 divisions and 250 tactical action programmes.
- *Sense of integrity.* Desire to maintain positive stable associations with all interest groups.
- *'Hands-on' top management.* Deep involvement in the assessment process of technological advance.

Information and communication technologies

The effects of ICT

Technological change, particularly the development of ICT, has been among the most important driving forces behind globalization. While developments in transport have played a major role in internationalizing industries and markets, by making it possible to transfer resources and goods between countries and continents, it is ICT probably more than any other single factor which has caused globalization. Developments like satellite television have helped to bring about convergence of customer wants and needs. ICT has had an even more significant impact on the ability of businesses to co-ordinate value-adding activities across national boundaries in remote geographical locations while still permitting local responsiveness when and where it may be required.

The key to successful global strategy can often be found in ICT. The technology is important because of the role that it plays in the processes of organizational learning and in knowledge management (Stonehouse and Pemberton, 1999). ICT is both a powerful competitive weapon and a major integrating force for the business. ICT can assist in building and leveraging core competences, in reducing costs and in differentiating products. The impact of ICT has not however been entirely positive, and it is cited as a major cause of hypercompetition and environmental turbulence (Chakravarthy, 1997).

Ironically, it is ICT in the context of organizational learning and knowledge management which offers the best hope to businesses seeking to acquire and sustain competitive advantage in turbulent environments (Stonehouse and Pemberton, 1999). This section examines the changes that have taken place in ICT and their impact on the global strategies of transnationals.

Developments in ICT

ICT alone has not driven the globalization of business activity, but without recent developments in ICT it is difficult to see how globalization could have developed to such an extent. For many years, the level of technology was a major factor for inhibiting those businesses seeking to achieve superior performance through their distinctive global architecture and co-ordination. According to Dicken (1992) 'both the geographical and organizational scale at which any human activity can occur is directly related to the available media of transport and communication.' The physical barriers to the movement of materials and products have been substantially reduced by improvements in transport technology. They have revolutionized logistics and resulted in global shrinkage, opening up the possibility of new configurations to transnationals.

Of even greater significance to the globalization of business activity have been the developments in ICT. In this context, 'convergent IT' (Hall and Preston, 1988), or the integration of computers and telecommunications into a unified system for the processing and interchange of business information, has been of singular importance. This convergence has opened new opportunities to transnationals for the acquisition of global competitive advantage.

The two most important contributions to the development of convergent IT have been in the areas of computing power and connectivity. There has been a 'radical change in information architecture' (Laudon and Laudon, 1991). There has been a move from centralized to distributed processing via PCs and workstations. Most of these have processing display and storage capabilities well in excess of some of their mainframe predecessors. Helms and Wright (1992) predicted that by the year 2000 over 15 million personal computers will be installed in businesses with 40% connected through far-reaching networks. In fact, this figure was greatly exceeded, such is the pace of change in ICT. The average personal computer has immeasurably more processing power and speed than the most powerful mainframe in the 1970s and at a tiny fraction of the cost. Thus, not only has computing power increased beyond recognition in the last 30 years, but information and knowledge have also become relatively cheap and far more accessible as resources.

Accompanying developments in software have the potential to empower individual managers and at a price that is no longer prohibitive. Spread-sheets, databases, word processors and the like have made powerful business software accessible to all managers. One of the major problems faced by managers in international enterprises is the volume and complexity of data which have to be analysed before decisions can be made. In this respect, decision support systems (DSS), expert systems, neural networks, multimedia, intelligent databases and artificial intelligence all have an important role to play. Parsaye (1989) stated that 'The implementation of intelligent databases was inconceivable prior to the implementation of hypermedia systems, advanced microcomputer workstations and expert systems. Now that these technologies have matured, intelligent databases can be used to respond to the needs of data rich and information poor users.' Software developments, allied to hardware, are at the root of executive information systems (EIS) and strategic information systems (SIS). From complex, conflicting and incomplete data such systems help to produce the information and knowledge which support improved decision making and enhance organizational responsiveness in increasingly chaotic and hypercompetitive environments.

The value of this individual power has been augmented by developments in connectivity. Local area networks and wide area networks are the basis of this connectivity. Developments in telecommunications, like satellite and cable links, have drastically improved inter and intra-company communications. They have made possible increased co-ordination of geographically dispersed organizations. Equally, they have improved linkages in the value chain between businesses, their suppliers and distributors. It is these developments that have made possible the development of the Internet, which has already had a dramatic impact on business activity, particularly on the links between businesses and their customers.

ICT and transnational strategy

The technological developments in ICT, particularly those that have improved networking and connectivity, have important implications for the architecture of transnational organizations, for the management of knowledge and for co-ordination of activities and for flexibility and responsiveness. According to Frankovich (1998) 'Any business seeking to globalise its operations has a major IT challenge on its hands. Never has the intelligent application of technology been more important to improving business performance.'

In Chapter 6 we identified several potential sources of global competitive advantage centred on the core competences, generic and transnational strategies of the organization. Knowledge and information have become the major resources underpinning competitive advantage (see Chapter 15). ICT plays a vital role in the collection of information, its manipulation, analysis, storage and interpretation and in the generation of new organizational knowledge which forms the basis of core competences. ICT has provided the infrastructure needed to support network organizational structures that can be important to both organizational learning and transnational business (Bartlett and Ghoshal, 1995; Stonehouse and Pemberton, 1999).

Core competences can be based on knowledge of customers and their needs, knowledge of technology and how to employ it in distinctive ways, knowledge of products and processes, etc. Microsoft's core competences are based on its knowledge of how to build and market operating systems and software. Equally, Microsoft's competitive advantage is based on its knowledge of computer hardware and networking, and its knowledge of the companies that produce those products. Microsoft has leveraged its competences in personal computer operating systems and software, and built new associated competences in order to build competitive advantage in computer networking and Internet software. Such competence building and leveraging is largely knowledge-based.

ICT has also assisted the process of building collaborative business networks that are also a valuable source of competitive advantage. Network members can concentrate on their individual core competences, and by pooling them together in network activities synergy is created. ICT has made it possible to integrate network activities far more effectively and efficiently, leading to the development of what are often called *virtual corporations* (Davidow and Malone, 1992). In the airline industry, alliances use ICT to co-ordinate and integrate flight schedules, bookings and prices.

As we saw in Chapter 6, according to Porter's model of global strategy (Porter, 1986a, 1990) competitive advantage is viewed as arising from the *configuration of organizational activities* (i.e., where and in how many nations each activity in the value chain is performed) and *co-ordination* (how dispersed international activities are co-ordinated). ICT has transformed the ability of transnationals to co-ordinate their activities in geographically remote locations. This has increased the range of alternative configurations of activities available to them, thus making it possible to gain global competitive advantage by choosing distinctive configurations for value-adding activities. In addition, ICT has made it possible to achieve co-ordination and integration at the same time as maintaining a high degree of flexibility and responsiveness.

Configuring ICT for transnational business

According to Frankovich (1998), IT in global business is typically configured in four basic ways:

- *Centralised:* strong control from headquarters;
- *Replicated:* identical country systems;
- *Autonomous:* dissimilar and uncoordinated country systems;
- *Integrated:* compatible and co-ordinated systems.

There is no ideal configuration for ICT and the configuration chosen will depend on the transnational strategy of the organization. The globalization drivers (Yip, 1992) will dictate the extent to which local responsiveness is required. A centralized configuration will suffer from lack of flexibility and is likely to hinder responsiveness. A replicated configuration will include unnecessary duplication. When responsiveness is the priority, an autonomous configuration may well be chosen, but this will hinder the co-ordination of global activities. A truly transnational strategy is likely to be associated with an integrated configuration where there is co-ordination combined with a degree of local variation to allow for local responsiveness.

Discussion and review questions

1. Define what is meant by the word 'technology'.
2. How can technology make products more competitive?
3. Explain how technology can assist in making production more competitive.
4. What is a technology audit and what does it contain?
5. Define and distinguish between technology development and technology transfer.
6. When might a company, having made a technological innovation, use a patent and when might it keep its development secret?
7. What is included in ICT and how has it contributed to globalization?
8. What is convergent IT and why has it been a major cause of globalization?

References and further reading

Abernathy, W.J. and Utterback, J.M. (1978) 'Patterns of industrial innovation'. *Technology Review*, June/July, 40–47.

Allen, T.J. (1984) *Managing the Flow of Technology*. Cambridge, MA: MIT Press.

Andrews, F.J. (1954) 'The learning curve as a production tool'. *Harvard Business Review*, January/February, 1–11.

Argyris, C. (1977) 'Double loop learning in organizations'. *Harvard Business Review*, September/October, 115–125.

Argyris, C. (1992) *On Organizational Learning*. Cambridge, MA: Basil Blackwell.

Argyris, C. and Schon, D. (1978) *Organization Learning: A Theory of Action Perspective*. Reading, MA: Addison-Wesley.

Avishar, B. and Taylor, W. (1989) 'Customers drive a technology-driven company: An interview with George Fisher'. *Harvard Business Review*, November/December.

Bagchi, P.K. (1992) 'International logistics information systems'. *International Journal of Physical Distribution and Logistics Management*, **22**(9), 11–19.

Barber, C. (1998) 'CRS information and competitive advantage in the airline industry'. Unpublished PhD thesis, University of Northumbria, Newcastle.

Barber, C.E., Pemberton, J. and Stonehouse, G.H. (1993) 'Airline developed computer reservation systems: A turbulent course ahead?'. *European Business and Economic Development*, November, **2**(3), 30–35.

Bartlett, C.A. and Ghoshal, S. (1995) *Transnational Management: Text, Cases and Readings in Cross-border Management*. Homewood, IL: Richard D. Irwin.

Beaumont, J.R. and Sutherland, E. (1992) *Information Resource Management.* Oxford, UK: Butterworth Heinemann.

Beaumont, J, R. and Walters, D. (1991) 'Information management in service industries: Towards a strategic framework'. *Journal of Information Systems,* **1**(3), 155–172.

Behrman, J.N. and Fischer, W.A. (1980b) 'Transnational corporations: Market orientations and R&D abroad'. *Columbia Journal of World Business,* **15**.

Benjamin, R.I. and Blunt, J. (1992) 'Critical IT issues: The next ten years'. *Sloan Management Review,* Summer, 7–19.

Bjornsonn, H. and Lundegard, R. (1992) Corporate competitiveness and information technology'. *European Management Journal,* September, **10**(3), 341–347.

Brown, J.K. and Elvers, L.M. (eds) (1983) *Research and Development: Key Issues for Management.* New York: The Conference Board.

Burns, T. and Stalker, G.M. (1961) *The Management of Innovation.* London: Tavistock Publications.

Camillus, J.C. (1984) 'Technology-driven and market-driven life cycles'. *Columbia Journal of World Business,* Summer, 56–60.

Caves, R.E. (1982) 'Multinational enterprises and technology transfer'. In: A.M. Rugman (ed.), *New Theories of the Multinational Enterprise* (pp. 254–293). London: Croom Helm.

Chakravarthy, B. (1997) 'A new strategy framework for coping with turbulence'. *Sloan Management Review,* Winter, 69–82.

Clark, K.B. (1989) 'What strategy can do for technology'. *Harvard Business Review,* November/December.

Cravens, D.W., Piercy, N.F. and Shipp, S.H. (1996) 'New organizational forms for competing in highly dynamic environments: The network paradigm'. *British Journal of Management,* **7**(3), September.

Cravens, D.W., Greenley, G., Piercy, N.F. and Slater, S. (1997) 'Integrating contemporary strategic management perspectives'. *Long Range Planning,* **30**(4), 493–506.

Daneke, G.A. (1984) 'The global contest over the control of the innovation process'. *Columbia Journal of World Business,* Winter, 83–87.

Davidow, W.H. and Malone, M.S. (1992) *Structuring and Revitalising the Corporation for the 21st Century The Virtual Corporation.* London: HarperBusiness.

Davidson, W.H. (1980) *Experience Effects in International Investment and Technology Transfer.* Ann Arbor, MI: UMI Research Press.

Davidson, W.H. (1983) 'Structure and performance in international technology transfer'. *Journal of Management Studies,* **20**, 453–465.

De Meyer, A. and Ferdows, K. (1985) 'Integration of information systems in manufacturing'. *International Journal of Operations and Production Management (UK),* **5**(2), 5–12.

Demarest, M. (1997) 'Understanding knowledge management'. *Long Range Planning,* **30**(3), 374–384.

Dicken, P. (1992) *Global Shift – The Internationalization of Economic Activity.* London: Paul Chapman.

Dicken, P. (1998) *Global Shift – Transforming the World Economy.* London: Paul Chapman.

Douglas, S. and Wind, Y. (1987) 'The myth of globalization'. *Columbia Journal of World Business,* Winter.

Earl, M.J. (1989) *Management Strategies for Information Technology.* Englewood Cliffs, NJ: Prentice Hall.

Frankovich, J. (1998) 'The techno-world'. *Mastering Global Business.* London: PriceWaterhouseCoopers/Financial Times/Pitman.

Galliers, R.D. (1990) 'Pinstripes at the Terminals'. *Times Higher Education Supplement,* p. 26, 29 June.

Gamble, P.R. (1992) 'The virtual corporation: An IT challenge'. *Logistics Information Management,* **5**(4), 34–37.

Ghoshal, S. and Butler, C. (1992) *Kao Corporation.* Fontainebleau, France: INSEAD-EAC.

Gomery, R.E. (1989) 'From the "ladder of science" to the product development cycle'. *Harvard Business Review*, November/December.

Goodman, R.A. and Lawless, M.W. (1994) *Technology and Strategy*. Oxford, UK: Oxford University Press.

Gresov, C. (1984) 'Designing organizations to innovate and implement'. *Columbia Journal of World Business*, **19**(4), 63–67.

Grant, R.M. (1997) 'The knowledge-based view of the firm: Implications for management practice'. *Long Range Planning*, **30**(3), 450–454.

Hakanson, L. (1983) 'R&D in foreign-owned subsidiaries in Sweden'. In: W. Goldberg (ed.), *Governments and Multinationals, The Policy Control Versus Autonomy* (pp. 163–176). Cambridge, MA: Oelgeschlager, Gunn & Hain.

Hall, P. and Preston, P. (1988) *The Carrier Wave: New Information Technology and the Geography of Information, 1846-2003*. Boston: Unwin Hyman.

Hamill, J. (1988) 'British acquisitions in the US'. *National Westminster Bank Quarterly Review*, August.

Harris, I.M., Shaw, R.W. and Sommers, W.P. (1984) 'The strategic management of technology'. In: R.B. Lamb (ed.), *Competitive Strategic Management*. Englewood Cliffs, NJ: Prentice Hall.

Helms, M.M. and Wright, P. (1992) 'External considerations: Their influence on future strategic planning'. *Management Decision*, **30**(8), 4–11.

Hilgard, E.R. and Bower, G.H. (1967) *Theories of Learning*. New York: Appleton-Century-Crofts.

Hirschey, R.C. and Caves, R.E. (1981) 'Internationalization of research and transfer of technology by multinational enterprises'. *Oxford Bulletin of Economic and Statistics*, **42**, May, 115–130.

Hopper, M.D. (1990) 'Rattling sabre: New ways to compete on information'. *Harvard Business Review*, **68**(3), 118–125.

Inkpen, A.C. and Crossan, M.M. (1995) 'Believing is seeing: Joint ventures and organisation learning'. *Journal of Management Studies*, **32**(5), 595–618.

Jackson. T. (1993) *Organisational Behaviour in International Management*. Oxford, UK: Butterworth-Heinemann.

Jelinek, M. and Golhar, J.D. (1983) 'The interface between strategy and manufacturing technology'. *Columbia Journal of World Business*, Spring.

Johnson, S.B. (1984) 'Comparing R and D strategies of Japanese and US firms'. *Sloan Management Review*, **25**(3), 25–34.

Kamoche, K. (1997) 'Knowledge creation and learning in international human resource management'. *International Journal of Human Resource Management*, **8**(3), April, 213–225.

Kay, J. (1993) *Foundations of Corporate Success*. Oxford, UK: Oxford University Press.

Keen, P.G.W. (1987) *An International Perspective on Managing Information Technologies* (ICIT briefing paper). Washington, DC: International Center for Information Technologies.

Kolb, D.A., Rubin, I.M. and Osland, J. (1991) *Organizational Behaviour: An Experiential Approach*. Englewood Cliffs, NJ: Prentice Hall.

Laudon, K.C. and Laudon, J.P. (1991) *Management Information Systems – A Contemporary Perspective*. London: Macmillan.

Levitt, T. (1983) 'The globalization of markets'. *Harvard Business Review*, May/June.

Liao, W.M. (1979) 'Effects of learning on resource allocation decisions'. *Decision Sciences*, **10**(1), January, 116–125.

Maidique, M.A. and Hayes, R.H. (1984) 'The art of high technology management'. *Sloan Management Review*, **25**(2), 17–31.

Mansfield, E., Teece, D.J. and Romeo, A. (1979) 'Overseas research and development by US-based firms', *Economica*, **46** (May), 187–196.

Martin, J. (1984) *An Information Systems Manifesto*. Englewood Cliffs, NJ: Prentice Hall.

Martin, J. (1990) *Information Engineering* (Vols 1, 2 and 3). Englewood Cliffs, NJ: Prentice Hall.

Martin, N. and Hough, D. (1992) 'The open systems revolution: Opportunities for the logistics industry'. *Logistics Information Management*, **5**(3), 19–23.

McMaster, M. (1997) 'Organising for innovation: Technology and intelligent capacities'. *Long Range Planning*, **30**(5), 799–802.

Parsaye, K. (1989) *Intelligent Databases*. New York: John Wiley & Sons.

Parsons, G.L. (1983) 'Information technology, a new competitive weapon'. *Sloan Management Review*, **25**(1), 3–13.

Pavitt, K. (1984) 'Technology transfer amongst the industrially advanced countries: An overview'. In: N. Rosenberg (ed.), *International Technology Transfer*. Chichester, UK: John Wiley & Sons.

Pavitt, K. (1986) 'Technology, innovation and strategic management'. In: J. McGee and A. Thomas (eds), *Strategic Management Research* (pp. 171–190). London: John Wiley & Sons.

Porter, M.E. (1985) *Competitive Advantage*. New York: Free Press.

Porter, M.E. (1986a) 'Changing patterns of international competition'. *California Management Review*, **28**(2), Winter, 9–40.

Porter, M.E. (1986b) *Competition in Global Business*. Boston: Harvard University Press.

Porter, M.E. (1990) *The Competitive Advantage of Nations*. New York: Free Press.

Porter, M.E. and Millar, V.E. (1985) 'How information gives you competitive advantage'. *Harvard Business Review*, **63**(4) 149–160.

Prahalad, C.K. and Doz Y.L. (1987) *The Multinational Mission: Balancing Local Demands and Global Vision*. New York: Free Press.

Prahalad, C.K. and Hamel, G. (1989) 'Strategic intent'. *Harvard Business Review*, **67**(3), 63–76.

Prahalad, C.K. and Hamel, G. (1990) 'The core competence of the corporation'. *Harvard Business Review*, May/June, 79–91.

Quinn, J.B. (1992) *The Intelligent Enterprise*. New York: Free Press.

Quintas, P. and Lefevre, P. (1997) 'Knowledge management: A strategic agenda'. *Long Range Planning*, **30**(3), 385–397.

Rogers, D.S., Daugherty, P.J. and Stank, T.P. (1993) 'Enhancing service responsiveness: The strategic potential of EDI'. *Logistics Information Management*, **6**(3), 27–32.

Roberts, E.B. and Berry, C.A. (1985) 'Entering new businesses: Selecting strategies for success'. *Sloan Management Review*, Spring, 3–17.

Ronstadt, R. (1977) *Research and Development Abroad by US Multinationals*. New York: Praeger.

Ronstadt, R. (1978) 'International R&D: The establishment and evolution of research and development abroad by US multinationals'. *Journal of International Business Studies*, **9**, 7–24.

Sanchez, R. and Heene, A. (eds) (1997) *Strategic Learning and Knowledge Management*. New York: John Wiley & Sons.

Senge, P. (1990) 'Building learning organizations'. *Sloan Management Review*, Fall.

Senge, P. (1990) *The Fifth Discipline. The Art and Practice of the Learning Organisation*. London: Century Business.

Severn, A.K. and Laurance, M.M. (1974) 'Direct investment, research intensity and profitability'. *Journal of Financial and Quantitative Analysis*, **9**, March, 181–190.

Steele, L.W. (1975) *Innovation in Big Business*. New York: Elsevier.

Stonehouse, G.H. and Pemberton, J. (1999) 'Learning and knowledge management in the intelligent organisation'. *Participation and Empowerment: An International Journal*, **7**(5), 131–144.

Stopford, J.M. and Turner, L. (1985) *Britain and the Multinationals*. New York: John Wiley & Sons.

Teece, D.J. (1977) *Technology Transfer by Multinational Firms*. Cambridge, MA: Ballinger.

Tsurumi, U. (1976) *The Japanese Are Coming: A Multinational Spread of Japanese Firms*. Cambridge, MA: Ballinger.

Turner, I. (1996) 'Working with chaos'. *Financial Times*, 4 October.

Volberda, H.W. (1997) 'Building flexible organisations for fast-moving markets'. *Long Range Planning*, **30**(2), 169–183.

Whitehill, M. (1997) 'Knowledge-based strategy to deliver sustained competitive advantage'. *Long Range Planning*, **30**(4), 621–627.

Wilson, I. (1986) 'The strategic management of technology: Corporate fad or strategic necessity'. *Long Range Planning*, **19**(2), 21–22.

Wiseman, C. (1985) *Strategy and Computers: Information Systems as Competitive Weapons*. Homewood, IL: Dow Jones/Richard D. Irwin.

Wyman, J. (1985) 'SMR Forum technological myopia – The need to think about technology'. *Sloan Management Review*, **26**(4), Summer.

Yip, G.S. (1992) *Total Global Strategy – Managing for Worldwide Competitive Advantage*. Englewood Cliffs, NJ: Prentice Hall.

Yelle, L.E. (1979) 'The learning curve: Historical review and comprehensive survey'. *Decision Sciences*, **10**(2), April, 302–328.

Zuboff, S. (1988) *In the Age of the Smart Machine*. London: Heinemann.

GLOBAL AND TRANSNATIONAL MARKETING MANAGEMENT

Introduction

Global marketing strategy is primarily concerned with the global scope and co-ordination of marketing activities, and the extent of standardization and adaptation of products, brands, and promotion and advertising. A global and transnational marketing strategy does not imply global standardization of all aspects of the strategy. Rather, it implies a global perspective, seeking to combine the benefits of global and local features. Marketing strategy is based on the appropriate global segmentation and positioning strategies, accompanied by a global marketing mix that is based on a global perspective of products, brands, advertising and promotion combined with local adaptation where it gives marketing advantages.

Global marketing strategy is based on analysis of the extent of globalization of various aspects of the market environment, like similarities and differences in consumer tastes, cultural similarities and differences, technical standards, levels of income, legislation and availability of advertising media.

The Internet has an increasingly important role to play in the marketing strategy and operations of global business organizations. It has the potential to transform relationships with customers, suppliers, agents and distributors on a worldwide basis.

The role of marketing in global and transnational strategy

Marketing and strategy

The study and practice of marketing have broadened considerably, from an emphasis on marketing as a functional management issue to a wider focus on the strategic role of marketing in overall corporate strategy. This broadening of the marketing concept, to include strategic as well as operational decisions, has resulted in an overlap between marketing and strategic management and has generated considerable controversy over the role and position of marketing in corporate strategy.

One view of strategy argues that strategic planning is the reserve of directors and corporate planners, managers who can take a broad-based view of the company's operations. In this context, marketing is seen as only one of several functional management areas providing important inputs into the strategic planning process. The primary role of marketing is to provide marketing information as an input into planning and the development of the tactical marketing mix.

Not surprisingly, the leading marketing authors dispute this view, arguing for a more central role for marketing in the determination of corporate strategy. For example, Baker (1985) argued for the adoption of a strategic marketing orientation:

It is my belief that while general managers do not see themselves as marketing managers, they should be just that, in the sense that they ought to subscribe to the philosophy of business encapsulated in the marketing concept. . . . Similarly, corporate strategists must be marketing strategists, for without a market there is no purpose for the corporation and no role for a corporate strategist (Baker, 1985, p. 29).

Toyne and Walter's (1993) perspective

The controversy regarding the role of marketing in corporate strategy has also emerged in global business. Toyne and Walters (1993), in their book *Global Marketing Management: A Strategic Perspective*, adopted a traditional view of marketing as a functional management area providing important inputs into the strategic planning process (and this despite the subtitle of the book *A Strategic Perspective*).

Marketing is seen as fulfilling the following roles in the overall global strategy of the business:

- identifying and making recommendations about future trends and opportunities in the markets where the company is already active;
- identifying and making recommendations about new marketing opportunities;
- providing estimates of the marketing resources (budget and staff) needed to exploit these opportunities;
- developing and implementing marketing strategies that are consistent with the overall strategic direction of the company in global markets.

Global marketing co-ordination

The second main perspective on the role of marketing in global strategy emphasizes the competitive advantages that can be derived from co-ordinating marketing on a global basis. Michael Porter's (1986a) work on the global configuration and co-ordination of value-added activities was reviewed in Chapter 6. Within the framework adopted, marketing is seen as an important source of value added which performs three important roles in the overall global strategy of the business:

- marketing configuration, which refers to the location of various marketing activities throughout the world (geographically concentrated or dispersed);
- marketing co-ordination, which refers to the extent of standardization or adaptation of the marketing mix globally;

- the strategic role of marketing, especially the link between marketing and the other value-added activities of the company (e.g., design, technology development, manufacturing).

Marketing and competitive advantage

According to Takeuchi and Porter (1986), significant competitive advantages can be achieved in each of these areas. Taking the first, the need to perform marketing in all countries implies a high level of geographical dispersion of activity. Important competitive advantages can be derived, however, by concentrating certain marketing activities globally, when conditions permit, including: the production of promotion material; central salesforce; central service support; centralized training; and global advertising.

There are a number of ways in which geographically dispersed marketing activities can be co-ordinated to gain competitive advantage, including:

- performing marketing activities using similar methods across countries;
- transferring marketing know-how and skills from country to country;
- sequencing of marketing programmes across countries; and
- integrating the efforts of various marketing groups in different countries.

Finally, the greatest leverage from taking a global view of marketing is its links to other upstream and support activities in the value chain. In particular, global marketing can allow significant economies of scale and learning in production and R&D, through uniform products for global markets.

The work of Takeuchi and Porter (1986), therefore, suggests a more central role for marketing in global business strategy. While recognizing its importance, marketing is seen as only one of several sources of competitive advantage, and the hypotheses concerning the role of marketing are secondary to the main argument concerning global configuration and co-ordination of all value chain activities.

Ohmae's (1989) view of marketing

Takeuchi and Porter's (1986) work can be contrasted with the work of Ohmae (1989), who argued that marketing is the core of any global strategy. Three distinct phases in the evolution of global business are identified.

Incremental multinational expansion

In the initial phase of multinational expansion, foreign markets were entered incrementally (according to Vernon's, 1966 international product life cycle model) through clone-like subsidiaries of the parent company in each new country of operation. These subsidiaries repatriated profits to the parent company, which remained the dominant force at the centre.

Competitor-focused expansion

This model of multinational expansion gave way by the early 1980s to a competitor-focused approach to globalization, associated mainly with the work of Michael Porter. According to Ohmae, this competitor-driven phase of globalization has been superseded by a customer-driven phase.

Customer-driven expansion

The needs and preferences of customers have globalized; that is why businesses need to globalize. Delivering value to customers, rather than pre-empting competitors, is the only legitimate reason for thinking global. Yip (1992) contended that global marketing can bring about four major benefits:

1. enhanced knowledge of customer preferences;
2. increased competitive leverage;
3. improved product quality; and
4. cost reduction.

To summarize these views, global marketing strategy is an essential element of an overall transnational strategy. It will be both customer and competitor-based and will be both globally and locally oriented.

Globalization of markets and marketing research

Customer needs, and therefore markets, are becoming increasingly global for many goods and services, but the extent of globalization varies considerably from market to market. Even in a market where customer needs are similar on a global basis there may be elements of the marketing mix (these being considerations over product design, price, place [i.e., segment], and promotion) which must be varied locally.

A global marketing strategy and the associated marketing mix must take account of the following factors in the market environment:

- *customer needs* – the extent to which they are global or to which there are specific local needs;
- *culture* – the products, brand names or advertising may have to be varied on a local basis to account for regional cultural differences;
- *language* – may require local variations in packaging, labelling, brand name and advertising;
- *technology* – the level of technology in a country or differing technical standards may require variations in product;
- *legal factors* – may demand variations in packaging, advertising, product features and so on.

In addition, analysis using Yip's globalization drivers (Chapter 4) will give an indication of which aspects of marketing strategy can be global and which must be varied locally. Global marketing research will indicate the extent to which aspects of marketing strategy can be standardized or the extent to which local variations must be introduced. The impact of these various factors on a global and transnational marketing strategy are explored further in the remainder of this chapter. Finally, marketing strategy (along with all other 'functional' strategies) must be an integral part of the overall transnational strategy of the organization.

Global marketing strategies

Different perspectives

Chapter 6 examined a number of approaches to global and transnational strategy which had been developed by different authors, from both a competitor and customer-oriented perspective. Global marketing strategy must also adapt to these perspectives. Drawing on Porter (1986a), a global marketing strategy must incorporate an appropriate degree of co-ordination and integration of geographically dispersed or concentrated marketing activities.

Although developed from a competitor-oriented perspective, Porter's view has important implications for global marketing. Hamel and Prahalad (1985) attributed the success of Japanese companies in global markets to their long-term strategic intent of global brand domination. Doz (1986) analysed the extent of global product standardization versus adaptation and found that success depends to a large extent on the type of global strategy adopted – multinational integration, national responsiveness and multifocal strategies.

In the same way that aspects of global marketing strategy have been developed from a competitor-oriented perspective, other authors have developed perspectives more closely based on customer orientation. This section examines three such typologies based on the work of Douglas and Craig (1989), Leontiades (1986) and Toyne and Walters (1993).

Douglas and Craig's (1989) typology

An important feature of global marketing strategy is the co-ordination and integration of marketing on a worldwide basis in the pursuit of global competitive advantage. The importance of co-ordination and integration issues were emphasized by Douglas and Craig (1989) who related global marketing to the evolution of global strategy over time. They identified three main phases in the evolution of global marketing with each stage presenting new strategic challenges and decision priorities to the firm.

Phase 1
Phase 1 represents the initial stage of international market expansion where the main strategic decisions facing the business include the choice of country to enter, the mode of entry adopted (see Chapter 7) and the extent of product standardization or adaptation.

Phase 2
Once the company has established a 'beachhead' in a number of foreign markets, it then begins to seek new directions for growth and expansion, thus moving to phase 2 of internationalization. The focus in this stage is mainly on building market penetration in countries where the company is already located. In consequence, the expansion effort is mainly directed by local management with marketing strategy being determined on a country by country or national responsive basis.

Phase 3
It is the third evolutionary phase that is the most important in the context of global marketing. In phase 3 the business moves toward a global

orientation. The country by country approach to marketing is replaced by one in which markets are viewed as a set of interrelated and interdependent entities. These are increasingly integrated and interlinked worldwide, and co-ordination and integration of global marketing becomes essential to fully exploit the competitive advantages to be derived from the company's global scope. According to Douglas and Craig (1989) there are two key strategic thrusts in phase 3.

First, the drive to improve the efficiency of worldwide operations through co-ordination and integration. This will not only cover marketing activities, such as product development, advertising, distribution and pricing, but also related production, sourcing and management. Standardization of product lines globally, for example, will facilitate the development of a globally integrated production and logistics network (see Chapter 9).

The second key strategic thrust is the search for global expansion and growth opportunities. This will involve a range of activities including: opportunities for transferring products, brand names, marketing ideas, skills and expertise between countries; identification of global market segments and target customers; and worldwide product development aimed at global markets.

Leontiades' (1986) perspective

While Douglas and Craig (1989) focused on the evolution toward global marketing, Leontiades (1986) focused more on the competitive marketing strategies of international businesses, identifying four generic international competitive marketing strategies (Figure 11.1).

Global high-share strategies

These strategies involve pricing, promotion, product and other elements of the marketing mix being geared toward the high-volume segments of global markets. The essence of global high-share strategies is the worldwide co-ordination of company resources behind global objectives. The global scope of marketing creates opportunities for competitive advantage through: lower costs and economies of scale; providing a global service; international sourcing; experience transfers; promoting an international corporate image; global resource focus; and improving the risk/return characteristics of the company's international business portfolio.

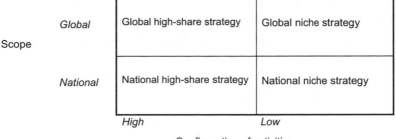

Figure 11.1 Four generic international marketing strategies
Source: Leontiades (1986)

Global niche strategies
These involve specialization by product, technology, stage of life cycle, market segment, etc. They avoid head-on competition with companies pursuing global high-share strategies.

National high-share strategies
These involve the use of nationally based competitive advantages, with marketing and production geared toward achieving high volume and lower costs relative to other national competitors.

National niche strategies
These involve specialization on a national scale to avoid competition with both global and national high-share companies.

Only the first two of these marketing strategies can be classified as being global. While Leontiades (1986) focused on the overall generic strategies of companies in global markets, Toyne and Walters (1993) provided a more comprehensive coverage of the main components of global marketing.

Four stages in a global marketing strategy

The development of a global marketing strategy involves four main stages:

- defining the global marketing mission;
- the global segmentation strategy;
- the competitive market-positioning strategy;
- the global marketing mix strategy.

Global marketing mission
The global marketing mission defines the major target markets to be attacked, the way these markets are to be segmented and the competitive position to be adopted in each market. In other words, the mission establishes the general parameters within which global marketing strategy decisions are made.

Segmentation strategies
In terms of global segmentation strategies, the three main alternatives identified are:

- *Global market segments* – where markets are segmented according to variables that largely ignore national boundaries (e.g., demographic, buying practices, preferences). The strategy concentrates on identifying similarities in customer needs across countries rather than emphasizing country/cultural differences. Some techniques for achieving this are examined in the next section.
- *National market segments* – which involves serving the same market segments in multiple markets but on a national basis. Segmentation is on the basis of geography/nationality, which emphasizes the cultural differences rather than similarities between countries.
- *Mixed market segments* – which is largely a combination of the first two. Some national markets may be of a sufficient size to warrant individualization. Others may be clustered into similar market segments.

Deciding on competitive position and marketing mix
Once the broad segmentation strategy has been established, the global company must decide on its competitive position within each market and its marketing mix strategy (see marketing mix strategy below).

Yip's (1992) view is that a global marketing strategy must be part of a global business strategy. A global strategy will be appropriate when customer needs are globally common, there are global customers and channels, and when marketing is globally transferable. In addition, cost drivers are likely to favour a global approach to marketing by creating economies of scale and scope. There are also competitive advantages (Table 11.1) to global marketing (e.g., through global branding). Yip did not advocate a marketing strategy that is global in every detail, rather one

Table 11.1   Potential advantages and limitations of a global marketing strategy

Advantages of global marketing	Comments
Unit cost reduction	Consolidation of the global-marketing function, economies of scale, experience curve economies, dilution of R&D and other fixed costs, etc.
Improved quality of products and programmes	Through concentration on key marketing activities, uniform products, etc.
Enhanced customer preferences	Through global customer knowledge of products, global availability, global serviceability, etc.
Increased competitive leverage	By focusing resources and unifying the approach to competition.
Risk reduction	Through reduced dependency on local demand, wider access to capital.
Global knowledge and information transfers	Transfer of experience, practice, etc.

Limitations of global marketing	Comments
Company-specific factors	For example, lack of resources, lack of global orientation, higher costs of co-ordination.
Environment factors	Linguistic, cultural, technological and legal factors.
Market factors	Customer need differences, channel differences, etc.
Product factors	Overstandardization can result in products that satisfy nobody.
Responsiveness	Overcentralization reduces responsiveness.

Source: derived from Toyne and Walters (1993) and Yip (1992).

that is global where there are evident advantages and local where necessary:

> *So global marketing is not a blind adherence to standardisation of all marketing elements for its own sake, but a different, global approach to developing marketing strategy and programs that blends flexibility with uniformity* (Yip, 1992).

In essence then, a global or transnational marketing strategy is concerned with devising a strategy that is global in scope and that is globally co-ordinated. The extent of globalization of each element of the strategy will be dependent on the transnational strategy of the organization, the relative advantages of globalization or localization based on such factors as customer needs.

Global market segmentation and positioning strategies

The key to successful global co-ordination and integration of marketing is effective market segmentation and product-positioning strategy. If the globalization hypothesis of Levitt (1983) and its 'converging commonality' of customer needs were accepted, then it could be seen as removing the need for market segmentation and product-positioning strategies, in that completely standardized products could be sold worldwide. Yet, it is evident that there remain important national differences between markets that require segmentation and positioning.

Segmentation bases

The traditional approach to international marketing segmentation was to segment a market on a country basis to take account of national differences in demand conditions. Kale and Sudharsham (1987), however, suggested a different approach for segmenting international markets which is more compatible with the requirement for global marketing co-ordination. The approach makes customers and their needs the basis for segmentation. It has the advantage of being consumer-oriented, while allowing global co-ordination of marketing, since it focuses on similarities rather than differences across groups of consumers in different countries. The basis of this approach is the 'strategically equivalent segmentation' (SES) of consumers. This is the identification of transnational segments of consumers, with similar needs, who will respond similarly to a given marketing mix. Four main stages are involved in identifying SES:

1. *the criteria to be used in segmenting markets* – develop qualifying and determining dimensions;
2. *country screening* – using qualifying dimensions to narrow down the list of countries as viable entry candidates;
3. *identifying market segments in each country* – develop microsegments in each qualified country;
4. *measuring segments* – develop factor score representation of microsegments and clustering analysis for SES.

The initial stage is the identification of qualifying criteria for identifying market segments (e.g., age, sex, income, etc.). This is followed by country screening to identify the relative size of the segments in each country. After these filtering processes to identify which segments in which countries are to be targeted, the target market segment is then aggregated across countries to provide the total market. The major advantage of this approach is that it permits a business to adopt a global marketing strategy in strategically equivalent segments without assuming the complete cultural convergence of countries. Examples of products which are offered in strategically equivalent segments across the world include Nike trainers, Calvin Klein jeans and Ferrari automobiles.

Market positioning

A useful review of the issues involved in global marketing positioning can be found in Perry (1988). Two main types of positioning are identified. First, market positioning which refers to the competitive position of a product in the market (e.g., market leader, strong number two, etc.). Second, product positioning which refers to the attributes of a product in comparison with other products or to consumer needs. These two types of positioning can occur at two levels: first, the marketplace and, second, in the consumers' mind. The first emphasizes the importance of competition; the second, customer orientation. A combination of these alternatives gives the model shown in Table 11.2. The importance of this to global marketing is that

Table 11.2 Positioning concepts and their meaning

	Market position (competitive standing)	Product position (profile attributes)
Measurements – marketplace	Market share	Comparison of attributes
Consumer's mind	Reputation	Image (perceptual map)
Possible positions	Leader (lion) Challenger (tiger) Leaper (frog) Nicher (groundhog) Follower (ant) Imitator (mouse)	Product category Price/quality vector Main features
Possible strategies	Enlarge Concur Advance Protect Withdraw	Reinforce Reposition

Source: derived from Perry (1988)

different positioning strategies can be adopted in different country markets in terms of market and product position.

There are advantages in having a common global perception of positioning. Nissan Motors, for example, is seen as a producer of good quality, reliable, reasonably priced products on a global basis. This is also linked to many standardized aspects of its marketing mix. There are, however, occasions when companies adopt different positions globally. Stella Artois is regarded as a standard beer in Belgium, but in some other markets it is positioned as a premium lager. In each case the advantages of uniform position have to be weighed against the advantages of differentiated positioning. Businesses adopting the same positioning strategy in all markets have adopted a *global-positioning strategy*, while those who vary position across markets are said to have adopted a *mixed-positioning strategy*.

Global marketing management

The adoption of global marketing strategies involving co-ordination and integration of worldwide marketing raises a large number of important issues concerning global management of the marketing mix. These are examined in this section covering global products, pricing, promotion and distribution. It should be noted that the issues involved are complex and varied, and all that can be attempted in the confines of this section is to present a brief overview of issues, together with a slightly more detailed discussion of some of the more important topics. Readers requiring a more comprehensive coverage should consult the further reading references at the end of the chapter.

Marketing mix strategy

Toyne and Walters (1993) identified four main categories of marketing mix strategy based on the global segmentation and positioning strategy of the business (Figure 11.2). The four options for marketing strategy are:

- *ideal global marketing strategy* – the marketing of a standard product to a global market segment using uniform marketing programmes;
- *ideal national marketing strategy* – the marketing mix is specifically tailored to meet the requirements of each national market;
- *hybrid I marketing strategy* – the standardization of products but the

Product strategy		National market segments	Global market segments
	Global product	Hybrid I marketing strategy	Ideal global marketing strategy
	National product	Ideal national marketing strategy	Hybrid II marketing strategy
		Segmentation strategy	

Figure 11.2 The global marketing strategy mix matrix
Source: adapted from Toyne and Walters (1993)

adaptation of other elements of the marketing mix to reinforce the product strategy;

- *hybrid II marketing strategy* – the standardization of one key element of the marketing mix but the adaptation of others.

Yip (1992) argued the case that *any* elements of the marketing mix can be standardized or varied as part of a global marketing strategy, according to the requirements of the global market.

The following sections consider the impact of alternative global or transnational marketing strategies on elements of the marketing mix. The emphasis of global marketing, however, remains focused on the identification of similarities between customer needs in particular market segments across countries rather than emphasizing differences. Thus the strategy of companies like McDonald's is centred on a core formula for its restaurants and food products but a degree of customization is allowed to meet different needs. For example, alcohol is served in McDonald's stores in some countries but not in others. The extent of standardization and customization of marketing strategy will depend on the competences of the business, the nature of its products, the nature of its markets and the importance of cultural, legal, technological and other factors.

McDonald's – globally homogeneous?

It is a myth that McDonald's assumes the world to have homogeneous demand for its standard products. In fact, it adapts its product offerings widely throughout the world to account for local taste and cultural preferences. Some of these are down to social culture while others are driven by religious and historical factors. Other parts of its format, retailing formula and marketing activity are the same throughout the world (e.g., the double arches logo, the restaurant layout and 'feel', etc.), but the product offering is sometimes modified to account for local tastes and sensibilities. In this respect, McDonald's can be said to pursue a hybrid II approach to global marketing. The following table describes a few of these local adaptations to illustrate the point.

Country	Example of 'unique' products
Chile	McNífica is a sandwich that includes tomato, ketchup, mayonnaise, onions, lettuce and cheddar cheese.
Cyprus	McNistisima is the promotional name for the Lenten period products offered to customers during the fasting period before Easter and Christmas. During this period, McDonald's customers can choose from a selection of Lent products, such as veggie burgers, country potatoes, shrimps and spring rolls.
India	McDonald's entered the market without the Big Mac, and local religious diet restrictions meant the company had to make a commitment not to introduce beef or pork products into its menu. Instead, products similar to the Big Mac with mutton and chicken patties were introduced (the Maharaja Mac and Chicken Maharaja Mac, respectively). With the large vegetarian population in mind, an entire vegetarian range was introduced including products using eggless mayonnaise.
Ireland	The Shamrock Shake – special shakes available for a period around the St Patrick's Day celebrations.
Israel	All meat served in McDonald's restaurants in Israel is 100% kosher beef. McDonald's operates kosher restaurants and non-kosher restaurants. Their non-kosher restaurants serve Israeli customers who do not keep strictly kosher and want to visit McDonald's on Saturdays and religious holidays. McDonald's Israel's seven kosher restaurants, where the menu does not

	include any dairy products and all food is prepared in accordance with kosher law, are not open on the Sabbath and all religious holidays.
Italy	A range of Mediterranean salads.
Japan	The Teriyaki McBurger – a sausage patty on a bun with teriyaki sauce.
South Korea	Bulgogi Burger – 100% pork patty on a bun with bulgogi sauce and lettuce.
Netherlands	The McKroket – 100% beef ragout with a crispy layer around it, topped with a fresh mustard/mayonnaise sauce.
Pakistan	The three McMaza meals (Chatpata Chicken Roll, Chicken Chutni Burger and Spicy Chicken Burger) – spicy and tangy tastes, developed keeping in mind the local palate.
Turkey	KöfteBurger – made of a spicy meat patty inside a specially prepared, flavoured bun enriched with a special yogurt mix and spiced tomato sauce. Also Ayran – a traditional Turkish soft drink.
UK	McBacon Roll – a breakfast product made with back bacon and traditional special brown sauce, served in a maize topped roll.

Global products

The importance of product decisions

Product decisions are probably the most important element of a company's marketing mix. They can have a major impact on the performance of the whole business in global markets. Products represent the most visible aspect of the company in foreign markets. Product design, quality, performance, etc. have a very significant effect on the global image and reputation of the company. In addition, other elements of the global marketing mix (pricing, promotion and distribution) need to be designed and developed on the basis of product decisions:

> *To a very important degree, a company's products define its business. Pricing, communication, and distribution policies must fit the product. A firm's customers and competitors are determined by the products it offers. Its research and development requirements depend upon the technologies of its products. Indeed, every aspect of the enterprise is heavily influenced by the firm's product offering* (Keegan, 1989).

Decisions on product strategy

A wide range of decisions need to be taken in the area of global product policy, including:

- *product range decisions* concerning the number, range and type of product sold throughout the world;
- *new product development* for global markets, including the process of research and development;
- *global product diffusion and adoption* concerning the rate of transfer and acceptance of new products in different markets;
- *managing the international product life cycle* which may be at different stages in different markets;
- *product standardization or differentiation* questions;
- *generic product strategies* which may be based on core competences and associated cost leadership, differentiation, hybrid or focus;
- *packaging, branding, after-sales service*, etc., decisions.

It is not possible to consider all of these issues in detail in this section. Indeed, two of these decisions – standardization versus differentiation and global market segmentation and positioning – were examined in the previous section. The remainder of this section focuses in more detail on one of the most important global product decisions facing any company: namely, that of global branding.

Global branding

A brand was defined by Thomas (1986) as 'a name, term, sign, symbol, mark, lettering or design (or any combination thereof) intended to differentiate a product from its competitors.'

Successful branding strategies can be an important source of competitive advantage in some marketplaces by differentiating the product from that of competitors, maintaining product quality and image, achieving strong brand loyalty and sustained consumer commitment, and erecting barriers to entry. Brands tend to be most important in consumer rather than industrial or intermediate markets. Whereas brands tend to cultivate confidence among consumers in FMCG (fast-moving consumer goods) or consumer durables sectors, intermediates such as petrochemicals, energy, aggregates and other industrial goods tend to be bought much more on the basis of technical specification or price.

The advantages of successful branding will be particularly important in global marketing given the intensity of the competitive environment in consumer goods sectors. One of the most important issues in branding for global markets is the choice between global or multiple country brands (i.e., whether a standardized global brand is sold worldwide or whether the brand is adapted to local market differences). The world's top brands are shown in Table 11.3.

It is noteworthy that few names appear in all four lists. Coca-Cola is one of the few names which does. There are some interesting omissions from the list, including Nike, Reebok and some others. These brands are undoubtedly well recognized on a global basis, particularly among groups of consumers in the global market segments that they serve. It is therefore a mistake to assume that global brands are insignificant. There are few people in the global consumer groups who purchase training shoes who are not aware of the Nike and Reebok brand names.

Advantages and constraints

There are several advantages to be gained from a global brand name. Brand names are often associated with consumer perceptions of quality, reliability, performance and other positive product features. Perhaps the most important advantage, therefore, is the positive perception that consumer's have of products associated with the brand name. Other major advantages to be derived from global branding are marketing efficiency through economies of scale, promotion of a global image and reputation and global consumer loyalty.

Table 11.3 The world's top 20 brands by triad region and world

World	USA	Europe	Japan
Coca-Cola	Coca-Cola	Coca-Cola	Sony
Sony	Campbell's	Sony	National
Mercedes-Benz	Disney	Mercedes-Benz	Mercedes-Benz
Kodak	Pepsi-Cola	BMW	Toyota
Disney	Kodak	Philips	Takashimaya
Nestlé	NBC	Volkswagen	Rolls-Royce
Toyota	Black & Decker	Adidas	Seiko
McDonald's	Kellogg's	Kodak	Matsushita
IBM	McDonald's	Nivea	Hibachi
Pepsi-Cola	Hershey's	Porsche	Suntory
Rolls-Royce	Levi's	Volvo	Porsche
Honda	GE	Colgate	Kirin
Panasonic	Sears	Rolls-Royce	Hotel New Otani
Levi's	Hallmark	Levi's	Fuji TV
Kleenex	Johnson & Johnson	Ford	Snow Brand Milk
Ford	Betty Crocker	Jaguar	Imperial Hotel
Volkswagen	Kraft	Fanta	Coca-Cola
Kellogg's	Kleenex	Nescafé	Mitsukoshi
Porsche	Jell-O	Black & Decker	Japan Travel Bureau
Polaroid	Tylenol	Esso	Disney

Source: Owen (1993)

The extent of global branding, however, is constrained by several factors, including:

- *Legal constraints* – in some developing countries, for example, foreign brands may be either banned or taxed more heavily.
- *Language and cultural factors* – which may lead to misleading connotations of certain brand names, requiring brand adaptation. In the automobile industry, for example, manufacturers have long tailored their product/brand names to individual countries or regions. The Volkswagen Golf is standard throughout most of Europe, Asia and Africa. In the USA, however, it is known as the Rabbit, as it is in Latin America and the Caribbean.
- *Consumer homogeneity* – the extent to which global branding is possible obviously depends on the extent of consumer homogeneity between markets or, to use Levitt's (1983) terminology, the extent of 'converging commonality'.
- *Counterfeiting* – this is one of the most serious problems faced by global branders. Pirating of video films, computer software, music recordings and designer clothing cost global business millions of dollars each year (see Kotabe and Helsen, 1998 for a detailed discussion).

Key branding decisions

The strategic decisions facing companies in global branding have been examined by Onkvisit and Shaw (1983). Four main strategic decisions are discussed, namely:

1. *whether to brand or not to brand* – which depends on whether the product has salient attributes that can be differentiated;
2. *whether to use the manufacturer's own brand or the distributor's/ retailer's private brand;*
3. *whether to use global or local brands* – which depends on the extent of intermarket differences;
4. *whether to use single or multiple brands* in the same market.

These decisions are summarized in Figure 11.3. The main advantages and disadvantages of each of these strategic options are listed in Table 11.4. The figure and table should be considered in conjunction with each other as they assist in the brand decision-making process. Particular attention should be paid to the advantages and disadvantages of worldwide branding. The framework can be used as the basis of analysis of the branding strategy of a particular business in global markets.

Some research (Kashani, 1997a; Rosen et al., 1989; Landor Associates, 1990) has cast doubts on the significance of brand names as a means of attracting customers. Some of the doubts are the result of research that targeted general consumers rather than consumers from the segments where brands are known. Kashani (1997) argued that successful brands can still be built and that brand building must involve:

- *getting lean* – pruning weak brands and concentrating resources on successful and potentially successful brands;
- *investment* – particularly in product innovation;
- *listening* – to consumers and understanding their needs

It is evident that the decision to brand globally or locally is not simple. Many businesses therefore adopt a hierarchy of global, regional and local brands (Kotabe and Helsen, 1998) to combine the benefits of global and local branding. The Swiss company Nestlé has, for example:

- 10 global corporate brands, including Nestlé, Carnation, Perrier;
- 45 global strategic brands, including Kit Kat, Polo, Smarties, After Eight;
- 140 regional strategic brands, including Macintosh, Vittel Contadina;
- 7,500 local brands, including Texicana, Rocky, etc.

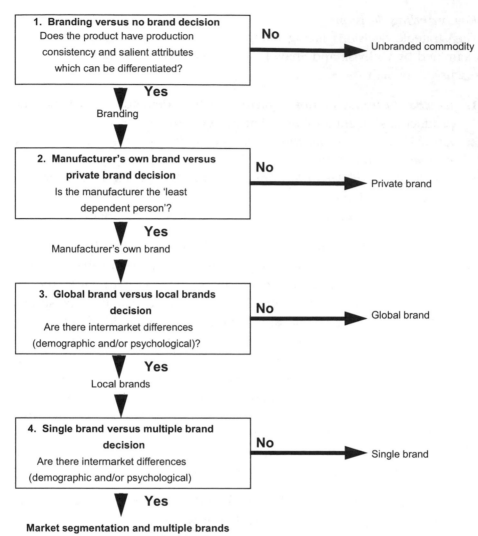

Figure 11.3 Branding decisions – from a manufacturer's perspective
Source: Onkvisit and Shaw (1983)

Global pricing

Pricing decisions

Like branding and advertising, *price* is an important element of a global marketing strategy. While price is heavily influenced by the overall strategy of the business, there is a need to ensure that it is sensitive to local market conditions. Price determination in international marketing is significantly

Table 11.4 Branding perspectives

Advantages		Disadvantages
Lower production cost Lower marketing cost Lower legal cost Flexible quality and quantity control	*No brand*	Severe price competition Lack of market identity
Better identification and awareness Better chance of product differentiation Possible brand loyalty Possible premium pricing	*Branding*	Higher production cost Higher marketing cost Higher legal cost
Better margins for dealers Possibly larger market share No promotional problems	*Private brand*	Severe price competition Lack of market identity
Better price – greater price inelasticity Better bargaining power Better control of distribution	*Manufacturer's brand*	Difficult for small manufacturers with unknown brand or identity Requiring brand promotion
Market segmented for varying needs Creating competitive spirits Avoiding negative connotation of existing brand Gain more retail shelf space Not hurting existing brand's image	*Multiple brands (in one market)*	Higher marketing cost Higher inventory cost Loss of economies of scale
Marketing efficiency Permitting more focused marketing Eliminator of brand confusion Good for product with good reputation (halo effect)	*Single brand (in one market)*	Assuming market homogeneity Existing brand's image hurt when trading up/down Limited shelf space
Meaningful names Local identification Avoidance of taxation on international brand Quick market penetration by acquiring local brand Allowing variations of quantity and quality across markets	*Local brands*	Higher marketing cost Higher inventory cost Loss of economies of scale Diffused image
Maximum marketing efficiency Reduction of advertising costs Elimination of brand confusion Good for culture-free product Good for prestigious product Easy identification/recognition for international travellers Uniform worldwide image	*Worldwide brands*	Assuming market homogeneity Problems with black and grey markets Possibility of negative connotation Requiring quality and quantity consistency Less developed country opposition and resentment Legal complications

Source: Onkvisit and Shaw (1983)

more complex than in domestic marketing as a result of such factors as variations in market demand and competitive conditions abroad, transport and distribution costs, tariffs and other government price controls, exchange rate fluctuations, etc. The need to integrate pricing with global strategy suggests that there should be global co-ordination of pricing policy, but the need to be locally responsive suggests variation in pricing. This section examines co-ordination and integration issues in relation to global pricing. Two of the most important issues in this respect are the locus of decision making regarding price determination and transfer pricing.

One of the most important price-related decisions in global marketing is the need for pricing policy to be developed within the context of the company's overall strategic objectives in global markets, and this is a powerful argument in favour of centralized co-ordination of pricing decisions. At the same time, however, prices need to be responsive to local environmental and market conditions in different countries, and this favours a decentralized approach, with pricing decisions being the responsibility of foreign subsidiaries. Decentralizing pricing decisions, on the other hand, may lead to intersubsidiary price competition.

Toyne and Walters (1993) identified three major groups of factors affecting international pricing:

- *company-specific factors* – these include the transnational strategy of the company, local variations to its strategy, research and development costs, and marketing and distribution costs;
- *external market-specific factors* – these include consumer tastes and behaviour, government regulations, the competitive environment, market structure and exchange rate fluctuations;
- *product-specific factors* – the stage of the international product life cycle, etc.

Becker (1980) identified four main factors as affecting international pricing:

- *costs* that establish a 'price floor';
- *demand and market factors* which set a 'price ceiling';
- *market structure and competition* which help to set a 'realistic price';
- *environmental constraints*, such as government price controls.

Yip (1992) made the point that, 'Charging the same absolute price can be very difficult because of inherent international differences in market price levels, laws, and the role of price, as well as differences in the business's market position and delivered costs.'

As an alternative to charging the same absolute price, businesses can opt to charge 'the same prices relative to their competitors in each market' (Yip, 1992). This, Yip argued, can help the business to maintain a consistent position in its markets.

Keegan (1989) identified three alternative pricing policies in global marketing:

- *the extension/ethnocentric pricing policy,* involving the uniformity of prices worldwide;
- *the adaptation/polycentric pricing policy,* where prices are determined by local subsidiaries and are responsive to local market needs;
- *the invention/geocentric pricing policy,* with prices determined in relation to the company's overall global marketing strategy.

The advantages and disadvantages of alternative pricing strategies are important to consider. Highly decentralized pricing has the advantage of being fully responsive to local market conditions. The main disadvantage is that decentralized prices may not be consistent with the overall global market objectives of the company and may encourage intersubsidiary price competition. This, in turn, may lead to opportunities for arbitrage and 'grey market' activities. The main advantage of centralized pricing is consistency with global strategy. The main disadvantage is that centrally determined prices may not take adequate account of local market conditions.

There are two intermediary situations between the two extremes of centralized, uniform pricing and decentralized, local market pricing. First, under the centralized pricing policy with decentralized price determination strategy, each national subsidiary is responsible for determining its own prices, but overall pricing policy is determined centrally. This may include decisions regarding rates of return to be achieved, market share and product-positioning objectives, etc. Second, prices may be determined decentrally but only within clearly defined limits laid down by the corporate centre.

Cross-subsidization is an important and controversial issue in global pricing. This occurs when a transnational or global company uses profits made in one country to subsidize prices elsewhere to gain market share. Thus, some Japanese companies have been accused of using surplus profits

Table 11.5 Pros and cons of different pricing strategies

	Advantages	Disadvantages
Standardized world pricing	Simple Equitable Removes possibility for arbitrage	Lack of responsiveness to local economic and demand conditions
Market-differentiated pricing	Market responsiveness	Creates opportunities for arbitrage and 'grey marketing'
Dichotomous pricing		Worst of both worlds

Source: adapted from Toyne and Walters (1993)

made in the protected Japanese market to subsidize prices on entry into the US and European markets, leading to accusations of 'dumping' (such as in the case of some semiconductors).

Toyne and Walters (1993) identified three alternative approaches (Table 11.5) to global pricing:

- *standard world pricing* – uniform pricing throughout the world;
- *market-differentiated pricing* – prices are customized for each market;
- *dichotomous pricing* – standardized foreign prices, separate from the domestic market price structure.

Toyne and Walters (1993) went on to argue that, subject to central co-ordination, a market-differentiated approach should be adopted in many cases, because:

- environmental factors affecting prices often vary significantly from market to market;
- pricing policy should be used proactively to achieve local market goals;
- the advantages of price uniformity are generally small;
- many of the drawbacks of price differentiation can be anticipated and managed.

Differentiated pricing can however create significant problems as it did in the late 1990s within the EU, where supermarket chains have used the 'grey market' to obtain and sell designer goods at lower prices. At the same time, many American products are sold in Europe for higher prices than in the USA.

Transfer pricing

The question of transfer pricing is an important and controversial one in global marketing. Transfer prices are the prices charged on intra-group trade. It occurs when there is a movement of parts, components, machinery, technology, etc., from one part of the global business network to another. The flow of goods and services is one-way; the flow of payment for these goods/services is the other way. The question then arises – what price is to be charged on such intra-group trade?

At this stage, it is worth pointing out the importance of the transfer-pricing issue since between 35 and 40% of all international trade takes the form of intra-company trade. The internal prices set for such trade can have a major effect on the value of exports and imports and, hence, on the balance of payments accounts of host and home countries. Keegan (1989) identified four main approaches to transfer pricing:

- transfer at direct cost;
- transfer at direct cost plus apportioned overhead and margin;
- transfer at a price derived from end market prices;
- transfer at an 'arm's length price' (i.e., a price that would have been negotiated by unrelated parties).

The crucial issue here is that international business can derive a number of benefits from the manipulation of internal transfer prices. These include reduced tax liability, circumventing restrictions on profit repatriation, reducing exchange risk and avoidance of import tariffs. The global tax liability of the business can be reduced by shifting declared profits from high-tax to low-tax countries. One way of achieving this is to manipulate transfer prices in order to increase the profits of subsidiaries in low-tax countries. Similarly, restrictions on profit repatriation may be overcome by 'overcharging' subsidiaries for goods and service transfers. Thus, money may be remitted from the country as payment for goods and services rather than as profits. In the same way, foreign exchange risk can be mitigated by manipulating transfer prices to siphon funds from countries where local currency depreciation is expected. Finally, where import tariffs are charged as a proportion of the value of goods, these can be reduced by artificially reducing the value of imports to subsidiaries through manipulating transfer prices.

Transfer pricing is also important in relation to management of exchange rate risk. This issue is discussed in Chapter 12 on global finance.

CHAPTER 11

Pricing decisions – a summary

The major issues in global pricing are:

- factors affecting global pricing;
- co-ordination of pricing;
- standardized versus differentiated pricing;
- transfer pricing;
- exchange rate risk and pricing.

Global pricing must be consistent with transnational strategy and with other elements of marketing strategy. Just as other elements of strategy can be standardized or localized, so can pricing. This allows the benefits of global strategy to be combined with those of local flexibility.

Global promotion

Marketing communications

Global promotion is defined here to include all forms of marketing communications that seek to influence the buying behaviour of existing and potential customers, including advertising, personal selling, direct mail, point of sale displays, literature, publicity and word of mouth communications (Keegan, 1989). Marketing texts have referred to these promotions as above-line (media promotions), below-line (more focused non-media promotions) and direct selling.

The major objectives of global promotion, as with domestic marketing, are 'to enhance the company's image vis-à-vis its competitors and/or to inform, educate, and influence the attitudes and buying behaviour of the individuals, companies, institutions, and/or government agencies that make up a target market' (Toyne and Walters, 1993).

Despite sharing the same objectives, global promotion is far more complex than domestic promotion due to the complexity of the global environment. This section explores:

- the extent of standardization of global promotion;
- the ways in which global promotion is organized and controlled (centralization versus decentralization);
- management of global promotional campaigns;
- the role and growth of global advertising agencies.

Standardization of global promotion

A concise summary of the arguments for and against the standardization of global advertising can be found in Mooij and Keegan (1991), summarized in Table 11.6. One of the most important factors constraining global advertising standardization is the relationship between the centre and subsidiary managers. This point was reinforced by Peebles (1989), who argued that the main obstacle to global advertising and the reason so many global campaigns fail is not because of cultural differences around the world, but rather because of interpersonal relationships between foreign subsidiaries and corporate headquarters (i.e., the 'not invented here' syndrome that can create subsidiary opposition to centrally designed campaigns).

Organization and control of promotions

Organization and control issues, therefore, are central to the debate on global advertising and have been well covered in the literature. Centralization of advertising decisions allows for greater co-ordination and integration of worldwide promotion, with the associated benefits listed in Table 11.6.

Table 11.6 Global advertising standardization

Arguments in favour of standardization	Arguments against standardization
Costs savings through economies of scale in promotion.	The heterogeneity of countries in terms of culture, mentality and product usage.
Promotion of uniform brand and corporate image.	The 'not invented here' syndrome (i.e., the desire of each country to create its own campaign).
Utilization of global media.	Differences in the media scene.
Simplified promotional planning through uniform objectives and simplified co-ordination and control.	Legal and regulatory constraints.
Maximum use of good ideas, transmission of know-how and continuous exchange of ideas.	Competitive position in different markets.
The tendency for global business to be centrally managed.	Product may be at different stages of its life cycle in different countries.
Better use of management abilities and resources.	Danger of being regarded as a foreign enterprise.
Universal guidelines and quality standards.	Higher co-ordination costs that need to be balanced against economies of scale.
Better access to stored know-how and experience of other countries, and improved ways of identifying global opportunities.	

Source: derived from Mooij and Keegan (1991)

Decentralization, on the other hand, will allow greater flexibility and responsiveness to local market needs.

The extent to which a business standardizes global promotion is governed by several external and internal factors. The major external factors are:

- *language differences* which may affect the translation of the advertising message and the appropriateness of trade names, brands, slogans, etc.;
- *cultural differences* which may affect behaviour patterns, values, tastes, fashions, etc.;
- *social differences*, especially the general attitude of society toward advertising;
- *economic differences*, including the stage of development of the country and its effects on education, levels of literacy, possession of radio, TV, etc.;
- *competitive differences* and the promotional campaigns of competitors;
- *promotion infrastructure differences* – the relative importance of different promotion channels can vary significantly between countries;
- *legal and regulatory controls*, including codes of practice and legislation, can vary considerably.

The most important internal factors are the overall global strategy of the business and the relationship between headquarters executives and foreign subsidiary management. The scope for global promotion is far greater when transnational strategy places greater emphasis on co-ordination of activities rather than when a locally responsive approach is adopted. Similarly, the greater the degree of centralized control the greater the standardization of promotion. When decision-making power is decentralized, then there is greater scope for local variations in promotion.

The choice of promotional strategy is, of course, not a simple choice between total standardization and complete local adaptation. As with other aspects of transnational strategy, it is more likely that a company will adopt an approach that combines a high degree of uniformity with local variations. Yip (1992) quoted the example of the Coca-Cola 'little boy gives Coke to sports hero' campaign. In the USA the hero was 'Mean' Joe Green of the Pittsburgh Steelers, in Latin America it was Diego Maradona so as to give an element of local appeal. At the same time, however, the major theme of the advertisement was globally consistent.

Mooij and Keegan (1991) and Toyne and Walters (1993) identified three broadly similar alternative options in relation to the decision as to the extent to which promotion should be centralized or decentralized:

- *the centralized organization* – centralization of all promotional decision making at corporate headquarters;
- *the decentralized organization* – decentralization of promotional decision making;
- *the mixed organization* – combining elements of centralized and decentralized promotional decision making.

Several factors will influence the choice between these three alternatives:

- *corporate and marketing objectives* – where global objectives predominate, promotion will tend to be centralized;
- *the uniformity of the product* – the greater the uniformity of the product the greater the centralization of promotion;
- *the appeal of the product or brand* – where this is widespread, decentralization will be increased;
- *legal constraints* – decentralization may be necessary to take account of different national regulations;
- *cultural aspects* – may dictate decentralization;
- *socio-economic conditions* – different tastes, habits and preferences may require decentralization;
- *the competitive situation* – where this differs from country to country promotional decisions will need to be at least partially decentralized.

Existing decision-making processes in global businesses vary considerably. Companies adopting global strategies (e.g., Coca-Cola, IBM, Sony, etc.) will be significantly more centralized in promotional decision making than nationally responsive ones. Generally speaking, however, the two extremes of complete centralization or complete decentralization are rare in practice, with most businesses adopting a variation of the mixed organization.

Generally, corporate (at the centre) staff are responsible for developing the core promotional objectives and core campaigns, and for providing advice and expertise to foreign affiliates. Decisions regarding the detailed implementation of core campaigns in foreign markets are often best left to subsidiary managers to achieve local flexibility. Certain local decisions, however, may still require the ultimate approval of the parent company.

(a) *Professional role:*

- positioning;
- stragety development;
- creative concept development and judgement;
- assisting local management in selecting the right target groups;
- giving an insight into the degree to which specific products and product attributes must be emphasized in local campaigns or in adapted campaigns;
- providing an insight into what kind of advertising is most effective in which country;
- selecting the media types to be used, both locally and internationally;
- drawing up procedures for reporting and internal communication between subsidiaries and head office;
- cultivating a feeling for cultural differences and thus increasing the possibilities of standardizing a creative approach;
- evaluating international media;
- co-ordinating advertising research and measurement of effect.

(b) *Management role:*

- providing worldwide planning systems, including worldwide production outlines or guidance;
- organizing worldwide co-ordination of local advertising plans;
- setting global budgets, dividing them according to region or country, evaluating country budgets and checking whether they meet the company's requirements;
- assisting with the selection of local advertising managers;
- developing documentation systems for registering successful multinational campaigns in order to help local subsidiaries develop their own campaigns;
- selecting advertising agencies (local, multinational or global);
- evaluating agency relationships and remuneration arrangements.

Figure 11.4   The role of corporate headquarters in global advertising
Source: derived from Mooij and Keegan (1991)

The role of corporate headquarters in global advertising was examined in detail by Mooij and Keegan (1991), where a distinction was drawn between the professional and management role. The former refers to the role of headquarters in creating and placing advertising. The latter refers to the importance of ensuring co-operation between headquarters and subsidiary and for evaluating campaign effectiveness. The role of corporate headquarters in these two areas is summarized in Figure 11.4.

The role of corporate headquarters in global advertising was also examined by Quelch and Hoff (1986). The main responsibilities of the centre included product/brand positioning and effect measurement. Foreign subsidiaries, on the other hand, were mainly responsible for media planning and media buying. Decisions that were jointly determined by both headquarters and foreign subsidiaries included advertising agency selection, concept development, execution and marketing research.

The management of global promotional campaigns

Toyne and Walters (1993) distinguished between strategic issues in promotion planning and management issues. The six main strategic issues are:

- *the market segment* at which the promotion is directed – in global marketing this refers mainly to the territorial boundaries or geographical scope of the campaign whether national, regional or global;
- *the objectives of the promotion campaign* – where a distinction can be made, for example, between building a global brand and increasing market share in a particular country;
- *the message(s)* communicated and whether this should be the same across countries;
- *the allocation of expenditure* to the campaign and the total budget;
- *the allocation of the total budget* across promotional mix elements – media, geographical areas, products and over time;
- *procedures for monitoring the performance* of the campaign.

The major managerial issues involved in implementing a campaign include:

- *the organization and control dimension* – as discussed in the previous section;
- *choosing an advertising agency* – where alternatives include using a domestic agency, using an agency with branches overseas, using local agencies in foreign markets or some combination of these alternatives. The choice between these alternatives will be influenced by three broad categories of factors including:
  - corporate factors, such as the extent of the company's internationalization, organizational structure and standardization policy;
  - market-specific factors, such as sociocultural, economic and legal differences; and
  - characteristics of the agency itself including its market coverage, quality and reputation.

Mooij and Keegan (1991) identified 10 steps in planning worldwide advertising:

1. *situation analysis* – analysis of the forces influencing promotional decisions, including organizational structure, brand portfolio, the extent of standardization, market share abroad and brand positioning;

2. *marketing communications strategy and objectives* – whether a brand is to be developed globally or multilocally;
3. *deciding on the target groups* – identifying similar market segments in each country (see the previous discussion on SESs);
4. *setting the total communications budget* – whether it is set centrally or locally, determine the basis on which the budget is determined (e.g., past experience, objectives);
5. *the message* – the choice between standardized and locally varied;
6. *the means of communication and their integration* – choices on sales, promotion, PR, media advertising, sponsorship and the interrelationships between these methods;
7. *centralized or decentralized control of the means of communication* – decisions governing who controls promotion;
8. *budget allocation* – between different promotional media and communications channels;
9. *organization and implementation* – of the strategy, including managing agency arrangements;
10. *control and evaluation* – measuring the effectiveness of the campaign in each country.

Choosing an advertising agency

The globalization of business and the attention focused on the opportunities for global promotion has resulted in a rapid internationalization of the advertising industry itself. Most of the early international advertising agencies originated from the USA, with expansion abroad being a gradual process in response to the internationalization of client companies. Since the mid-1980s, internationalization of the advertising industry has accelerated at an unprecedented rate, with the emergence of a number of global, 'mega'-agencies. This has mainly been a consequence of the wave of cross-border mergers and acquisitions which have swept the industry in recent years.

The rapid internationalization of the advertising industry and the emergence of global, 'mega'-agencies can be attributed to three main causes:

1. *Globalization* – some agencies have explicitly adopted the globalization hypothesis of Levitt (1983). Indeed, Theodore Levitt was appointed to the board of Saatchi & Saatchi in 1986. Once the premise of 'converging commonality' has been accepted, the opportunities for

global promotion become apparent. To exploit such opportunities, agencies have established geographically dispersed subsidiaries throughout the world – sometimes through establishing new branches, but more commonly through mergers and acquisition.

2. *The benefits of size* – closely related to the advantages of globalization are the benefits of size. Global 'mega'-agencies, due to their size and geographical scope, can exert considerable influence over media groups and can achieve considerable economies of scale in operations.

3. *Synergy* – a third factor in the emergence of global 'mega'-agencies has been the view that substantial benefits can be derived from the provision of an integrated marketing communications service to clients. Thus, most of the rapidly expanding agencies have diversified their operations to include not only advertising and promotion but also other services including public relations, market research, consultancy, design, executive recruitment, etc.

Jaben (1994) suggested that 'think globally, act locally' is still the 'dominant strategy of international advertisers but with a slight revision: "think globally, act regionally".' This implies that the global headquarters has a central role to play in ensuring a globally consistent message while regional managers must have the autonomy to adapt advertising to local markets.

ICT and global marketing

It has been claimed that 'Commercialisation of the WWW will revolutionise the study and practice of international marketing' (Hamill, 1997). Certainly, the Internet has the potential to revolutionize many aspects of global marketing and strategy. Hamill (1997) identified three main strategic applications of the Internet in the context of internationalization:

- *a communications tool* supporting network relationships with overseas customers (actual and potential), agents, distributors, suppliers, etc.;
- *a low-cost export market research resource*;
- *a global marketing and promotions tool* through the design and effective marketing of company websites and the development of integrated Internet-supported strategies.

The Internet is potentially useful to both large and small companies operating in or wishing to enter global markets. It is a valuable tool for

Table 11.7   Ten effects of the Internet on global marketing

Effect	Comment
1. Improved global communications with customers	The Web allows businesses greater opportunity to communicate directly with their customers all over the world.
2. Improved global communications with other businesses	Suppliers and distributors all over the world can be contacted electronically. Materials, etc. can be globally sourced via the Web at low cost.
3. Improved internal communications	The Internet can be used to provide cheap and quick worldwide internal communications within a global business.
4. Improved corporate image	The website of a business can be used to present its corporate image.
5. Finding new global customers	New customers can be attracted by the company's website. Additionally, new customers can be approached directly via the Web on a worldwide basis.
6 Reduced market entry costs for small businesses	Small businesses were often deterred from entering global markets on the basis of the costs of market research, agents charges, etc. The Internet has reduced these costs substantially.
7. Global price standardization	Marketing on the Internet increases the advantages of and need for global price standardization.
8. Global market niche strategies	Niche markets can be accessed through groups on the Web. Customers are also more able to access specialist services and products by searching the Web.
9. Global-marketing research tool	Access to information sources available on the Internet.
10. Reduced importance of traditional-marketing intermediaries	Agents, etc. will be of less value to businesses entering international markets.

Source: adapted from Hamill and Gregory (1997)

communicating both with customers and with other businesses. It is inexpensive to use and is therefore of particular value to small and medium-sized enterprises wishing to operate internationally. Table 11.7 summarizes the most significant effects of the Internet on global marketing strategies.

One thing is certain. The impact of the Internet on global marketing has increased and will increase further, particularly among small and medium-sized enterprises. As we have seen, it is likely to influence global promotion, pricing, logistics and distribution. Indeed, it permeates most aspects of global marketing. Managers in global businesses must assess the potential role of the Internet in their global marketing strategies.

Axis Communications Inc. – the Internet and global marketing

Axis communications has its headquarters at Lund in Sweden. It develops and manufactures a range of products designed to support network-centric computing. The company's flagship products, the StorePoint CD Network CD-ROM Server and the NetEye 200 Network Camera, are part of the first wave of network and Web appliances designed to increase productivity by enabling users to access and share computer resources more efficiently. The company, which in year 2000 employed 200 people, has experienced an average annual sales growth of 43% since its foundation in 1984. In 1995–96 its sales were $49 million and it had an installed base of 500,000 products worldwide. Major customers include 'Fortune 500' companies, such as Ford, GM, AT&T, Pepsi, ABC News, Microsoft, GE and Boeing, and many more smaller organizations worldwide.

The rapid growth of the company has been to a large extent dependent on the establishment of 'strategic technology relationships' with customers and with leading hardware vendors and software developers, such as Hewlett-Packard, IBM, Canon, Fujitsu, Sony, Xerox, Microsoft, Netscape, Oracle and Sun. Maintaining good relationships and communications with their existing customer base is vital for Axis.

Despite its success, Axis remains a relatively small company in global terms, and this has created two major challenges: how to support its existing global customer base and how to achieve greater global brand awareness and sales volume on a small promotion budget compared with major global competitors. Axis sees the Internet as providing a low-cost solution to both problems and one that is highly relevant to the changing nature of procurement in the IT industry.

Axis's website has become central to its global marketing strategy. It contains full and comprehensive product information, sales contacts by region, corporate news, new product developments and a jobs-vacant section. The site is fully interactive and the company relies heavily on email to support existing customers and to develop relationships with new ones. An innovative feature of the Axis website is the Axis electronic newsletter that is widely accessible and provides new product information to existing and potential customers around the world. The ultimate aim of the site is to create a virtual community of customers, distributors, resellers and suppliers in order to supply the Axis brand globally.

Review and discussion questions

1. Explain what you understand by the term 'global marketing'. What are the major potential advantages and drawbacks of adopting a global marketing strategy?
2. Why are many markets becoming more global? How is the extent of globalization of a market assessed?
3. Choose a market with which you are familiar. Assess the extent to which it is globalized and the extent to which it is localized.
4. What is meant by a 'strategically equivalent segment'? How can one be identified?
5. Select a product that is globally available. What are the limitations on its standardization?
6. Why are global products often not sold at a globally standardized price? What are the major factors affecting the pricing decisions of a global business?
7. What factors affect the extent of globalization of promotion of a good or service? What are the relative advantages and disadvantages of global promotion?
8. Explain the growth and importance of global advertising agencies.
9. Discuss the impact of the Internet on global marketing.

References and further reading

Aaker, D.A. (1992) *Strategic Market Management*. New York: John Wiley & Sons.

Akhter, S.H. and Laczniak, G.R. (1989) 'The future US business environment with strategic marketing implications for European exporters'. *European Journal of Marketing*, **23**, 5.

Ayal, I. and Zif, J. (1979) 'Market expansion strategies in multinational marketing'. *Journal of Marketing*, **43**(2).

Baker, M.J. (1985) *Marketing Strategy and Management*. London: Macmillan.

Barnard, P. (1982) 'Conducting and co-ordinating multicountry quantitative studies across Europe'. *Journal of Market Research Society*, **24**(1), January.

Bartlett, C.A. and Ghoshal, S. (1989) *Managing Across Borders: The Transnational Solution*. Boston: Harvard Business School Press.

Bartlett, C.A. and Ghoshal, S. (1990) 'Matrix management: Not a structure, a frame of mind'. *Harvard Business Review*, July/August.

Becker, H. (1980) 'Pricing: An international marketing challenge'. In H. Thorelli and H. Becker (eds), *International Marketing Strategy* (Chapter 25). New York: Pergamon Press.

Becker, H. and Thorelli, H. (eds) (1980) 'Strategic planning in international marketing'. *International Marketing Strategy* (Chapter 45). New York: Pergamon Press.

Benjamin, R. and Wigand, R. (1995) 'Electronic markets and virtual value chains on the Information Superhighway'. *Sloan Management Review*, Winter, 62–72.

Boddewyn, J.J., Soehl, R. and Picard, P. (1986) 'Standardisation in international marketing: Is Ted Levitt in fact right?'. *Business Horizons*, November/December.

Bolt, J.F. (1988) 'Global competitors: Some criteria for success'. *Business Horizons*, January/February.

Cavusgil, T.S. and Nevin, J.R. (1981) 'State-of-the-art in international marketing: An assessment'. In: B.M. Enis and K.J. Roering (eds). *Review of Marketing 1981.* Chicago: American Marketing Association.

Chakravarthy, B.S. and Perlmutter, H.V. (1985) 'Strategic planning for a global business'. *Columbia Journal of World Business*, Summer.

Chan, P.S. and Justis, R.T. (1991) 'Developing a global business strategy vision for the next decade and beyond'. *Journal of Management Development*, **10**(2).

Czinkota, M.R. and Ilkka, A. (1992) 'Global marketing 2000: A marketing survival guide'. *Marketing Management*, **1**(1), 36–45.

Daniels, J.D. (1987) 'Bridging national and global marketing strategies through regional operations'. *International Marketing Review*, **4**(3).

Day, E., Fox, R.J. and Huszagh, S.M. (1988) 'Segmenting the global market for industrial goods: Issues and implications'. *International Marketing Review*, **5**(3), Autumn.

Diamantopoulos, A. and Schlegelmilch, B.B. (1987) 'Comparing marketing operations of autonomous subsidiaries', *International Marketing Review*, **4**(4), Winter.

Douglas, S.P. and Craig, C.S. (1989) 'Evolution of global marketing strategy: Scale, scope and synergy'. *Columbia Journal of World Business*, Fall, 47–59.

Doyle, F.P. (1990) 'People power: The global human resource challenge for the '90s'. *Columbia Journal of World Business*, Spring/Summer.

Doz, Y. (1986) *Strategic Management in Multinational Companies.* NewYork: Pergamon Press.

Edwards, F. and Spawton, T. (1990) 'Pricing in the Australian wine industry'. *European Journal of Marketing*, **24**(4).

Espey, J. (1989) '"The Big Four": An examination of the international drinks industry'. *European Journal of Marketing*, **23**(9).

Fayerweather, J. (1981) 'Four winning strategies for the international corporation'. *Journal of Business Strategy*, fall, **1**(2).

Glaum, M. (1990) 'Strategic management of exchange rate risks'. *Long Range Planning*, **23**(4).

'Going global', selected excerpts from a conference organized by the Economist Conference Unit. *European Management Journal*, **4**(1), 1986.

Gregson, J. (1987) 'How Cadbury Schwepped into worldwide markets'. *Financial Weekly*, March.

Hamel, G. and Prahalad, C.K. (1985) 'Do you really have a global strategy?' *Harvard Business Review*, July/August.

Hamill, J. (1992) 'Global marketing'. In M.J. Baker (ed.), *Perspectives on Marketing Management* (Vol. 2). New York: John Wiley & Sons.

Hamill, J. (1997) 'The Internet and international marketing'. *International Marketing Review*, September.

Hamill, J. and Gregory, K. (1997) 'Internet marketing in the internationalisation of small and medium sized enterprises'. *Journal of Marketing Management*, January.

Henzler, H. and Rall, W. (1986) 'Facing up to the globalization challenge'. *McKinsey Quarterly*, Winter.

Herbert, I.C. (1988) 'How Coke markets to the world'. *Journal of Business Strategy*, September/ October.

Howard, D.G. and Ryans, J.K. (1989) 'Advertising executives' perceptions of satellite TV's potential impact on the European market'. *European Journal of Marketing*, **23**(5).

Huszagh, J.D., Fox, R.J. and Day, E. (1986) 'Marketing: An empirical investigation'. *Journal of World Business*, **20**(2).

Jaben, J. (1994) For business, the global arena is the greatest show on earth. *Business Marketing*, **79**(8).

Jatusripitak, S., Fahey, L. and Kotler, P. (1985) 'Strategic global marketing: Lessons from the Japanese'. *Columbia Journal of World Business*, **20**(1), Spring.

Jeelof, G. (1989) 'Global strategies of Philips'. *European Management Journal*, **7**(1).

Kahani, K. (1997) 'Why marketing still matters'. In: T. Dickson (ed.), *Financial Times Mastering Management*. London: Pitman.

Kale, S.H. and Sudharsham, D. (1987) 'A strategic approach to international segmentation'. *International Marketing Review*, Summer.

Kashani, K. (1990) 'Why does global marketing work – or not work'. *European Management Journal*, **8**(2), June.

Kashani, K. (1997a) 'A new future for brands'. In: T. Dickson (ed.), *Financial Times Mastering Management*. London: Pitman.

Kashani, K. (1997b) 'Why marketing still matters'. In: T. Dickson (ed.), *Financial Times Mastering Management*. London: Pitman.

Keegan, W.J. (1989) 'Five strategies for multinational marketing'. In: H. Thorelli and H. Becker (eds), *International Marketing Strategy*. New York: Pergamon Press.

Keown, C.F., Synodinus, N.E. and Jacobs, L.W. (1989) 'Advertising practices in northern Europe'. *European Journal of Marketing*, **23**(3).

Killough, J. (1980) 'Improved payoffs from transnational advertising'. In: H. Thorelli and H. Becker (eds), *International Marketing Strategy* (Chapter 28). New York: Pergamon Press.

Kotabe, M. and Helsen, K. (1998) *Global Marketing Management*. New York: John Wiley & Sons.

Kreutzer, R.T. (1988) 'Marketing-mix standardisation: An integrated approach in global marketing'. *European Journal of Marketing*, **22**(10).

Lancioni, R.A. (1989) 'The importance of price in international business development'. *European Journal of Marketing*, **23**(11).

Landor Associates (1990) *The World's Most Powerful Brands*. San Francisco: Landor Associates.

Larreche, J.C. (1980) 'The international product/market portfolio'. In: H. Thorelli and H. Becker (eds), *International Marketing Strategy* (Chapter 38). New York: Pergamon Press.

Leontiades, J. (1985) *Multinational Corporate Strategy: Planning for World Markets*. Lexington, MD: Lexington Books.

Leontiades, J. (1986) 'Going global – global strategies vs national strategies'. *Long Range Planning*, **19**(6).

Levitt, T. (1983) 'The globalization of markets'. *Harvard Business Review*, May/June.

Luqmani, M., Yavas, U. and Quraeshi, Z. (1989) 'Advertising in Saudi Arabia: Content and regulation'. *International Marketing Review*, **6**(1).

Mahmoud, E. and Rice, G. (1988) 'Use of analytical techniques in international marketing'. *International Marketing Review*, **5**(3), Autumn.

Main, J. (1989) 'How to go global – and why'. *Fortune*, 28 August.

Martenson, R. (1987) 'Is standardisation of marketing feasible in culture-bound industries? A European case study'. *International Marketing Review*, **4**(3).

Mayer, S. (1978) 'Multinational marketing research: Methodological problems'. *European Research*, **6**, March.

Mooij, M.K. and Keegan, W.J. (1991) *Advertizing Worldwide: Concepts, Theories and Practice of International, Multinational and Global Advertizing.* Englewood Cliffs, NJ: Prentice Hall.

Moyer, R. (1968) 'International market analysis'. *Journal of Marketing Research,* **5**.

Naylor, T.H. (1985) 'The international strategy matrix'. *Columbia Journal of World Business,* Summer.

Ohmae, K. (1985) *Triad Power: The Coming Shape of Global Competition.* NewYork: Free Press.

Ohmae, K. (1989) 'Managing in a borderless world'. *Harvard Business Review,* May/June.

Ohmae, K. (1990) *The Borderless World: Power and Strategy in the Interlinked Economy.* London: Collins.

Onkvisit, S. and Shaw, J.J. (1983) 'An examination of the international product life cycle and its application within marketing'. *Columbia Journal of World Business,* **18**(3), Fall.

Onkvisit, S. and Shaw, J.J. (1989) 'The international dimension of branding: Strategic considerations and decisions'. *International Marketing Review,* **6**(3).

Owen, S (1993) 'The London Image Power Survey®: A global assessment of brand strength'. In: D.A. Aaker and A.L. Biel (eds), *Brand Equity and Advertising: Advertising's role in Building Strong Brands.* Hillsdale, NJ: Lawrence Erlbaum.

Papavassiliou, N.K. (1989) 'The involvement model in advertising consumer products abroad'. *European Journal of Marketing,* **23**(1).

Peebles, D.M. (1989) 'Don't write off global advertising: A commentary'. *International Marketing Review,* **6**(1).

Perlmutter, H.V. (1969) 'The tortuous evolution of the multinational corporation'. *Columbia Journal of World Business,* January/February.

Perry, A.C. (1990) 'International versus domestic marketing: Four conceptual perspectives'. *European Journal of Marketing,* **24**(6).

Perry, M (1988) 'Conceptual overview and applications of international marketing positioning'. *European Management Journal,* **6**(4), Winter.

Pitts, R.A. and Daniels, J.D. (1984) 'Aftermath of the matrix mania'. *Columbia Journal of World Business,* Summer.

Porter, M.E. (ed.) (1986a) *Competition in Global Industries.* Boston: Harvard Business School Press.

Porter, M.E. (1986b) 'Changing patterns of international competition'. *California Management Review,* **28**(2), Winter.

Quelch, J.A. and Hoff, R.J. (1986) 'Customizing global marketing'. *Harvard Business Review,* May/June.

Raffée, H. and Kreutzer, R.T. (1989) 'Organisational dimension of global marketing'. *European Journal of Marketing,* **23**(5).

Ratnatunga, J., Hooley, G.J. and Pike, R. (1990) 'The marketing–finance interface'. *European Journal of Marketing,* **24**(1).

Rau, P.A. and Preble, J.F. (1987) 'Standardisation of marketing strategy by multinationals'. *International Marketing Review,* Autumn.

Rosen, B.N., Boddewyn, J.J. and Louis, E.A. (1989) 'US brands abroad: An empirical study of global branding'. *International Marketing Review,* **6**(1).

Sanders, P. (1989) 'Global managers for global corporations'. *Journal of Management Development,* **7**, 1.

Schmittlein, D. (1997) 'Customers as strategic assets'. In: T. Dickson (ed.), *Financial Times Mastering Management.* London: Pitman.

Shulman, J.S. (1980) 'Transfer pricing in the multinational firm'. In: H. Thorelli and H. Becker (eds), *International Marketing Strategy* (Chapter 40). New York: Pergamon Press.

Sims, C., Phillips, A. and Richards, T. (1992) 'Developing a global pricing strategy'. *Marketing and Research Today,* **20**(1), 3–15.

Spawton, T. (1990) 'Development in the global alcoholic drinks industry and its implications for the future marketing of wine'. *European Journal of Marketing*, **24**(4).

Takeuchi, H. and Porter, M.E. (1986) 'Three roles of international marketing in global strategy'. In: M.E. Porter (ed.), *Competition in Global Industries*. Boston: Harvard Business School Press.

Terpstra, V. (1987) 'The evolution of international marketing'. *International Marketing Review*, Summer.

Thomas, M. (1986) *Pocket Guide to Marketing*. London: Economist Publications.

Toyne, B. and Walters, P.G.P. (1993) *Global Marketing Management: A Strategic Perspective*. Boston: Allyn & Bacon.

Tuncalp, S. (1988) 'The marketing research scene in Saudi Arabia'. *European Journal of Marketing*, **22**(5).

Turnbull, P.W. and Doherty-Wilson, L. (1990) 'The internationalisation of the advertising industry'. *European Journal of Marketing*, **24**(1).

Vernon, R. (1966) 'International investment and international trade in the product cycle'. *Quarterly Journal of Economics*, **80**.

Yip, G. (1992) *Total Global Strategy*. Englewood Cliffs, NJ: Prentice Hall.

GLOBAL FINANCIAL MANAGEMENT

Introduction

The purpose of the chapter is to discuss the major financial issues faced by a global business and to relate these to other aspects of international management reviewed elsewhere in this book. It is assumed that the reader is familiar with the basic finance topics that can be found in many elementary textbooks. Readers who wish to learn in detail about the international monetary system, foreign exchange markets and how businesses can reduce the associated risks should consult an up-to-date textbook on international finance, such as Eiteman et al. (1998).

Finance, as one of the key resources under management of a global or transnational business, is one of the key strategic areas to address in the implementation of strategy and in internal analysis. Financing investments and working capital can be complicated in domestic business, but, for international companies, factors such as political uncertainty and exchange rate fluctuations mean that certainty can be even more elusive. This has implications for all parts of international business strategy because operational investments and changes to the stock of fixed assets all require significant input from the financial function.

Finance management and the global enterprise

The key issues in international financing

In other parts of this book we have seen that all functions within a business are affected by the overall strategy of the business in international markets. Lessard (1986) examined some international finance activities within a business to show how they would differ between a US-based business following an export/import strategy, a multidomestic strategy and a pure global strategy (Table 12.1).

Table 12.1 Global competitive strategy and international finance functions

Function	Export/Import	Multidomestic	Global
Investment evaluation	Domestic perspective; few 'foreign' considerations	Yes/No decision to enter market or change mode to serve local market	Mutually exclusive global choices; currency and tax issues central
Funding operations	Meet domestic norms	Meet local norms	Match global competitors' cost of capital
Exchange risk management	Focus on exposure of foreign currency contracts	Focus on exposure of converting foreign profits into dollars	Focus on exposure of home and foreign profits to competitive effects of exchange rate shifts
Output pricing responses to exchange rate movements	No change in home currency price	No change in local currency price	Change in home and local price to reflect global competitive position
Performance measurement	Measure all operations in dollars at actual exchange rates	Measure foreign operation in local currency	Measure all operations relative to standards that reflect the competitive effects of exchange rate changes

Source: Lessard (1986)

Investment evaluation

While the business following a multidomestic strategy can take decisions in one country which have little or no effect on its operations in another country, the global company is faced with a complex and interdependent set of choices. For example, the decision to locate a plant in China to take advantage of low labour (and hence production) costs must also take into account the associated logistical costs of shipping to other markets as well as strategic issues, such as locating in that country before competitors and the potential for organizational learning.

Funding operations

A global enterprise has (by definition) access to a wide range of sources of finance with lower costs than domestic sources as well as opportunities to reduce taxation through the use of 'creative' transfer pricing. Access to lower cost of capital can be a source of competitive advantage, but the company may be restricted by the degree of choice available to it. Host government legislation, for example, may prevent the use of resources from other parts of the business in other countries. While this may not be a significant drawback for the multidomestic company, it does limit the ability of the global company to achieve the lowest possible costs of capital.

Exchange risk management: output/pricing responses to exchange rate movements

Changes in the exchange rate for a country will affect the operating costs and the revenues of the company's subsidiary in that country. Lessard (1986) pointed out that for the company following a multidomestic strategy, the costs and revenues move together because most of the value-adding costs are locally incurred and the revenues are locally generated. Thus, profits move in simple proportion to the exchange rate. On the other hand, the sourcing costs, value-adding activities and revenues of the global enterprise may be associated with a number of countries. Thus a change in the exchange rate of one country will have a much more complex effect on the profits of the global business.

Foreign exchange risk management at British Airways (BA)

The overall foreign exchange position of a company may be complex, as illustrated by the position of British Airways. BA does business in approximately 140 foreign currencies, which account for approximately 60% of group revenue and approximately 40% of operating expenses (the rest being UK sterling). The group generates a surplus in most of these currencies (i.e., revenues are greater than costs). The principal exceptions are the US dollar and the pound sterling in which BA has a deficit, arising from capital expenditure and the payment of some leasing costs, together with expenditure on fuel, which is payable in US dollars, and the majority of staff costs, central overheads and other leasing costs, which are payable in pounds sterling.

BA consequently has a highly complex foreign exchange position, but it is imperative to the profitability of such a company that this exposure to foreign exchange rate movements is recognized and managed appropriately. In all cases, risk attributed to foreign exchange rate movements arises out of uncertainty about the future exchange rate between two currencies. This risk would be minimized if it were possible to predict future rate movements. Unfortunately, however, it is not possible to do so with any degree of accuracy, and for a company to try to do so it can be financially dangerous. Therefore, given that foreign exchange rates cannot be predicted, another option might be to pass on to the customer the effects of any adverse movements in exchange rates and, hence, the company would incur no impact. In most cases, however, the highly competitive nature of international business prevents higher costs being passed on to the customer in this way.

The broad spectrum of currencies in the business, many of which are linked in their movements to the US dollar and the pound sterling, gives BA a measure of protection against exchange rate movements and reduces the overall sensitivity of the company's results to exchange rate fluctuations. Nonetheless, BA can experience adverse or beneficial effects. For example, if the pound sterling weakened against the US dollar and strengthened against other major currencies, the overall effect would be likely to be adverse, while the reverse would be likely to produce a beneficial effect. The company seeks to reduce its foreign currency exposure arising from transactions in various currencies through a policy of matching, as far as possible, receipts and payments in each individual currency. Surpluses of convertible currencies are sold either immediately (spot) or forward for US dollars and pounds sterling.

Performance measurement
The financial performance of a global or transnational company can be measured in terms of the host country currency or the currency of the parent country. Operational performance can be partly masked by exchange rate changes during the accounting period, making it difficult for the global enterprise to compare performance in different countries. Global strategic financial targets and control systems are usually therefore set up in such a way as to permit the effect of rate changes to be removed, thus exposing the underlying financial performance. Lessard and Lorange (1977) advocated a system where budgets are established based on the projected exchange rate over a period and performance is tracked using the same projected rate. This does not shield the business from unexpected exchange rate changes, but does at least provide a fair measure of the effectiveness of the operating managers.

Centralization versus decentralization of the finance function

Different approaches to decentralization

As with all the functions of an international business, a compromise has to be found between the need for global co-ordination (implying centralization) and local responsiveness (implying decentralization) of the finance function. The above discussion of multidomestic and global strategy helps us to understand how the function should be organized depending on the strategy the company is pursuing. According to Asheghian and Ebrahimi (1990) there are three approaches used (based on the EPRG [ethnocentric, polycentric, regiocentric, geocentric] framework – see Chapter 2).

Polycentric approach
Decision making is decentralized to the subsidiaries with the parent company's role limited to decisions on financing new projects. This is most likely to be used by companies following a multidomestic strategy.

Ethnocentric approach
Strategic decision making and operational control are centralized and remain the responsibility of the parent company. This is the approach adopted by the business following a purely global strategy. While this approach can optimize the financial performance of the company as a

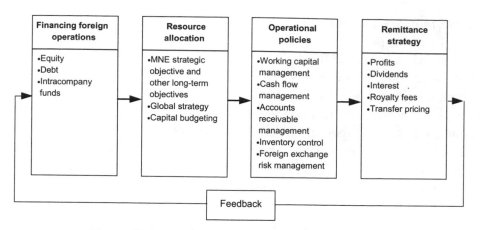

Figure 12.1 Fundamental decisions in financial strategy
Source: Asheghian and Ebrahimi (1990). MNE = multinational enterprise

whole, it can have an adverse effect on the apparent performance of individual subsidiaries. This approach can also create difficulties in meeting local financial-reporting requirements.

Geocentric approach
Each subsidiary is treated differently according to factors such as the local financial environment, the quality of local management and the nature of the business. This approach could be compared with the transnational strategic approach in that the centre is permitting some adaptation to suit local conditions while maintaining a degree of central co-ordination.

In practice, as suggested by Table 12.1, different parts of the financial function tend to be centralized (e.g., capital budgeting) while other parts tend to be decentralized.

In order to look more closely at the different elements of the financial strategy of an international business, we will examine the four fundamental decision areas (see Figure 12.1).

Decision area 1: financing foreign operations

The options

The global or transnational business, like any other company business that wants to grow, needs access to funds to finance land, plant and equipment as well as the additional working capital required for the day to day operations of the business. The three main sources of funds are:

1. equity capital raised by selling shares on the stock exchange;
2. debt capital raised by borrowing from a lender;
3. internal funds generated through the normal operation of the business (retained profits).

The options of sources of funds to choose from are summarized in Figure 12.2.

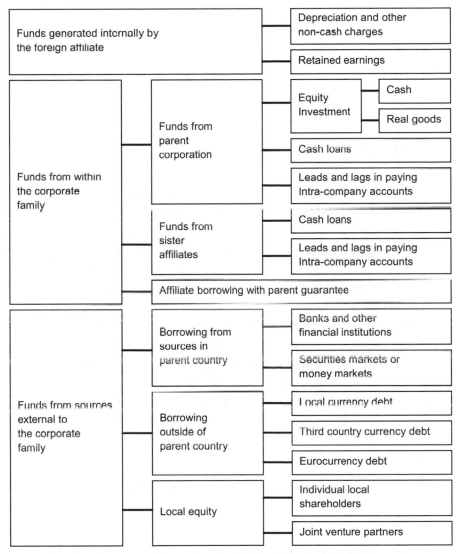

Figure 12.2 Potential sources of capital for financing foreign operations
Source: Eiteman et al. (1998)

Table 12.2 Advantages and disadvantages of different sources of equity capital for international companies

Sources of equity financing	Advantages	Disadvantages
Parent company	Possibility of enhancing debt capacity of overseas subsidiaries. Higher parental controls on subsidiary operations.	Higher foreign exchange exposure risks. Higher risks for remittance of earning and repatriation of invested capital. Higher risks for expropriation and nationalization.
Host country	Lower foreign exchange exposure risks. Stronger identity with host country and local interest groups.	Less parental control on overseas operations.

Source: Davidson (1982)

Equity capital

The international company has the opportunity to raise capital not only on its home stock exchange but also through cross-listing (i.e., listing its shares on other stock exchanges). The underlying objective of listing on additional stock exchanges is to lower the weighted average cost of capital. The main drawback to obtaining additional listings is that other stock exchanges, in particular the New York Stock Exchange, may require the company to disclose much more detail about its financial operations that its home stock exchange requires. An alternative approach is to raise capital by selling shares directly to foreign investors. This can include the sale of rights issue stock to a joint venture partner based in the host country in which the company wishes to invest. Table 12.2 summarizes the advantages and disadvantages of raising equity capital through the parent company and through host country sources.

Debt (or loan) capital

There are a number of possible sources of debt capital for foreign investment (Asheghian and Ebrahimi, 1990).

Development banks and government agencies in the host country
These sources are most relevant for developing countries. There are often

restrictions on what may be purchased (e.g., the subsidiary may be constrained to source from local suppliers).

Investment and commercial banks in host countries

The interest rate chargeable on debt capital varies between countries, and it can sometimes be preferable to borrow locally if monetary pressure is lower in the host country. One of the advantages of international development is the ability to borrow in a range of countries, depending on the attractiveness of interest rates at the time the finance is needed.

Financial markets

There is a wide range of sources for finance as well as a wide range of instruments through which the loan may be raised. The three major sources of funding are *international bank loans*, the *Euronote market* and the *international bond market*. The last of these 'sports a rich array of innovative instruments created by imaginative investment bankers, who are unfettered by the usual controls and regulations governing domestic capital markets' (Eiteman et al., 1998).

Table 12.3 summarizes the advantages and disadvantages of domestic and host country sources of debt financing for international businesses. From this we can see that a company has to balance the opposing factors of exchange rate risks and political risks.

Table 12.3 Advantages and disadvantages of home versus host sources of funding for financing

Source of debt financing	Advantages	Disadvantages
Home base (parent company, home country)	Tax deductions on interest paid. Ease in remittance and repatriation. Access to low-cost funds.	Higher foreign exchange exposure risks.
Host country	Low political risk. Tax deduction on interest paid. Elimination of foreign exchange exposure risks. Possibility of establishing a good relationship with local businesses and other financial institutions.	Availability of capital. Less control over subsidiary operations.

Source: Davidson (1982)

Decision area 2: resource allocation and capital budgeting

Uncertainties constraining the certainty of choice

Any business needs to plan how it is going to invest its capital in order to meet its long-term objectives. New opportunities for investment may come from a variety of sources inside and outside the business. One of the key activities of the finance function is to evaluate the financial aspects of each proposal to determine, first if they meet company set criteria for the return generated and, second, to rank the proposals so that the most attractive can be identified. The standard tools used in such evaluations include calculation of the net present value (NPV) or the internal rate of return (IRR). A company using the latter approach will specify a 'hurdle rate' for all investment decisions; any project with an IRR below this rate will not be considered further.

Investment decisions for international businesses are made in a similar way to those for domestic companies; differences are mainly caused by the greater complexity present in the international environment. Asheghian and Ebrahimi (1990) identified the following causes of this additional complexity:

- political risks are higher and more varied;
- variations in the sources and forms of financing;
- foreign exchange rate fluctuations;
- restrictions on capital, exchange and profit flows in many countries;
- differences in taxation systems between home and host countries;
- differences in the economic systems and conditions between countries;
- differences in inflation rates;
- varying interest and discount rates;
- uncertainty in the estimation of salvage value (the value of project assets at the end of the project).

Because investment appraisal for international business can be more complex than for purely domestic decisions, a number of 'softer' criteria are sometimes applied to the decision. Non-financial criteria can be applied to an investment proposal and such tools as impact analysis and cost/benefit analysis can provide information as useful as the financial calculations that are often based on unreliable projections of revenue flows.

The conclusions reached by these three approaches could be different. Multiple evaluations do not necessarily make decision making any easier, but at least the final decision should be made on the basis of a wider range of information than the basic NPV approach. A further important factor in the decision is how the company is able to address the risks posed by political and exchange rate uncertainties – problems very commonly encountered by global and transnational businesses.

Political risk

The political environment has already been discussed in Chapter 5. Political factors vary by country, by industry and by individual business. The greatest risk that any international business faces is the expropriation, without compensation, of assets held in a foreign country. This threat is a major deterrent to investment in late developing countries. There are other ways in which host governments can directly influence the operations of global companies; the imposition of currency restriction introduced by the Malaysian government in 1998 following the collapse of the 'tiger' economies is a dramatic example of this. Kobrin (1982) defined two different types of political risk:

1. country-specific (macro) risks that apply to all foreign businesses in that country;
2. company-specific (micro) risks that apply to an industry, a particular company or even a particular project.

Figure 12.3 summarizes the various components of political risk.

Assessing and forecasting political risk

Two different types of risk have to be assessed – macro-risk and micro-risk.

Macro-risk
The international business will need to know the degree of political stability in a host country and the current attitude of the various political forces toward foreign investors. Some estimates of this can be gained from examining the country's history as well as such sources as radio, television and newspapers. However, in countries where the media is controlled by political forces, an incomplete or (at worst) totally misleading picture may

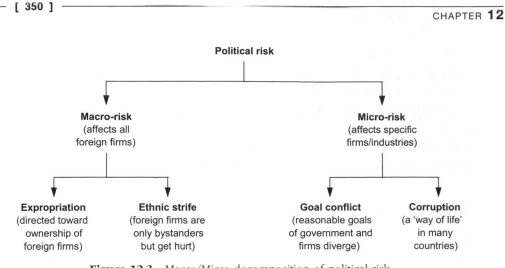

Figure 12.3 Macro/Micro decomposition of political risk
Source: Eiteman et al. (1998)

be gathered. Alternative sources of information are professional analysts, recent visitors and business contacts within the country. The problem is that political change can be very sudden and overwhelming, as events such as the break-up of the USSR demonstrated.

Micro-risk

Even if some degree of accuracy can be made in forecasting political events, the impact of these on specific companies or industries may be even harder to predict. Eiteman et al. (1998) suggested that international companies with significant exposure to micro-risk are likely to employ in-house political analysts who understand the industry well and can focus their attention on each country. Knickerbocker (1973) suggested that, in many cases, international companies make little attempt to make independent risk assessments, but instead will tend to watch what other companies do and then copy them.

Dealing with political risk

It is demonstrably obvious, then, that political risk cannot be avoided. For companies seeking to expand in other countries, strategy formulation is more concerned with finding appropriate approaches to dealing with the risk. An obvious way to minimize such risk is to invest only in those countries that have a historically low level of risk. Unfortunately, this may deprive the company of the opportunity to invest in many countries where the potential returns are very high. An alternative approach is to accept that risks are present and plan investment and operations in such a way that the consequences of unexpected political changes can be minimized. Such plans might include:

- *negotiating investment agreements* with the host country government, covering as many aspects as possible (the implication here is that a compromise must be reached which offers acceptable benefits for the investor *and* the host country government; this does not of course eliminate the possibility of a new government ignoring agreements made with its predecessor);
- *adapting to host country goals and cultural norms,* so that the investor is seen as a benefit to the country rather than an exploiter;
- *planning disinvestment,* so that ownership of the project will be acquired by the host government after an agreed period of time;
- employing *operating strategies,* such as local sourcing, keeping ownership of key technologies, building market control, investing using funds sourced from the host country, etc. to strengthen the company's bargaining position.

Decision area 3: operational policies

Working capital and cash flow management

Working capital has the value of assets required for the normal operations of the business. In practice, this means the value of stock, creditors (including trade creditors and short-term debts), debtors and cash-in-hand. Businesses need working capital to ensure that the day-to day operations of the business are properly financed. There is usually a lag between the purchase of the input stocks and the recovery of the added value through payment by customers for the final product.

Businesses will hold cash balances (and other liquid assets) in order to fund the normal day-to-day operations of the business (*transaction* motive) and as a buffer against unexpected variations in cash requirements (*precautionary* motive). However, all working capital is an asset tied up in the business which is not earning a useful return (the opportunity cost of working capital). Thus the purpose of cash flow management is to ensure that while the business has sufficient cash to cover the transaction and risk motives, it does not hold excess cash that might be better employed elsewhere in the system and in another form.

All businesses, whether domestic or international, engage in some form of cash flow management. The international business must deal with a more complex situation because of the additional uncertainties posed by exchange rate changes, government restrictions on the flow of funds in and out of the country, differences in tax systems and the costs and other difficulties involved in transferring funds across national boundaries. It may not therefore be able to make the maximum use of such opportunities as transfer of cash into stronger currencies or into areas with more favourable tax systems.

Eiteman et al. (1998) summarized the main differences between domestic and international business cash management.

Planning

An international business usually prepares three cash budgets – one for each individual national entity, one for each currency used within the system and one for the parent company as a whole. In order for the last of these budgets to be prepared, the company must use a forecast set of exchange rates.

Collection

Delays between customer payment and the cash being actually available to the company should be minimized. The availability of a multinational banking system with a presence in each host country can facilitate this process.

Repositioning

Funds collected have to be transferred to where they are of most use to the business. The international business may face restrictions (see above) in its ability to do this to maximum effect. A variety of direct and indirect techniques may be used to effect transfers and reduce restrictions, including intra-company transfer pricing.

Disbursement

This is similar to the collection of cash; the aim is to keep the cash within the business for as long as possible while ensuring that it reaches the recipient at the agreed time. Again, the selection of an appropriate banking system is important.

Covering cash shortages
Cash shortage at a subsidiary can be covered either by the subsidiary itself borrowing locally or by an internal transfer of funds from another part of the parent company. The opportunity here is that other parts of the business may be able to borrow at much more favourable rates of interest than others.

Investing surplus cash
The various parts of an international business may hold cash in local currency which represents a surplus generated from normal operations. Subsidiaries may have responsibility for managing this surplus themselves, but many companies accumulate these surpluses into a 'pool' and may then set up a financial subsidiary to manage the pool effectively.

Foreign exchange exposure

There are three main types of risk associated with unexpected foreign exchange rate movements which are faced by an international company with subsidiaries in several countries. One of the objectives of the finance department is to estimate the potential of such movements to affect the profitability and other key measures of financial performance (in other words, gain an estimate of the company's *exposure*) and to take steps to ensure that these key measures are maximized.

Transaction exposure
If the company agrees to some sort of financial transaction where payment will be made some time after the agreement, then the value of the transaction will change as the exchange rate changes. For example, a British company may agree to purchase machinery from an American supplier for $150,000 with delivery in six months. If the exchange rate at the time of the agreement is £1 = $1.50, then the value of the transaction is £100,000. If in six months the rate rises to £1 = $2.00, then the value of the transaction will be only £75,000 which is a significant saving. On the other hand, if the rate drops to £1 = $1.00, the value of the transaction will rise to £150,000 which would make the deal much less attractive. Thus, transaction exposure arises from cash flows generated by current financial obligations.

Operating exposure

This is also related to cash flows but in a much wider sense; unexpected changes in exchange rates will affect not only a company but also its suppliers, customers and competitors. This, in turn, could affect the company's international competitiveness, future sales and costs. Thus, operating (or economic) exposure is a measure of how much the present value of the company is altered by unexpected rate changes.

Translation exposure

A global or transnational business with subsidiaries in several countries must prepare consolidated accounts in its domestic currency. In order to accurately report figures in the financial statements, they must all be translated into the domestic currency. Exchange rate changes may therefore have a significant effect on the value of the shareholders' equity. Note that this is only an accounting change and not a realized gain or loss.

Reducing exposure

There are many methods that can be used to reduce the exposure of a business to exchange rate changes; the reader is referred to any standard textbook on international finance for details. One technique that is commonly used to reduce risk is *hedging*. If we return to the example above, the business may consider the risk of the sterling price increasing to £150,000 unacceptable. It may therefore buy $150,000 immediately the deal is agreed. The drawback with this is the opportunity cost of tying up this amount of capital for six months.

An alternative is to buy $150,000 in the forward market for delivery in six months at the six-month forward rate – say, £1 = $1.20. The company's capital is not tied up during this time and the company knows exactly how much it will have to pay for the machinery. Thus, hedging places an upper limit on the detrimental effect that adverse changes of exchange rates will have on the company's cash flows. One drawback is that the business cannot benefit from favourable exchange rate movements. It is up to the finance function to determine which method(s) of managing the company's exposure are most appropriate.

Decision area 4: remittance strategy

Types of funds transfer

In the above discussion on operational policies we referred to the movement of cash between different parts of an international company. A remittance strategy refers to the company's policies and procedures for implementing the flow of funds around the business and, in particular, the repatriation of funds to the parent company. Table 12.4 summarizes the conduits that an international business has for moving funds.

Problems with transferring funds

Unlike a purely domestic company the global or transnational company may face a number of restrictions that impede its ability to freely transfer funds around the organization.

Political constraints

Just as an exporter may face tariff and non-tariff barriers to trade, so an internationalized business may be subject to direct and indirect constraints. The currency may become unconvertible or else the government may impose a fixed exchange rate which makes conversion to the home country's currency impossible or not economically viable. Governments may also place limits on the total amount of funds that may be transferred out of the country. Less obvious limitations may be present through the imposition of complex and time-consuming processes that must be followed in order to gain permission to transfer funds.

Table 12.4   Conduits for moving funds

Type of funds flow	Methods of performing the flow
Flows as compensation for invested capital	Payment of dividends, interest payment on inter-company loans, principal repayment on inter-company loans.
Flows for goods and services received	Payment for purchased materials and components, payment for purchase or services, royalty payments, licence fees, management fees, overhead compensation
Flows for both categories	Leading or lagging of payments.

Source: Eiteman et al. (1998)

Tax constraints

In addition to foreign exchange losses, the international company can be subject to taxation in the host country and any other country whose borders the funds cross. Even within countries there may be regional taxation in addition to national taxation which causes extra complexity. The threat by the State of California to tax local subsidiaries of foreign-based companies on the profits of the parent rather than the subsidiary is an interesting example of this. Some companies establish subsidiaries in *tax havens* in order to defer the payment of taxes.

Transaction costs

Even when exchange rates themselves are not a constraint, the conversion from one currency to another incurs a cost. Although for a single conversion the cost is only a small percentage of the total value of the transaction, these costs can become significant if funds are repeatedly converted. The effects can be reduced by planning funds flow so that instead of going from subsidiaries to the parent then back to subsidiaries, the funds flow directly between subsidiaries. Another approach is to use *netting*: instead of several unconnected exchanges of funds between a parent and a subsidiary, the transactions over a period are grouped together so that only one transfer of funds, representing the net value of all the transactions, is required.

Liquidity needs

We mentioned above the need for each subsidiary to hold funds for transaction and precautionary motives. The level of funds held by the subsidiary will vary from one country to another due to local conditions and may sometimes have to be somewhat higher than the optimum level for the company as a whole.

Blocked funds

If exchange or other controls severely restrict the normal movement of funds out of a country, then the business may still be able to effect a transfer through indirect means. Eiteman et al. (1998) described a number of alternatives.

'Unbundling' services

Instead of repatriating profits the company can split the transfers up into a number of categories as shown in Table 12.4. Host governments may be more willing to permit at least some of these payments.

Transfer pricing

If a parent company wishes to relocate funds from a subsidiary, it can charge artificially high prices for goods and services purchased from the parent by the subsidiary. This may, however, result in additional tax complications.

Leading and lagging payments

The parent can delay payments to the subsidiary (lag) but accelerate some payments by the subsidiary to the parent (lead). This has the effect of a temporary transfer of funds to the parent, but some countries set limits on the timings that may be used.

Reinvoicing centres

This could be viewed as a method of implementing the first three approaches. Intra-company transfers of goods and services are all made through a reinvoicing centre, a separate corporate entity that buys from the supplier in the supplier's home currency and then resells to the buyer in the buyer's home currency. The main use of this technique is to manage the company's exposure to movements in exchange rates. Where there are restrictions on funds transfers, the reinvoicing centre can handle the unbundling, transfer pricing and lead/lag methods discussed above with the added benefit of masking the ultimate destination of funds transferred out of the subsidiary.

Fronting loans

Loans from a parent to a subsidiary are made through a financial intermediary (usually a large international bank) and interest payments from the subsidiary are made to that intermediary. The idea is that foreign governments are less likely to restrict payments to a large international bank than to the parent.

Unrelated exports

The blocked funds are used to pay for goods or services used by other parts of the business and provided by the host country. Eiteman et al. (1998) gave the example of an international company's employees using the host country's state airline for international flights. The tickets are paid for in the host country's currency using the blocked funds. Other more sophisticated techniques, such as bartering and countertrade (Hennart, 1990), have also been used. The underlying theme is finding ways to improve the host country's economy whose poor state was the original cause of the block.

Discussion and review questions

1. When might a decentralization of financial decision making be preferable to centralization?
2. What are the options available to international companies seeking to find finance for foreign investment?
3. Describe the pros and cons of the three options for financing foreign investment.
4. Why might an international company have an advantage over a domestic business when raising debt finance in an overseas country?
5. Why is an international company more vulnerable to political risks than purely domestic producers?

References and further reading

Aharoni, Y. (1966) *The Foreign Investment Decision Process*. Boston: Harvard University Press.

Asheghian, P. and Ebrahimi, B. (1990) *International Business, Economics, Environment, Strategies*. New York: Harper & Row.

Brigham, E. and Gapenski, L.C. (1985) *Financial Management: Theory and Practice* (4th edn). Hinsdale, IL: Dryden Press.

Buckley, A. (1986) *Multinational Finance*. Oxford, UK: Philip Allan.

Chakravarthy, B.S. and Perlmutter, H.V. (1985) 'Strategic planning for a global business'. *Columbia Journal of World Business*, Summer, 3–10.

Davidson, W.H. (1982) *Global Strategic Management*. New York: John Wiley & Sons.

Eiteman, D.K., Stonehill, A.I. and Moffett, M.H. (1998) *Multinational Business Finance* (8th edn). Reading, MA: Addison-Wesley.

Fayerweather, J. (1978) *International Business Strategy and Administration*. Cambridge, MA: Ballinger.

Hennart, J.-F. (1990) 'Some empirical dimesions of countertrade'. *Journal of International Business Studies*, second quarter, 243–270.

Knickerbocker, F.T. (1973) *Oligopolistic Reaction and Multinational Enterprise*. Boston: Harvard Business School Press.

Kobrin, S.J. (1979) 'Political risk: A review and recommendations'. *Journal of International Business Studies*, Spring/Summer, 69–80.

Kobrin, S.J. (1982) *Managing Political Risk Assessment: Strategic Response to Environmental Change*. Berkeley: University of California Press.

Lessard, D.R. (1986) 'Finance and global competition: Exploiting financial scope and coping with volatile exchange rates'. In M.E. Porter (ed.), *Competition in Global Industries*. Boston: Harvard Business School Press.

Lessard, D.R. and Lorange, P. (1997) 'Currency changes and management control: Resolving the centralization/decentralization dilemma'. *Accounting Review*, July, 628–637.

Murrenbeeld, M. (1975) 'Economic factors for forecasting foreign exchange rate changes'. *Columbia Journal of World Business*, Summer, 81–95.

Robbins, S. and Stobaugh, R. (1973) *Money in the Multinational Enterprise*. New York: Basic Books.

Robock, S.H. (1971) 'Political risk: Identification and assessment'. *Columbia Journal of World Business*, July/August, 6–20.

Robock, S.H. and Simmonds, K. (1989) *International Business and Multinational Enterprises* (4th edn). Homewood, IL: Richard D. Irwin.

Rummel, R.J. and Heenan, D.A. (1978) 'How multinationals analyse political risk'. *Harvard Business Review*, January/February, 67–76.

Shapiro, A. (1986) *Multinational Financial Management* (2nd edn). Boston: Allyn & Bacon.

ORGANIZATIONAL STRUCTURE AND CONTROL IN GLOBAL AND TRANSNATIONAL BUSINESS

13

Learning objectives

After studying this chapter students should be able to:

- describe two key variables that distinguish forms of organizational structure from each other;
- explain the contingency and configuration approaches to determining structure;
- explain the types of structure adopted by international and global businesses;
- describe the routes by which structures develop, particularly into complex forms such as matrix structures;
- describe the influences behind, and forms of, transnational structures;
- explain how performance measures can be used to appraise the performance of transnational businesses.

Introduction

Chapter 13 is important to the main themes of the book since it provides the link between global strategies, global management, strategy implementation and global competitiveness. There are particularly strong links, therefore, between this chapter and those on global strategy, human resource management and networks. The chapter explores the determinants of organizational structure, summarizes the alternative organizational structures available to international organizations, introduces recent alternative configurations and examines the important links that exist between global strategies and organizational structure and control.

The essence of a global and transnational strategy is the co-ordination and integration of geographically dispersed operations in the pursuit of global competitive advantage. This chapter examines the complex interrelationships between global strategy and the organization, and control issues associated with its implementation.

Some essentials of organizational structure

Key variables

Organizational structure concerns the shape adopted by the business in the pursuit of its strategic objectives. For international businesses the importance of structure is brought into focus because of the distances between the various parts and the need to co-ordinate activities between them. Structures are usually distinguished according to two variables:

1. the height and width of the structure;
2. the extent to which hierarchical management is observed.

Before we begin our discussion of the importance of structure in global and transnational businesses, we will review these two key themes in general terms.

'Height' and 'width' of structures

Height of structures
It is perhaps obvious to say that different organizations adopt different 'shapes'. 'Height' refers to the number of layers that exist within a structure. Larger organizations are higher than smaller ones. The guide to how high an organizational structure should be depends on the complexity of the tasks that a proposed strategy entails. A small, single site manufacturer will typically be involved in competing in one industry, sometimes with a single product type. This scenario is much less complex than a transnational

chemical company that competes in many national markets, in several product types and with a high dependence on research and legal regulations.

Height facilitates the engagement of specialist managers in the middle of an organization who can oversee and direct the many activities that some large organizations are involved in. Not all organizations have this requirement, and it would be more appropriate for such organizations to have a flatter structure. Companies with a high requirement for specialist professional staff often have several layers of management (thus increasing its height), and, accordingly, civil engineering consultancies, accountancy firms, chemical and specialist engineering companies often have this feature.

Width of structures

The 'width' of organizational structures refers to the extent to which the organization is centralized or decentralized. A decentralized organizational structure is one in which the centre elects to devolve some degree of decision-making power to other parts of the organization (see the EPRG [ethnocentric, polycentric, regiocentric, geocentric] framework in Chapter 2). A centralized organization is one in which little or no power is devolved from the centre. In practice, a continuum exists between the two extremes, along which the varying extents of decentralization can be visualized (see Figure 13.1). Transnational business tend toward the right-hand side of the continuum.

As with the height of structures, there is a trade-off between the costs and benefits of width. The advantages of centralization are mainly concerned with the ability of the centre to maintain tighter direct control over the activities of the organization. This is usually more appropriate when the organization is smaller and engages in few product or market segments. Some degree of decentralization is advantageous when the organization operates in a number of markets and localized specialized knowledge is an important determinant of overall success.

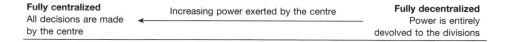

Figure 13.1 The centralization–decentralization continuum

Hierarchical configuration of structures

It would be wrong to assume that all organizations observe a strict form of structural hierarchy. Strict hierarchy is not always an appropriate form of organization, especially when it cannot be automatically assumed that seniority guarantees superior management skill.

In some contexts, formal hierarchy is entirely appropriate in implementing strategy. In others, however, allowing employees to act with some degree of independence can in fact enable the organization to be more effective in its various spheres of activity. The use of matrix structures, for example, can result in the organization being able to carry out many more tasks than a formal hierarchical structure. Many companies go 'halfway' in this regard by seconding employees into special task forces or cross-functional teams which are not part of the hierarchical structure and which act semi-independently in pursuit of its brief.

Determinants of organizational structure

Mintzberg's determinants

According to Mintzberg (1979; Mintzberg et al., 1998) there are two basic approaches to the formation of organizational structure, the *contingency approach* and the *configuration approach*.

According to the contingency approach, the structure of an organization will depend on factors like the nature of its business and its strategy, its size, the geographical span of its activities, its age and history and the nature of its environment. Mintzberg argued that, rather than adopting a contingency approach, it is sometimes better to base structure on a configuration approach. Factors like spans of control, the need for formalization, centralization or decentralization, and planning systems should be logically configured into internally consistent groupings.

Peters and Waterman (1982) argued that 'excellent' organizational performance depends on strategy, systems, culture (shared values), skills, leadership, staff and structure (drawing on what has become known as the McKinsey 7S framework). As these organizational features are interdependent, each was thought to play an important part in determining the others, so that structure will be affected by strategy, systems, culture, etc. Equally, structure will help to shape strategy, culture and systems. It is therefore evident that there are many complex factors shaping the structure of organizations.

The contingency approach

Contingency theory (as it relates to organizational structure) suggests that the most important determinants of organizational structure will include a number of factors. The key point with contingency theory is that the structure adopted will *depend*. This is in contrast to the configuration approach which seeks to proactively determine.

The structure that an organization adopts (which may be a domestic or internationalized business) will depend on several determining factors:

- the nature of the business;
- the environment of the organization;
- the global strategy of the business;
- the age and history of the organization;
- the size of business and limitations of span of control;
- the level of technology in the organization;
- the geographical span of activities;
- the culture of the organization;
- leadership and leadership style.

We will briefly consider each of these determining factors in turn.

The nature of the business
Businesses whose value-adding activities are largely repetitive, and which may be centred on a production line, are likely to adopt hierarchical structures with centralized decision making. Hierarchical structures are better suited to standardization of procedures. Organizations whose activities are diverse, creative or innovative are more likely to be based on flatter structures that encourage horizontal communication and devolve decision-making powers.

The environment of the organization
The more dynamic, turbulent and complex the environment the more adaptable the organization will usually need to be. In these circumstances, decision making is likely to be decentralized so as to increase responsiveness. On the other hand, Mintzberg (1979) argued that organizations will

tend to centralize decision making under conditions of extreme environmental hostility. In the international environment, a market that is globally homogeneous will permit greater centralization of authority while diversity of market conditions will increase the need for local responsiveness and will require decentralized decision making.

The global strategy of the business

When a business has a globally standardized strategy its structure will tend to concentrate power at the centre as this facilitates global co-ordination and integration of activities. A strategy that is centred on local responsiveness will require devolution of power to local managers. A transnational strategy, combining global co-ordination with local responsiveness, will require a complex structure allowing a degree of global control to be combined with the ability to respond locally. Developments in information and communications technology have made possible new organizational structures designed to achieve these dual, but somewhat conflicting, objectives (see Chapter 10).

The age and history of the organization

Mintzberg (1979) found that older organizations and businesses in mature industries tended to have more formalized structures. Few structures are designed 'from scratch' and, consequently, most structures evolve alongside the business itself. Accordingly, a small, new organization will have little need for a formal or complex structure, but, as an organization grows, the need for formalization and the observance of hierarchy increases.

The size of business and limitations of span of control

Larger organizations have more formalized and complex structures with greater specialization of tasks and clearly defined methods of communication. Tasks will be clustered into related groupings and the relationships between these groupings will be well established. The size of any cluster of activities will be dictated by the limitations of a manager's effective span of control (i.e., the number of subordinates he or she can directly control). Activities are often typically grouped by functional area, so that marketing and sales-related activities will be grouped together, and activities like recruitment, training and payroll are often grouped under the banner of human resources management.

The level of technology in the organization

Information and communications technology (ICT) has widened the potential span of control of an individual manager, making possible flatter organizational structures. Similarly, ICT makes it possible to centrally co-ordinate activities while simultaneously allowing decentralization of decision making, assisting local responsiveness. Before the advent of ICT, most international businesses operated on a multinational basis – allowing considerable autonomy to national subsidiaries because it was almost impossible to co-ordinate activities across boundaries with such constraints on effective communication.

The geographical span of activities

The greater the geographical span of an organization's activities the greater the need for formalization and complexity of structure. Again, ICT has increased the ability of organizations to increase the geographical span of their activities. Developments in telecommunications, like satellite and cable technology, have been critical in allowing businesses to integrate and manage their activities on a worldwide basis.

The culture of the organization

The values, attitudes and beliefs of the members of the organization will play an important part in moulding organizational structure. Thus a creative organization like a software house or an advertising agency will often have a flexible structure (less observance of hierarchy), whereas a production based manufacturing company is likely to have much more precisely defined and formalized groupings of activities with a much firmer observance of hierarchy. Organizational culture also often has its origins in the national culture of the country of origin of the business. The organizational culture of many Japanese businesses, for example, is often strongly influenced by values, attitudes and beliefs like loyalty and obedience which are prominent features of traditional Japanese society.

Leadership and leadership style

Larger organizations with strong leadership will tend to adopt structures that concentrate power at the centre of the organization. Smaller organizations have structures that spread from the leader at the centre. There will also be a close relationship between leadership style and organizational culture.

The configuration approach to organizational design

Although the factors discussed in the previous section contribute to understanding of how organization structures evolve, Mintzberg (1979; Mintzberg et al., 1998) proposed a 'configuration approach' to organizational design. The configuration of an organization (according to Mintzberg) must take account of the following design parameters:

1. *job specialization* – to logically divide up the tasks of the organization;
2. *behaviour formalization* – standardization of work processes;
3. *training* – instructional programmes to provide employees with the skills and knowledge to do their jobs;
4. *indoctrination* – to inculcate organizational norms in workers;
5. *unit grouping* – according to (i) business function (e.g., marketing, finance, production, etc.) and (ii) market served (these may conflict with each other as grouping by business function centres on the efficiency of the processes of the organization, while grouping by market increases organizational flexibility but encourages duplication, in turn reducing efficiency);
6. *unit size* – the number of positions contained in a single unit of the business;
7. *planning and control systems* – used to plan and control the activities of the organization;
8. *liaison and integrating devices* – devices like task forces and committees can integrate the units of the business (the logical conclusion of such devices is a matrix structure);
9. *the need for centralization or decentralization* – the extent to which it is necessary or desirable to diffuse decision-making power.

In addition, it is important to consider both the horizontal and vertical communication requirements and systems within the organization. In an international business unit grouping, particular importance is attached to planning and control systems, integrating devices, the need for centralization or decentralization, and indoctrination. The way in which units are grouped is one of the most significant decisions to be made in the design of international organizations. It is not simply a decision between grouping by functional area or by market, but rather how to integrate the two. The structures of global organizations must also take account of the need to co-ordinate and integrate geographically dispersed activities, at the same time as making possible local responsiveness where and when it is required. The matrix and the transnational (Bartlett and Ghoshal, 1987) are alternative forms of organization which attempt to resolve these conflicting requirements.

There is no ideal organizational structure. There are several commonly found types of structure which incorporate the parameters above and which reflect the range of internal and external factors that influence the evolution of organizational structure.

Types of international organizational structure

International businesses can theoretically choose from a range of alternative organizational structures, as summarized in Table 13.1. Each structure has its own inherent strengths and weaknesses.

Table 13.1 Types of transnational organizational structure

International structures	Characteristics
Export department	Responsibility for foreign sales transferred from domestic product divisions to a separate export department reporting directly to the group CEO.
Mother–daughter structure	Parent company acts as holding company for largely autonomous foreign subsidiaries. Subsidiary management report directly to CEO, but on an informal and personal basis. Subsidiaries are granted substantial operating freedom subject to satisfactory performance evaluation.
International divisional structure	Responsibility for all foreign operations transferred to a separate international division based at the corporate centre. Foreign subsidiaries report directly to the international centre.
Global structures	Characteristics
Functional	Responsibility for foreign operations allocated to functional line managers at the centre. Foreign subsidiaries report directly to functional executives at the centre (production, marketing, human resources, finance, etc.).
Product	Responsibility for foreign operations allocated to product divisions based at the centre. Foreign subsidiaries report directly to product divisions.
Geographic/Regional	Responsibility for foreign operations allocated to area executives. Foreign subsidiaries report directly to geographic/regional division based at the centre or abroad.
Matrix	Responsibility for foreign operations divided between product and geographic divisions. Foreign subsidiaries report directly to both product and geographic centres.

International structures

Export departments
The establishment of a separate export department to control and co-ordinate foreign sales is most frequently found in companies in the early stages of internationalization where foreign production is minimal and foreign markets are supplied mainly through domestic production and exports. The creation of a separate export department allows a greater degree of control and co-ordination of the export drive by concentrating knowledge of foreign markets in a single department and by ensuring that foreign sales are included in the planning process.

Export departments, however, suffer from two main weaknesses. First, conflicts of interest may arise between domestically oriented product divisions and the export department regarding the relative importance of foreign as opposed to domestic sales. The export department will be dependent on domestic product divisions for both products and technology. Since the latter are mainly concerned with domestic sales, less attention may be devoted to enhancing foreign markets. Second, export departments are ill-suited to further foreign market expansion through licensing, subcontracting and FDI (foreign direct investment) because of the lack of expertise in managing foreign operations as opposed to foreign sales. Largely because of the second of these disadvantages, most export departments are relatively short-lived. Continued foreign market expansion through FDI has led most international businesses to replace their export departments with international divisions, or, in the case of some European businesses, with mother–daughter structures.

Mother–daughter structures
This type of structure is particularly suited to two types of international enterprise: first, new foreign investors, where foreign operations are not of crucial importance to the parent company; second, businesses with extensive FDIs, but limited central resources, as with some European businesses. The main advantage of the mother–daughter structure is that it encourages subsidiary innovation and motivation by substituting subsidiary autonomy for centralized control. Its main disadvantage, on the other hand, is the lack of global planning and co-ordination of activity.

International divisional structures
The majority of US businesses (and some European and Japanese businesses) have used this type of structure at some stage in their inter-

nationalization. The strengths and weaknesses of the international division are similar to those of export departments. Thus, the international division provides a focal point for the growing foreign involvement of the company (through FDI) by concentrating international knowledge and expertise in a single division. This allows greater control and co-ordination of foreign operations as well as ensuring that the interests of foreign subsidiaries are taken into account in the corporate planning process. On the negative side, however, the same conflict of interest evident between domestic product divisions and export departments will also exist in the relationship between the former and the international division. International divisions are also usually short-lived in most international companies. Indeed, the very success of the international division in stimulating FDI may sow the seeds of its own destruction. The continued foreign expansion of the company through FDI will result in the need for closer control and planning of foreign activities by the parent company. This has led most international organizations to replace their international divisions with global structures aimed at providing a greater degree of co-ordination and integration of their worldwide activities. Such global structures may be organized on functional, product or geographical lines of responsibilities.

Global structures

Functionally based structures

Global organization along functional lines is rare among US companies, although it has been used successfully by some European and US international businesses with extremely narrow product lines (e.g., oil companies). The global functional organization allows tight control over specific functions worldwide, which may be of particular importance to businesses whose competitive strengths lie in superior technology, marketing or personnel practices. Such advantages, however, are often outweighed by the disadvantages of this type of structure. First, co-ordination of functions is difficult, leading to the potential separation of, for example, production and marketing. Second, subsidiaries will be reporting to several different divisions at the corporate centre, resulting in the duplication of effort and a possible breakdown of communications. Finally, the structure is unsuitable for multiproduct or geographically dispersed organizations. As a consequence of such disadvantages, most international companies have incorporated functional responsibilities within global divisions based on product or geographical lines.

Product-based structures

Under the global product organizational structure, product divisions at the corporate centre are given worldwide responsibilities for their own products and services, including both functional and geographical responsibilities. The global product structure is particularly suited for global businesses with diverse product lines, when products go to a variety of end uses and when a high degree of technology capability is required. Organization by product may also permit significant economies of scale to be achieved through the co-ordination and integration of production in different countries. It also allows the business to respond quickly to the actions of competitors. The principal weaknesses of global product divisions relate to the lack of emphasis placed on international or geographical planning. Global product divisions may be staffed by executives with particular product expertise but with limited knowledge of international/geographic markets. Thus, the emphasis of the division may be on the domestic market to the detriment of foreign markets. Similarly, the lack of international knowledge may create difficulties in assessing changes in environmental and political conditions in overseas markets, leading to lost opportunities for expansion. Finally, co-ordination and integration of the subsidiary companies in a particular geographical area is difficult to achieve under global product divisions.

Geographic/Regionally based structures

The problems associated with the lack of regional co-ordination can be overcome by adopting global regional/geographic structures. Under this structure, subsidiary companies (regardless of product line) report directly to corporate executives responsible for a particular geographical area. Each area division has both product line and functional responsibilities for all operations within its area. Such area divisions may be based at the centre. More commonly, however, separate regional headquarters will be established in the relevant areas. Many US companies, for example, have established separate regional headquarters based in Europe.

A survey by Daniels (1986) identified various reasons for the establishment of such offices, including:

- *pooling of resources* – the provision of specialist staff support to operating divisions;
- *product rationalization* – the management of product integration on a European basis;

- *size of reporting structures* – to reduce the number of subsidiaries reporting directly to the parent company;
- *day-to-day control* – to exert greater operating control over subsidiaries than is possible from a distant parent company;
- *management development* – the regional headquarters is used to develop a cadre of highly trained managers with global orientations;
- *unification of external relations* – the consolidation of public relations efforts.

The global regional/geographic structure is particularly suited for international companies with narrow product lines but with geographically dispersed operations. The structure allows co-ordination and integration of activities within particular regions, as well as allowing greater responsiveness to local or regional market conditions. The concentration of knowledge of particular regions within a separate division may allow scope for the further development of the organization's operations in that area. Many global businesses have established separate regional head offices for Europe since the development of the single market in 1993. The weaknesses of the global regional/geographic structure relate to the lack of integration of product lines and the possible duplication of functional and product specialists at each regional headquarters.

Matrix structures
In order to preserve the strengths of each of these international structures and to overcome their disadvantages, many global businesses adopted global matrix structures that attempted to co-ordinate and integrate worldwide functional, product and area responsibilities. Under this structure, responsibility for foreign operations is divided between global product and regional divisions with subsidiary managers reporting to two bosses (thus confusing the hierarchy of the organization). Co-ordination and integration of product and area responsibilities is achieved through frequent interchanges between the product and regional divisions and through the CEO. The drawbacks of the global matrix structure are that it can be difficult to manage because of conflicts of interest between product and regional groupings. Decision-making procedures are also complex because decision making is a group process. The advantages and disadvantages of global matrix structures are examined in more detail in the next section.

The development of global and transnational matrix structures

Stimuli to matrix development

The link between corporate strategy and corporate structure has become firmly established in the literature since the pioneering work of Chandler (1962) who showed that as a company's product/market strategy changed so too did its organizational structure to support implementation of the new strategy. The work of Stopford and Wells (1972) established patterns of development found in the structures of many multinational businesses. When only a limited range of products are sold abroad and when foreign sales are only a small proportion of sales, many companies initially manage their overseas activities through an international division. Organizations that then broaden the range of products offered abroad tend to establish a worldwide product division. Those that expand sales abroad without broadening product range will often do so by establishing an area division structure. When sales abroad reach a high percentage of total sales and a broad range of products are offered for sale, then businesses often opt for a matrix structure. These developments in structure are illustrated in Figure 13.2, which shows Stopford and Wells' 'international structural stages model'.

According to the Stopford and Wells model, development through path 1 or path 2 will culminate in the development of a global matrix structure. The extent to which global matrix structures provide a solution to the complex organizational and control problems of transnationals has been the subject of the extensive debate that is explored below.

Global matrix structures

At some point in the internationalization process, the introduction of global structures becomes necessary to achieve co-ordination and integration of geographically dispersed activities. One possible approach to this situation is the global matrix structure, which is one means of achieving global co-ordination and local responsiveness.

Benefits of a matrix structure
One of the key benefits of a matrix structure is that co-ordination and integration of activity on a global scale can be achieved through global

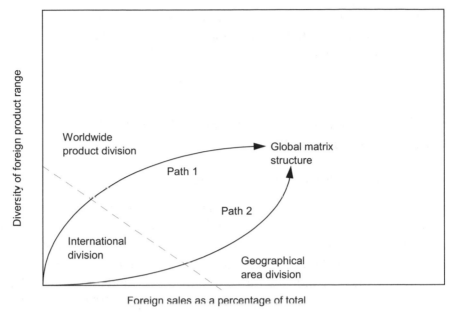

Figure 13.2 International structural stages model
Source: adapted from Stopford and Wells (1972)

product divisions. Local responsiveness can be achieved through global regional or geographic structures. Thus, global matrix structures that combine both product and geographic divisions can achieve both global co-ordination and national responsiveness simultaneously. The main advantage of matrix compared with strict hierarchical structures is that they are able to accommodate managers with worldwide (product) responsibilities for particular businesses and country managers responsible for specific area markets.

Disadvantages of matrix structures
Bartlett and Ghoshal (1995) observed that many companies that had previously adopted matrix structures like Dow Chemical and Citibank have now abandoned them. This is because of the problems inherent in managing through such structures that include:

- overlapping responsibilities;
- reporting duplication with managers reporting to two or more bosses, often with conflicting objectives;
- survival of the fittest with one decision-making centre emerging as dominant;

- excessive time spent on reaching compromise decisions;
- duplication of information, communications and activities;
- increased administrative costs.

The development of the transnational organizational structure

National influences on structural form

The weakness of traditional organizational structure in an international and global context gave rise to Bartlett and Ghoshal's view that 'formal structure is a powerful but blunt instrument of strategic change' (1995). They argued that to 'develop multidimensional and flexible strategic capabilities, a company must go beyond structure and expand its fundamental organizational capabilities.' Bartlett and Ghoshal (1987, 1988, 1989, 1992, 1995) developed the concepts of the transnational business and transnational management, which are explained in this section.

European businesses
A company's organizational structure is shaped by its tasks, its environment and its administrative heritage or the history that, in turn, has shaped its culture (Bartlett and Ghoshal, 1995). European businesses, which expanded abroad in the 1920s and 1930s in a time of protectionism and limited transport and communications technology, developed as *decentralized federations*. Within these federations, headquarters provided capital investment, while national subsidiaries were integrated business units with considerable management autonomy.

American businesses
American businesses which experienced their greatest period of growth in the 1950s and 1960s, based on technological superiority, developed as *co-ordinated federations* where knowledge was passed to subsidiaries, structures were rigid and centralized planning prevailed. Subsidiaries were allowed limited freedom to modify products to reflect local market differences.

Japanese businesses
Japanese companies, internationalizing in the 1970s, grew as *centralized hubs* because their strategies depended on cost advantages requiring tight centralized control of activities.

Limitations of the three forms
Each of these solutions to the problems of international structure has disadvantages. The decentralized federation achieved local responsiveness but at the cost of duplication of activities and a failure to gain the efficiencies possible with international co-ordination of activities. At the other extreme, centralized hubs realized the advantages of co-ordination but at the expense of local responsiveness. The failure of the matrix to reconcile these problems meant that an alternative solution had to be sought.

'Anatomy' and 'physiology'

As global and transnational strategies became more sophisticated, the problem became one of organizational incapacity to implement such sophisticated strategies. In other words, strategic thinking has far out-distanced organizational capabilities. The main problem facing global companies is not one of designing appropriate global strategies. Rather, it is one of organizational incapability to implement complex strategies. Matrix structures provide no solution since they can sometimes result in excessive conflict and confusion.

The key organizational task, therefore, is not to design ever more elegant and complex structures, but to capture individual capabilities and motivate the entire organization to respond co-operatively to a complicated and dynamic environment. To achieve this, Bartlett and Ghoshal (1995) suggested a reversal in the traditional organizational sequence that emphasizes organizational anatomy (formal structure), physiology (communications and decision processes) and psychology (corporate beliefs and norms that shape managers' perceptions and actions).

Rather than searching for the 'ideal' organizational anatomy (structure), the first task is to alter organizational psychology; then to enrich communications and decision processes through improvements in organizational physiology. Only then should these changes be consolidated and confirmed by realigning organizational anatomy through changing the formal structure. The companies that respond most successfully to the complexities of the global business environment are those that emphasize the need to change organizational psychology in the broad corporate beliefs and norms that shape managers' perceptions and actions. These changes can be reinforced by changing organizational physiology by enriching and clarifying communications and decision processes. Only then should these be consolidated by realigning organizational anatomy (i.e., the formal structure).

Features of transnational structures

Bartlett and Ghoshal (1995) made the case that industries have changed from being international, multinational or global to being 'transnational'. In such an environment, organizations themselves must become *transnational*. According to Bartlett and Ghoshal (1995), successful international corporations must 'optimize efficiency, responsiveness and learning simultaneously in their worldwide operations.' The difficulty is to achieve 'a three way balance of organizational perspectives and capabilities among product, function and (geographical) area' (Bartlett and Ghoshal, 1987).

The issue is not whether to be globally integrated *or* locally responsive but how to be *both* simultaneously. Authoritative global corporate management is required to integrate activities and ensure global efficiencies are obtained. Corporate managers must determine the overarching strategy of the organization, stress the interdependence of its functional and geographical parts, and co-ordinate its activities. The development and transfer of core competences requires capable functional management. Functional managers must facilitate learning and innovation within their domain of the business. Strong geographical management is required to ensure local responsiveness to national and regional markets. Local managers, in turn, must develop locally determined competences that must then contribute to company-wide competences. Only a multidimensional organization can provide these three strands of management simultaneously. Accordingly, the transnational is multidimensional by ensuring that:

- tasks are systematically *differentiated* by treating different businesses, functions and areas differently and by allowing them to be organized differently;
- relationships between the different parts of the business are based on *interdependence* rather than independence;
- *co-ordination and co-option* of differentiated and interdependent

organizational units are achieved through shared vision and integrative mechanisms.

The transnational model

Bartlett and Ghoshal (1995) gave several examples of organizations that were, at that time, becoming transnational:

- Unilever adopted a differentiated organization of tasks. In Europe, activities were closely integrated (recognizing the similarities between national markets), while in Latin America there was greater local autonomy to cater for greater market diversity. In other words, Unilever moved from being an organization that is symmetrical to one that is differentiated in terms of product, function and geography.
- NEC developed co-ordination of its activities through a clearly communicated global vision and strategy rather than through tight management controls.

In both these cases, creating a transnational is more concerned with creating an organizational culture based on a global vision, emphasizing differentiation and co-ordination, rather than a specific structure that incorporates tight controls.

Bartlett and Ghoshal (1995) developed the transnational model further by suggesting that transnationals possess integrated networks with three major characteristics:

1. multidimensional perspectives;
2. distributed, interdependent capabilities;
3. flexible integrative processes.

We will briefly consider each of these characteristics.

Multidimensional perspectives
The cultural diversity and increasing volatility of the international business environment have increased the need for organizations to sense and respond to environmental changes. This depends on developing strong global, subsidiary and functional management without domination by any one of these groups. Strong *subsidiary management* is required to identify the changing needs of local customers. Strong *global management* is

required to respond to the global strategies of competitors and to co-ordinate an appropriate response. Strong *functional management* is required to provide focus for areas of organizational knowledge and to ensure its transfer among units of the organization.

Distributed, interdependent capabilities

In devising its response to changes in the environment, a transnational seeks to avoid the problems of other international configurations. The global centralized hub makes it difficult to respond to diverse local demands while the decentralized federation results in duplication, inefficiency and barriers to organizational learning. Within a transnational it is not seen as necessary to centralize activities that require global scale or specialized knowledge. Global scale can be achieved by making a local plant into a global production centre serving all the company's worldwide markets. A particular research and development centre can become the centre of excellence for the whole business. A local marketing group with proven expertise may be given the role of developing a global marketing strategy for a particular product. In this way the company becomes an *integrated network* (Figure 13.3(d)) of distributed but interdependent capabilities that benefit the whole organization.

Flexible integrative processes

Once the network of distributed and integrated capabilities has been created alongside the management groups that represent the multiple perspectives of the organization's environment, then flexible integrative management processes are required that integrate these diverse perspectives and capabilities. These processes must be flexible to allow differentiated operating relationships, adaptable operating relationships and functional decision-making roles which can change over time in response to changing circumstances. This flexible integration is achieved by three separate but interdependent management processes:

- *centralization* – which is sensitive to the groups within the organization but allows senior management to intervene in certain decisions to ensure co-ordination;
- *formalization* – which allows different parts of the organization to have influence on key decisions;
- *socialization* – which is a set of cultural norms and procedures which

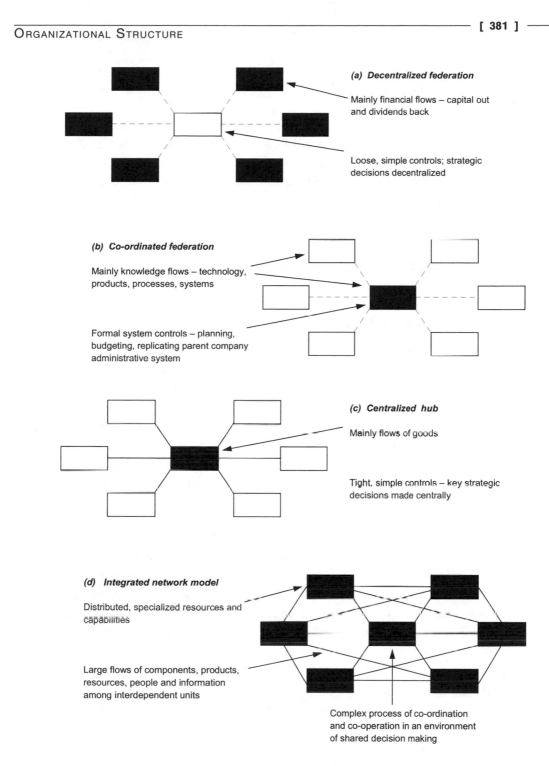

Figure 13.3 Organizational configuration models
Reproduced from Bartlett and Ghoshal (1995)

provides the framework for delegated decision making in the context of the overall organization.

There is no prescribed structure for a transnational. Rather, there are a set of principles which guide the managers of global businesses in the design and configuration of their organizations. These principles assist in achieving simultaneous global co-ordination and local responsiveness, alongside organizational learning and competence building.

Decision making and control in international business

Decentralization and control

The issue of decision making within the transnational is closely related to the discussion of organizational structures presented above. In traditional multinationals, for example, decision making is largely decentralized at the level of the foreign subsidiary. In global structures, on the other hand, greater centralization of decision making may be expected, although this will vary between different businesses and across functional areas. In a transnational corporation the issue is how to combine centralization and decentralization so as to achieve global co-ordination and local responsiveness.

Too much centralization may prevent the utilization of local initiative and have an adverse effect on the motivation of local management. Overcentralized decision making may also result in a lack of adaptation to local market needs and may create political problems with host country governments. Decentralizing certain decision making to the local subsidiary may overcome many of these difficulties. By granting subsidiary autonomy the transnational may encourage the use of local initiative and the flexibility of the subsidiary to changes in local market conditions. Pressures on the corporate centre are also reduced as are the potential tensions with host country governments. The identification of a 'local' image may also be important in a number of industries. National units can develop new products and new techniques locally which can then be used throughout the transnational.

Centralization of some decision making may be necessary to achieve the benefits of global co-ordination through global economies and efficiencies.

In the transnational model this centralized decision making would include representation of different local, functional and business areas rather than only central management. Typically, the centre of any organization is concerned with establishing its overall vision, mission and its broad strategy. At the same time, within a transnational the centre plays an important role in co-ordinating activities, improving efficiency through benchmarking and setting standards, promoting innovation and encouraging a learning and interdependent culture.

Empirical studies

Several studies have investigated the centralization/decentralization of decision making within transnationals (Brooke and Remmers, 1976; Goehle, 1980; Hedlund, 1981; Young et al., 1985). The general conclusion emerging from these studies is that the locus of decision making varies significantly across functional areas and between different transnationals.

A survey of 154 foreign-owned subsidiaries operating in the UK highlighted the variation in decision-making procedures across functional areas, with financial decisions being the most centralized and personnel decisions the most decentralized (Young et al., 1985). Production and marketing decisions generally fell within these two extremes, with strategic production/marketing decisions being more centralized than operational decisions. Research and development decisions were also closely controlled by the parent company in a large proportion of the sample companies. Such variations in the locus of decision making across functional areas can be explained in terms of the relative importance of each decision to the parent company. Decisions that draw on or directly affect central resources (e.g., most financial decisions), decisions that constitute long-term obligations for the transnational (e.g., the introduction of new products and entry into new markets) and decisions that attempt to standardize and establish a common framework of organizational routines and procedures (e.g., the setting of financial targets and rates of return on investment) are the most likely to be centralized.

In addition to establishing appropriate organizational structures and decision-making procedures, transnationals must also establish evaluation and control procedures for assessing subsidiary performance and ensuring the conformity of the subsidiary to corporate objectives. Internal benchmarking of performance is an important feature of a transnational organization. It is one means by which best practice can be spread throughout the organization from one geographical area to another and from one functional area to another.

Evaluating performance

Performance evaluation within the transnational serves a number of functions (Hedlund and Zander, 1985):

- Ensuring the co-ordination and integration of strategy. Global and local strategy are integrated.
- Assisting in the internal benchmarking of performance. This acts as a mechanism to spread best practice throughout the organization.
- Ensuring a realistic level of profitability. Performance of parts of the organization may be measured against some target variable (e.g., actual profit, return on investment, etc.).
- Early identification of problems. Failure to meet targets provides an early warning system in order that corrective action may be taken.
- Resource allocation. Limited resources channelled into areas of highest return.
- Information. The performance evaluation system provides essential information on the operations of the different parts of the business.
- Long-run planning. Information acts as an input into strategic planning.
- Motivation. Performance evaluation used to motivate management in different parts of the organization.
- Communications. Performance evaluation stimulates discussion between different parts of the organization regarding performance, problems, long-run trends, etc.

While each of these functions may be important, surveys by the BIC (1982) and Hedlund and Zander (1985), covering both US and European trans-nationals, showed that the three most important functions performed by the evaluation procedure are:

1. ensuring subsidiary profitability;
2. identifying potential problems; and
3. facilitating resource allocation.

Hedlund and Zander (1985) also suggested that the importance of these three objectives varies with the nature of the international involvement of the company. Large, geographically dispersed transnationals emphasized the problem identification and resource allocation roles, while early internationalizers emphasize profitability as an objective.

In terms of the actual performance measures used, the transnational has the same alternatives available as a domestic company, including return on investment, income/profit contribution, market share, cash flow measures, etc. The use of these measures, however, is usually more difficult in a transnational due to exchange rate variations, differences in accounting procedures, variations in national inflation rates and tax rates, transfer pricing and restriction on remittances (see Chapter 12).

Global and transnational strategies, organization and control

Several references have already been made in this chapter to the link between corporate strategy and the internal management and control of the transnational. This final section examines this relationship in more detail by linking the discussion in this chapter to Chapter 6 on global strategy.

Many factors influence the internal management and control systems adopted by transnationals. The most important are:

- the global or transnational strategy of the organization;
- the strategic predispositions and value systems of the transnational as identified in the EPRG profile (see Chapter 2);
- the geographical extent of its operations;
- the nature of its international business environment.

The influence of strategy on structure and control systems

According to Porter's (1986, 1990) classification of international strategies, the organizational and control challenge facing the transnational is the need to balance the conflicting forces of country responsiveness and global direction. The relative importance of these and the impact on organization and control will vary with the type of international strategy. Thus, country-centred strategies (geographically dispersed operations with minimum co-ordination) imply an organizational structure that is country-responsive, such as a geographic divisional structure, with considerable decision-making autonomy being devolved to the local subsidiaries.

Performance evaluation within international businesses with country-centred strategies will normally be confined to ensuring subsidiary profitability.

In geographically dispersed but highly co-ordinated businesses, on the other hand, the need for global planning and co-ordination will be reflected in the organizational structure that will be based on factors like global product, geographic or matrix systems. This, in turn, will depend on the company's product range and its geographical spread of activities. Similarly, authority over a range of both strategic and operational decisions will be transferred to a higher level in the organization which has a global perspective. Decision making, therefore, will be highly centralized, with a hierarchical chain of command between subsidiary and parent. Finally, performance evaluation within such organizations will serve several functions relating to resource allocation, problem spotting and planning, in addition to the short-run measurement of subsidiary profitability.

In the Yip (1992) model of 'total global strategy' and the model of transnational strategy presented in this book, co-ordination and responsiveness are *both* viewed as essential to the achievement of competitive advantage. In this context it is necessary to build an organization that is 'transnational'. This will imply, as discussed in the previous sections of this chapter:

- strong global, subsidiary and functional management and multidimensional perspectives;
- distributed, interdependent capabilities; and
- flexible integrative processes.

Discussion and review questions

1. Discuss the contributions made by contingency theory and the configuration approach to our understanding of organizational structures.
2. Discuss the major organizational and control problems specific to international businesses.
3. Explain the international structural stages model (Stopford and Wells, 1972). Is the matrix structure the inevitable outcome of the process?
4. Why are export departments and international divisions unlikely to be structures permanently adopted by an international business?
5. What are the problems inherent in simply adopting a global functional or product division structure?

6. To what extent does a geographical structure solve the problems inherent in a global functional or product division structure?
7. Explain the relative advantages and disadvantages of the decentralized federation, the co-ordinated federation, the centralized hub and the integrated network.
8. Explain what Bartlett and Ghoshal meant by the 'transnational solution'. What are the main characteristics of a transnational? What are its advantages and disadvantages compared with a global matrix structure? Give examples in support of your answer.
9. Explain the functions of performance evaluation systems in transnationals.
10. What is the relationship between global and transnational strategy and organizational structure?

References and further reading

Bartlett, C.A. and Ghoshal, S. (1988) 'Organizing for a worldwide effectiveness. The transnational solution'. *California Management Review*, **30**, 54–74.

Bartlett, C.A. and Ghoshal, S. (1989) *Managing Across Borders: The Transnational Solution*, Boston: Harvard Business School Press.

Bartlett, C.A. and Ghoshal, S. (1987) 'Managing across borders: New organizational responses'. *Sloan Management Review*, Fall, 45–53.

Bartlett, C.A. (1981) 'Multinational structural change: Evolution versus reorganisation'. In: L. Otterbeck (ed.), *The Management of Headquarters – Subsidiary Relationships in Multinational Corporations* (Chapter 6). Aldershot, UK: Gower Press.

Bartlett, C.A. and Ghoshal, S. (1990) 'Matrix management: Not a structure, a frame of mind'. *Harvard Business Review*, July/August, No. 4, 138–145.

Bartlett, C.A. and Ghoshal, S. (1992) 'What is a global manager?'. *Harvard Business Review*, **70**(5), 124–132.

Bartlett, C.A. and Ghoshal, S. (1995) *Transnational Management: Text, Cases and Readings in Cross-border Management*. Homewood, IL: Richard D. Irwin.

BIC (1981) *New Directions in Multinational Corporation Organisation*. Clichy, France: Business International Corporation.

Brooke, M.Z. and Remmers, H.L. (1976) *The Strategy of Multinational Enterprise*. London: Pitman.

Chandler, A. (1962) *Strategy and Structure*. Cambridge, MA: MIT Press.

Daniels, J.D. (1986) 'Approaches to European regional management by large US multinational firms'. *Management International Review*, **26**(2).

Davidow, W. and Malone, M. (1992) *The Virtual Corporation*. London: Harper Business.

Franks, L.G. (1976) *The European Multinationals*. New York: Harper & Row.

Ghertman, M. (1984) *Decision-making in Multinational Enterprises: Concepts and Research Approaches* (ILO Working Paper No. 31). Geneva: International Labour Organization.

Goehle, D.G. (1980) *Decision-making in Multinational Corporations*. Ann Arbor, MI: UMI Research Press.

Hedlund, G. (1981) 'Autonomy of subsidiaries and formalisation of headquarters – Subsidiary relationships in Swedish MNCs'. In: L. Otterbeck (ed.), *The Management of Headquarters – Subsidiary Relationships in Multinational Corporations*. Aldershot, UK: Gower Press.

Hedlund, G. (1984) 'Organisation in-between: The evolution of the mother–daughter structure of managing foreign subsidiaries in Swedish multinational corporations'. *Journal of International Business Studies*, Fall.

Hedlund, G. and Aman, P. (1983) *Managing Relationships with Foreign Subsidiaries – Organisation and Control in Swedish MNCs*. Stockholm: Sveriges Mekunforbund.

Hedlund, G. and Zander, U. (1985) *Formulation of Goals and Follow-up of Performance for Foreign Subsidiaries in Swedish MNCs* (Institute of International Business RP 85/4). Stockholm: School of Economics.

Hulbert, J.M. and Brandt, W.K. (1980) *Managing the Multinational Subsidiary*. New York: Holt, Rinehart & Winston.

Jarillo, J.C. (1993) *Strategic Networks: Creating the Borderless Organisation*. Oxford, UK: Butterworth-Heinemann.

Jennings, D. and Seaman, S. (1994) 'High and low levels of organisational adaptation: An empirical analysis of strategy, structure and performance'. *Strategic Management Journal*, **15**(6), 459–475.

Johnson, G. and Scholes, K. (1999) *Exploring Corporate Strategy*. Englewood Cliffs, NJ: Prentice Hall.

Journal of International Business Studies (1983) Special issue on management and culture in the transnational, Fall.

Miller, D. (1987) 'The genesis of configuration'. *Academy of Management Review*, **12**(4), 686–701.

Miller, D. (1990) 'Organisational configurations: Cohesion, change and prediction'. *Human Relations*, **43**(8), 771–789.

Mintzberg, H. (1979) *The Structuring of Organizations*. Englewood Cliffs, NJ: Prentice Hall.

Mintzberg, H. (1983) *Power in and around Organizations*. Englewood Cliffs, NJ: Prentice Hall.

Mintzberg, H. (1984) *Mintzberg on Management: Inside Our Strange World of Organizations*. New York: Free Press.

Mintzberg, H., Quinn, J.B. and Ghoshal, S. (1998) *The Strategy Process* (revised European edn). Englewood Cliffs, NJ: Prentice Hall.

Mullins, L. (1996) *Management and Organisational Behaviour*. London: Pitman.

Naylor, T.H. (1985) 'The international strategy matrix'. *Columbia Journal of World Business*, **20**(2), Summer.

Otterbeck, L. (ed.) (1981) *The Management of Headquarters – Subsidiary Relationships in Multinational Corporations* (Chapter 6). Aldershot, UK: Gower Press.

Perlmutter, H.V. (1969) 'The tortuous evolution of the multinational corporation'. *Columbia Journal of World Business*, January/February.

Peters, T. and Waterman, R. (1982) *In Search of Excellence*. New York: Harper & Row.

Pitts, R.A. and Daniels, J.D. (1984) 'Aftermath of the matrix mania'. *Columbia Journal of World Business*, **19**(2), Summer.

Porter, M.E. (1986) 'Changing patterns of international competition'. *California Management Review*, **28**(2), Winter.

Porter, M.E. (1990) *The Competitive Advantage of Nations*. New York: Free Press.

Prahalad, C.K. and Doz, Y.L. (1986) *The Multinational Mission: Balancing Local Demands and Global Vision*. New York: Free Press.

Rugman, A.M., Lecraw, D.J. and Booth, L.D. (1985) *International Business: Firm and Environment*. London: McGraw-Hill.

Stopford, J.M. and Wells, L.T. (1972) *Strategy and Structure of Multinational Enterprise*. New York: Basic Books.

Yip, G.S. (1992) *Total Global Strategy – Managing for Worldwide Competitive Advantage*. Englewood Cliffs, NJ: Prentice Hall.

Young, S., Hood, N. and Hamill, J. (1985) *Decision-making in Foreign-owned Multinational Subsidiaries in the United Kingdom* (ILO Working Paper No. 35). Geneva: International Labour Organization.

Managing Global Mergers, Acquisitions and Alliances

Introduction

Sirower (1997) made the point that 'The 1990s will go down in history as the time of the biggest merger and acquisition wave of the century.' At the same time as this boom in mergers and acquisitions, there was a similar increase in the numbers of strategic alliances and collaborative business networks involving international organizations. In this chapter we begin by explaining the motivations that underlie international mergers and acquisitions and collaborative business networks. We then explore the reasons for the success and failure of such ventures before considering how global managers can seek to increase the chances of successful integration or collaboration.

An overview of integrations and alliances

Perspectives on external growth

De Wit and Meyer (1998) presented an interesting review of the factors underlying merger and collaborative activity from two opposing perspectives: the *portfolio perspective* and the *core competence perspective.*

The portfolio perspective
The portfolio perspective stresses that the major benefits of integration are the leveraging of financial resources, entry to new businesses and markets, and the spreading of risks. Successful management of a diversified business will accordingly depend on responsiveness. There is, therefore, an emphasis on devolving responsibility for strategy to each of the strategic business units that comprise the corporation so as to increase their ability to respond flexibly to changes in the environment.

The core competence perspective
The core competence perspective is based on the view that mergers, acquisitions and alliances improve performance by creating synergy between the businesses involved. This synergy arises from the leveraging of resources and core competences between the businesses. For example, the reputation or brand name of a company can produce shared benefits. The involvement of the German Volkswagen Group in Skoda of the Czech Republic helped to improve the latter's reputation. Similarly, the sharing of Volkswagen's knowledge, skills and technology improved Skoda's productivity, quality and products. De Wit and Meyer (1998) listed the other potential sources of resource leveraging as increased bargaining power in relation to customers and suppliers, improved linkages to distributors, shared marketing, shared finance, etc.

From a core competence perspective, a successful merger or collaborative agreement must create greater value through synergy and co-ordination than the value lost through reduced responsiveness. In fact, it is not the case that increased co-ordination will necessarily result in decreased responsiveness. In the case of horizontal or diversified integration and alliances, there may well be some resultant loss of responsiveness to the business. Vertical integration or alliances between a business and its suppliers and distributors is likely to increase responsiveness due to more reliable access to inputs and outlets (this being a major factor in many just-in-time alliances between businesses and their suppliers). The advent of information and communications technology and its impact on organizational learning (Stonehouse and Pemberton, 1999) has further enhanced the ability of networks of collaborating or integrated organizations to sustain responsiveness at the same time as achieving synergy through co-ordination.

Types of integrations and alliances

A major factor in the boom in the 1990s in integrations and collaborative ventures was their increasing importance in the global and transnational strategies of many businesses. Despite the potential benefits of competence leveraging and synergy, improved co-ordination and responsiveness, cross-border deals suffer from a very high failure rate (20–50% according to some empirical studies). It is, therefore, important to consider the possible reasons for the success and failure of integration and collaboration.

Although there are many similar concerns in the setting up and management of integrations (mergers and acquisitions) and alliances, there are also many differences. These arise from the fact that alliances involve collaboration between two or more organizations who may continue to compete in one form or another as well as collaborating in global markets. Integration and collaboration can be split into four distinct categories (Figure 14.1):

Vertical backward or upstream integration or collaboration
Such integrations and alliances take place when a business engages with its suppliers. The major motivations for vertical backward integration or upstream collaboration are mainly related to resource leveraging by improving access to and control of resources and better supply chain

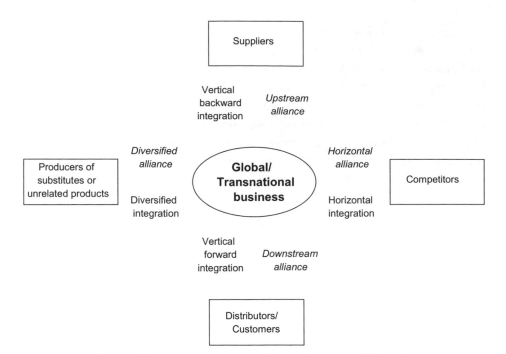

Figure 14.1 A categorization of integration and collaboration

linkages. Many motor vehicle manufacturers, for example, are involved in vertical alliances with suppliers. Collaboration with suppliers improves access to materials and parts. This, in turn, allows greater control of quality and delivery.

Vertical forward or downstream integration or collaboration
This form of integration or alliance takes place when a business engages with its distributors or customers. Collaboration with distributors provides improved access to customers and allows greater marketing synergies between a business and its distributors.

Horizontal integration or collaboration
When two companies at the same stage of the supply chain or value system collaborate or integrate, it is horizontal in direction. Thus the collaboration between Honda and Rover or the later acquisition of Rover by BMW are classified as horizontal collaboration and a horizontal acquisition, respectively. Here the major advantages relate to synergy rather than responsiveness. There are opportunities for competence leveraging through brand names, shared finance, etc.

Diversified integration or collaboration
Diversified integrations and collaborative ventures take place between a business and other businesses in other industries. Here the major advantages also relate to leveraging of brand names and access to finance.

Transnational mergers and acquisitions

The key definitions

It is important to begin by understanding the terms *merger, acquisition* and *integration.* In a *merger,* two organizations agree to join together and pool their assets in a new business entity. Both of the previous entities 'disappear' into the new organization. Shares in the previous entities are commuted into new stock, usually revalued to account for the new market value. In practice, the two partners in a merger are usually of comparable size and, importantly, they are entered into willingly by both parties.

An *acquisition* is a joining of unequal partners. A large organization purchases all (or a controlling share interest in) a smaller business and then subsumes it into its structure. Acquisitions can be either agreed or hostile, depending on the attitude of the smaller company:

- An *agreed acquisition* is one where the directors of the target company accept that the offer for the shares are in the best interests of the shareholders and they accordingly recommend that shareholders accept the price offered.
- A *hostile acquisition* (sometimes called a hostile takeover in the press) is an attempt to acquire a controlling shareholding in a public limited company which is not recommended by the target company's directors. In this case, acceptance of the offer price by shareholders represents a difference of opinion between directors and shareholders, and questions are often raised as to the extent to which directors are or are not acting in the shareholders' best interests.

Whichever of these routes is taken, the result is a larger and more financially powerful company. The word *integration* is the collective term used to describe these growth mechanisms.

Motivations for transnational M&As

Transnational M&As are motivated by a range of business considerations and will depend on the strategic intent and transnational strategy of the business. The more common motivations include:

- market entry – M&As are often used as a method for entering and servicing a new national market;
- market share – M&As can increase market share by combining the market shares of the two businesses (in addition the selling power of the two businesses is likely to be increased resulting in further increases in market share, especially in the case of horizontal integrations);
- product and market portfolio – M&As can be used to increase an organization's product portfolio, thus rendering the business more robust in the event of trauma in one or more of its product or market sectors;
- reduction of competition – competition can be reduced if the integration target is a competitor;
- leveraging of core competences – control can be gained of key inputs and brand names can be leveraged;
- access to supply or distribution channels – backward and forward integration can improve access to resources and customers, respectively;
- product development – new products can often be acquired more rapidly than could be achieved by the internal R&D function;
- technology acquisition – new technology can be acquired, such as that employed in production or IT applications;
- economies of scale and scope – these can be achieved, especially if the integration involves an increase in capacity;
- resource utilization – resources can be successfully and fruitfully deployed, such as underused cash deposits;
- reputation enhancement – reputation can be enhanced if the acquisition or merger is with a business of some repute in a key market or with a key stakeholder group.

Each separate integration will have its own specific objectives at the strategic level. For many transnationals the major motivations are access to new markets or to resources, competences and skills.

Synergy is intended to facilitate an enhancement in the value-adding capability of the business. Kay (1993) made the point that, 'Value is added, and only added, [in an integration] if distinctive capabilities or strategic assets are exploited more effectively. A merger adds no value if all that is acquired is a distinctive capability which is already fully exploited, as the price paid will reflect the competitive advantage held.' Accordingly, integrations that do not enable the 'new' organization to produce higher profits or consolidate a stronger market position are usually deemed to have been relatively unsuccessful.

Hoechst and Rhône-Poulenc merge to form Aventis, a new global leader in life sciences

On 1 December 1998 the CEOs of France's Rhône-Poulenc and Germany's Hoechst Atkiengesellschaft announced a merger that would create one of the largest life science companies in the world. On 15 December 1999 the merger actually came about. It was claimed that the new company, Aventis, would create a worldwide leader in pharmaceuticals and agricultural businesses with combined annual sales of US$20 billion. In addition, it was hoped that the merger would provide a platform for sustainable growth through combining R&D resources, the creation of a robust product pipeline and the employment of powerful emerging technologies and synergies in global marketing. By the time of the merger in 1999, the combined management team was reported to have already identified to drive new strategy and required culture change.

The merger appealed to the boards of both companies because they believed it would create an innovation-driven leader in life sciences. Neither Hoechst nor Rhône-Poulenc could have achieved such a position alone in a similar time frame. The combination of Hoechst and Rhône-Poulenc was expected to provide a foundation for increased value for the shareholders of both companies, particularly because of the hoped-for improvements in profitability that would accrue by taking advantage of a broader product portfolio and stronger product pipeline, enlarged marketing and salesforce, and the realization of operational efficiencies.

Hoechst and Rhône-Poulenc, both of which had prominent positions in the pharmaceutical and crop science industries, believed that in the turbulent global business environment the only life science companies that would succeed in maintaining global leadership positions were those that:

❑ had a high innovation potential and broad access to new technologies;

❑ were able to rapidly develop and launch new products worldwide; and

❑ had a strong global marketing and distribution network for marketing products worldwide.

In the late 1990s the life science industry was experiencing two significant trends, both of which would affect the future composition of the industry. First, new companies with innovative products and smaller companies with positions in niche markets were emerging at a rapid pace. Second, rising R&D, sales and marketing costs and faster product obsolescence made it increasingly difficult for existing companies to maintain a leading position in life sciences solely on the basis of their own resources. This led to an intense consolidation within the pharmaceutical and crop science industry.

1994 – American Home Products (USA) acquired American Cyanamid (USA);

1995 – Glaxo (UK) acquired Wellcome (UK) to form Glaxo Wellcome;

1995 – Upjohn (USA) merged with Pharmacia (Sweden) to form Pharmacia & Upjohn;

1996 – Sandoz (Switzerland) merged with Ciba-Geigy (Switzerland) to form Novartis;

1997 – Roche (Switzerland) acquired Boehringer Mannheim (Germany);

1999 – Zeneca (UK) merged with Astra (Sweden) to form Astra-Zeneca;

1999 – Sanofi (France) merged with Synthélabo (France) to form Sanofi-Synthélabo.

Such a restructuring of the industry placed enormous pressures on smaller companies to merge and thereby gain the scale economies in R&D and marketing enjoyed by the other players in the industry. This was an important motive in driving the merger between Hoechst and Rhône-Poulenc.

Problems with integration

A number of academic studies have been undertaken with regard to the successes and failures of external growth, and the balance of evidence is that more fail than succeed (e.g., Porter, 1985; Ravenscraft & Scherer, 1987; Kay 1993). Many acquisitions ended in subsequent disposal because performance of the post-integration organization was not as hoped. Of those integrations that did survive, Kay (1993) found that when profitability before and after the integration were compared, a 'nil to negative effect' was achieved.

What causes failure?

We suggest that there are six reasons why some integrations fail to add value and become subject to subsequent 'divorce':

1. *lack of research* into the internal and external environmental features of the target company (and hence incomplete knowledge);
2. *cultural incompatibility* between the acquirer and the target – especially important when the two parties are in different countries;
3. *lack of communication* within and between the two parties;
4. *loss of key personnel* in the target company after the integration;
5. *paying too much for the acquired company* and hence overexposing the acquiring company to financial risk;
6. *assuming that growth in a target company's market will continue indefinitely* – market trends can fall as well as rise.

A seventh reason for failure, albeit one that is outside the control of the organization, is legislative or regulatory frameworks that prevent the integration from happening or from fully performing as it might. Most developed economies have frameworks in place to regulate M&A activity. Article 86 of the Treaty of Rome 1957 (the primary legislation of the EU) is one such instrument. It enables the EC to review proposed M&As resulting in a combined national market share of 25% or when the combined turnover in EU markets exceeds a certain financial figure (which at 1998 was ECU 250 million). The UK has similar legislation (the Fair Trading Act, 1973).

Successful M&As

The high failure rate of M&As (Sirower, 1997) obviously indicates that managers of transnationals must evaluate potential mergers and acquisitions carefully before entering into them. Once the decision to merge or acquire has been taken, it is then necessary to plan the integration process carefully.

The chances of successful integration are increased when seven 'success factors' are observed:

1. find a suitable target partner;
2. fully evaluate the target's competitive position;
3. fully evaluate the target's management and culture for compatibility with the initiator;
4. investigate the compatibility of the two companies' structures;
5. ensure that key resources (including key human resources) can be locked in after the integration;
6. ensure the price paid for the target's stock is realistic;
7. plan the post-merger process carefully.

Sources: based on Payne (1987), Shelton (1988) and Sirower (1997)

Each of these success factors is discussed below.

Finding a suitable target

First, success depends on the identification of a suitable 'target' candidate with whom to merge or acquire. This is often problematic as the initiating organization – with specific strategic intentions in mind – may have to wait for many years or consider international M&A in order to find such a partner. In practice, some compromise is necessary.

Evaluation of the target's competitive position

Second, a preparation for an approach should involve a detailed evaluation of the target company's competitive position. This would typically comprise a survey of its profitability, its market share, its product portfolio, its competitiveness in resource markets, etc. Key success factors are identified and the core competences of key competitors are addressed.

Cultural compatibility

Third, consideration should be given to the compatibility of the two companies' management styles and cultures – a process that may require significant preintegration discussions. As integrations often involve the merging of the two boards of directors, it is usually important that the directors from the two companies are able to work together. In addition, the cultures, if not identical in character, should be able to be brought together successfully.

Structures

Fourth, there should be the possibility of a successful marriage between the two corporate structures. Integrations work best where the two structures in question are comparably decentralized and have similar 'height' and 'width'.

Locking in resources

Fifth, any key resources that the target company has must be guaranteed to still be available post-integration. Key human resources who helped to build the target's core competences must be locked in so that their use can be continued after the integration. In many organizations these key resources will be human, but in others they may also be key locations, processes, patents, brands or sources of finance.

Valuing the stock price

Sixth, the initiating company will need to be certain that its valuation of the target company is reasonable in so far as it will enable a satisfactory return to be made on the investment. This is one of the most difficult matters to sort out in advance of an integration. While the balance sheet value of a company can be easily ascertained, attention will need to be given to the value of the target's *goodwill* – a figure over and above the balance sheet value to take account of its future prospects and a valuation of its intellectual resources (brands, patents, licences, etc.). For large acquisitions, the value of goodwill is often the matter of intense debate between the parties. Accordingly, the importance of detailed information gathering before the integration cannot be overemphasized. The acquisition of Wellcome plc by Glaxo (Holdings) in the mid-1990s was one in which the majority of the price paid was goodwill. Although Wellcome's balance sheet value was ca £2.5 billion, Glaxo paid around £9 billion for the target company. While some of this £6.5 billion difference can be accounted for by asset revaluation, the majority was goodwill, reflecting Wellcome's capabilities in promising pharmaceutical areas such as virology and its product range which contained some of the most important drugs in the world.

Planning the integration

Finally, the post-merger process must be carefully planned. Olie's (1990) study identified poor integration of merged businesses as the major cause of poor performance. Obstacles to successful integration were found to include resistance to change, a focus on personal security rather than organizational goals, culture shock and resentment of management. Olie concluded that even when a merger was initially flawed, it could then be made successful by effective management of the post-merger process.

DaimlerChrysler

With the breakdown of international trade barriers, transnational mergers are becoming commonplace, and, yet, they remain among the most poorly understood phenomena in the business world. On the outside, the newly merged colossi pose as robust giants with the market power to strike fear into the hearts of the competitors they dwarf. On the inside, however, they are often turbulent with strong cultural identities fighting for supremacy. Car manufacturers, furthermore, are viewed in a highly symbolic way as instruments of national prestige. The case of the DaimlerChrysler merger (which resulted in the formation of a company with a turnover of over $150 billion per annum) represented not only the winners and losers in the 1939–45 war but also the winners and losers in post-war motor production. The merger also served to demonstrate some of the cultural complexities of transnational mergers. The German company Daimler, represented by famous and successful brands such as Mercedes, had exhibited consistent international growth, whereas the American company Chrysler was very much the third-ranked US manufacturer despite a relatively successful performance during the 1990s. Newspaper articles pointed to the cultural differences of the two companies often resorting to stereotypical images of Germans and Americans and questioning their ability to work harmoniously.

In agreeing to the merger that took place in 1999, Chrysler's CEO Robert Eaton named a 'non-negotiable' condition – the company must be a 'merger of equals'. DaimlerChrysler would have two chief executives for three years and its board would consist of executives from both companies. From the beginning, industry experts viewed this plan with scepticism. Daimler was contributing 57% of the stock market value to the merger and Chrysler 43%, and so analysts' expectations were that Daimler would control the new entity. This prediction turned out to be true – Daimler called the shots in terms of the new company's logo, the company's headquarters would be in Stuttgart and DaimlerChrysler would be a German 'AG' and not an American 'Inc.'. One after another, all the members of the Chrysler team that led Chrysler in the

1990s left. To Americans, it seemed obvious that Daimler's Germans – contrary to their promises – had taken over Chrysler despite adopting English as the company's primary language.

By 2002 it had become clear that the Chrysler part of the company had grown bloated and inefficient. The company's production costs in the former Chrysler plants were too high and too few new products were introduced. Financial commentators again alluded to the cultural tensions. Was this a case of the Americans being duped into selling one of their prize companies to a ruthless German predator, or on the contrary had the Germans been tricked into paying too much in order to acquire an ailing American company?

The truth seems to have been that there was indeed a cultural problem but that it was rather different to the story that had often been portrayed by the press. It was precisely because the Daimler executives feared being seen in the USA as arrogant, 'know-it-all' Germans that they failed to intervene in the Chrysler operation in time. For two years the German executives failed to become fully involved with the Chrylser operations in the belief that the Americans must know what they were doing, despite the high-level departures from the company. Because they were so eager to do the right thing they were hesitant to intervene. Their belated and hurried intervention, when it did come, appeared authoritarian and to some sections of the media, 'typically German'. Before a successful turnaround was achieved by decisive management actions initiated in the German headquarters in Stuttgart, the company's managers had underestimated the situation not only economically but also culturally.

Collaborative ventures and strategic alliances

What are collaborative ventures and strategic alliances?

The terms *collaborative venture* and *strategic alliance* are used to describe a family of arrangements between two or more organizations to collaborate across organizational boundaries with the express purpose of gaining mutual competitive advantage. Conventional models of business behaviour have tended to emphasize the role of the individual business in gaining competitive advantage. Some core competence theorists (Heene and Sanchez, 1997) identified collaboration between businesses as an important potential source of competitive advantage.

According to Contractor and Lorange (1988a), it is important to view a transnational business as a member of various open and shifting coalitions, each with a specific strategic purpose, rather than as a closed internalized system that straddles national boundaries. Competitive advantage can result from the effective management of such international and global coalitions.

As we saw in Chapter 6 resource-based strategy theory argues that superior performance is based on the development and deployment of core competences and distinctive capabilities. Quinn et al. (1990) suggested that it is best for a company to concentrate on activities that are directly related to its core competences and that other non-core activities can be outsourced to other businesses for whom those activities are core. According to Quinn et al. (1990), 'outside vendors can supply many important corporate functions at greatly enhanced value and lower cost. Thus many of those functions should be outsourced.' Consequently, outsourcing is often associated with collaborative behaviour.

Porter (1986, 1991) stressed the importance of *configuration* of business activities and their *co-ordination* to achieving global competitive advantage. Collaboration has made it possible for businesses to adopt new configurations that are difficult for competitors to emulate and that can also sometimes enhance organizational responsiveness.

In broad terms, then, the acquisition of competitive advantage through collaborative ventures and strategic alliances will require:

- identification of the core competences of the organization;
- identification and focus on activities that are critical to the core competence of the organization and outsourcing those that are not to collaborating businesses;
- achieving the internal and external linkages in the value/supply chain which are necessary for effective co-ordination of activities and which permit responsiveness.

The remainder of the chapter explains the different categories of alliance that exist, the motivations behind them and how such alliances can be best managed.

Motivations for forming strategic alliances

It is possible to identify several rationales for collaboration (Contractor and Lorange, 1988a):

- the sharing of different but linked core competences;
- international expansion and market entry;
- vertical quasi-integration – access to resources, skills, materials, technology, labour, capital, distribution channels, buyers, regulatory permits;
- sharing of risks;
- the acquisition of economies of scale and scope;
- access to complementary technologies and technology development;
- the blocking or reduction of competition;
- overcoming government-mandated investment or trade barriers.

The second of Contractor and Lorange's motivations is the most important in the context of this book. As organizations seek out new markets for their products, many recognize skill or knowledge deficiencies where an in-depth knowledge of a foreign market is required. The need to develop local knowledge is increased if overseas production (with an overseas alliance partner) is being considered to meet market demands. While local knowledge can be hired (say, through a local importing agent), it is often quicker and more reliable to seek assistance from an already established producing organization of the host country. It should also be noted that a legal requirement of many countries is that foreign organizations must have host partners before they can trade, thus making a collaborative agreement a prerequisite for market entry.

Types of strategic alliance and collaborative venture

Directions of alliances

Like M&As collaborative ventures can be categorized as vertical backward (or upstream), vertical forward (or downstream), horizontal or diversified. Vertical backward or upstream alliances are between a business and its suppliers. Vertical forward or downstream alliances are between a company and its distributors or customers. Horizontal alliances are between a business and other companies at the same stage of the value system, while diversified alliances are between companies in industries which are not closely related to each other. Collaborative ventures are always entered into willingly and all participating parties expect the alliance to work toward their own specific strategic purposes. They vary from highly formal, long-term agreements linking two or more organizations, to short-term consortia of organizations engaged together in a relatively short-term project.

The legal status of an organization need not be a barrier to its participation in an alliance. While many are between two business organizations, many countries have witnessed an increase in alliances between governmental bodies and privately owned companies. In the UK, for example, the Private Finance Initiative (PFI) has been responsible for collaboration in the building of roads, hospitals and other public sector investments. The channel tunnel between Britain and France was constructed by a number of companies working together in an alliance referred to as a *consortium*. In some circumstances, collaboration between companies can result in the creation of a new and jointly owned enterprise. Cellnet, for example, was founded as a jointly owned mobile telephone business by two British companies, BT and Securicor.

Strategic alliances can therefore assume a number of different forms depending on the participants' structures, the mechanism of decision making, the nature of the capital commitment, the apportionment of profit and the legal status of the venture. Some exist for a particular project only and are short-term in timescale, while others are more permanent. The choice of arrangement will depend on the specific objectives that the participants have at the time.

Horizontal networks and alliances
Alliances between businesses at the same stage of the value system are generally intended to strengthen the participating companies against outside competition. Partners in such alliances can benefit from:

- shared skills and competences;
- shared technologies;
- access to some new market segments;
- reduced risks;
- reduced costs, particularly development costs;
- increased entry barriers and reduced danger from new entrants;
- forces that create synergy;

- advantages in vertical relationships (e.g., a voluntary retail group can obtain discounts from suppliers for bulk buying).

The company must always retain control of its core strategic assets and activities but can outsource other activities to partners. From a portfolio perspective, this form of alliance gains synergy through leveraging shared financial resources.

Diversification alliances

Alliances between businesses in unrelated areas are often used by one or more of the businesses to take them into a new competitive arena. This form of alliance is viewed as important from a portfolio perspective in so far as the key advantage of diversification is to broaden product and market portfolio in order to reduce the risk of trauma in any one sector.

Vertical networks and alliances

These can be upstream in the supply chain toward suppliers or downstream toward distributors and customers (see Figure 14.1). These alliances produce the following potential benefits:

- the ability for each collaborating business to concentrate on its own core competence, while at the same time benefiting for the core competences of the other businesses in the alliance, creating synergy;
- improved responsiveness if just-in-time management techniques are employed;
- creation of new barriers to entry;
- production of logistical economies of scale;
- generation of superior information on activities at all stages of the supply chain;
- tying in of suppliers, distributors and customers to the business.

The extent and timescale of collaboration

There are several other methods that can be used to distinguish alliances.

The extent of co-operation – focused and complex alliances

It is possible to distinguish alliances by where they are positioned in respect to the number of areas in which the parties co-operate with each other. Some alliances are set up between businesses in order to collaborate in only one area of activity, such as joint purchasing, shared research or shared distribution. A continuum exists between the two extremes of fully focused (collaboration in one activity only) and complex (collaboration in all activities – the parties act in concert to the point where they appear to be one single organization). As with all continua, the majority of real life cases fall somewhere between the two extremes.

Timescales of the collaboration

The second way in that we can subdivide strategic alliances is by asking how long they are intended to last. Some are set up for a specific project only, and we tend to refer to these as 'joint ventures' – time-limited arrangements for the joint accomplishment of a shared aim or project. Others can last for many years and are intended to enable both (or all) parties to intensify the strength of their strategic position on an ongoing basis. Longer term alliances tend to be more common when the partners are from different countries, as the interpenetration of markets can take many years to achieve and consolidate.

Consortiums

One particular type of (usually) short to medium-term alliance is the consortium. Consortiums are often created for time-limited projects, such as civil engineering or construction developments. The channel tunnel was constructed by a number of construction companies in a consortium that was called Trans Manche Link (TML). TML was dissolved on completion of the project. Camelot, the first UK National Lottery operator was another example of a consortium.

Choosing the most appropriate type of alliance

The form of alliance chosen by the parties will depend on several factors. The complexity of the alliance will depend on the objectives that the two parties are pursuing. Alliance partners tend to seek co-operation on the minimum number of areas that are needed in order to avoid overexposure to the risk of one of the parties leaving abruptly or 'finding out too much'. The selection of partners for a consortium will depend on matching the resource and skill requirement of the project with those organizations that are willing to contribute to the effort. Organizations with previous experience of projects of the type proposed will obviously be among the most in demand as consortium participants.

Collaborative strategy in the international airline industry

The airline sector has a long history of working in partnerships, exemplified by the International Air Transport Association's (IATA) annual conference bilateral agreements (which split markets equally between pairs of national airlines). Under the auspices of IATA, on a global scale, a tradition of co-operation between airlines has been built up, and on individual routes co-operation has commonly included revenue-pooling agreements between the carriers operating a route. Airlines have, in recent years, rushed to form alliances in the fear of being left behind, and the stage has now been reached where the international airline sector is coalescing into a small number of large alliance groupings, such as the *Star Alliance* which includes Lufthansa, United Airlines and Scandinavian Airlines System (SAS); the *Oneworld Alliance* which includes British Airways, American Airlines and Qantas; and the long-standing alliance between KLM (of Holland) and North-west Airlines. It is not only the number of airline alliance agreements being made that is significant but also the deepening relations between partners in these alliances.

The development of airline strategic alliances is one of the most fundamental developments in the airline industry over recent years. After the initial rush to form alliances, many companies later changed their partners as they became more sophisticated at identifying the potential 'strategic fit' between partners. To some degree, alliance formation can be viewed as an inevitable result of the regulatory framework within which the international airline industry operates. Regulatory and legal restrictions often prevent the full ownership of airlines by foreign companies, and, in consequence, alliances have often been perceived as the only viable market entry mechanism, at least in the short to medium term.

Indeed, some observers have viewed strategic alliances as inherently unstable and as transitory forms of organization – a 'second-best' solution that is disturbingly likely to break up under commercial pressure. Porter (1990), for instance, suggested that alliances rarely result in a sustainable competitive advantage being established, whereas Hamel (1991) viewed them as a race to learn, in which the winner will eventually establish dominance in the partnership thereby leading to instability. Certainly, the airline industry has been subject to a number of examples of failed alliances and alliances that have been discussed, but never actioned.

However, the commercial logic for airlines to form alliances, at least in the short to medium term, seems to have been established as a range of drivers exert pressure on companies:

❑ The existence of 'economies of scope,' related to the size and nature of operations, which help to explain the growing market concentration and the move toward alliances. Economies of scope occur when the cost of producing two (or more) products jointly is less than the cost of producing each one alone. Such economies can be achieved if alliance partners link up their existing networks, so that they can provide connecting services for new markets, and if marketing costs can be shared between alliance partners who may have strong, entrenched positions in certain markets. In forming alliances, airlines are seeking to maximize their 'global reach', in the belief that those that offer a global service (with a competitively credible presence in each of the major air travel markets) will be in the strongest competitive position.

❑ Specific resource, skill or competence inadequacy or imbalance can be addressed by collaborating with partners who have a different set of such attributes and can therefore compensate for internal deficiencies. The regulatory framework of 'bilateral agreements' between governments (concerning landing rights) and congestion at certain airports means that airlines possessing licenses to operate on a route and slots at congested airports have important and marketable assets that are attractive to alliance partners. Alliances can thus offer relatively easy access to a route through allowing access to a partner's assets which may have been established over prolonged periods and which may have been protected by government intervention.

❑ Strategic alliances are seen as an attractive mechanism for hedging risk because neither partner bears the full risk and cost of the alliance activity. The need to spread the costs and risks of innovation has increased as capital requirements for development projects have risen. Developing new or existing routes, for instance, becomes far less risky if the partners operating the routes have firmly entrenched marketing strengths in the two markets at either end of the routes.

❑ Strategic alliances may be used as a defensive ploy to shape the competitive environment by reducing competition, since an

> obvious benefit of strategic alliances is converting a competitor into a partner. Furthermore, relatively weak airlines may view alliances as the only viable way in which to compete with larger more sophisticated rivals.
>
> ❑ Consumers receive several benefits from those alliances that are successful in producing integrated products. Consumers are provided with an enhanced choice of destinations through the marketing of alliance partners' route networks. Schedule co-ordination between partners often produces shorter transfer times between connections, and co-ordination of flight timings can avoid bunching of flight schedules. Additionally, consumers benefit from: one-stop check-in for passengers (although they are taking an onward connecting flight provided by the partner airline); the pooling of frequent flyer programmes; shared airport lounge facilities; ground-handling arrangements and the improvement in technical standards brought about through the sharing of expertise.

Successful alliances

The success of an alliance is attributed to a number of factors, some of which are similar to the factors present in a successful integration (M&As). The failure of an alliance often results from problems, like incompatibility of objectives, the ending of the basis for the collaboration as a result of competitive, environmental or organizational change, cultural differences and problems of co-ordination.

Faulkner (1995) suggested that the following factors are critical to the success of collaborative ventures:

- complementary skills and capabilities of the partners;
- the degree of overlap between the parties' markets be kept to a minimum;
- a high level of autonomy, with strong leadership and commitment from the parent organizations (if appropriate);
- the need to build up trust and not to depend solely on the contractual framework of the relationship;
- recognizing that the two partners may have different cultures.

Researchers in this area have noted that alliances seem to work best when the partners are from related industries (or the same industry) or when the objective of the alliance is the development of a new geographical region. Success is further enhanced when the parties are of a similar size and are equally committed (in resource terms) to the alliance. Strict adherence to the initial objectives of the alliance can often limit its success, as modification of the original purpose may become necessary if the business environment changes. There is thus a need to continually reappraise the parameters of the agreement. Reve (1990) argued that alliances are more likely to succeed when a *behavioural approach* is adopted which emphasizes the value of the relationship to the parties and which places a high value on trust and personal contacts. An *economic approach*, emphasizing only a profit motive, is likely to create a much less stable alliance.

Brouthers et al. (1993) advanced a more succinct version of Faulkner's success factors in the 'three Cs' of successful alliances. The two parties should have:

- complimentary skills;
- compatible goals;
- co-operative cultures.

The termination of an alliance should of course not always lead us to conclude that it has been a failure. For fixed-term alliances, such as joint ventures for the purposes of a research or marketing project, the conclusion date may have been set at the start of the alliance. Similarly, consortium partners, such as those who form an alliance for a large civil engineering project, will dissolve the alliance on successful completion of the project.

The success of the venture should be judged in terms of the extent to which it improves the performance of the partner businesses over its lifetime. Similarly, not all partners in an alliance will benefit from it equally. Nevertheless, it can be viewed as successful if they realize benefits from the alliance in terms of improved performance.

The strategic management of networks and alliances

The concept of the 'focal' business

Many collaborative networks are centred on what can be regarded as a *focal business*. Toyota, for example, is at the heart of a network of suppliers and distributors and can be regarded as the focal business in its arrangements. It is the strategy of the focal business which will have the greatest influence in determining the overall strategy of the network and the other businesses which will comprise it.

According to Reve (1990), the focal business will have three major elements to its strategy. The first element is the strategic core which consists of core skills that are high in specificity and are managed internally. Such activities are central to the core competences of the organization and are managed via internal contracts and organizational incentives. The second element of strategy consists of the strategic alliances in which the focal business is involved. These are used to acquire complementary skills of medium asset specificity but which are not viewed as central to core competencies. Such activities are managed by external contracts governed through alliances.

Finally, all assets of low specificity are obtained through the appropriate markets. Strategic management within a network or alliance is therefore concerned with:

- determining which activities and assets are core and should therefore be carried out by the focal business;
- determining which activities are of medium specificity and should be obtained via alliances and outsourcing;
- determining which activities are of low specificity and should be obtained through the market;
- co-ordination and integration of core and alliance activities;
- management and operation of the alliances.

Information and communications technology has played an important role in improving the management of collaborative networks (see Chapter 10) by improving co-ordination and responsiveness and by facilitating learning across organizational boundaries. As network relationships change over time, the survival of a strategic alliance will depend on its ability to co-ordinate activities and adapt relationships.

Discussion and review questions

1. Define and distinguish between a merger, an agreed acquisition and a hostile acquisition.

2. What is the difference between the horizontal and vertical directions for integrations and alliances?
3. What is a consortium?
4. Explain the strategic reasoning behind a horizontal integration and a forward vertical arrangement.
5. What preintegration practices, if adopted, might reduce the failure of the integration?
6. Why is the identification of the focal business important in understanding alliances?

References and further reading

Alexander, M. (1995) 'Managing the boundaries of the organisation'. *Long Range Planning*, **30**(5).

Bengtsson, A.M. (1992) *Managing Mergers and Acquisitions: A European Perspective*. Aldershot, UK: Gower Press.

Bishop, M. and Kay, J. (1993) *European Mergers and Merger Policy*. Oxford, UK: Oxford University Press.

Bleek, J. and Ernst, D. (1993) *Collaborating to Compete*. New York: John Wiley & Sons.

Bowerson, D.J. (1990) 'The strategic benefits of logistics alliances'. *Harvard Business Review*, **90**(4), 36–47.

Brooke, M.Z. (1986) *International Management: A Review of Strategies and Operations*. London: Hutchinson.

Brouthers, K.D., Brouthers, L.E. and Wilkinson, T.J. (1993) 'Strategic alliances: Choose your partners'. *Long Range Planning*, **28**(3), 18–25.

Buckley, A. (1975) 'Growth by acquisition'. *Long Range Planning*, August.

Buckley, P.J. and Casson, M. (1988) 'A theory of co-operation in international business'. In: F.J. Contractor and P. Lorange (eds), *Competitive Strategies in International Business*. Lexington, MD: Lexington Books.

Buckley, P.J., Pass, C.L. and Prescott, K. (1990) 'Foreign market servicing by multinationals – An integrated treatment'. *International Marketing Review*, **7**(4), 25–40.

Buckley, P.J., Pass, C.L. and Prescott, K. (1992) 'Foreign market servicing strategies of UK retail financial service firms in continental Europe'. In: S. Young and J. Hamill (eds), *Europe and the Multinationals: Issues and Responses for the 1990s* (Chapter 7). Aldershot, UK: Edward Elgar.

Chai, T. and McGuire, D.J. (1996) 'Collaborative ventures and value of learning: Integrating the transaction cost and strategic option perspectives on the choice of market entry modes'. *Journal of International Business Studies*, **27**(2).

Contractor, F. and Lorange, P. (eds) (1988a) 'Why should firms co-operate?'. *Co-operative Strategies in International Business*. Lexington, MD: Lexington Books.

Contractor, F.J. and Lorange, P. (1988b) 'Competition vs. cooperation: A benefit/cost framework for choosing between fully-owned investments and cooperative relationships'. *Management International Review*, **28**(Special issue), 88.

Davidson, K.M. (1990) 'Mergers and acquisitions: Anatomy of the fall'. *Journal of Business Strategy*, **11**(5), 48–51.

Davidson, K.M. (1991) 'Mergers and acquisitions: Innovation and corporate mergers'. *Journal of Business Strategy*, **12**(1), 42–45.

De Noble, A.F., Gustafson, L.T. and Hergert, M. (1988) 'Planning for post-merger integration – Eight lessons for merger success'. *Long Range Planning*, **21**(110), 82–86.

Devlin, G. and Bleackley, M. (1988) 'Strategic alliances – Guidelines for success'. *Long Range Planning*, **21**(5), 18–23.

De Wit, B. and Meyer, R. (1998) *Strategy – Process, Content, Context, An International Perspective.* Florence, KY: International Thomson Business Press.

Doz, Y.L., Hamel, G. and Prahalad, C.K. (1986) 'Strategic partnerships: Success or surrender? The challenge of competitive collaboration'. Paper presented at *Joint Academy of International Business/European International Business Association Conference, London, November.*

Faulkner, D. (1995) *Strategic Alliances: Cooperating to Compete.* New York: McGraw-Hill.

Firth, M. (1991) 'Corporate takeovers, stockholder returns and executive rewards'. *Managerial and Decision Economics*, **12**.

Foot, R., Robinson, T.M. and Clarke-Hill, C.M. (1993) 'The entry of UK firms into the former East German market through acquisitions in the Treuhand: A case approach'. *European Business and Economic Development*, **2**(3), November.

Franck, G. (1990) 'Mergers and acquisitions: Competitive advantage and cultural fit'. *European Management Journal*, **8**(1), March.

Franks, J. and Harris, R. (1989) 'Shareholders wealth effects of corporate takeover: The UK experience 1955–85'. *Journal of Financial Economics*, **23**.

Gall, E.A. (1991) 'Strategies for merger success'. *Journal of Business Strategy*, **12**(2), 26–30.

Geroski, P.A. and Vlassopoulos, A. (1990) 'Recent patterns of European merger activity'. *Business Strategy Review*, Summer.

Ghoshal, S. and Bartlett, C.A. (1990) 'The multinational corporation as an interorganisational network'. *Academy of Management Review*, **15**, 603–625.

Glaister, K. (1993) 'UK joint venture formation in Western Europe'. *European Business and Economic Development*, **2**(3), November.

Glaister, K.W. and Buckley, P. (1994) 'UK international joint ventures: An analysis of patterns of activity and distribution'. *British Journal of Management*, **5**.

Gogler, P. (1992) 'Building transnational alliances to create competitive advantage'. *Long Range Planning*, **25**(1), 90–99.

Gulati, R. (1998) 'Alliances and networks'. *Strategic Management Journal*, **19**, 293–317.

Hamel, G. (1991) 'Competition for competence and inter-partner learning within international strategic alliances'. *Strategic Management Journal*, **12**(Special summer issue), 83–104.

Hamel, G., Doz, Y.L. and Prahalad, C.K. (1989) 'Collaborate with your competitors – and win'. *Harvard Business Review*, January/February, 133–139.

Hamill, J. (1988) 'British acquisitions in the US'. *National Westminster Bank Quarterly Review*, August.

Hamill, J. (1988) 'US acquisitions and the internationalisation of British industry'. *Acquisitions Monthly*, November.

Hamill, J. (1991) 'Strategic restructuring through international acquisitions and divestments'. *Journal of General Management*, **17**(1), Autumn.

Hamill, J. (1991) 'Changing patterns of international business: Crossborder mergers, acquisitions and alliances'. *Proceedings of the UK Region, Academy of International Business Conference, London, April.*

Hamill, J. (1992) 'Crossborder mergers, acquisitions and strategic alliances in Europe'. In: S. Young and J. Hamill (eds), *Europe and the Multinationals: Issues and Responses for the 1990s* (Chapter 6). Aldershot, UK: Edward Elgar.

Hamill, J. and Crosbie, J. (1989) 'Acquiring in the US food and drink industry'. *Acquisitions Monthly*, May.

Hamill, J. and El-Hajjar, S. (1990) 'Defending competitiveness'. *Acquisitions Monthly*, April, 36–39.

Haspeslagh, P. and Jemison, D. (1991) *Managing Acquisitions: Creating Value through Corporate Renewal*. New York: Free Press.

Heene, A. and Sanchez, R. (eds) (1997) *Competence-based Strategic Management*. New York: John Wiley & Sons.

Hennart, J.F., Roehl, T. and Zietlow, D.S. (1999) 'Trojan horse or workhorse? The evolution of U.S.–Japanese joint ventures in the United States'. *Strategic Management Journal*, **20**, 15–29.

Jain, S.C. (1987) 'Perspectives on international strategic alliances'. *Advances in International Marketing* (pp. 103–120). Greenwich, CT: JAI Press.

Jarillo, J.C. (1988) 'On strategic networks'. *Strategic Management Journal*, June/July.

Jarillo, J.C. and Stevenson, H.H. (1991) 'Cooperative strategies – The payoffs and pitfalls'. *Long Range Planning*, **24**(1), 64–70.

Jemison, D.B. and Sitkin, S.M. (1986) 'Corporate acquisitions: A process perspective'. *Academy of Management Review*, **11**(1).

Jemison, D.B. and Sitkin, S.M. (1986) 'Acquisitions: The process can be a problem'. *Harvard Business Review*, March.

Johanson, J. and Mattson, L.G. (1992) 'Network positions and strategic action'. In: B. Axelsson and G. Easton (eds), *Industrial Networks: A New View of Reality*. London: Routledge.

Kay, J. (1993) *Foundations of Corporate Success*. Oxford, UK: Oxford University Press.

Khanna, T., Gulati, R. and Nitin, N. (1998) 'The dynamics of learning alliances: Competition, cooperation, and relative scope'. *Strategic Management Journal*, **19**, 191–209.

Kitching, J. (1974) 'Why acquisitions are abortive'. *Management Today*, November.

Lorange, P. (1988) *Cooperative Strategies: Planning and Control Considerations* (WP-S12). Centre for International Management Studies.

Lorange, P. and Roos, J. (1991) 'Why some strategic alliances succeed and others fail'. *Journal of Business Strategy*, **12**(1), 25–31.

Lorange, P. and Roos, J. (1992) *Strategic Alliances: Formation, Implementation and Evolution*. Oxford, UK: Basil Blackwell.

Lorenzoni, G. and Baden-Fuller, C. (1995) 'Creating a strategic center to manage a web of partners'. *California Management Review*, **37**(3).

Love, J.H. and Scouller, J. (1990) 'Growth by acquisition: The lessons of experience'. *Journal of General Management*, **15**(3), Spring.

Luostarinen, R. (1979) *The Internationalisation of the Firm*. Helsinki: Acta Academica Oeconomicae Helsingiensis.

Lyons, M.P. (1991) 'Joint ventures as strategic choice – A literature review'. *Long Range Planning*, **24**(4), 130–144.

Malekzadeh, A.R. and Nahavindi, A. (1990) 'Making mergers work by managing cultures'. *Journal of Business Strategy*, **11**(3), 55–58.

Medcof, J.W. (1997) 'Why too many alliances end in divorce'. *Long Range Planning*, **30**(5).

Meeks, G. (1977) *Disappointing Marriage: A Study of the Gains from Mergers*. Cambridge, UK: Cambridge University Press.

Morgan, N.A. (1988) 'Successful growth by acquisition'. *Journal of General Management*, **14**(2), winter.

Morris, D. and Hergert, M. (1987) 'Trends in international collaborative agreements'. *Columbia Journal of World Business*, Summer.

Ohmae, K. (1989) 'The global logic of strategic alliances'. *Harvard Business Review*, March/April.

Olie, R. (1990) 'Culture and integration problems in international mergers and acquisitions'. *European Management Journal*, **8**(2), June.

Oman, C. (1984) *New Forms of International Investment in Developing Countries*. Paris: Organization for Economic Co-operation and Development.

Payne, A.F. (1987) 'Approaching acquisitions strategically'. *Journal of General Management*, **13**(2), Winter.

Pearson, M. (1985) *Managing Acquisitions*. London: British Institute of Management.

Perlmutter, H.V. and Heenan, D.H. (1986) 'Cooperate to compete globally'. *Harvard Business Review*, March/April.

Porter, M.E. (1980) *Competitive Strategy*. New York: Free Press.

Porter, M.E. (1985) *Competitive Advantage*. New York: Free Press.

Porter, M.E. (ed.) (1986) *Competition in Global Industries*. Boston: Harvard Business School Press.

Porter, M.E. (1990) *The Competitive Advantage of Nations*. London: Macmillan.

Porter, M.E. and Fuller, M.B. (1987) 'Coalitions and global strategy'. In: M.E. Porter (ed.), *Competition in Global Industries*. Boston: Harvard Business School Press.

Preece, S. (1995) 'Incorporating international strategic alliances into overall firm strategy: A typology of six managerial objectives'. *The International Executive*, **37**(3), 261–277.

Quinn, J., Dooley, T. and Paquette, P. (1990) 'Technology in services: Rethinking strategic focus'. *Sloan Management Review*, winter.

Ravenscraft, D.J. and Scherer, F.M. (1987) *Mergers, Sell-offs and Economic Efficiency*. Washington, DC: Brookings Institution Press.

Reve, T. (1990) 'The firm as a nexus of internal and external contracts'. In: M. Aoki, M. Gustafsson and O.E. Williamson (eds), *The Firm as a Nexus of Treaties*. London: Sage Publications.

Shelton, L.M. (1988) 'Strategic business fits and corporate acquisitions: Empirical evidence'. *Strategic Management Journal*, **9**.

Shleifer, A. and Vishny, R. (1986) 'Large shareholders and corporate control'. *Journal of Political Economy*, **94**, 461–488.

Shleifer, A. and Vishny, R. (1991) Takeovers in the '60s and the '80s: Evidence and implications'. *Strategic Management Journal*, **12**.

Sirower, M.L. (1997) *The Synergy Trap: How Companies Lose the Acquisition Game*. New York: Free Press.

Stonehouse, G.H. (1995) 'International collaborative business networks and the virtual corporation'. Paper presented at the *Conference of the British Academy of Management, Sheffield*.

Stonehouse, G.H. and Pemberton, J.D. (1999) 'Learning and knowledge management in the intelligent organisation'. *Participation and Empowerment: An International Journal*, **7**(5), 131–144.

Sudarsanam, P.S. (1995) *The Essence of Mergers and Acquisitions*. Englewood Cliffs, NJ: Prentice Hall.

Walsh, J. and Ellwood, J. (1991) 'Mergers, acquisitions and the pruning of managerial deadwood'. *Strategic Management Journal*, **12**.

GLOBAL BUSINESS – PRESENT AND FUTURE TRENDS

Introduction

In the future, global strategy will continue to be centred on new sources of competitive advantage for transnational organizations. The acquisition of competitive edge will depend on the ability of businesses to build and leverage new competences in the context of a rapidly changing global business environment. This chapter therefore examines potential developments in the forces that shape the global environment, their effect on transnationals and the means by which they compete. First, the future of globalization and its limitations are explored before potential new sources of competitive advantage including knowledge, collaborative networks and e-commerce are considered.

The global business environment – limits of globalization

The real state of homogenization

Levitt (1983) presented his seminal vision of a 'global village', characterized by standardized products and services, and global strategies built on economies of scale and scope. There are a growing number of industries and markets that display some of the characteristics thought to typify a global market. At the same time, Segal-Horn (1992) argued that there is actually little evidence of the homogenization of markets, rather 'the differences both within and across countries are far greater than any similarities which may exist.'

The question for the future is whether the differences that currently exist between national markets will continue or whether there will be ultimate convergence into a series of global markets for goods and services. Parker (1998) presented a discussion of factors that he argued will always inhibit, and indeed prevent, convergence of markets. His argument is based on physioeconomic theory.

Physioeconomic theory

Physioeconomic theory dates back to the 18th century and the work of Adam Smith (1723–90) and the French philosopher Montesquieu (1689–1755). Its roots are in natural history which recognizes that there is a hierarchy of phenomena. For example, solar climate precedes and determines physical climate, while the natural resources that a country possesses place a theoretical limit to its ultimate wealth. As Parker (1998) put it, 'Each level in the hierarchy is a necessary condition for the next: culture depends upon the existence of terrestrial life, which depends upon the existence of marine life, which depends on a particular climate.' Physioeconomic theories use both physiological and physiographic (physical-geographic) factors to explain differences between cultures, tastes and needs. To put this another way, similarities and differences in human behaviour will depend on similarities and differences in climatic conditions, terrain and endowments of natural resources which will help to predetermine cultural, political and economic conditions.

According to Parker (1998), 'solar climate alone . . . has a stronger correlation than income per head with many economic behaviours that are usually thought of as "development driven".' Milk, cereal, flour, coffee and cigarette consumption per head are better explained by solar climate than by income per head. People in colder climates consume more alcohol than those in warmer climates. Furthermore, 'Physiological adaptations across populations affect dietary preferences ..., housing preferences (heating, insulation, architecture) and clothing preferences ...; overall they influence 30–50% of total household consumption in developed economies and up to 90% in less developed economies (Parker, 1998). Climatic differences also explain differences in consumption of psychological products like entertainment products, which are more strongly demanded in colder climates.

In essence, physioeconomic theory suggests that, although countries with similar physioeconomic characteristics like climate, terrain and natural resources, will tend to converge in economic and social terms, those facing different physioeconomic conditions will preserve many of their differences. Thus, although cultures may converge in some respects, physioeconomic factors will ensure that differences between many national markets persist. There are therefore natural limitations to globalization.

Challenging the presuppositions

As well as forces beyond the control of humankind, there are other factors that challenge some of the assumptions on which globalization is based. For Levitt (1983) organizations must sell high volumes of standardized products on a global scale so as to enjoy the benefits of economies of scale. Yet, 'Developments in factor automation allowing flexible, lower cost, lower volume, high variety operations are challenging the standard assumptions of scale economy benefits by yielding variety at lower costs' (Segal-Horn, 1992). When this is coupled to the fact that consumers in many markets are becoming increasingly fickle, some of the perceived benefits of globalization to business seem to disappear. According to Martin (1997) the increasing volatility of markets means that there may be advantages in dispersion of manufacturing activities rather than concentration. Having a manufacturing facility located near to a market increases responsiveness and, while concentration of activities may bring the benefits of economies of scale, it may be at the cost of local adaptability.

Even some of the supposed benefits of globalization are not so great as might be assumed. While the OECD argued in 1996 that globalization 'gives all countries the possibility of participating in world development and all consumers the assurance of benefiting from increasingly vigorous competition between producers', the argument fails to take into account that consumers are also producers. From the viewpoint of producers, increased competition drives down prices, wages and, potentially, employment.

Further, Elliot (1996) made the point that 'Liberalisation and globalisation in industrial countries have not resulted in increased growth, nor are they likely to do so.' In fact, it is often the case that those countries that have prospered most in recent years have been those with high levels of government intervention (such as Germany, Japan and Korea). Professor Alit Singh of Cambridge University made the point in Elliot's (1996) article that records for growth, employment, living standards and investment were much poorer in the period from the mid-1970s to mid-1990s than they were between 1945 and 1973 when interventionism based on the Keynesian economic model was common practice.

At the level of the individual business there are also drawbacks in being global. Global companies are sometimes blamed for many of the world's ills. Jackson (1997) gave the examples of oil companies like Exxon being blamed for the world's pollution problems after the *Exxon Valdez* sank in 1989, McDonald's for rainforest destruction and Nike for exploiting child labour. These accusations are often unjust but arise because the names of these businesses are known globally.

A global approach to strategy and management?

There have been various attempts to make the case that the management philosophy and techniques of one country or region are superior to those of others. For example, American and Japanese techniques are often held up as examples of good practice. If this were the case, then it might be reasonable to assume that some form of global approach to management might develop. There are certainly global trends in management theory like total quality management, knowledge management and others, but there remain fundamental differences in approach between managers.

Doyle (1996) argued that the focus of international management varies from country to country. American and British managers emphasize seeking to maximize 'shareholder value', which is achieved when an attractive rate of return on capital expenditure is achieved. This differs from Japanese, German and Korean companies who tend to place greater emphasis on achieving market leadership by seeking to build customer satisfaction with their products. There are therefore important differences in the way that strategy is determined in businesses in these two groups. In the Anglo-American group, the approach adopted focuses on arriving at the financial budget necessary to achieve the target return on capital employed. This has been criticized as representing a short-term approach to business strategy. In the other group, businesses emphasize the importance of R&D, innovation, brand building and supply chain management so as to increase customer satisfaction. In other words, it is patently obvious that there is not a single global approach to management and strategy in businesses around the world.

Martin (1997) pointed out that, 'Going global is not the only possible approach to the 21st century business challenge. It is also feasible to build a company strategy around defending a home market.' For the trans-national business, the strategic challenge of the 21st century is to combine global scope with the responsiveness and flexibility necessary to compete with local domestic producers. Further, it is necessary to balance the pressures for globalization resulting from the benefits of economies of large-scale production against the need to respond flexibly to increasingly erratic customer preferences. On the other hand, companies that choose to defend their domestic positions rather than going global will only do so successfully if they remain alert to the changes taking place at a global level.

There are many examples of global players facing successful local competitors. In the global fast food market McDonald's faces strong local competition in France and Belgium from Quick and in Greece from Goody's who hold a significant share of the market but who are by no means a global competitor. Similarly, Coca-Cola and Pepsi-Cola face competition in Scotland from Barn's Irn Bru soft drink which holds a 25% market share but which is virtually unknown outside of the UK. It may therefore be necessary to make local variations to strategy to cope with local competitors.

Global competitive advantage in the future

The increasingly turbulent and hypercompetitive business environment has made it correspondingly difficult to generate and, even more importantly, sustain competitive advantage. Companies must develop and leverage core competences that meet the realized and unrealized needs of customers. At the heart of such core competences is organizational learning. To put this another way, core competence is normally founded on organizational knowledge. The pace of change means that knowledge changes rapidly over time so that organizations must 'learn' in order to build new knowledge. Organizations must become 'intelligent' and remain focused on the creation and management of knowledge that forms the basis of competitive advantage (Stonehouse and Pemberton, 1999).

Knowledge-based strategy: the intelligent organization

As the pace and unpredictability of change in the global business environment increase, flexibility and adaptability become more and more critical to sustaining a competitive edge. Responsiveness and proactivity are dependent on the ability of both individuals and organizations to learn more quickly than their rivals. Organizations must become 'intelligent' by actively attempting to learn about their internal and external environments and the relationships between them. In order to learn more quickly than competitors, it is necessary to develop understanding of the nature and processes of organizational learning and knowledge management.

Stonehouse and Pemberton (1999) developed a model of knowledge management and organizational learning (Figure 15.1). As organizational learning is not linear (Argyris, 1977, 1992), it is represented in a series of loops. Organizational learning and knowledge are based on individual knowledge, which must be formalized and stored in appropriate formats for dissemination and diffusion throughout the organization. Knowledge management in an 'intelligent organization' will be founded on a culture, structure and infrastructure which encourage and support the creation and development of knowledge.

Types of knowledge
Organizational knowledge can be defined 'as a shared collection of principles, facts, skills, and rules that inform organizational decision making, behaviour and actions', forming the basis of core competences. Raising the level of knowledge in the organization will increase its competitiveness. Knowledge can be either explicit or implicit.

Explicit knowledge is knowledge whose meaning is clearly stated, details of which can readily be recorded and stored. *Implicit* or *tacit knowledge* (Demarest, 1997) is often unstated and is based on individual experience. It is difficult to record and store but is often a vital source of competitive edge.

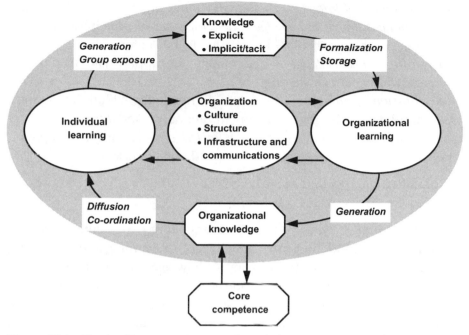

Figure 15.1   The intelligent organization   knowledge management and organizational
learning loops
Source: Stonehouse and Pemberton (1999)

One of the major challenges of knowledge management is the transformation of individual and tacit knowledge into organizational knowledge. A
second major challenge is creating an organizational context that encourages and facilitates the development of new knowledge through
organizational learning. The process of knowledge management is
highly contingent on organization culture, structure and infrastructure. An
important factor to be borne in mind when attempting to build a learning
organization through knowledge management is that 'knowledge is ... one
of the few assets that grows most – usually exponentially – when shared'
(Quinn, 1992). For this reason an intelligent organization must create a
context in which learning and sharing of knowledge throughout the organization are supported.

Managing knowledge in an intelligent organization
Knowledge management is therefore concerned with the following
processes:

- *the generation of knowledge* – individual and organizational learning;
- *the formalization of knowledge* – development of principles, rules and procedures which will allow knowledge to be shared;
- *the storage of knowledge* – determining the appropriate medium for storage which permits sharing;
- *the diffusion of knowledge* – sharing of knowledge within the organization and limiting sharing across organizational boundaries;
- *the co-ordination and control of knowledge* – ensuring that organizational knowledge is coherent and applied consistently.

The organizational context of such activities is vital to effective knowledge management. This context consists of:

- *Organizational culture* – this must encourage experimentation, the sharing of ideas and must place a high value on learning and knowledge;
- *Organizational structure* – this must allow experts to share ideas but must also be holistic, allowing ideas to be shared across the whole organization. It favours a network structure or the use of project teams and task groups (see Chapter 13 where organizational structure is discussed);
- *Organizational infrastructure and communications* – this will depend on the efficient and effective use of information and communications technology (ICT), particularly networks (internal and external, the Internet), expert system neural networks and multimedia. ICT has an important role to play in the storage and diffusion of knowledge (see Chapter 10 where technology strategy is discussed).

Core competences and knowledge
Core competences must be distinctive, complex, difficult to imitate, durable and adaptable if they are to be a source of sustained superior performance. Knowledge can be an important source of these characteristics. Knowledge, particularly tacit or implicit knowledge, is both complex and difficult to imitate. Organizational learning can make knowledge a durable and adaptable source of competitive advantage. There are numerous examples of the ways in which knowledge acts as the foundation for competence building and leveraging. Microsoft's competitive advantage in the software sector, for example, is largely knowledge-based (Stonehouse and Pemberton, 1999).

The number of organizations seeking to become 'intelligent' by fostering organizational learning through knowledge management is increasing.

Grant (1997) pointed out that 'companies such as Dow Chemical, Andersen Consulting, Polaroid and Skandia are developing corporate wide systems to track, access, exploit and create organisational knowledge.' The distinctive features shared by these organizations are that they encourage questioning and creativity, and place a high value on trust, teamwork and sharing. At the same time, they have created infrastructures that support learning, which assist in the storage and controlled diffusion of knowledge and which co-ordinate its application in creating and supporting core competences.

The idea of knowledge as an important source of competitive advantage is not new, but renewed interest in it is partly due to rapid change in the macroenvironment, turbulence and hypercompetition. Collectively, these factors mean that organizations must learn more quickly than their rivals if they are to stay ahead in the competitive game. Knowledge that is distinctive is vital to the building and leveraging of core competences. In these circumstances it is inevitable that managers in transnational businesses will be seeking better ways of fostering learning through knowledge management.

The 'virtual' corporation

The 1990s witnessed an increase in interest in the potential of collaboration between businesses, coupled with the use of ICT as a potential source of competitive edge. This interest is again linked to the rise of the core competence school of thought in strategic management. The development of core competences within an organization requires a degree of specialization so as to focus the development of knowledge and skills which are relevant to a particular form or aspect of business. Collaboration allows businesses to share knowledge and core competences so as to create synergies and new sources of competitive advantage. The development of ICT and e-commerce has further increased possibilities for collaboration both between businesses and between businesses and their customers.

Davidow and Malone (1992) were among the first to highlight the role of information and ICT in the management of collaborative activities, stressing the improved service flexibility and responsiveness made possible by the sharing of information. Since their article in 1992 the rapid expansion of the Internet and developments in e-commerce have sparked a revolution in the use of technology to support business in general and collaboration in particular. For these reasons, information technology is hailed as having given birth to the virtual corporation.

The virtual corporation can be viewed as a collaborative network comprising of a focal business, its suppliers and customers whose activities are integrated and co-ordinated by the extensive use of ICT. There are several key characteristics that may be viewed as essential to the existence of a virtual corporation:

- a network of collaborative businesses and customers centred on a focal business;
- concentration on core business activities by individual network members;
- shared complementary goals;
- alignment of network business strategies;
- integration of business and information strategies;
- shared technology which often includes computer networks, satellite or cable communications, common software standards and electronic data interchange.

The truly virtual corporation will be centred on a focal business that shows a high degree of integration of internal activities with considerable blurring between functional business areas. The external linkages of the focal organization will also demonstrate a high degree of integration, both upstream with suppliers and downstream with customers and distributors, in the value system.

The potential benefits to the network include more effective co-ordination of activities, reduced costs, greatly enhanced responsiveness, ability to compete more effectively on the basis of time and, equally as importantly, information that leads to superior knowledge of customers, products and markets. Thus, ICT, while usually not the major underlying motivation for a network, has the ability to transform its competitive performance from the acceptable to the exceptional.

Discussion and review questions

1. Discuss the potential for further globalization of business activity. What limitations are there on globalization?
2. What impact might limitations on globalization have on the strategies of transnational organizations?
3. Why is there increasing interest in knowledge as a source of competitive advantage?

4. What factors must be taken into account in building an intelligent organization?
5. Explain the main features of a virtual corporation.

References and further reading

Argyris, C. (1977) 'Double loop learning in organizations'. *Harvard Business Review*, September/October, 115–125.

Argyris, C. (1992) *On Organizational Learning*. Cambridge, MA: Basil Blackwell.

Argyris, C. and Schon, D. (1978) *Organization Learning: A Theory of Action Perspective*. Reading, MA: Addison Wesley.

Chakravarthy, B. (1997) 'A new strategy framework for coping with turbulence'. *Sloan Management Review*, Winter, 69–82.

Davidow, W.H. and Malone, M.S. (1992) *Structuring and Revitalizing the Corporation for the 21st Century – The Virtual Corporation*. London: Harper Business.

Demarest, M. (1997) 'Understanding knowledge management'. *Long Range Planning*, **30**(3), 374–384.

Doyle, P. (1996) 'The Loss from Profits'. *Financial Times*, 25 October.

Elliot, L. (1996) 'Putting Trade in its Place'. *The Guardian*, 27 May.

Financial Times (1997) 'Non-global Markets', 27 September.

Graham, G. (1997) 'The Difficulty of Banking on the World – Is there a Life for the Non-global'. *Financial Times*, 29 October.

Grant, R.M. (1997) 'The knowledge based view of the firm: Implications for management practice'. *Long Range Planning*, **30**(3), 450–454.

Hilgard, E.R and Bower, G.H. (1967) *Theories of Learning*. New York: Appleton-Century Crofts.

Inkpen, A.C. and Crossan, M.M. (1995) 'Believing is seeing: Joint ventures and organisation learning'. *Journal of Management Studies*, **32**(5), 595–618.

Jackson, T (1993) *Organisational Behaviour in International Management*. Oxford, UK: Butterworth-Heinemann.

Jackson, T. (1997) 'Facing up to Challenging Opposition'. *Financial Times*, 31 October.

Kamoche, K. (1997) 'Knowledge creation and learning in international human resource management'. *International Journal of Human Resource Management*, **8**(3), April, 213–225.

Kolb, D.A., Rubin, I.M. and Osland, J (1991) *Organizational Behaviour: An Experiential Approach*. Englewood Cliffs, NJ: Prentice Hall.

Levitt, T. (1983) 'The globalization of markets'. *Harvard Business Review*, May/June.

Martin, P. (1997) 'A Future Depending on Choice – The Global Company in the 21st Century'. *Financial Times*, 7 November.

McMaster, M. (1997) 'Organising for innovation: Technology and intelligent capacities'. *Long Range Planning*, **30**(5), 799–802.

Parker, P. (1998) 'Why markets will not converge'. *Mastering Marketing*. London: Financial Times.

Parsaye K. (1989) *Intelligent Databases*. New York: John Wiley & Sons.

Quinn, J.B. (1992) *The Intelligent Enterprise*. New York: Free Press.

Quintas, P. and Lefevre, P. (1997) 'Knowledge management: A strategic agenda'. *Long Range Planning*, **30**(3), 385–397.

Rushde, D. and Oldfield, C. (1999) 'E-mania'. *Sunday Times*, 19 September.

Sanchez, R. and Heene, A. (eds) (1997) *Strategic Learning and Knowledge Management*. New York: John Wiley & Sons.

Segal-Horn, S. (1992) 'Global markets, regional trading blocs and international consumers'. *Journal of Global Marketing*, **5**(3).

Senge, P. (1990) 'Building learning organizations'. *Sloan Management Review*, Fall.

Stonehouse, G.H. and Pemberton, J.D. (1999) 'Learning and knowledge management in the intelligent organisation'. *Participation and Empowerment: An International Journal*, **7**(5), 131–144.

Turner, I. (1996) 'Working with Chaos'. *Financial Times*, 4 October.

Volberda, H.W. (1997) 'Building flexible organisations for fast-moving markets'. *Long Range Planning*, **30**(2), 169–183.

Whitehill, M. (1997) 'Knowledge-based strategy to deliver sustained competitive advantage'. *Long Range Planning*, **30**(4), 621–627.

MCDONALD'S AND ITS INTERNATIONAL EXPERIENCE

Appendix 1

A brief history

It is thought that the first meat burgers (minced or ground meat formed into flat 'pats') were developed in 1904 for a World Fair exhibition in St Louis, Michigan. The idea of a burger as a fast and convenient food, especially when served in a bun, caught on in America and a number of entrepreneurs opened mobile stands at various events and in some city centres.

By 1943 Wimpy (named after a character in the children's comic strip, *Popeye*) was the US market leader. Also in 1943 the 'Big Boys' chain was credited with developing the double burger and the drive-through. It was in the post-war climate (i.e., after 1945), however, that the whole idea of fast food took off.

During the late 1940s, while much of Europe was still under reconstruction and enduring food rationing, Southern and Central California were beginning to enjoy the benefits of mass car ownership. For the first time, people's lives began to revolve around their cars and the idea of 'nipping out' for a meal became possible. The concept of the drive-through was ripe for the time. The drive-throughs of the time involved driving into a parking area and a waitress (a 'car hop') would take the order and then bring out the food (perhaps more like a 'drive-in' than the way we understand 'drive throughs' today). These grew out of California and across the USA as car ownership increased and other drive-ins and drive-throughs became a feature of American life (e.g., the drive-in movie). The growth of edge-of-town housing developments and the development of the American suburban culture around the time were also conducive to the fast food industry.

Brothers Dick and Maurice McDonald were two entrepreneurs who, in 1948, opened a hamburger 'stall' in San Bernardino, California. Their idea was to sell their food cheaper than competitors by saving on the 'car hops' and persuading customers instead to go to a counter to order their food. This also made for a faster turnround for the customer (it saved the time of the 'car hop' going back and forward to the car, and the food 'queueing' in the kitchen). This simple innovation proved popular with customers and Dick and Maurice soon realized they were taking business off the other local drive-through businesses.

Later observers pointed out that the McDonald brothers were pioneers in their industry by employing a 'Fordist' approach to the production of hot food. They saw burger cooking as a production line rather than a kitchen task, and on a good day, in contrast to conventional restaurant cooking, the burgers were effectively produced on a production line. Staff became committed to one task at a time – cutting buns, flipping burgers, packing burgers, serving customers, etc.

The McDonald brothers were not especially ambitious, however, and it took Chicago-based businessman Ray Kroc to take the business on to its next stage of development. Kroc was a risk taker by nature and had previously remortgaged his home and invested his entire life savings to become the exclusive distributor of a five-spindled milkshake maker called the Multimixer. In 1954, when he was 52, he heard about the McDonald brothers' burger stand and that it ran eight Multimixers at a time. He went to San Bernardino to see the McDonald's business for himself.

Kroc later reported that he had never seen so many people served so quickly than those at the McDonald's stall. It quickly dawned on him that if there could be more stalls like the McDonald's one, each running eight Multimixers, then he could become very wealthy, very quickly. When Kroc suggested the idea of opening other McDonald's stalls, Dick and Maurice told Kroc it wouldn't be possible because they were already too busy running the one they already had. Kroc saw the opportunity and volunteered to run the first new outlet himself, paying Dick and Maurice a royalty for the use of their business idea.

Ray Kroc opened his McDonald's outlet in Des Plaines, Illinois in 1955 (in the north-eastern part of the USA – a long way from San Bernardiino). His first day's takings of $366.12 soon grew and Kroc saw his investment grow not only through the sale of burgers but also through the Multimixers. By paying Dick and Maurice for the use of their business idea, Kroc's store was, in effect, a franchise, and it became the first of many.

Kroc differed from Dick and Maurice in many ways in addition to his more aggressive and risk-taking attitude. It was he who realized that small things were often valued more by customers than some of the other restaurant chains of the time had realized. 'If you've got time to lean, you've got time to clean,' Ray Kroc said to his employees in Des Plaines. Cleanliness, he suggested, was not only good for hygiene, it also showed customers that McDonald's was a business that cared about detail. By way of example, Kroc himself was sometimes seen sweeping up in the car park.

Kroc's initiative soon meant that he became the franchise manager for what was fast becoming a medium-sized business. As Kroc sold more franchises in the USA, he became the effective founder of what we now know as McDonald's. Ted Turner became a McDonald's franchisee in 1956 and Kroc soon realized that Turner was a man he could deal with. Together they built McDonald's into an international business.

Kroc and Turner realized that the key to success was rapid expansion. The best way to achieve this, they realized, was not through direct investment from the company itself but rather through offering franchises. This was also the way that both men had become involved in the idea, and it would involve private individuals or other (smaller) businesses putting up the capital for each new store and bearing the risk of failure in each case. By using this approach, they realized that the potential for expansion was almost limitless.

The major domestic (i.e., in the USA) growth of McDonald's began in the 1960s. It is likely that, among others, one cause of the increased demand for cheap takeaway food at the time (Kentucky Fried Chicken was also ascendant at that time) was a decline in the real (i.e., after inflation) value of the US minimum wage. Beginning in 1968 the decline had the effect of reducing the minimum wage by 40% in real terms over the next 20 years. Because McDonald's was from the outset a mass market product, the falling disposable incomes of the large numbers of unskilled and manual workers worked in McDonald's favour and against the more mid-priced restaurants and food outlets.

The McDonald's product range grew steadily throughout the 1950s, 1960s and 1970s with many product ideas coming from the growing numbers of franchisees. The 'Big Mac' was launched in 1968 (the brainchild of Jim Delligatti, one of Ray Kroc's earliest franchisees, who by the late 1960s operated a dozen stores in Pittsburgh) and the 'Egg McMuffin' was introduced in 1973 (the idea of another franchisee, Herb Peterson). The 'Happy Meal', a product aimed particularly at children, was introduced in 1979. This included an appropriately portioned burger, fries and drink together with one of a range of small toys in the hope that customers would be tempted to 'collect the set' through repeat visits. Throughout the development of the menu, however, an emphasis was placed on a limited choice of products that could, over time, become familiar to customers. This became increasingly important as the company internationalized.

McDonald's and franchising

The franchise concept has been key to McDonald's worldwide success. This has ensured consistency of quality and uniformity of product from location to location and country to country. As the arrangement developed over the years, the nature of the agreement between franchisor (McDonald's) and the franchisee developed and changed. Through observing both successes and some failures, an agreement was eventually developed that involved McDonald's itself having a large influence on store location, while the normal term for a franchisee was limited in the first instance to 20 years. The franchisees, in exchange, agreed to:

- use McDonald's recipes and specifications for menu items;
- comply to specific standards of operations, including systems of inventory control, financial record keeping and marketing;
- display and use of McDonald's trademarks and other registered logos and marks;
- meet McDonald's standards for such things as restaurant and equipment layout and display signage.

From the outset, McDonald's made franchises expensive. This was partly not only to guarantee that each new store development would be of a quality and in a situation consistent with the company's reputation but also to ensure that the amount risked by each franchisee was sufficient to guarantee a lot of effort to make the franchise a success. The costs included an initial fee paid to McDonald's at the commencement of the franchise, a refundable deposit as security for faithful performance of the franchise, costs while the franchisee and staff underwent initial training and the costs of establishing the restaurant in terms of fixtures, fittings and landscaping. Such a cost was beyond the reach of the casual investor and required a detailed financing package to be drawn up and presented, possibly involving elements of both private and borrowed capital.

In exchange, the franchisee would benefit from the parent company in terms of the provision of the fabric of the building (i.e., franchisees rarely owned the building itself), advice on the various aspects of the McDonald's 'way' and a very high chance that the venture would be a success, drawing as it did on the proven McDonald's business formula and marketing.

Despite the reciprocal advantages of franchising, McDonald's adopted a dual approach to its expansion. While the majority (about 70%) of stores were franchised, the company chose to operate some (the remainder) as directly controlled operations from its national centres.

International growth

By 1970 there was at least one McDonald's store in each of the 50 states of the USA. This amounted to about 1,000 stores in the USA.

International expansion occurred steadily rather than in a 'big bang'. The most obvious first candidate for foreign expansion was Canada (in the late 1960s), and by the early 1970s McDonald's had made its first forays into Europe. The UK, as a country traditionally open to symbols of American culture, was one of the first overseas targets for McDonald's. During the 1960s, when fish and chips was the staple takeaway food, the Wimpy brand had become established. The first McDonald's in the UK was opened in 1974 in Woolwich, South London and, spreading initially in the south-east, restaurants were eventually rolled out across the UK to reach a total (as at 2003) of 1,200. Other early overseas 'targets' were Germany (1971), Netherlands (also 1971) and Sweden (1973).

From a slow start, international expansion accelerated in the 1980s and 1990s. One explanation for this was that McDonald's had saturated its home markets – there was a McDonald's restaurant at most intersections and in all town centres in the USA and many in Canada. Future growth could only come through finding new national markets and through finding new markets for McDonald's products within existing national markets. In the UK, for example, McDonald's started to grow out of town centres into suburbs and onto its motorway network (replacing the traditional 'transport cafe' as the choice of refreshment stop for many people).

McDonald's continued to develop internationally (Table A1.1). In some regions of the world, the franchise became not only a useful mode of market entry but also an important part of the company's reputation management. The fact that McDonald's had become a symbol of American

Table A1.1 Selected international McDonald's developments

Country	First store opened	Number of stores as at 2003*	Employees	Percent franchised
Europe				
Austria	1977	159	7,350	90
Belgium	1978	57		
Croatia	1996	16	800	
Cyprus	1997	13	600	
Czech Republic	1992	68		
Finland	1984	93		
France	1979	900	35,000	
Germany	1971	1,152		
Greece	1991	48	1,500	
Hungary	–	69	3,700	
Ireland	1977	60	3,000	
Italy	1985	230	10,000	
Netherlands	1971	193	15,000	
Poland	1992	200	10,000	21
Portugal	1991	106		45
Romania	1995	48	2,300	
Serbia	1988	16	700	
Slovenia	1993	17	600	
Sweden	1973	220		
Switzerland	1976	115	5,900	
Turkey	1986	98	3,500	
UK	1974	1,200	68,000	34
South and Central America				
Argentina	1986	173	11,000	
Bolivia	1997	8	850	
Brazil	1978	530		53
Chile	1990	70	3,000	
Colombia	1995	25	1,000	
Guatemala	1974	27	2,000	
Mexico	1985	270	11,000	
Paraguay	1996	6		
Peru	1996	10		
Uruguay	1991	20		
Middle East				
Bahrain	1994	9		100
Egypt	1994	50	3,000	100
Israel	1993	80	3,000	100
Jeddah	1994			100
Kuwait	1994	34		100
Oman	1994	4		100
Qatar	1995	7		100
Saudi Arabia	1993	71		100
UAE	1994	25		100
Pacific Rim				
Australia	1971	680		
Hong Kong	1975	158	9,000	
Japan	1971	2,400		
New Zealand	1976	147	6,000	
Singapore	1979	129	6,000	

Table A1.1 (*cont.*)

Country	First store opened	Number of stores as at 2003*	Employees	Percent franchised
North America				
Canada	1969*	1,200	77,000	
USA	1954			
Asia				
India	1996	34		
Korea (South)	1988	270		
Pakistan	1998			
Russia	1990	90		

*Approximate or estimated. In total there are more than 30,000 McDonald's restaurants in 121 countries (as at 2003)

culture in many parts of the world represented both an opportunity and a threat. Where American culture was seen as glamorous and exciting, the company was able to choose between granting franchises and operating the stores directly. In other regions, however, where America was perceived less favourably, the local marketing initiatives stressed the local ownership and management of restaurants. In the Islamic Middle East in particular, where America's support for Israel had made it unpopular with some Muslim and Arab communities, it was stressed that all McDonald's were owned and operated by local nationals. All McDonald's in the region were franchised to enable this claim to be made.

The idea that a standard product range could be offered in all countries came under strain early in the company's international development. While it remained an objective to offer a standard range as far as possible (to support global marketing and scale economies in production and supply), national, cultural and religious differences necessitated some product variations in some countries (Table A1.2). One such problem was in the make-up of the company's major product. Despite its name, the standard American 'hamburger' was actually made by McDonald's of 100% beef. In India, for example, where cattle are sacred to the Hindu majority, a variation on the product was devised using lamb and with a greatly enhanced vegetarian menu. In Israel, with its Jewish majority, products were introduced which conformed to the kosher rules of diet and food preparation. Where local taste preferences were a factor, additions to the standard menu were made to cater for them. Similarly, McDonald's stores in some countries sold alcoholic beverages, while in other countries they did not.

Table A1.2 Examples of variations on the menu

Country	Example of 'unique' products
Chile	McNífica is a sandwich that includes tomato, ketchup, mayonnaise, onions, lettuce and cheddar cheese.
Cyprus	McNistisima is the promotional name for the Lenten period products offered to customers during the fasting period before Easter and Christmas. During this period, McDonald's customers can choose from a selection of lent products, such as veggie burgers, country potatoes, shrimps and spring rolls.
India	The market was entered without the brand's flagship product, the Big Mac. Keeping in mind the religious sentiments of the local population, a commitment was made not to introduce beef or pork products into the menu. Instead, a product similar to the Big Mac with mutton and chicken patties was created and christened the Maharaja Mac™ and Chicken Maharaja Mac™, respectively. With the vegetarian population in mind, an entire vegetarian range in the menu was created. Also developed was an eggless mayonnaise that made the vegetable burgers vegetarian in the true sense of the term.
Ireland	Introduced in 1970 the Shamrock Shake is a unique item for Ireland. These special shakes are only available for a period around the St Patrick's Day celebrations.
Israel	All meat served in McDonald's restaurants in Israel is 100% kosher beef. McDonald's operates kosher restaurants and non-kosher restaurants. The non-kosher restaurants serve Israeli customers who do not keep strictly kosher and want to visit McDonald's on Saturdays and religious holidays. McDonald's Israel's seven kosher restaurants, where the menu does not include any dairy products and all food is prepared in accordance with kosher law, are not open on the Sabbath and all religious holidays.
Italy	A range of Mediterrannean salads.
Japan	If meeting the demands of local culture means adding to its regular menu, McDonald's will do it. In Japan it added the Teriyaki McBurger . . . a sausage patty on a bun with teriyaki sauce.
South Korea	The Bulgogi Burger was the first adaptation of the McDonald's menu to meet the demands of local Korean culture. The burger consists of a 100% pork patty on a bun with bulgogi sauce and lettuce. Another sandwich unique to Korea is the Tukbul Burger with two, 100% pork, patties and cheese on a bun with bulgogi sauce and lettuce.
The Netherlands	The McKroket is a McDonalized version of a unique Dutch product. The burger is made of 100% beef ragout with a crispy layer around it. It's topped with a fresh mustard/mayonnaise sauce.
Pakistan	The three McMaza meals are Chatpata Chicken Roll, Chicken Chutni Burger and Spicy Chicken Burger, all three are served with Aaloo fingers and a regular drink. The spicy and tangy taste of the meals has been specially developed, keeping in mind the local palate. The combination of local taste and great value for money makes these meals very popular.
Turkey	In addition to the standard products of McDonald's, KöfteBurger is also offered for those who are looking for a different and local flavour. KöfteBurger is made of a spicy meat patty inside a specially prepared flavoured bun enriched with a special yogurt mix and spiced tomato sauce for those McDonald's customers seeking variety. Ayran is a traditional soft drink which is offered as another local taste at McDonald's restaurants in the country.
UK	The McBacon Roll is a popular breakfast product made with back bacon and traditional special brown sauce, served in a maize-topped roll. Fish fingers are available with children's Happy Meals.

NIKE INC.

Company development

In 1998, with sales exceeding $9 billion and a market share of 33%, Nike was the brand leader in the global training shoe market. These figures represented an increase of 5% compared with its market share figure of 28% in 1995. This figure of 28% was 10 percentage points ahead of Reebok's 18% share and was more than double that of Adidas's 11% share. Nike faced continued competition from Reebok and faced increased competition from a revived Adidas. Nevertheless, Nike remained the market leader and its 'swoosh' trademark was the most recognized in the industry ahead of the famous three stripes of Adidas.

Since its foundation by Phil Knight, Nike's record of growth has been strong. For the first 10 years of its history, its sales grew at an average rate of 82% a year, while its profits doubled every year. Accordingly, by 1980 it had overtaken Adidas as the largest seller of sports shoes in the USA. The 1980s and early 1990s saw the internationalization of Nike, and by 1993 20% of sales were outside the USA, mainly in Europe where Nike held the largest market share at 20% ahead of Reebok (17%) and Adidas (16%). Sales in the Far East also increased, so that by 1996 Nike had a 12% share of the Japanese market, while Nike products also became widely available in the former Soviet Union. Nike was very much an American brand that became global.

Nike began life as Blue Ribbon Sports in 1957 selling cheap, but technically advanced, running shoes out of the back of a van. The company's founders, Phil Knight and Bill Bowerman, met at the University of Oregon, where Knight was a student and moderate middle-distance athlete and Bowerman was his coach. Bowerman had developed the practice of modifying his athlete's shoes because he felt the original products were poorly designed. Knight capitalized on this idea and developed a business plan while at Stanford Business School, deciding that rather than manufacturing his own product, he would buy and market Japanese-made running shoes. This was a particularly bold idea as, at the time, Japanese products had a reputation for poor quality.

The Nike product concept

The brand name Nike was launched in 1972 at the US Olympic track and field trials where Knight and Bowerman sold running shoes targeted at serious athletes. The name Nike was taken from that of the Greek goddess of victory, and the 'swoosh' trademark was introduced as a symbol of speed and the achievement of excellence. Initially, success came slowly, but, when in the mid-1970s Nike invented the impact-absorbing sole, there followed a sizeable increase in sales among both serious athletes and joggers. It was this development that allowed Nike to replace Adidas as the number one sports shoe company in the USA by 1980.

Since this time, product design and development has remained at the heart of Nike's competitive strategy. Large sums are spent on developing materials that will wear for longer and absorb the damaging impacts of sporting activity on the body. The original concept of the impact-absorbing sole was further enhanced with the development of the air principle, based on a sole and heel which incorporated an air cushion. Although the benefits of this system may be questioned, it quickly became very popular with athletes and with fashion-conscious youth.

Product design and development take place at Nike's headquarters in Portland, OR on its 75-acre World Campus. So well known is Nike's trademark that there is no nameplate on the entrance to the Campus. A red swoosh is the only sign identifying the site's occupants. The swoosh also appears on the door handles and is even engraved into the after dinner chocolates served in the executive restaurant! There are 2,500 employees on site, working primarily in R&D and marketing. Nike is reported to take good care of the workforce at its headquarters, which features state-of-the-art sports facilities, lakes, woods, restaurants, a hairdresser, a cobbler, a cashpoint and a nursery for employee's children. So strong is the loyalty to the company that some employees have a swoosh tattooed on their body.

Nike has always regarded itself as a business run by athletes for athletes. For this reason, product development has always been regarded as vital. Teams of designers work in informal and picturesque surroundings to develop new concepts to keep the company ahead of its rivals. There are laboratories and test tracks to test out new products. The product range expanded from running shoes into a range of high-performance sports shoes covering most sporting activities. In addition to shoes, it began to produce a full range of sports apparel, including shorts, T-shirts, tracksuits, etc. As the training shoe and sports apparel became fashion items, sales of all these products quickly expanded. More importantly, Nike accepted that the training shoe market has matured and embarked 'on a strategy to transform itself from a shoemaker into a global sports and fitness company.'[1]

Nike is proud of its claim to be the technological leaders in the industry. Continuous product development is considered necessary because Knight believes that there are seven-year brand cycles in the industry. Accordingly, Nike continuously innovates to stay ahead Nike's success followed that of Converse and Adidas. It has not always been plain sailing; Nike lost direction in the mid-1980s when Reebok took over from Nike as market leaders in 1986. This was seen as the height of the crisis. It was this that galvanized Nike into action and led to the launch of the Air Jordan range of products linking 'shoes, colours, clothes, athlete, logo and television advertising.'[2] Such is Nike's commitment to R&D that some commentators have suggested that trainers could eventually measure the runner's pulse when running and cool the feet at the same time. *The Independent* newspaper (25/06/96) reported that 'it is Nike's designs that are the most sought after by trainer connoisseurs.'

Vertical linkages and outsourcing

Although Nike briefly flirted with the idea of manufacturing its own products, it quickly realized that the main source of its competitive advantage lay in the design, development, marketing and distribution of sport apparel, rather than in manufacture. The products are manufactured more cheaply and to a higher quality standard in countries other than the USA. Once a new product has been designed and developed in Portland, its manufacture is then outsourced to countries like Taiwan, China and Brazil (Figure A2.1). Nike imposes stringent quality control standards on its manufacturers. Nevertheless, Nike, Adidas and Reebok have come in for criticism of the allegedly low wages paid to workers in the factories producing their shoes, particularly when these are compared with the sums paid to the athletes promoting these products. This was highlighted by a report completed by Christian Aid, which drew attention to 'the plight of many of the workers in

[1] *International Business Week*, 17 June 1996.
[2] Katz, D. (1993) 'Triumph of the Swoosh'. *Sports Illustrated*, 16 August.

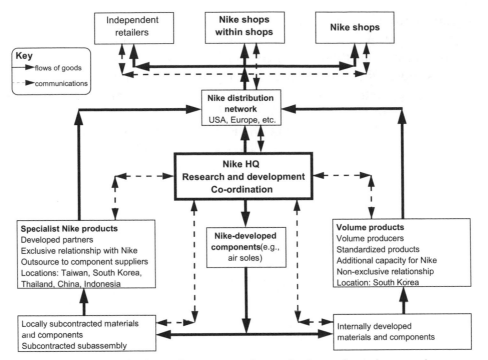

Figure A2.1 Nike's value system – the production and supply network
Source: Adapted from Dicken (1998)

these subcontracting factories. Its survey of conditions for workers in China, the Philippines and Thailand found that discrimination against trade unions, forced overtime, poor health and safety provision, and low wages were recurring problems.'[3] In response, Nike pointed to the fact that the wages in the factories were well above average earnings in other occupations in the same countries and that it insisted on health care programmes for workers in its factories.

Nike also carefully vets the retailers who are allowed to sell its products. Not only are retailers checked for creditworthiness they are also for their expertise in sportswear. This is because Nike values its reputation as an authentic sportswear company and believes that retailers must be able to advise knowledgeably on Nike products. This expertise is felt necessary to strengthen the Nike brand image. Nike is valued by retailers not only because its products are popular among consumers but also because of the service that Nike provides to the retailers. Nike representatives have computers that provide information on the entire range of Nike products

[3] *Ethical Consumer*, 1 February 1996.

and the advertising campaigns that support them. Although Nike products command a premium price, a 'generous' proportion of this premium price goes to the retailer as well as to Nike itself. This is designed to encourage retailers to promote Nike products over other brands. Retailers also benefit from Nike's association with top athletes and the large-scale advertising campaigns to promote the products.

In recent years Nike has ventured into retailing itself. It opened a number of Nike Town Stores throughout the USA. There are a growing number of such superstores that exclusively sell Nike products. Those in Chicago and New York bear a strong resemblance to theme parks. They are heavily decorated with sports memorabilia and feature video walls showing famous sports events with prerecorded crowd noises. These stores are devoted to Nike products and are based on the twin themes of Nike's history and that of its athletes. They include high technology and feature Nike's Ngage laser machine which not only measures the size of a customer's foot to the nearest millimetre but also indicates which Nike products would be most suitable for the foot size. Nike Town Stores have expanded beyond the USA. London was the site of the first European branch. Nike Town Stores are regarded as the 'temples' of the business and are 'shrines' to its products. As Nike extended its product range and entered new market segments, influence over the retailing of its products was seen as vital to preservation of the reputation of the brand.

Promotions and endorsements

Marketing, promotion and brand name are as important to Nike's success as are product development and quality. Nike signed a number of top athletes to endorse and promote its products. In the USA, Michael Jordan is the supreme example of a Nike athlete but other top names like John McEnroe and Andre Agassi are also endorsees. In Europe, footballers Ian Rush and Eric Cantona were among those signed by Nike. Such athletes are paid substantial sums to wear and promote Nike products. This approach has shown some signs of success as, in the USA, 265 out of 320 NBA players wear Nike shoes. A sign of the loyalty of Nike's athletes, or perhaps of the sums of money paid to them, is illustrated by an incident at the Barcelona Olympics when Nike-endorsed athletes refused to wear Reebok shoes (the official shoes of the US team) when they went to collect their medals. It is also interesting to note that Nike did not seek out the most 'clean-cut' athletes but tended to opt for controversial characters like McEnroe and Cantona who, Nike believed, would generate more interest in its products, particularly among young people. There is evidence to support this view – Nike's UK advertisements were found to be the most popular among the key age range of 7 to 16-year-olds.

As well as endorsements from athletes, Nike used slogans and television advertising to enhance its brand identity. The best known of its advertising campaigns is the 'Just do it' slogan, and more recently 'Think global – dunk local.' The company spends substantial sums on television and other media advertising. Nike's campaigns often generate controversy. The campaign timed to coincide with the Euro '96 football championships showed Eric Cantona leading a team of humans to victory over a team of demonic monsters. The evidence suggests that the controversy generated as much publicity for Nike as the campaign itself. A survey by British Market Research Bureau suggested that many people believed that Nike was an official sponsor of Euro '96 when it was not. This is a convincing demonstration of the success of Nike's publicity machine.

In 1996 Nike launched a new campaign based around its top athletes using the Iggy Pop song *Search And Destroy*, while in 1998 it sponsored Ronaldo and Brazil in their World Cup campaign. Once again Nike was perceived as sponsors of the tournament in France when in fact it was not, but arch rivals Adidas were. In the late 1990s Nike sponsored such personalities as Tiger Woods, Michael Schumacher and Pete Sampras. In 1997 the company spent $5.6 billion on marketing and $4 billion on individual sponsorships. Michael Jordan alone was paid $70m.

Markets and structure

Saturation of the US market was a major factor in stimulating Nike's expansion overseas. Nike's internationalization into Europe initially entailed the establishment of virtually autonomous subsidiaries. Each subsidiary had marketing, sales, distribution, IT and accounting functions. Each subsidiary also had a warehouse from which Nike products, obtained from factories mainly in Asia, were distributed to retailers throughout the country in question. Products offered to retailers varied from country to country and there was considerable variation in operational strategies between countries.

In the 1990s, however, the company brought in control procedures that allowed for much greater central control from the USA of both strategy and operations. At the same time, greater centralization of activities within Europe itself was introduced, reflecting the increasing similarity of the markets in which Nike operated. The company aimed to reduce the number of European distribution warehouses from 32 in 1994 to 5 by 1997, with European headquarters in the Netherlands and a main distribution warehouse in Belgium. Product ranges were also more standardized as were advertising and promotion. It is interesting to note, however, that there were still variations between the product ranges offered in Europe and the USA, and to some extent between the advertising and promotional campaigns. These differences reflected differences in the popularity of different sports between Europe, where soccer is the number one sport, and America, where it is still a minority game. There were also differences in the athletes signed to endorse Nike's products, reflecting the popularity of different athletes within Europe as compared with the USA.

Changes in the 1990s

It has not always been plain sailing. In 1997 Nike issued two poor profit warnings and made 1,000 redundancies among US employees. This downturn had a number of causes. There was evidence of a shift in demand away from training shoes to 'brown shoe goods'. These hybrid walking/training shoes were manufactured by companies like Caterpillar, Timberland and Rockport. Rockport had a turnover of $500m in 1997 and, ironically, was owned by Reebok who lost the training shoe wars with Nike. There was also evidence that the sports apparel and training shoe markets had also become saturated.

Accordingly, Nike found itself with large quantities of unsold stock with the inevitable consequence that stock had to be sold at heavily discounted prices. To make matters worse, sales of Nike products on the 'grey market' increased. Tesco began to import Nike shoes into the UK to sell them at a reduced rate. Its advertisements added insult to injury for Nike by parodying Nike's 'Just do it' slogan with 'Just do it for less'.

Nike's troubles were exacerbated by economic problems in Asia where the majority of Nike's products were manufactured. There had been some bad publicity surrounding the conditions of employment of the workers employed by factories producing goods for Nike in the Asian region. There were claims that employees, including children, were forced to work for up to 14 hours a day for subsistence wages. Moreover, there were reports that workers suffered beatings at the hands of their employers. 'Anti-Nike' groups referred to 'The curse of the swooshstika.' These reports severely damaged Nike's image among young and middle-aged people who had become increasingly concerned about allegations of exploitation in the Third World.

The problems were not all of external origin. The size of the company had begun to cause communication problems and there was some evidence of low morale. Many employees felt that they had little say in the running of the business and felt that they had become remote from its management. There was also some evidence that Nike's American managers interfered rather too much in the running of the business in other parts of the world, particularly in Europe. For example, when Nike installed its new information systems in Europe, its American managers took over the project because they were unhappy with the progress being made by their European counterparts.

Nike at the end of the 1990s

Despite these problems, Nike had regained its market leadership by the turn of the millennium. Its swoosh logo ranked alongside the red can of Coca-Cola and the twin arches of McDonald's as the three most globally recognized logos. In fact, so well recognized was the logo that Nike sometimes used it without the name itself. It became perceived as the most fashionable sportswear company in the world.

The threat from Adidas increased in the late 1990s, particularly when Mel C of the Spice Girls regularly appeared wearing Adidas products. Nike was seemingly taken by surprise and reacted relatively slowly. Nevertheless, Nike reacted to this challenge and to the other threats to its business. The company lost a little of what some observers perceived as its arrogance and it made attempts to recultivate its workforce's goodwill. Nike also sought to improve the working conditions of workers in Asia and began to exert far greater control over its suppliers, forcing them to become model employers in their regions.

Nike once more became highly design-oriented and took advantage of the blurring between the markets for sportswear and fashion wear. It became successful in the growing fashion market which is no longer confined to those below 30 years of age. So strong is the Nike name that

Americans often refer to their 'Nikes' rather than their training shoes. There are both advantages and dangers associated with Nike's entry into the fashion market. The market is characterized by the built-in obsolescence of its products, and this has the advantage that new products can regularly be designed and sold at higher prices and that competition is more based on design and brand than on price. The danger arises from the fact that fashion changes rapidly and a brand can become unfashionable very quickly. At the same time, development costs of new products are high.

Perhaps to counteract this problem, Nike sought to regain its association with its grassroots athletes by introducing the Alpha range which represented the most scientifically designed and high tech of its products centred on the new Air Zoom Citizen trainer. Nike even changed its logo for these products. Alongside the swoosh were five circles to denote excellence of performance. This symbolized a return to the core values of the business, which has always represented itself as the athlete's company. There was also a softening of the message conveyed in its advertising slogans from the harsher 'Just do it' to the more gentle slogan 'I can'.

Nike looked set to retain its position as a world market leader having fought off successive challenges from Reebok and Adidas. There were plans to expand the scope of Nike's business both geographically and in terms of the range of its activities. Phil Knight said that 'sport is the culture of the United States' and that 'before long it will define the culture of the entire world.' This may prove to be an accurate extension of the concept of cultural convergence. Equally, it may be indicative of the kind of cultural arrogance that can precede the decline of such a business.

References and further reading

Dicken, P. (1998) *Global Shift – Transforming the World Economy*. London: Paul Chapman.
Jones, D. (1998) 'No More Mr Nike Guy'. *Sunday Times*, 23 August.

INDEX